MODERN AMERICAN HISTORY ★ A

Garland Series

Edited by
ROBERT E. BURKE
and
FRANK FREIDEL

MYTHS AND MORES
IN
AMERICAN BEST SELLERS
1865–1965

Ruth Miller Elson

Garland Publishing, Inc.
New York & London ★ 1985

Library of Congress Cataloging-in-Publication Data

Elson, Ruth Miller.
  Myths and mores in American best sellers, 1865–1965.

  (Modern American history)
  Bibliography: p.
  Includes index.
  1. Books and reading—United States—History.
2. Best sellers—United States—History. 3. Popular
literature—United States. 4. American literature—
History and criticism. 5. Social values in literature.
I. Title. II. Series.
  Z1003.2.E47 1985   028'.9'0973   85-16254
  ISBN 0-8240-5667-1

All volumes in this series are printed on acid-free,
250-year-life paper.

Printed in the United States of America

To

Merle E. Curti

"The best books . . . are those that tell you what you know already."

George Orwell, <u>1984</u>

CONTENTS

Chapter 1: WHAT BEST SELLERS SELL

To discover what ideas were held by ordinary people in
any period is one of the persistent problems of history.
The ideas and ideological development of literary figures,
statesmen, intellectuals can be analyzed without serious
methodological problems. But the ordinary person, a-verbal
or at least a-vocal beyond his/her neighborhood leaves no
direct expression of her/his beliefs. Household furniture
and artifacts offer source material for social history, but
the intellectual furnishings of most of us rarely appear
in a form capable of survival. Nor can one assume that
spokesmen and spokeswomen for a particular group in society
necessarily represent the ideas and attitudes of their
constituents on particular issues. Did Elizabeth Cady
Stanton in her day or does Betty Friedan in hers mirror
the thoughts of most American women? The most enthusiastic
wishful thinking cannot assure us that they did. Did
Frederick Douglass or Martin Luther King, Jr. express the
thoughts of most American blacks? And we are all aware of
the frequent repudiation by organized labor of candidates
endorsed by their Unions. Leaders and followers are not
necessarily of one mind on all subjects.

In shifting the focus of history from extraordinary to
ordinary people, the contemporary historian has unearthed
a flood of evidence relevant to the status of blacks, women,
children, manual workers and other submerged groups hitherto
more or less ignored in the writing of history. Such
artifacts have been particularly fruitful in revealing the
material conditions of their lives, the roles they played
in society and what other classes thought of them. But how
does one find out what they thought of themselves and their
world? If they recorded their ideas, they were, by that

very fact, a-typical. Educated people and the upper classes were at least consistent letter writers, but one cannot assume that letters of the middle and upper classes speak either the language or the minds of those beneath them.

Although there seems to be no way to discover directly what most people of the past thought about anything, one can at least find out what books they favored and what ideas they encountered therein. There is, of course, no way to know how much of popular culture was absorbed by its consumers, but one can at least discover what concepts were most frequently and forcefully available to the public at large. This study is not an examination of what in American culture made a book a best seller; there are several excellent analyses of best sellers from this point of view by James Hart, Frank Luther Mott, Alice Payne Hackett and James Henry Burke.[1] My central concern is not why people bought these books, but what they discovered about their world when they read them. One may pick up a novel for a relaxing read, but in the process one also absorbs ideas along with the narrative. One may choose a non-fiction book on religion and find theology accompanied by advice not only on man's relation to God, but on man's relation to man, current social questions, how to get along with one's spouse, and even on how to achieve monetary success in this world.

The best selling books, then, should offer clues to the world view of that mythical creature--the average American. Intellectuals, then and now, see the essence of the 1920s in such writers as F. Scott Fitzgerald, Theodore Dreiser and T. S. Eliot, and in many ways they are right. But the books most widely read in that decade were written by Edgar Rice Burroughs, Harold Bell Wright and Gene Stratton Porter.

Major writers in any culture reveal the fundamental values with which the culture operates, the basic assumptions it makes about itself. Literary artists with

imagination and style offer insights not just into the
nature of men and women in a particular society, but into
the nature of man. Theirs is a profound vision, both
individual and universal. Their writings presuppose a
reader willing to expend intellectual, emotional and moral
effort to comprehend what the author has to say. The
insights of artists are likely to disturb rather than merely
edify. The diction of artists is expressive of what they
wish to say, and in a rhythm of their own; they are unlikely
to choose an idiom because it offers easy access to an
audience. Literature as art is likely to have profound
effects on individual readers, but it is unlikely to attract
a mass audience. Sometimes a work of art penetrates the
best seller list inadvertently. Any book that offered
sensational or unusual sex scenes for its day attracted
American buyers en masse: undoubtedly this accounts for the
popularity of Guy de Maupassant's short stories in 1889,
Hemingway's Farewell to Arms in 1929, D. H. Lawrence's Lady
Chatterly's Lover in 1932 and Nabokov's Lolita in 1958. In
literary quality these are not typical best sellers. One
might wish that the literary artist did have great effects
on the ordinary reader, but sales figures belie this hope.

Popular literature, on the other hand, offers entertainment rather than art. The reader becomes a spectator rather
than a participant; he is to be pleased but never shaken up.
Some best sellers, especially those John Cawelti calls
"formulaic"[2], are written with their primary and sometimes
only purpose to attract a wide audience: the Erle Stanley
Gardner detective story or the Barbara Cartland romance.
These authors produced hosts of best sellers year after
year, all following the same formula. Whatever the motive
of the writer, the reader of best sellers is looking for an
idiom he or she can understand without difficulty, and a
situation to relate to in comfort. So the reader creates
the best seller which, according to Leo Lowenthal, offers

both ". . . models for the way of life for the masses, and an expression of their actual way of life."[3]

Who reads these books? While the public school had not wiped out illiteracy in the United States, it had provided a large reading public apparently not fully defined by class. The worker who put in a twelve hour day seven days a week (as in the steel industry until 1923) was obviously limited by time and energy from reading much of anything whatever his inclinations. At the other extreme the middle class wife with household help could indulge herself as she pleased, and farmers had long winter evenings not entirely occupied with farm chores. Nor need one live near a book store. Just after the Civil War publishers began sending out door-to-door salesmen; most of Mark Twain was sold this way until the 1880s.[4] Many of the novels appeared in serial form in cheap magazines in the nineteenth century. And the great mail order houses established in the late nineteenth century offered popular books in their catalogues. That readers ordered these along with clothing and farm equipment is evident from their sales: in 1913 Sears Roebuck and Co. ordered and sold one million copies of Ben-Hur.

Cost was probably not a major factor. Technological changes in printing made cheap books possible by the middle of the nineteenth century. They were printed on newspaper presses, paper-bound and sold at newsstands. In 1873 the New York Tribune began publishing major novels including Hardy and Blackmore at ten cents a copy. Most major publishers of the 1870s and 1880s began to issue cheap reprint "Libraries" of novels; by 1887 Mott estimates there were twenty-six such libraries selling their books priced from ten to twenty cents. Furthermore until the international copyright law of 1891 foreign books were easily and blithely pirated and sold very cheaply. Evidence that international piracy made for heavy sales is clear in the best seller lists: foreign titles are prominent indeed

before 1891. Quo Vadis with a defective copyright sold at
seven cents a copy. Pirating of books printed in the United
States was also not unknown. Finally in the 1890s the paper
back book industry collapsed because stiff competition had
produced a glut on the market. Nor was it revived in this
country until the advent of Pocket Books in 1939. There is
some evidence that the reading taste of those who patronize
public libraries is much the same as that of those who buy
books. A study made by the American Library Association in
1975 indicates similar choices in libraries and bookstores,
but there is little evidence on this point in earlier
periods.[5]

Books bought are not always books read. Some books are
bought for social prestige, for display rather than reading,
and may become unread best sellers. I suspect that H. G.
Wells' The Outline of History and Will Durant's The Story
of Philosophy graced more coffee tables than minds in the
1920s.

In evaluating these books as clues to popular culture
one must also take into account the heterogeneity of the
reading public. The Gothic romance and the tough private-
eye stories appeal to quite different tastes, and in some
areas offer quite different values. But then it is all the
more significant when one finds the same attitudes or values
embodied in both. Sado-masochism in sexual matters, for
example, is clearly manifested in both genres. They differ
in the language in which it is expressed and the situations
in which it is palpable, but the basic attitudes are much
the same.

Ideally a study of best sellers should be coordinated
with studies of schoolbooks, newspapers and magazines,
movies, radio and television programs. Most of these novels
were made into movies, some with spectacular success as in
the case of The Sheik in the 1920s and Gone With the Wind
in the 1930s. The basic Tarzan story has been made into

movies four times and is currently a television serial. One cannot, however, assume that the cinema version carries the same message as the book. Tom Mix appeared in 1925 in a movie version of Zane Grey's Riders of the Purple Sage; the novel centers on the evil machinations of the Mormons, but the movie doesn't even mention Mormons. An analysis of such shifts in social values of the same tale in different media would in itself shed light on American popular culture and the function of these different media.

While popular literature probably influenced its readers, it was not the single or even the most important source of popular values, but it did reflect and reinforce them. Institutions that spoke with authority--church and school-- as well as personal experiences and psychic needs were probably more important in shaping basic concepts. But constantly repeated stereotypes in popular literature could fix a picture firmly in the reader's mind. And if the reader had no personal experience in a particular area, books were likely to have major effects. For example, Jews appeared as peripheral characters in many best sellers, but until 1948 always as conspirators or money-grubbers.[6] Their very success, unlike that of the self-made WASP was regarded as a sinister accomplishment, a result of a subversive racial plot rather than a result of the virtue that allowed the WASP to attain such status. In reading best sellers one becomes so used to the Jew as money-lender that it is startling to come across an instance where a money-lender is not so identified. Most Americans, including many who read these books had never met a Jew, and when they did probably perceived him through an already familiar stereotype.

Besides the values consciously espoused in these books, the reader was likely to ingest ideas and ideals accepted axiomatically by the author. Uncle Tom's Cabin consciously promulgated abolitionist sentiment, but at the

same time it also unconsciously expressed racism and other
values endemic in the United States at the time. While the
abolitionism had rather spectacular effects, the racism
revealed even more basic beliefs--the unexpressed values by
which Americans lived. The reader of Tarzan of the Apes
was probably attracted to the book by the promise of an
exciting adventure story, but along with adventure he
inadvertently exposed himself to particular ideas of race,
class, nature, success, etc. Certainly the white American's
view of Africa, after the publication of this book, had its
source in this novel. And the Darwinism accepted by the
ordinary American was filtered largely through Edgar Rice
Burroughs and Jack London.

Some myths persist through long periods of time in
popular literature; others disappear or are replaced. In
some instances the change is clearly related to economic
and social change, in others to changes in the intellectual
climate. The degree of change can be observed if one
compares two best sellers (both, as it happens, written by
women), one at the beginning of the period, an 1864 novel
by Mrs. Southworth and the other in 1966 by Jacqueline
Susann.[7] Although specifically anti-Semitic material had
faded by the latter date, the inherited characteristics of
national stereotypes had not (see Susann on the Italian,
Gino; Southworth on the Italian, Faustina). In Southworth
the hero, and he is a hero, is "intensely conscious of the
innate majesty of man" (116); in Susann heroes are incon-
ceivable, and "men are animals" (170). In Southworth the
main male character works hard, is independent, generous,
honest and ambitious. In Susann two of the better men will
deny any of the above virtues in order to achieve success
in their professions. In Southworth the main female character is a busy, self-effacing housewife whose whole life
is devoted to making the hero happy. Southworth also
includes in her novel two ambitious women; both come to

grief. In Susann the three women at the center of the
novel are also ambitious; unlike the ambitious women drawn
by Southworth they have successful careers, but like
Southworth's career women, they also come to grief. In a
sense both convey the same message to professional women.
In Susann their careers are built on an exploitation of sex,
but of a peculiarly mechanical, a-sensual sort, and there
is not a single happy male-female relationship in the book.

In his speech accepting the Nobel prize for literature
(December 12, 1930) Sinclair Lewis remarked:

> To be really popular and beloved in America, a
> novel should assert that all American men are still
> handsome, rich and honest and powerful at golf;
> that all the country towns are filled with neighbors
> who do nothing from day to day except be kind to one
> another; that although American girls may be wild,
> they change always into perfect wives and mothers
> and that geographically America is composed solely
> of New York which is inhabited only by millionaires;
> of the West which retains unchanged all the bois-
> terous heroism of 1870, and of the South, where
> everyone lives on a plantation perpetually glossy
> with moonlight and scented with magnolias.

And, for most best sellers this was true. They presented a
more ordered world than the one the reader inhabited, one
in which worth was surely rewarded and vice punished, a
world of problems, but "happy problems", problems with
solutions requiring no fundamental readjustments of values
already held by the readers. The reader, soothed by the
confirmation of his/her prejudices, was freed from the
necessity of coping realistically with life as it was.
Q. D. Leavis notes that the readers of best sellers in
England (and there is no reason not to apply this to the
United States as well) used them as wish fulfillment, often
writing to the author in gratitude to say how "real" the

book was.[8] Most best sellers told the reader what he wanted
to know, his problems changed into "shapes which tame them"
as Michael Wood says of the movies.[9] Americans could use
the myths and conventions in best sellers sometimes as
escape from their world, but often as a way to avoid more
complex, realistic and possibly painful explanations.

If best sellers are a clue to the intellectual history
of the ordinary American then the early 1940s are a water-
shed. Up to that time almost all of the best sellers
plucked the reader from his complex world and set him down
in the never-never land described by Sinclair Lewis. From
the 1940s on most of the popular books were still of this
sort, but the best seller list now included books that
seriously faced many of America's most unhappy problems:
rural poverty in John Steinbeck's Grapes of Wrath (1939);
racism in Lillian Smith's Strange Fruit (1944); urban slums
and juvenile delinquency in Nelson Algren's Never Came
Morning (1942), Willard Motley's Knock on Any Door (1947),
Irving Shulman's The Amboy Dukes (1947), William Barnard's
Jailbait (1949), Hal Elson's Duke (1949); modern war in
John Hersey's Hiroshima (1946), Norman Mailer's The Naked
and the Dead (1948); sex in D. P. Geddes and E. Currie, An
Analysis of the Kinsey Report (1954), Vin Packer's Spring
Fire (1952). These did not replace the romances of the long
ago and far away. Anthony Adverse, Gone With the Wind,
Forever Amber, the novels of Frank Yerby and Daphne
DuMaurier reached extraordinary popularity in the same
period. The neat world of Agatha Christie and Ellery Queen
and the simple romances of Fannie Hurst, Taylor Caldwell
and Barbara Cartland coexisted on the best seller lists.

There were a few best sellers before the 1940s that
revealed American problems with some realism and a program
of reform: Henry George, Progress and Poverty (1879), Edward
Bellamy, Looking Backward (1888) and William Harvey, Coin's
Financial School (1894). But unlike those after 1940, these

earlier realists assumed that economic and social problems
could be handled rationally. However fanciful their
remedies the authors all believed that solutions were both
possible and probable. Many of the later books are deeply
embedded in pessimism. Theirs was an intricate, unsatis-
fying and painful world, full of problems but devoid of
solutions. The planned society changed from a nineteenth
century Utopia to a twentieth century nightmare as in
Huxley's Brave New World and Orwell's 1984.

Why suddenly were such books attractive to so many
Americans? Some probably reached the best seller list
through required reading lists in college English courses.
Courses in contemporary literature, instituted in most cases
in the 1920s, became increasingly popular in American
colleges. Hemingway's The Sun Also Rises undoubtedly found
a place on the lists through this avenue. Furthermore if
college attendance may be considered an index, the reading
public was noticeably better educated. The number of
college students increased dramatically in the 1940s and
thereafter, financed by the G. I. Bill for veterans of
World War II. Perhaps there is a causal connection between
this change in popular books and the paperback revolution
in American publishing; they are exactly contemporaneous.
With lower publishing costs publishers may have been more
willing to undertake large paper-bound editions of more
serious books. The sensationalism inherent in such a
subject as juvenile delinquency with its inevitable violence
and sex might also help to explain the popularity of books
on this subject. But why hadn't such subjects attracted the
attention of earlier popular writers? Or, why hadn't
writings on such subjects become best sellers in an earlier
period? By the 1890s the social conflicts of urban society,
racism, the poverty stricken farmer and monopoly in business
were sharp enough to produce the Populist Party, militant
labor groups, socialist parties, the Haymarket affair, the

Pullman and Homestead strikes and to make reform a national issue. Such subjects were indeed available to writers, and were used by Crane, Dreiser, Lewis, Howells, but until the 1940s most Americans avoided buying these books. Only after 1940 did popular culture catch up with the realism of the late nineteenth century literary world.

The most credible explanation for this half-century retardation seems to be the unique combination of the depression of the 1930s and the war of the 1940s. We had been involved in wars and depressions before, but never on quite such a scale and in a single generation. The hardships of both were thoroughly democratized; the perennial problems of the proletariat were, at least temporarily, problems of the upper classes; and with national conscription war affected most American families. Social problems here and abroad now became personal dilemmas. The changes in lifestyles--everybody's-- engendered by the Depression and the War rubbed most noses in rather grim realities, realities not actually new, but newly perceived. Slums were old but now they had new, formerly middle class inhabitants. If it didn't happen to you, it happened to friends. The war and its concomitant issues became personal problems because of the draft, rationing, commodity shortages, organizing industry and the community for defense, etc. Middle class America now had to relate to problems they had assumed happened to other people. Now both of these events affected all intimately: when one got up in the morning, what one ate and wore, how one got to work, how one spent the day, and, probably, what one chose to read. The American still read widely in literature that offered a more ordered world, but he/she was also evidently ready to read about the worlds she/he inhabited. Many Americans were now willing to acknowledge that their Garden of Eden was no more, if it had ever been. American belief in the uniqueness of their country as a land untroubled by the problems faced by the rest of the world, the land for the common man, the land of justice where virtue is invariably rewarded had eroded. Interestingly enough these catastrophes--Depression and War--increased both the size of the reading public and the amount of time people could devote to reading. The leisure of unemployment and the necessity to fill one's recreation time while in the army away from one's usual haunts encouraged more extensive reading.

One aspect of American culture is revealed immediately in the value placed on best sellerdom. In the United States the concept of the best seller creates best sellers. Alexis de Tocqueville, aware of the American's need for conformity in a uniquely competitive world, would have been delighted to read today's book advertisements. The major appeal to the potential customer is not that the book is interesting, relevant, exciting, well-written or has any of the other qualities that might make one wish to read a particular book, but rather that it is a best seller. If one buys it one joins the great majority, and need not seek the strength to defend one's individual taste, even to oneself.

There are certain problems in considering which books are to be regarded as best sellers. I have adopted the criteria of Frank Luther Mott in Golden Multitudes: a book that sold copies equal in number to one per cent of the population of the United States in the decade in which it was published. But sales figures are not always accurate; as we have seen books were often pirated and came out in unauthorized and uncounted editions, and publishers were, and often are, reluctant to issue accurate sales figures, and, in some cases, any figures at all. For the older books it is apparently impossible to discover which were best sellers in the years immediately following publication. War and Peace was a best seller by Mott's definition, but many decades passed before it reached this peak. There are no

neat figures in such cases to distinguish between the steady
and the best seller, and I have used my own judgment in
emphasizing those that achieved more immediate popularity.
Although they are major contributors to popular culture I
have not included juveniles, cookbooks or the Bible. I have
found it necessary to modify the best seller list in several
ways. I have included several enormously popular pamphlets:
Acres of Diamonds by Russell Conwell and A Message to Garcia
by Elbert Hubbard, not included in many best seller lists
simply because they are not book length although in every
other way they rank as best sellers. Some authors produced
many best sellers: Pocket Books reported in the New York
Times Book Review for December 24, 1978 that Erle Stanley
Gardner is the best selling American author of all time;
they had sold 185 million copies of ninety-six of his
detective stories. In such cases I have arbitrarily limited
my analysis to two by so popular an author, particularly
when they were written by formula. Both the reader and the
writer of this study should remember that while Pasternak
and Hersey were widely read, Erle Stanley Gardner might be
described as fifty times more popular. Some authors whose
total production was vast produced no single book that
qualified as a best seller by Mott's criterion: F. Marion
Crawford, Fannie Hurst and Grace Livingston Hill are
examples. While Grace Livingston Hill produced no single
book that qualified, her total production included eighty-
nine volumes of popular fiction. In cases of this sort I
included at least one representative novel. I have also
added a few books outstanding on a particular subject though
slightly deficient in number sold: Helen Hunt Jackson's
Ramona on the American Indian, John Hay's The Breadwinners
on labor organization, Bruce Barton's biography of Jesus,
The Man Nobody Knows. And in one instance I have gone
beyond my own time span; it would be absurd to discuss
racial attitudes in late nineteenth century best sellers

without using one of the best of all sellers, the 1852
Uncle Tom's Cabin. So Harriet Beecher Stowe has also been
added.

The reader should be warned that this study is not
concerned with aesthetic criticism. To arrive at Nabokov's
Lolita after reading a series of books whose literary
quality could be labeled mediocre at best was both a relief
and a delight. But I have tried not to let such pleasure
intrude on the fundamental intention of this study. Nor am
I interested here in the authors' attitudes as such.
Whether Hemingway is anti-Semitic or not is not my concern.
But that Robert Cohn in The Sun Also Rises exactly and
fulsomely fits the stereotype of the Jew in twentieth
century anti-Semitism is very much to the point. Fundamentally this is an examination of what the American reader
could learn of nature, man and society from the best sellers
of his generation. It is, if you will, a history of
American clichés.

Part I: NATURE AND NURTURE

Chapter 2:   THE NATURAL WORLD: PARADISE LOST?

In the late nineteenth century the American's relationship to nature as well as his ideas about nature changed
drastically. The hypothesis of evolution by natural
selection backed by a great weight of empirical evidence in
Darwin's 1859 presentation challenged older theories of the
origin of life on earth. A non-teleological, truly Darwinian evolution had few adherents. By the 1880s, however,
the theory in a version Christianized by Asa Gray, John
Fiske and other popularizers was generally accepted as
revealing the pattern of God's creation. With the Scopes
trial in the 1920s Fundamentalist opposition to even this
watered-down version became nationally prominent, and still
functions in the laws of some states.

Almost as upsetting to Americans was the discovery that
the frontier had been swallowed up by the westward movement.
In 1893 Frederick Jackson Turner's formulation of a theory
of the frontier was a seminal paradigm of American
nationality--a doctrine thoroughly in accord with what
Americans already thought of their West. But could America
remain a land of opportunity without a western frontier?
Furthermore the accelerating industrial revolution changed
in fundamental ways the relationship of the American to the
land, its natural inhabitants and its products. Technology
and new business methods produced revolutionary revisions
in farming, cattle-raising, and finally in the landscape
itself. These changes not only produced changes in ways of
making a living, but new ways of living as the city
developed into a metropolis.

Although Darwin's Origin of Species came out in 1859, the
nineteenth century American who restricted his reading to
best sellers would be completely innocent of that hypothesis

or any of its ramifications unless he happened to read
Rider Haggard's She or Hall Caine's The Deemster. The
latter contains a mild hint of something other than
beneficence in nature when a clergyman and a sailor,
watching a large fish devour a smaller one, recognize but
deplore the fact that the strong consume the weak in the
animal kingdom. Rider Haggard in She also offers an
instance of the same kind with somewhat greater vigor.[1]
But not until Jack London published The Call of the Wild in
1903 was the battle for existence in a harsh world used as
a central theme. In this stirring novel the struggle for
survival and the survival of the strong are vividly
illustrated when Buck, a town dog from California is forced
to make his way in primitive Alaska. The attitude of the
book is symbolized in the title of the second chapter:
"The Law of Club and Fang." The book offers a brutal
nature; survival is won not by the virtuous or the humane,
but by the physically strong. London's other best seller
The Sea Wolf (1904) transfers this principle from animals
to human beings. The poems of Robert Service (1907) carry
much the same message as the writings of London; in fact,
one of his poems is titled "The Call of the Wild." Edgar
Rice Burroughs' Tarzan of the Apes (1914) was a runaway
success (and still is) with its human parallel to London's
Buck: an orphaned child of civilization becomes king of a
Darwinian jungle. Burroughs, knowing nothing of Africa,
invented it so successfully that most Americans after 1914
were convinced that Africa was made up entirely of impene-
trable jungle enlivened by both lions and tigers and peopled
only by wild men. London and Burroughs caught the imagination of their readers and stamped an indelible impression
on their minds. It is worth noting however that "nature
red in tooth and claw" seems to be located only in exotic
places: Alaska, Africa, the high seas.

Evolution by natural selection is discussed in two works
of non-fiction: H. G. Wells' The Outline of History (1921)
and Billy Graham's Peace with God (1953). Wells applies his
rationalistic, sceptical approach to an outline of evolution
allowing the reader to exercise his own judgment. Graham,
on the other hand is polemical; he denies that the first man
was a "cave-dweller . . . a creature of the forest trying
to subdue the perils of the jungle and the beasts of the
field." That Adam walked with God is his refutation of
Darwin (44). Curiously enough the two popular books
(Graham's Peace with God and The Magnificent Obsession by
Lloyd Douglas) that specifically reject evolution are not
from the period when Darwinism was first introduced, but
are of fairly recent publication, and both authors are
Protestant clergymen.

In best sellers the portrayal of the natural world that
the American reader was likely to encounter is saturated
with a benevolent, Emersonian tone. It was not only to the
heroine of St. Elmo (1866) that nature "brought messages of
God's eternal love and wisdom"; this was a universal message
message. To Harold Bell Wright nature "is the great book
wherein God has written in the language of mountain, and
tree, and sky, and flower, and brook the thing that makes
truly wise those who pause to read."[2] Nature is the great
teacher. Nature is also a testing ground for manhood, not
just in the wild struggle for existence as in London and
Burroughs, but in working with and ordering the forces of
nature. According to Marie Corelli, success in such
endeavors produces "the joy of manhood."[3] A favorite motif
throughout this hundred years of best sellers is the
redemptive power of nature. A Grace Livingston Hill
heroine recovering from an attempted seduction flees to the
woods: "into the lap of mother earth who, true to all her
children, receives the poor child with open arms." Nature

heals both physical and psychic ills by mothering, fathering or merely by "the healing silence of the wilderness."[4]

Nature also comes to be used as a measure for the good, the true, and finally it becomes a measure of man. Corelli criticizes Americans for their restlessness; her judgment is that this is wrong because it is unnatural. Wright describes the admired Dan as "well-born; he was natural. He was what a man-child ought to be."[5] The nature against which men and women can measure themselves is obviously not that of Burroughs and London; it is a peaceful, balanced and moderate nature. From the 1940s on best selling handbooks on how to live life successfully stress the natural from diet to child-rearing. The proliferation of such books has produced to date a veritable landslide.[6]

One curious aspect of nature presented in these books, curious precisely because it is universal, is the personification of animals. This is as common in the fierce world of London and Burroughs as in the highly sentimentalized nature described by James Whitcomb Riley. London talks of the dog Buck's "fear of the future," his recurring thoughts of his old home in California, and his "moral nature."[7]

The high priestess of what can only be described as a cult of nature was Gene Stratton Porter--one of the most popular early twentieth century authors. She too personifies animals (note especially her courtship of birds) and yet simultaneously thinks she advocates a scientific approach to the animal kingdom. Hers is truly a religion of nature, a prayerful approach. The redemptive powers of nature are overwhelming. Ethics comes from the trees: the girl of the Limberlost announces that the beeches tell you "'to be patient, to be unselfish, to do unto others as I would have them do unto me'"; the oak trees say: "'be true'", "'live a clean life.'"[8] And certain natural products--buttermilk, tomatoes--would seem to have the miraculous powers of the wine and wafer in the Mass. Yet

at the same time she treats nature the way women's magazines
used to treat food--as bland, pretty, neat and tidy.

Scientific studies of nature are rare on the best seller
list. Paul de Kruif's The Microbe Hunters in 1926, a collection of biographies of microbiologists, was the first.
Its popularity may have stemmed from interest in the lives
rather than the scientific work of the microbe hunters, but
it did introduce the reader to the problems and prospects
of scientific research. Then two books--Kon-Tiki by Thor
Heyerdahl in 1950 and The Sea Around Us by Rachel Carson in
1951 appeared in a world newly aware of the importance of
the scientist's view of nature. The devastating effects of
the atom bomb had been detailed by John Hersey in Hiroshima
in 1946, and atomic power had become the major issue in the
Cold War. Heyerdahl, an ethnologist, set out to test his
hypothesis that Polynesians had originally migrated from
South America. He writes of his journey across the Pacific
from Peru to Polynesia using only the implements and balsa
rafts available to stone age people. This book, offering
the reader adventure as well as scientific analysis became
very popular. The next year Carson, author of several scientific studies of marine life produced The Sea Around Us,
an investigation of the sea, its denizens, its relation to
land, wind, and to human beings, and finally to changing
human perceptions. It is a quiet book, imaginative and
poetic as well as scientific--an unlikely book to find best
seller status. Perhaps the popularity already achieved by
Heyerdahl's exciting voyage stimulated a particular interest
in the sea. Curiously enough Carson's later book Silent
Spring (1962) which had tremendous impact on the recent
ecology movement was rather a steady than a best seller.
On the whole, science in these books appears most often not
in studies of nature but in the practical application of
technology and gadgetry. Utopias and Utopias-in-reverse
from Edward Bellamy to Huxley and Orwell all foresee a world

changed beyond recognition by applied science. In most of
the novels science appears not in contemplation or understanding of nature, but in an admiration for technology
applied to the production of goods, or in the simple gadgetry of James Bond's car. It is as though the Thomas Jefferson
of Monticello with his many gadgets for comfortable living
had outlasted the Thomas Jefferson of Notes on Virginia and
his many writings on science and natural history.

Throughout the period nature is related to people and
usually in a benevolent way. The idea of a neutral nature,
current in late nineteenth century literature occurs rarely
until the 1940s in best sellers. Before this the sun shines
on man with indifference only in The Deemster (1888) and in
Crane's The Red Badge of Courage (1895).[9]

NATURE IN AMERICA

That nature in America was unspoiled by man at the time
the Europeans came is regarded not only as a distinction
reserved for America, but a blessing bestowed by God on a
chosen people. A Zane Grey character, observing the
"sweetness and content of this wild land" echoes a theme
constant in American culture from the Puritans on: "'Here
is the promised land.'"[10] Successful migration from Europe
to America is assumed to be clear evidence that God meant
America for them rather than for its native inhabitants.
The enormous size of American physical features--the Rocky
Mountains, the Mississippi, the Great Plains, Niagara
Falls--indicates the superiority of this land to that of
Europe; it is a land suitable to a superior people.

The everpresent theme in these books of the superiority
of those who live close to nature over those warped by
civilization appears most often in contrasts between East
and West. The West sheers away the past and allows the
western migrant the possibility of becoming a new Adam. He
is independent not only of the past but of the rest of the

world. The only standard in the West is "'What can you
do?'" according to one admired Wright character.
Addressing an Easterner, Barbara Worth, the title character
of one of Wright's novels, defines differences between
Western attitudes and those of the East: "'You are praised
and take rank because of what your forefathers did; we are
proud and take rank because of what we are doing.'" And:
"'Ancestors are to be counted as a valuable asset, but not
as working capital.'"[11] Destry of Destry Rides Again
observes that going West changes ways of thinking as well
as behavior: "'Eastern thinkin' never raised western crops'"
(55). Most of these writers were apparently unconscious
followers of Frederick Jackson Turner. Clearly the American
West will produce a superior people: individualistic,
equalitarian, ambitious, hard-working. The very difficulties of pioneering are an advantage to the nation in that
they will produce a stronger race. The one dissent comes
from Steinbeck who comments in The Grapes of Wrath in 1937
that as Americans took up land in the West ". . . their
love [of the land] was thinned with money . . . and they
became not farmers but little shopkeepers of crops" (316).
He fears the Easternization of the West.

     Actual changes from wilderness to garden to factory are
reflected in these books, but interpreted with ambivalence.
On the one hand there is vast pride in American accomplishments in bringing civilization to the wilderness; on the
other hand the conquest of the wilderness removes the
American from God's world and from the redemptive power of
nature. Many writers refer in some way to this problem;
two authors, John Fox Jr. and Harold Bell Wright use it as
a central theme in many of their books. An ominous note is
sounded by Wright, who advises an artist to work fast:
". . . while the book of God is still open, and God's
message is easily read. When the outside world comes, men
will turn the page and you may lose the place."[12]

If one wished to write a novel that would sell well in the United States a western locale for at least part of the story was a good idea. Even Anthony Adverse, that cosmopolitan financier, made a foray into the trans-Mississippi wilderness. And the twentieth century saw a great proliferation of western novels. Historical accuracy was evidently irrevelant to a western. The reader of best sellers who didn't live in the West was likely to imagine "the West" as one enormous ranch encompassing everything west of the Mississippi River and peopled by highly individualistic cowboys riding the open range, whereas that stage of the cattle industry was over by 1890. The cattle industry had become a business like any other and the cowboy an employee whose time was spent on a ranch rather than on the Long Drive. Only Shane in 1949 challenges this mythical view of cattle raising; furthermore the author, Jack Schaefer, accepts the change as a desirable one because the beef raised on a settled ranch is better than that subjected to the Long Drive. Up to the 1940s the West appears mainly as cattle-raising country, but in 1939 Steinbeck uses the West in the odyssey of the Okies, dispossessed mid-western farmers looking for a new life. Other western industries rarely appear: Las Vegas gambling (Richard Prather, Find This Woman, 1951); Texas oil (Edna Ferber, Giant, 1952); chicken raising in the Northwest (Betty MacDonald, The Egg and I, 1945). In the 1940s and thereafter California cities are used as background for the new, tough detective stories. But essentially throughout the period the West is the West of the cattle industry as it existed between the late 1860s and the late 1880s.

That God has assigned to Americans the task of taming a wilderness into a garden will not only strengthen the American, but may be taken as a sign of divine recognition of American superiority: the conquest of the wilderness was ". . . a task that had been too great for other blood,--a

task of bringing into civilization in the compass of a
century of wilderness 3,000 miles in breadth."[13] The
Americans are a chosen people, chosen not as superior beings
who deserve a soft life, but chosen as superior beings
capable of accomplishing a hard task. Loss of the wilderness to the garden is unfortunate, but necessary to build
a strong nation.

Although the change from wilderness to garden is shown
to be a major factor in American culture, the transition
from garden to factory was obviously more upsetting. In
losing the wilderness to the farm, one did not lose one's
roots in nature and through nature in God. Wilderness was
fresh from the hand of God. Although the garden was cultivated by man, nonetheless in the garden man was caring for
the works of God. It would be hard to put such a case for
an industrialized America engaged in the process of changing
the products of nature beyond recognition; man was now
caring only for the works of man.

The glories of American technology are celebrated as a
manifestation of American mechanical and business genius.
Progress is ordinarily equated with technology. In the
early books the building of the railroad becomes the focus
for American industrial development. But as time goes on
the best sellers give increased attention to technology
until one reaches the absurdity of Goldfinger (1959) which
illustrates ad nauseum a kind of obsession with technology
in the innumerable gadgets used to equip James Bond's car
for all contingencies (87). Except for the nature writers
at the turn of the century (John Fox Jr., Gene Stratton
Porter and Harold Bell Wright) pride in American industrial
progress dominates the best seller list until the 1940s.
Perhaps stimulated at that time by war-time discussions of
the possibilities of a post-war Utopia a number of books
offer discussions and debates on the advantages and
disadvantages of accelerating industrialism. For example,

in a Taylor Caldwell novel of 1946 one character foresees
in a technological America the end of vitality, diversity
and joy; he fears Americans will become "ant-men"
relinquishing their independence for stability and
mechanical order. "'An economy based on the soil is an
economy of natural rhythm. . . .'" The response offered in
this book is that industry will liberate man from "stulti-
fying labor", give him leisure and more freedom.[14] Such
debates occur in a number of books at that time. A few take
note in passing of the dangers to the environment from the
factory.[15] But none except Edward Bellamy in his Utopian
novel <u>Looking Backward</u> proposes reform to counteract these
problems.

What might be unconscious protest at the increasing
complexities of the new economy produced a major wave of
nostalgia in the 1890s. Of the twenty-four best sellers of
that decade six recreated and extolled a simple village
life. Three were laid in Scotland: J. M. Barrie, <u>The Little
Minister</u> (1891) and <u>A Window in Thrums</u> (1982); Ian MacLaren,
<u>Beside the Bonnie Brier Bush</u> (1894); these followed the
tradition of R. D. Blackmore's <u>Lorna Doone</u> on 1874. The
other three were laid in American villages: Opie Reade, <u>The
Jucklins</u> (1896); Edward N. Westcott, <u>David Harum</u> (1898);
and Irving Bacheller, <u>Eben Holden</u> (1900). Escape to the
bucolic past must have been attractive and soothing to
Americans faced with violence in labor strife at Pullman and
Homestead, Coxey's Army, the Populist Party and increasingly
visible urban ills.

Three books--and it is interesting to note the calibre of
their authors--see only the ruin of man and civilization in
industrialization. Henry Miller: "Whatever there is of
value in America Whitman has expressed, . . . the future
belongs to the Machine, to the robots." Mellors in D. H.
Lawrence's <u>Lady's Chatterly's Lover</u>: "'I'd wipe the machines
off the face of the earth again, and end the industrial

epoch absolutely, like a black mistake.'" They are joined
by Steinbeck whose condemnation while not so sweeping, sees
the "dead tractor" taking the joy out of work and love out
of the land.[16]

There is one celebrant of the industrial revolution
whose worship of technology intrudes in every chapter. Ayn
Rand asks herself why machines inspire in her "that joyous
sense of self-confidence," and decides it is because:
"Every part of the motors was an embodied answer to 'Why?'
and 'What for?' The motors were a moral code cast in
steel." Effects of industry on nature do not bother her:
when one of her characters sees steel rails going through
beautiful woods and beds of flowers "what she felt was an
arrogant pleasure at the way the track cut through the woods
. . . ." Another of Rand's creations longs to see a bill-
board, and expresses hatred of those who object to them.[17]
Rand's attitude toward the machine is quite as mystical as
Gene Stratton Porter's toward nature.

CITY AND COUNTRY

The ambivalence of most of these authors toward the
conquest of the American landscape is not reflected in their
attitudes toward the development of the city. If best
sellers are an index to culture, contemporary American
hostility to the city is heir to a long, strong tradition
of disdain. The theoretical basis for this contempt lies
in the myth that God made the country but man made the town.
Actually, in contrasting city and country the country that
these writers have in mind was not wilderness untouched by
human hands but villages and farms planned and cultivated
by men and women. The dogma persists, however, through the
whole century of best sellers. The city becomes the true
opposite and enemy of nature.

Cities are described as noisy, restless and hard on their
inhabitants, but the major accusation is that they are the

center of vice. The word "city" is so often preceded by
the word "wicked" that one misses it when it is not there.
The atmosphere of the city is, at the least, "unwholesome."[18]
Conan Doyle describes the city of London as "that great
cesspool."[19] Any city is a place of peril for the innocent;
all are full of "two-legged skunks."[20] Even Horatio Alger's
Ragged Dick, a success in an urban environment warns: "'A
feller has to look sharp in this city, or he'll lose his
eye-teeth before he knows it.'" To Holden in 1900 the
country offers truth, but not the city: "Here the lie has
many forms--unique, varied, ingenious. The rouge and powder
on the lady's cheek--. . . the multitude who live by their
wits and the lack of them in others--they are all liars;
. . . It is bound to be so in great cities, and it is a
mark of decay." In 1902 Owen Wister makes a curious
distinction between the city saloon and the country saloon:
"More of death it [the country saloon] undoubtedly saw, but
less of vice than did its New York equivalent. And death
is a thing much cleaner than vice."[21]

Nor are the perils of the city all external; the city
offers temptations hard for even the most virtuous to
resist. The dangers of moral subversion are all the greater
because city people "are bent on nothing but pleasure."
Furthermore the loneliness of the individual in a crowded
city makes it hard to protect oneself from the "salesmen of
souls" so common to the city.[22] Newcomers must also steel
themselves against the derision with which they are greeted
by urban natives. Fulton Oursler writes that even Jesus
Christ was described by city folk as "that yokel Messiah"
(164, see also 23). This universal contempt for country
people is another example of the cynical arrogance of the
city-slicker. The girl of the Limberlost, Elnora, taunted
for her country ways at school vows to show ". . . those
city girls and boys how to prepare and recite lessons, how
to walk with a brave heart; and they could show her how to

wear pretty clothes and have good times."[23] Thus, whatever
city people may think, "real" values come from the country.
In considering the frequency of diatribes against the city,
it should be kept in mind that books designed to be popular
were likely to stress the perils of the city if for no other
reason than that they were colorful, indeed sensational.

Rarely is the city described as a seat of national power.
The Vixens in 1947 accuses "men of dishonor" of taking over
the South after the Civil War "in their smokey offices in the
great bleak cities." And the growing power of urban centers
is sometimes a menace.[24] But frequently the city is seen as
a seat of both economic power and economic powerlessness.
In The Robe (1942) Lloyd Douglas' description of ancient
Rome with "greed and gluttony at the top" and "poverty and
degradation growing more and more desperate" at the bottom
of the society appears clothed in different words about many
cities in all of these books. Sheldon, the mid-western
preacher, who hoped to arouse the populace to live in the
modern world as Christ would have lived, noted that Chicago
as all great cities showed "the marked contrast between
riches and poverty, between culture, refinement, luxury,
ease, and ignorance, depravity, destitution and the bitter
struggle for bread. . . ." Carvel in describing what he
called "This Sodom of London" believes "Sin levels rank."[25]
To him the urban rich and poor are equals in vice, and the
wealth and power of those at the top of urban society are
no help to those at the bottom. The power of the city
inclines rather to malevolence than benevolence.

Nostalgia leads a few authors to view city poverty as
unfortunate but also as a spur to ambition, and, especially
in Jewish culture, as the natural environment of wit. Betty
Smith in 1943 suffuses Brooklyn with nostalgia; Harry Golden
in 1958 does the same thing for the Lower East Side of New
York City. Golden, describing himself as an indoor person,
celebrates the institutions only the city can harbor; of

the New York Public Library he says: "history was made in
that library" (128). Both he and Smith reveal a snug ethnic
community surrounded by a tough, often hostile environment.
Damon Runyon in 1938 and Polly Adler in 1953 in their
different ways also create cozy communities out of the very
people the law-abiding city dweller fears. Here tough
criminals, operating with more or less success in the city,
delight the reader with their obsessive attempts to
establish a kind of respectability on their own terms.
Nostalgia is present here too but so are the dangers of the
city, however wittily presented.

But in the late 1940s and 1950s a series of books take
a much more dismal view of the city; it is not just a den
of iniquity but a brutal environment, the ambience of
despair, and it creates monsters. The city slum as a
breeding place of lethargy, juvenile gangs, drug addiction,
crime of all sorts is the major theme of Never Come Morning
(1942), Knock on Any Door (1947), The Amboy Dukes (1947),
Jailbait (1949), Duke (1949), The Blackboard Jungle (1954),
Another Country (1962). Slums had appeared in earlier best
sellers (as In His Steps in 1897), but it was generally
assumed that the effects if poverty even in an urban
environment were not all deleterious and that they could be
counteracted by reforms. No such expectation remains in
these later books; to its natives the slum is the death of
all hope.

Those who inhabit the city but not its slums have other
problems also stemming from their city turf. What Roe in
1874 calls the "artificial metropolitan society" is to
Oursler "unnatural and overcivilized" and to Bret Harte an
"effete" society. Such an environment is deleterious to
both sexes. The city woman tends to artificiality: Ellery
Queen describes one female as "pure metropolis, insolent
and bored and trying to conceal both."[26] But the effects
of the city are not as serious for women as for men because

qualities assigned by the society to "ladies" can still be
maintained, at least in theory, in the city whereas the city
saps qualities regarded by the society as essential to
masculinity. In an America that still had a western
frontier Roe points out that city men are "so emasculated
that they are quite vain of being blasé." And Grace
Livingston Hill perceives something "womanish" in the way
a New York City man knocks on a door.[27] Country living
allows none of the softness associated with city living;
according to Edward Eggleston: "'It takes a man to boss
this deestrick [sic]'" (3). In Ben-Hur the provinces
produce "active, hardy men", and according to Edgar Guest:

> Forests were ever the cradle of men
> Manhood is born of a kinship with trees.[28]

And indeed in American culture the rugged American countryside was a land of opportunity only for the male; it
required qualities associated with masculinity--courage,
endurance, strength, ingenuity. Actually the American
countryside required the same qualities from the woman; as
both female and human being she too had to be strong,
courageous, persevering, ingenious. But since the American
concept of femininity did not include these qualities, the
rough countryside did not enhance her value to herself or
the world. It is interesting to note that only Kerr and
MacDonald, two women writing of their experiences in the
country, make fun of the mystical feelings Americans display
when talking of nature.[29] That the frontier is a man's
world is stated explicitly in only one book, but is implicit
in the others.[30]

The man who leaves the farm to make a living in the city
leaves honesty behind:

> He barters a natural for an artificial pursuit;
> and he must be the slave of the caprice of customers,
> and the chicane of traders, either to support himself
> or to acquire a fortune. The more artificial a man's

pursuit, the more debasing it is morally and physically.[31]

America's culture heroes from George Washington to Henry Ford are invoked to give prestige to the idea that only the possession of land guarantees independence. Such testimonials continue right through periods when midwestern farmers were losing both independence and their farms in the depression of the 1930s.[32] Kains who gives advice in 1935 on how to run a farm to city people who have lost their jobs, observes that most of the people in Who's Who in America were reared on farms. The country is the cradle of character. Zhivago notes that Christ himself was "emphatically human, deliberately provincial."

One might expect the role of the city as a cultural center to compensate for other disadvantages. And, in some instances it does: Zhivago, in returning to Moscow notes ". . . cities are the only source of inspiration for a new, truly modern art."[33] Amber, in Forever Amber rejects America because there are no cities or theatres or palaces. In a few instances the Puritan attitude toward the stage surfaces and produces an opposite effect. In 1874 Roe describes a young man on his way to perdition: ". . . the theatre had become his church."[34] The city as cultural center attracts surprisingly little attention; its advantages often appear only obliquely in describing the sheer monotony and isolation of the country. Love for a particular city appears in some instances as in Trilby's lust for Paris. But the predilection she and Madame Bovary feel for city life is hardly a recommendation to the puritanical American. Evidently the production of "masculine" men (men capable of dealing directly with nature rather than merely representing it) was much more important than producing or experiencing art. Indeed one might assume from these books that the two are antithetical.

The two authors who have undisguised admiration for the city are two who have much in common in other ways: Horatio Alger (Ragged Dick, 1867) and Ayn Rand (The Fountainhead, 1943; Atlas Shrugged, 1957). To Horatio Alger the city is the land of opportunity, its perils merely a school for sharpening the wits, thus increasing one's arsenal for the battle to get ahead in the world. Ayn Rand celebrates the city as the locus of the industrial revolution. She not only admires the efficiency of the new technology, but makes it the basis for a new aesthetics and a new religion. Rand's feeling for technology is akin to the feeling Pearl Buck, Erskine Caldwell, John Steinbeck and Zane Grey have for land. To Rand there is a mystical and beneficent relationship between man and the machine, and the machine is most visible in the city.

The American view of nature is of peculiar importance because it played a major role in creating a national identity. In every country outstanding physical features become symbols of the nation and so Niagara Falls, the Grand Canyon, the Rockies, etc. stand for America. But America came to be symbolized to herself and to the world not primarily by physical features as such, but by the functional relationship of nature to man. What man did with nature and what nature did to man, and the myths thereof, became major steps in the definition of the American. Increasingly in popular literature America was personified in the frontiersman and the cowboy, at home in nature, ill at ease in society. These stereotypes were perpetuated not only in popular novels, but in the movies made of them. Frontiersmen and cowboys existed in other cultures, but Americans appropriated them exclusively for themselves. The legend of the cowboy and frontiersman shows them living in harmony with unspoiled nature rather than attempting its conquest.

But at the same time American identification with the unspoiled West was challenged in popular culture by national pride in her tremendous and exceedingly rapid industrial development. Progress is equated with the railroad cutting through the frontier, the machine conquering nature. These divergent views of what is uniquely American exist side by side.

There seems to be a time lag of about half a century in portraying some of the social realities of the American use of land. When the independent cowboy entered popular fiction, his existence was already confined to legend. The long drive had ended by 1890, but the popularity of the cowboy in books and movies is a twentieth century phenomenon. The reality of the industrial slum antedates its exploitation in popular literature by about fifty years. Curiously the frontiersman, the cowboy and the slum dweller have one quality in common--loneliness, but with vastly different connotations. The frontiersman and the cowboy of popular literature have freely sought to escape to nature, and their high moral character, even heroism, reflects this closeness to nature and therefore to God. The slum dweller is just as alone, even when a member of a juvenile gang, but his/hers is the loneliness of abandonment and aliena-tion. The city is incapable of providing a nurturant environment.

So the readers of these novels, living in a highly industrialized society, were quite prepared to retain Uncle Sam as their symbol, and Uncle Sam is no city dweller.

Chapter 3:   THE FEMALE SHROUDED IN FEMININITY

While nature determines biological differentiation
between male and female, it is society that invents the
concept of "femininity" and "masculinity." These terms
cover no natural distinctions between the sexes, but the
modes of thought and behavior prescribed by the society and
taught to their children as proper to each sex. Such codes
are far from being mere code of etiquette; they establish
spheres within which each sex must operate, they provide
both opportunities and limitations carefully defined by
sexual classification. And the society that creates these
categories sanctions them by assuming that the differences
they have fabricated are innate; these spheres are not only
those within which each sex must live, but the only fields
in which each can operate with any degree of success.
Needless to say sex roles are so deeply ingrained and
institutionalized in culture that they have only recently
been challenged, and displacing them will involve a truly
revolutionary process. There may be instinctive personality and character differences between men and women, but
we have found no hard evidence that this is so. Differences
in attitude and behavior are apparent, but these are usually
traceable to the quite different environments the sexes
occupy even in the same family. The proces of masculiniza-
tion and femininization begins at birth with the gift of
boxing gloves to the male infant and a doll to the female
in the maternity hospital, with the differences in vocal
intonation in talking to the female infant, and in the quite
different ways babies are held and handled. But all
societies seem to accept axiomatically the notion that the
different roles they have established for male and female
are bestowed by nature--genetic and, therefore, immutable.

Popular literature probably plays a major role in cultivating such stereotypes in both conscious and subconscious
American minds.[1]

It would seem fair to say that the sphere of the woman
has been immeasurably smaller and more confining than that
of the man. One of the clearest illustrations of this is
the contrast between the phrase "bad girl" and "bad boy" in
American popular culture. Applied to a boy the adjective
"bad" has all sorts of possibilities: he may lie, cheat,
steal, physically attack--the possibilities are endless.
Applied to a girl it posits only one: a "bad girl" is a
girl involved in sexual activities not accepted by the
society.[2] It was the 1920s with their more flexible sexual
standards that accepted as a best seller a novel entitled
Bad Girl whose heroine is trying to cope with her guilt on
finding herself a "bad girl." A "bad woman" (distinct from
an evil woman) is one who is paid for such activity.[3]
Furthermore when a female "loses her virtue," as she does
in Donald Henderson Clarke's 1929 novel Louis Beretti (51-
52), the reader knows exactly what the author means since
both have accepted the idea that the virtue of a female is
vested entirely in her vagina. Both in virtues and vices
women's options are limited, and the limitations are so
thoroughly accepted that they affect ordinary diction.

The language of popular literature not only reflects
the narrowness of the sphere assigned to women, but also
her natural inferiority to the male. The application of
the adjectives "frail" and "weak" to persons whose normal
activities include childbirth, major responsibility for the
heavy physical and mental burdens of rearing children,
taking physical care of the home and administering the
complexities of family life would seem particularly
incongruous. And in a land where women shared the
unremitting physical labor required in settling a frontier
ludicrous, but these women rarely appear in best sellers.

Only one book, Louis Beretti in 1929 specifically refutes
this when in describing Ma Beretti's activities in childbirth and in keeping a family and house together the author
concludes: "Ma Beretti was one of those women who prove
that the feminine is the stronger sex" (156). The picture
of Ma Joad in Grapes of Wrath is another illustration of
this idea. Perhaps old mothers were exempt from female
weaknesses. When men exhibit a lack of courage they are
termed effeminate. In The Prisoner of Zenda in 1894 men
afraid of a particular undertaking ask themselves "Are we
women?"[4] Conversely the phrase "like a man" appears in
almost every novel as the highest compliment to be paid a
woman for an admired action or quality. If she exhibits
intelligence she is said to "think like a man"; when she
shows courage she is "behaving like a man"; when she
achieves success in business she earns the accolade of
acting "like a man"; if she is straightforward and decent:
"Why, she's as upright and straight and honorable as a
man!"[5] In all things except childbirth the man is the
standard against which the woman is measured.

In many instances the term "girl" is used for a grown
woman, probably because the image of the adult woman is the
image of a child--weak and without the virtues associated
with the male. The frontispiece of The Trail of the
Lonesome Pine in 1908 shows a physically grown woman, but
calls her a "little girl." Adult prostitutes in a house
are collectively referred to as "girls" though individually
known as bad women. The term apparently applies only to
the unmarried adult woman. The use of "Miss" (rather than
the European "Madame") as the common address to an adult
woman reminds one of the use of the term "boy" applied to
adult black males. The Citadel in 1937 offers the most
curious use of this nomenclature when a secretary is
described as "'a nice elderly girl, neat and composed'"
(212).

According to most of these authors, female as well as male, the qualities assigned by nature to women include whatever qualities might help to produce the comfort of the male. The Royal Path of Life, an 1876 manual on how to get the most out of life, sets the tone of the first fifty years of these books in several essays on women. Being female means that she is endowed intrinsically with tenderness, affection, mercy, timidity, self-sacrifice, intuition, morality and piety (14-15, 28, 82, 436-37, 447-48, 522-23). She has no ambition for herself, only for her husband (18). She is weaker in intellect than the male, but stronger in the affections. Another quality generally assigned to women is a "'Home-making instinct which lies dormant in every woman.'"[6] Ilg and Ames in their 1955 book Child Behavior seem to give scientific backing to this in pointing out that even in nursery school little girls prefer dolls and little boys trucks. They do not, however, also note that already each child has had several years' exposure to the sex roles he/she is expected to fulfill before ever seeing a nursery school.

In best sellers there is general agreement on the natural limitations as well as the natural gifts of women. One area in which they are assumed to be conspicuously lacking is in capability of rational thought and intellectual activity in general.[7] That women follow "instinct," "the heart" rather than the head is generally assumed for the whole period of this study. In 1946 Taylor Caldwell characterizes feminine reasoning as "utterly illogical" (362). Scarlett O'Hara, one of the few independent women in these books is warned by her grandmother that being smart about dollars and cents is "'a man's way of being smart'", "'intuitive knowledge'" is that of a woman (719). In Not as a Stranger, Morton Thompson's saga of a modern hospital, this sentiment is appropriately expressed: a woman "thinks with her uterus" (380). Obviously, then, education, except in the business of making a home, is wasted on women. In 1909 <u>Girl of the Limberlost</u> one character says in disgust that girls want to go to college just to learn bridge, embroidery and other small and foolish things (287). One man in Brinkley's <u>Don't Go Near the Water</u> in 1956 sees only dire consequences coming from higher education for women; he refuses to send his daughter to an Eastern college because he believes that all they do is change women into men (225). And Paul Leicester Ford in <u>Janice Meredith</u> in 1899 suggests that with women's intuition they do not need much education; Eve probably knew more than Adam before she tasted the fruit of the tree of knowledge (40). Few intellectual women appear in these best sellers: Edna in <u>St. Elmo</u> in 1866 and Evadne in <u>The Heavenly Twins</u> in 1893. Mme. de Stael appears in <u>Anthony Adverse</u> in 1933 and in <u>Desirée</u> in 1953, but in both cases in a most unflattering light; she is characterized in <u>Desirée</u> as "dreadful", garrulous and fat (83).

There are several women who use unfeminine reasoning power to become a success in business. Scarlett O'Hara in <u>Gone With the Wind</u> and Cara in Marian Castle's <u>The Golden Fury</u> in 1949 both realize that they are better at mathematics than their husbands and excellent business women. Ayn Rand's Dagny Taggart in <u>Atlas Shrugged</u> in 1957 is a successful engineer and administrator unique in these books. <u>I Never Promised You a Rose Garden</u> in 1964 offers a marvellously intelligent psychiatrist, but because of the nature of her work her success might be ascribed by the reader to feminine intuition. It may be significant that all four of these books are by women, although in general I find no correlation between an expressed belief in equality for women and the sex of the author. There are three other women inhabiting these best sellers whose extraordinary business success came in running brothels: <u>Mamie Stover</u> in 1951, Dora in <u>Cannery Row</u> in 1945 and the actual Polly Adler in 1953. Adler's autobiography shows her to be an astute

business executive who offered to her employees most of the
fringe benefits provided by paternalistic employers of the
day.

Some of the qualities assigned to the female sex in these
books might lead to consequences in the arts. But this too
is denied them in the books where women confront the arts.
In Reade's A Terrible Temptation in 1871 one of the male
characters suggests the fact that women read so many novels
indicates that they have more imagination than men. But the
response this elicits is that this proves the opposite is
true: their lack of imagination attracts them to novels in
which the artist supplies substitutes for imagination (248).
Haines and Yaggy in 1876 caution women against reading
novels because, as females made up mainly of feelings they
will find themselves "disheveled . . . hands trembling,
bursting into tears at midnight . . ."; novels are altoge
altogether too much for their delicate nervous systems (163-
(163-64). Gunter in 1887 and Ford in 1899 offer the same
cautions. Of the professional women who appear in these
books fourteen are writers, but only two write imaginative
literature: Jo in Little Women and Edna in St. Elmo; the
rest are journalists and these people the more recent books.
Somerset Maugham in Of Human Bondage admires a woman who
writes cheap best sellers to support her husband and child
(390). Although 23.8% of the best sellers in the first
fifty years and 24.4% from 1915 to 1965 were written by
women they didn't weave their profession into their books.

Women in the graphic arts come out very badly. The woman
artist in Roe's 1872 Barriers Burned Away is carefully
described as capable of imitating with skill and taste, but
incapable of creating new effects or of invention of any
kind (110, 265). In Robert Elsmere in 1888 a woman painter
who wants to try oil instead of watercolor is told to stick
with watercolor because it is more suitable to ladies than
oil (12). In Rudyard Kipling's The Light That Failed Dick

advises Maisie to design decorative medallions because she is not truly an artist, but has only "cheap little impulses" (172-76, 91, 85). And Maugham in 1915 believes that "women have no feeling for art. . . . They only pretend they have" (388). And in The Razor's Edge he suggests that a female painter should "paint like a woman. Don't aim to be strong; be satisfied to charm" (197). In these books art is quite clearly mortgaged to sex.

Of all the arts the one in which more women are engaged than any other in the best sellers is music. In fact professional singers make up the largest number of women in any profession in these books, nineteenth and twentieth century as well. There are more professional singers than teachers or nurses, and only one male singer. One can only suppose this the result of a holdover in popular culture of the Romantic view of singing as the spontaneous expression of the soul, and women were believed to be peculiarly well-endowed with soul. One particularly bizarre attitude toward women and the arts comes out in Evan Hunter's The Blackboard Jungle in 1954. A man with ambition but no talent for creative work envies his pregnant wife and all women, and muses: "Creation has been given to them as a gift . . ." (135). This identification of the creativity of giving birth with the creativity of the artist seems nothing short of ludicrous when one considers the role of the two instruments: in the case of pregnancy and birth the woman is essentially a passive vehicle whose inspiration, will and hand have nothing to do with the result, whereas the artist shapes, tends and determines the work produced. This was a way to explain why women were not and did not need to be active in the arts--they are deflected by nature.

The feminization of the female also creates a life style dependent on her being irresponsible and fickle by nature. Gunter in 1887 characterizes women as "natural gamblers" because their capriciousness accords so well with gambling

(111). It is also generally assumed that the female nervous system is more sensitive than a man's, and women get upset more easily than the male.[8] Perry Mason, Erle Stanley Gardner's detective-lawyer, describes a client to his secretary in 1941: "'She's intensely emotional, Della. She's a woman'" (278). Women are also said to be stubborn-- "a trait peculiarly feminine"; given to foolish argument-- "'Don't let us wrangle like a pair of women'"; and their love of gossip and idle talk is "a feminine characteristic . . . an inherited quality."[9] In Kenneth Roberts' Lydia Bailey in 1947 a man is cautioned to stop "'quibbling like an old woman'" (52). Zane Grey in Riders of the Purple Sage in 1912 assures the reader that such qualities come from nature rather than nurture; Bess, brought up in isolation, shows in her behavior that she "inherited certain elements of the eternal feminine" (296). So the feminine nature accorded to women sets up a life-style that can only be regarded as annoying at best to the more stable male.

Throughout this century of best sellers a particularly persistent quality assigned uniformly to women is devious-ness, in dramatic contrast to the straightforward and honest attitudes and behavior of men. The feminine woman normally teases, fools and deceives. Griffith Gaunt in 1866 sets the tone for later books:

Drive a donkey too hard; it kicks.

Drive a man too hard; it hits.

Drive a woman too hard; it cajoles. (124)

Haines and Yaggy in 1976 contrast men and women in conver-sation; women talk to please not to persuade (14). Doyle agrees with Maupassant's description of the "native, simple cunning and tranquil duplicity" of women. That all women are liars by nature is frequently said.[10] One author, Edison Marshall in 1947 sees female deceit as not entirely lacking in social virtue because it often produces a peaceful atmosphere: "Plainly she was not without deceit, a natural and perhaps excellent thing in women worth their salt" (61). Chesser's sex manual of 1947 notes that women use coquetry and teasing habitually: "Women know such things instinctively" (78). Few books recognize these machinations as a normal response, a necessary mechanism to permit dependent persons to inhabit in some comfort the niche society has assigned to them. In Janice Meredith, in 1899, a book full of coquettes, the title character is told by her mother that women must live up to the picture men have of them, but then "secretly do otherwise" (6). Kenneth Roberts in 1947 marvels at the terrible things women will do for money and security (69). And Scarlett O'Hara's mother in discussing woman's lot in a man's world says that while the man owns the property, the woman manages it. "The man took credit for the management and the woman praised his cleverness" (58). When Scarlett's husband finally realizes that she is much better than he at managing a business, but that she has carefully hidden this talent from him, ". . . he felt the usual masculine indignation at the duplicity of women" (616). Women are regarded as manipulative by nature. Most writers assume women dissimulate to get their way: as Lindsay puts it in a 1932 novel: "The secret of subjecting the male is a pose of meek submission" (104).

Beauty is of particular importance to a woman because worldly success in money and esteem is dependent on her attractiveness to the male. If she is a "bad woman" she will use her sex appeal to further a career, as did Nana, and Amber (of Forever Amber); if she is a "good woman" she will use it to entice a rich man into marriage. And the importance of beauty to a woman is universally acknowledged in all of these books. Apparently the potentiality for beauty is granted by nature only to women; it is never ascribed to men. To Haines and Yaggy "Beauty and virtue are the crowning attributes bestowed by nature upon women"

(428). Even Elizabeth Stuart Phelps in her 1868 description
of life after death is gratified that in Heaven all bodies
are beautiful: "The loss or presence of beauty is not as
slight a deprivation or blessing as the moralists would make
it out" (123). Only the maverick Henry Miller in Tropic of
Cancer scorns the idea that beauty inheres in the female; he
talks of "the natural homeliness of the female" (162). Interestingly enough even a man of the cloth, Norman Vincent
Peale in 1952 considers a woman's careful attention to her
appearance vital to her happiness. In advising a woman
troubled because no one seems to want to marry her, he does
mention that spiritual life will light up one's face, but he
also suggests that she fix up her hair and take to using
perfume (113-14). Dale Carnegie in 1936 advises men to win
friends in the office not by complimenting the work of the
female office force, but their clothes; he tells how Calvin
Coolidge used this technique to make his secretary feel good
and therefore do well (186, 242). In some instances intellectual activity and beauty are regarded as antithetical.
In Jaffe's 1958 The Best of Everything when a young woman
describes herself as a studious type, her male boss responds
"'I don't believe that. You're too pretty'" (161). Female
beauty is generally seen as a source of power, and in some
of the more melodramatic novels it is a power fraught with
danger for men. Ouida in 1867 observes that behind the ruin
of every man is a woman whose ". . . beauty must come . . .
out of hell itself."[11] What makes a woman beautiful is
never defined, but it is noticeable that nineteenth century
heroines tend to be blondes with blue eyes, and evil women
tend to be brunettes. From the 1920s on the physical
glories of women become more explicitly sexual. Dale
Carnegie in 1936 uses Florenz Ziegfeld as an example of a
successful man whose success came from transforming "drab
little girls" into glamorous creatures (37). The first
sentence in the 1953 novel Desirée is: "A woman can usually

get what she wants from a man if she has a well-developed figure," and the novel is about a woman doing exactly that. In the tough private-eye crime stories female beauty is reduced almost entirely to sexual characteristics and the female breast becomes an obsession. Prather's 1951 description of a woman shows her as "a body that was sex boiled and distilled till only the essence was left" (35). One unusual novel, The Rosary in 1910, must have been seized upon with joy by every female reader who considered herself homely; the heroine is "a beautiful woman in a plain shell" (9). She is rational, independent, strong and calls a spade a spade and not "a garden implement" (160); she is, because of these qualities, referred to as "boyish" (11), and when abroad as "lady-gentleman" (135). But with all of these admirable traits she is also tall, heavy and homely. She falls in love with an artist, but cannot believe he could love so homely a woman in spite of his fervent protestations, and so they part. Years later, after he has been blinded by an accident she returns, incognito, as his nurse. In the end, of course, her inner beauty wins and love conquers all. One wonders if the homely female reader noticed that there wasn't quite so much to conquer since her homeliness was now invisible.

The function of the female throughout these books is to soothe, and comfort the male and to help him achieve his goals and hide hers. The kind of comfort she offers shifts a bit in emphasis, from the earlier books offering the comfort of a well-run home and obedient children to sexual satisfaction in the later books.

The woman who chooses not to marry or is not chosen--the spinster--is unsuccessful as a woman, and, therefore, in these books as a person. But there is a dramatic contrast between the attitudes toward the spinster in the earlier and later halves of this century of best sellers. In the first fifty years, "old maids", as Eggleston expresses it in 1871,

are "a benediction to the whole town" because their
frustrated mother-love is turned on the community, and
"There is no nobler life possible to anyone than to an
unmarried woman." By the 1940s a simplified Freudian
interpretation changes the humanitarian spinster into a
twisted, love-starved neurotic. A character in The Chinese
Room by Vivian Connell in 1942 sees "weeds . . . growing
in her mind."[12]

The true role for a woman throughout the period is to
be a wife--a wife prepared to sacrifice herself for her
husband. The 1866 novel St. Elmo the story of am ambitious
woman who gives up a successful career happily for a man,
is preceded by a long quotation on the title page from
Ruskin. Its message:

> ". . . a true wife in her husband's house is
> his servant . . . whatever of best he can conceive,
> it is her part to be; whatever of the highest he
> can hope, it is hers to promise . . . in her,
> through all the world's warfare, he must find his
> peace."

James Barrie's A Window in Thrums in 1892 illustrates the
degree of self-sacrifice expected of women in the story of
a woman whose energies are spent keeping secret her
husband's vices, with the author's comment that no man could
be so self-sacrificing (118). Examples of female selfless-
ness are legion. The success manual Think and Grow Rich by
Napoleon Hill in 1937 points out that most of the men who
achieve success were motivated and aided by women (177). I
In almost every case the scientists discussed in the 1926
The Microbe Hunters by Paul de Kruif had the uncomplaining
and invaluable aid of their wives. Haines and Yaggy in 1876
believe that "woman equips man for the voyage of life.
. . . She is seldom a leader in any prospect but meets her
peculiar and best attitude as helper" (28). This book
suggests that sisters are also useful to the male, and

offers the rather dubious example of Byron's sister who
"cheered the poet's dark soul" (91). Maugham in 1944 has a
sympathetic character root this quality of self-sacrifice
in nature: "'I suppose it's more in a woman's nature to
sacrifice herself than in a man's'" (100). Marie Corelli
in her 1888 novel A Romance of Two Worlds uses Mary, the
mother of Jesus, as an example to be emulated by all women.
She "loved to hold a secondary position; she placed herself
in willing subjection to Joseph" (231). Her subservience
is then not only to be accepted but enjoyed. These books
are full of stories of women who committed themselves to a
career, but then happily subsided into marriage when the
opportunity offered. Marjorie Morningstar in 1955, for
example, ends up a contented suburban matron. All of the
nurses in Dariel Telfer's 1959 story of a hospital, The
Caretakers, fervently hope to marry and leave the
profession.

The subservience of a woman to her husband is seldom
challenged. In Edward Westcott's David Harum in 1898 a
woman questions the limitations marriage imposes on women;
she would like the same opportunities men have, although as
she is careful to point out, she has never wanted to be a
man. She resents the conventional response to such wishes
that women have opportunities too by their influence on
their husbands' careers, and says: "'The career was the
man's after all, and the fame and visible reward. A man
will sometimes say "I owe all my success to my wife, or my
mother or my sister," but he never really believes it, nor,
in fact does anyone else'" (70-71). Another challenger of
the conventional role of the married woman is Evadne in the
1893 novel The Heavenly Twins. At one point Evadne's mother
tries to persuade her to marry a reprobate to reform him.
Evadne points out that her mother wouldn't even consider
advising a son to marry a woman with a comparable past (89).
"'Women have practiced self-sacrifice when they should have

been teaching men self-control'" (92). She proposes a new
principle to be adopted by married women: "'Whatever we do
we should do openly and fearlessly--we are not the property
of our husbands, they do not buy us'" (116).

But essentially it is accepted that success for a woman
lies in marriage and marriage should be every woman's
primary goal. In Niven Busch's Duel in the Sun in 1944 a
young woman is advised: "'I'm sure you'll be successful if
you go to Mrs. Withington's. . . . I mean that you'll be
able to attract a man'" (86). This is very little different
from Meg's statement in Little Women three-quarters of a
century earlier: "'Men have to work and women marry for
money'" (136). In seeking a husband Dale Carnegie advises
women to tone down their efficiency and to remember that
men don't want an executive but "someone with allure and
willingness to flatter their vanity and make them feel
superior" (241). And in discussing Disraeli's wife whom
he considers stupid he praises her as "a positive genius at
the most important thing in marriage: the art of handling
men" (235). Success for a woman is success as a wife
catering to her husband. In The Caretakers, in 1959 a
sympathetic female character still maintains the house
servant concept in saying that women marry not just to go
to bed with the man and have his children, but "'We want to
iron his shirts and clean his kitchen and polish his shoes'"
(92). [See also 1950 The Cardinal (85-86).] In choosing a
mate, Hill's Manual in 1905 suggests that a good marriage
should imitate nature in which the male is the stronger and
protects the female and the woman helps him to carry out his
decisions (165).

Besides providing comfort and helping a husband to world
worldly success, women have another function--as redeemer.
On the title page of St. Elmo in 1866 there is a quotation
from Ruskin on the woman redeemer. She has the opportunity
to "'purge into purity'" his dark nature which is exactly

what the novel is about. It is generally assumed that the
spiritual side of the male is underdeveloped and that of
the brute overdeveloped. Even Jack London in the 1904
The Sea-Wolf believes men without women are blighted by
"coarseness and savagery" (128). In the first sixty years
of these best sellers there are innumerable examples of the
redemptive power of women to tame and civilize men and to
save them from corruption.[13] More recent books are just as
sure of women's faith in their redemptive powers, but less
sure of the efficacy of those powers. In a 1957 novel a
woman finally persuades her husband to move from Greenwich
Village to the suburbs where she will expose him to "the
true, the important, the abiding things--home, family,
community." He follows her advice to no particular end,
although he was quite content with his previous environment.[14] Fulton Oursler in 1949 gives a Biblical rationalization to the role of woman as redeemer: Mary knew that
death had come into the world by the action of a woman, but
thought "She had been given Eve's second chance, through
His son to bring salvation" (104). But this is a lonely
voice among recent books because redemption requires the
concepts of both virtue and sin, and by this time it would
seem that faith in man's potentiality for virtue had eroded.

The power of women is also exhibited in motherhood which
is sentimentalized ad nauseum. In Ben-Hur Lew Wallace
purports to quote a rabbi: "'God could not be everywhere
and therefore he made mothers'" (223). Haines and Yaggy in
1876 point out that motherhood offers women even more power
than men have because they "mould the character and destiny
of the child" (436-37). The mother is sometimes endowed
with magical powers as in The Little Minister in 1891 where
the mother's powers extend to the body and mind as well,
through her mind. A baby born without a chin has one in a
few months because the mother willed it (11). Rudyard
Kipling dedicates The Light That Failed in 1891:

> If I were hanged on the highest hill,
> Mother o' mine, o mother o' mine
> I know whose love would ·follow me still
> Mother o' mine, o.mother o' mine.

And, of course, Mother's Day is celebrated fittingly in the
verse of Edgar Guest in 1916. Kathleen Norris' 1911 novel
Mother centers entirely on the joys of motherhood with the
intertwined stories of many women with various attitudes
toward children. The views of the author are made quite
clear. Norris is adamantly opposed to contraception and
offers an idyllic picture of motherhood, with the mother in
the home devoting her every thought to her children. One
much-admired woman ". . . welcomed the fast coming babies
as gifts from God" (20). Norris fears the moral decline
that she sees in the modern woman who wants fewer children
so that she can indulge her own fancies. The ideal mother
is "old-fashioned, hopelessly out of the modern current of
thoughts and events" (20).

Contraception is routinely handled in books published in
the last thirty-five years of this period. Kathleen Norris'
hostility is well matched in 1937 in The Citadel when a
doctor, enraged by the request of a minister for contracep-
tive information, shouts: "'Get out--quick--you--you--dirty
little man of God'" (193). He considers the production of
children the only reason for marriage. But Mary McCarthy's
The Group in 1963 has an extended piece on the sociology,
mythology and mores of the diaphragm in modern life (52-77).
These are two extremes; most books accept the existence of
contraception without particular comment. Illegitimacy, a
major issue in the nineteenth century, as in the novels of
Charles Reade and John Fox Jr., is little remarked in
twentieth century books. Abortion appears first in Louis
Beretti in 1929 and frequently thereafter. Chesser's sex
manual in 1947 contains a chapter called "The Abortion
Racket" in which he stands for the woman's right to choose

an abortion if she likes. He points out that laws against abortion do not make them less frequent, only more dangerous. Three years later Henry Robinson's The Cardinal tells of several instances of Roman Catholic doctors choosing to allow the mother to die rather than to abort or hurt the baby (91, 320). By 1961 Robbins has Jonas, his principal male character, pay routinely for three abortions a year; his father says he must pay "for every bitch you plug" (12).

The most unsentimental and realistic picture of motherhood appears in an 1876 book, Helen's Babies, a hilarious account of a young man's baby-sitting experience with two small boys. He finds himself "reduced to physical and mental worthlessness by the necessities of two boys not over-mischievous or bad." The task requires more strength than that of young male athletes, more heroism than "fort and field", more decisiveness and more diplomacy than that of statesmen. The mother who survives is "far above warrior, rabbi or priest" (144). That women have a maternal instinct is unquestioned in all books, but that men have a paternal instinct is mentioned only in one book and that is to deny that such a thing exists. The narrator of the book Mr. Adam in 1946 explains that the instincts of the male are physical and of the moment and, therefore, cover the act of sex only whereas females prefer babies to sex (85). Parenthood is a matter for rejoicing, incidentally, only if the child is a boy. In every instance but one in which the birth of a baby is recorded in these books, the parents either exult that it is a boy or lament that it is a girl. The exception is in The Young Lions in 1948, but the prospective father expressing this opinion recognizes it as unusual when he writes to his pregnant wife: "'Please don't worry about its being a girl--I will be delighted with a girl'" (410).

There are two instances when the mother is indifferent
to motherhood, but neither Mildred in Of Human Bondage in
1915 nor Scarlett O'Hara of Gone With the Wind are
considered by their creators as models of virtue. In his
other best selling novel, The Razor's Edge in 1944 Maugham
offers a mother with a fairly rational approach to motherhood. She admits that she does not love the children as
much as their father does, but she is still an excellent
mother. She understands that she is a human being and so
are they and "A mother only does her children harm if she
makes them her only concern in life" (180). Dr. Spock
would seem to disagree with this in his 1946 book which
immediately became the child care bible. Here he seems to
give Freudian backing to the complete responsibility of the
mother for all aspects of the child's development. This
responsibility was undoubtedly the source of a tremendous
burden of guilt in many a Spock mother in spite of his
common sense guidance in most matters. In Spock quite as
much as in the books that tout the maternal instinct, the
father's role is minor.

There are two instances of mothers who hate and try to
harm their children. In the 1944 Leave Her to Heaven the
woman gets pregnant as a means of keeping her husband, but
after the birth hopes the baby will die (191). But Ellen
has been shown to be an evil woman anyway. A Girl of the
Limberlost in 1909 offers a more complex bad mother. She
hates her daughter, Elnora (the girl of the title), because
when she was pregnant with Elnora she saw her husband sink
into a swamp, but because of the pregnancy was incapable of
helping him. Her hatred for the child is so intense that
she finds it impossible to perform the ordinary duties of
the mother of a schoolgirl: she cannot get herself to attend
a performance of the school play, or buy her a graduation
dress (185). But this mother recovers herself and her love
for her daughter only when she is told that her husband fell

into the swamp while returning from an assignation with another woman (215).

As one would expect, sexual attitudes go through a dramatic change from the end of the nineteen twenties on, but, although women's relationships to sexual activities change, their relationship to men doesn't. One is tempted to say they come out of the home into the house, serving the male not so much as a house servant and helpmeet, but as a sex object.

In the first half of the period of this study most of the fictional heroines are feminized into potential mothers rather than women; they are so a-sexual that one wonders how they are to achieve their maternal destiny. The word commonly used to describe a state of chastity is "clean"; "dirty" is the adjective applied to one with a serious interest in sexual activity, and the latter continues to be used well into the twentieth century.[15] Haines and Yaggy, using euphemisms common at the time note that women have "weaker appetites and weaker intellects" than men (15). They are passive in sex as in everything else. Only Ouida's Cigarette in 1867 is as free and active in sex as in every-thing else: she has had a "thousand lovers" (182), she swears, rides, drinks, is loyal, truthful, and is a good shot. In these books all of these activities and qualities are "masculine", and indeed she is termed in the book "unfemi-nine" (484) and "a poor little unsexed child" (461). For a woman to engage happily in sexual activity would seem then to unsex the woman because she is not living up to her proper feminine role. For most of the heroines of this period sexual activity has only one function--the begetting of children--and any other interest in the process is "dirty."

"Bad women" (prostitutes) appear as early as 1870 in the writings of Bret Harte. They are often pictured sympa-thetically. The good "bad women" have been forced into

prostitution by otherwise insoluable poverty or, in the
later books, by rape, and they often have hearts of gold.[16]
Robert Service in a poem about prostitutes in 1907 sees the
prostitute as victim of the male's base sexual desires:
"For every man since life began is tainted with the mire"
(119). In the 1880s the importation of translations of
Maupassant, Flaubert and Zola introduced more frank and
more tolerant treatments of sex. (It goes without saying
that descriptions of sexual encounters of any sort at any
time was likely to create a best seller.) But Madame Bovary
and Nana who use illicit sex successfully for social and
professional advancement both die ghastly deaths described
in precise and vivid detail. In a preface to the 1880
edition of Nana (the edition that became a best seller in
the United States) the translator, Mary Neal Sherwood,
emphasizes the lessons to be extracted from this denouement.
Sherwood avers that Zola wrote Nana to show the youth of
France the inevitable consequences of so loose a life, and
"The jeunesse dorée of this country need the reproof and the
warning quite as much as that of France, is the belief of
the translator" (22). This sentiment then allowed the
reader to eat his cake and have it too.[17]

The Evil Woman as opposed to the "bad woman" appears in
a few novels; one great difference between the two is that
the prostitute hurts only herself, whereas the evil woman
hurts others. She is clearly the daughter of Eve or Lilith,
rather than of either Mary, and her function in life is to
ruin men by any means.[18] In King Solomon's Mines in 1886
and She in 1887 H. Rider Haggard creates two superwomen:
Gagaoola described as a "fiend" in King Solomon's Mines
(243) and Ayesha who rules by terror in She (134). They
are witch-like in both power and attributes. They seem
designed to stimulate male fears of what might really lie
under femininity.

Then in 1907 Eleanor Glyn broke new ground with her
account of a passionate sexual affair of three weeks between
a young man and an older woman, witch-like and with a
background of mystery and power, and, like Haggard's
superwomen, "beyond ordinary laws of morality" (1). But
unlike Haggard's witches she uses her power over men for
their pleasure. While she comes from the realm of fantasy,
any male reader would find it easy to identify with the
ordinary young man on whom she bestows her favors. She is
described as having witches eyes (208) and in movements she
is compared to an undulating snake (78, 121, 61) and a tiger
(121, 191). In one conversation with the young man she
announces that the women who have really ruled the hearts
of men are not simple wifely types but Cleopatra, Theodora,
Lady Hamilton and the mistresses of the French kings. Paul
then asks if all clever women are immoral, and she introduces him to a doctrine of morality new to these best
sellers: to lie, to cheat or steal is immoral, but for a
woman to help a man in any way including offering him sexual
pleasure is moral (193-94). Accepted American sexual mores
in 1907 were outraged, and when Boston banned the book it
became an immediate best seller. In this portrait of the
mysterious seducing woman one can see the outlines of the
vamp who soon appeared in early films.[19] One scene in the
book presages many in vamp movies: the young man arriving
for an assignation is greeted by the woman lying on a tiger
skin in front of the fireplace with a single stemmed rose
held between her lips (76-77). The movie vamp, like Glyn's
was dark, with a mysterious past, elusive, melodramatic,
sexy and a peril to the male's moral well being.

In the last thirty years of these best sellers the woman
as instigator of sexual encounters becomes more common.
Different from her 1907 predecessor, she is more often
sexual aggressor rather than subtle seducer. By the 1940s
many authors acknowledge a female sex drive missing in their

predecessors' female characters. These women are far from
the passive brides who suffered sex in order to produce
children, or the enigmatic vamp, and like the male they can
even separate sexual gratification from affection.[20]   In
the 1946 Mr. Roberts a doctor observes that women discovered
sex during World War II and are now often the aggressors
(198). The sexual revolution of the 1920s, limited at the
time to urban middle and upper classes was apparently spread
throughout society by World War II and finally reached the
best sellers. Casual sex encounters of war-time abound in
novels about the army with women appealing only as sex
objects. One wonders how prostitution could flourish with
as much private, unpaid competition as appears in these
books. And in many best sellers but especially in the tough
private eye crime stories of Hammett, Cain, Chandler,
Spillane and the slum tales of Algren and Shulman women are
not merely sex objects, but objects of violence.

It must, however, be remembered that best seller lists
were bifurcated on this issue. While most equated sex with
violence there was also during the war years the popular
Mrs. Miniver, the quintessential feminine woman of the old
style, concerned hardly at all with basic drives, but
absorbed in a world made up of the small bits of gracious
living possible in war-time. She must have been a
reassuring figure, especially to women, in a world of
social turmoil.

Language used to describe sexual activity had also gone
through a revolution. Quo Vadis in 1896 is the first of
these books to offer specific physical aspects of love-
making. But by the 1940s most books describe men and women
largely in terms of their sexual characteristics. In some
books females seem to appear mainly as breasts--"rising
beauties" as Erskine Caldwell calls them in God's Little
Acre (26, 38, 69, 90). Robbins offers a veritable catalogue
of female sexual characteristics, and in The Carpetbaggers

in 1961 his concern with the female breast (pages 183,
192-96, 221, 223, 224, 243, 257, 258, 294, 301, 306, 312)
is obsessive. Encounters between the sexes are increasingly
depicted as meetings not of whole persons but of bodies;
genitals make love rather than people. Sexual activity
appears in infinite variety. Masturbation is freely
described as a normal experience in novels and in the books
of Spock, Ilg and Ames and Chesser as they advise on child
care and relations between the sexes. Sex slang--"fuck",
"pimp", etc. become commonplace and even monotonous.,

Homosexuals appear first in Quo Vadis (226) with a gay
marriage, and often from the 1940s on. In 1959 Goldfinger
describes Pussy Galore's gang of Lesbian burglars, and James
Bond thinks the development of Lesbianism is a result of
sex equality (269). Two books offer a sympathetic view of
Lesbians. In Tereska Torres' Women's Barracks in 1950 they
are pitied because of their social ostracism, but are
regarded by the author as respected human beings. Spring
Fire by Vin Packer in 1952 is a story of Lesbians, again
sympathetically treated. Susan, the woman most people in
the novel assume to be Lesbian by nature, is heavy and
homely, but has both strength and grace. Her lover, Leda,
is beautiful and attractive to men as well. In the end
Susan, the admired one of the two, realizes she never really
loved Leda and isn't really therefore a Lesbian whatever she
looks like. And Leda, the true Lesbian ends up hopelessly
insane. Packer's treatment is likely to disturb some
stereotypes of the Lesbian but confirm others.

It is important to remember that alongside such books
were the romances and Gothics harking back to earlier
descriptions of sexual relations. Cartland in 1961, at her
most sexual describes a "burning, passionate kiss upon her
lips--a kiss which seemed to have seared its way right into
her very soul" (156). "She felt, too, as if a streak of
lightning passed through her body making her quiver and

tremble" (164). These books evidently appealed to a different segment of the public.[21]

In the twentieth century both the romantic and the tough modes of expressing sex turn to sado-masochism with women rejoicing in the brutality of their lovers. Novels with a particular appeal to women--Gothic romances--and those with a particular appeal to men--tough detective stories--differ enormously, yet both embody sado-masochism. Robert Elsmere in 1888 hints at the coming trend when one woman, admired in the novel, describes her ideal man: he will have "'the temper of a fiend'" and will be "'odious, insufferable for all the world besides, except for me; and for me it will be heaven'" (71). Here the emphasis is on the relationship in which the woman enjoys being spiritually dominated. The twentieth century version sets up what is essentially a rape situation, but one in which the woman glories in the violence to which the male subjects her. The Sheik by E. M. Hull in 1921 set up a pattern endlessly repeated in popular literature. Sex becomes not an act of mutual pleasure, or communication, or reproduction, but an act of violence--a violence the female finds thrilling as her lover "works his will" on her. The taming of the female is made more provocative by having her appear as a woman of unusually independent spirit. In The Sheik Diana was raised as a boy, and at the moment of her adbuction, is riding alone in the desert--a singularly daring act. She is not enticed, but forcibly kidnapped by the sheik who tells her "'What I want I take'" (78). His "brutal hands" invade her to her mingled horror and delight (57). (She doesn't completely succumb until she realizes he is not an Arab after all, but a self-exiled Englishman living as an Arab.) The importance of this book would be hard to exaggerate. It was imitated in print many times and was made into a sensationally successful movie, a movie that faithfully followed the book in both story and dialogue.[22] Rudolph Valentino, as the

sheik, was literally adored by vast numbers of American
woman and became the center of an international cult. The
effect on men was also widespread; the compliment most
sought by the young male of the 1920s was to be termed "a
sheik."

That this theme has not died out of popular fiction is
clear when one reads the novels of Ayn Rand. In Atlas
Shrugged in 1957 her heroine, Dagny, is not merely
independent in manner as is Diana in The Sheik, but is a
success in male roles, as a graduate engineer and a business
executive. Her lover frequently "throws" her down (251,
255), his kisses are "viciously painful" (957); he offers
"shocking intimacy that needed no consent from her, no
permission" (108), and she is thrilled "to submit" (107).
In The Fountainhead in 1943 Rand's heroine appraises the
violence visited upon her by her lover, as ". . . the act
of a master taking shameful, contemptuous possession of her
was the kind of rapture she wanted" (230, 290). Both the
ideas and the rhetoric differ not at all from that of
E. M. Hull. Another novel, The Bramble Bush, by Charles
Mergendahl in 1958 suggests that a rape may produce highly
desirable long-term results by endowing a rather tough
female with femininity: her eyes are now "the eyes of a
woman" (259). Crime and spy tales usually view sex relations as reported in Goldfinger in 1959: "Their eyes met
and exchanged a flurry of masculine/feminine, master/slave
signals" (181). The reader of best sellers might well be
persuaded to see violence perpetrated on the woman as both
normal and desirable. She invites rape and should be
grateful for it.

In most books women appear mainly as wives, comforters
of men, sex objects or mothers, but always in a position
subservient to men. On the whole the reader of best sellers
might indeed agree with Bertha, the manager of a successful
brothel in William Bradford Huie's 1951 novel, The Revolt

of Mamie Stover who says: "'Life for every woman is just a matter of what she has to let men do to her to get what she wants'" (123-24). Most women made their lives by their marriages, but the women in these books who had the most successful careers outside the home built their careers very carefully by their manipulation of the men attracted to them: Nana in 1880, Scarlett O'Hara in 1936, Kitty in the 1943 novel of the same name, Amber in Forever Amber in 1944, Roxanne in Yankee Pasha in 1947.

Professional women in best sellers lead lives probably as ambivalent as those they led in real life. As noted before, women appear in greater numbers as professional singers than in any other profession. Singing was considered peculiarly suited to the spiritual nature of the female; the discipline and hard work involved was hardly noticed. Actresses come along in the 1940s, but do not have the unqualified approval given female singers. There is one detective, Bertha Cool in the detective stories of Erle Stanley Gardner under the nom de plume A. A. Fair. In a 1953 novel, Some Women Won't Wait, Bertha Cool is fat, stupid, ugly and incompetent. When she does manage to detect something, she realizes it is her "feminine instinct" not rationality that led her to that conclusion (149). Her cases are all solved by Donald Lam, her male assistant. In many of these popular novels most of the women who start out in a career eventually retreat happily into domesticity from June in Fox's Trail of the Lonesome Pine in 1908 to Marjorie Morningstar in 1955. Ayn Rand's Dagny Taggart is supremely efficient as a business woman, and stays with her career, but at the same time is happily submissive to sadistic sex encounters. There are, of course, many teachers, nurses and librarians. Six women are business successes, and some are writers. Although one fourth of the writers of these best sellers were women, most of the

writers they write about produced not fiction, but newspaper
stories.[23]

In menial occupations outside the home servants in other
people's houses are common. Factory work rarely occupies
women in best sellers although it did in life, but then male
factory workers are quite as scarce. Perhaps routine
factory labor hardly offered the proper background for the
kind of melodrama that made a book sell well. Yet the
United States from the 1870s on was the scene of violent
confrontations between labor and management and women were
deeply involved as in the 1912 Lawrence textile strike, and
the Triangle fire in New York. Perhaps actual labor conditions were too threatening to attract the general reader--
these were not "happy problems." Although office work
employed great numbers of women by 1900 they don't appear
in best sellers until Bad Girl in 1928. Della Street, Perry
Mason's secretary in the novels of Erle Stanley Gardner,
is probably the best known.

The few women willing and able to push aside the curtain
of femininity to achieve independence in judgment and
action are clustered mainly at the beginning and near the
end of this century of best sellers. Charles Reade's 1866
Griffith Gaunt describes Catherine Peyton "writhing and
rebelling against the network of female custom that
entangled her, and would not let her fly out of her cage
even to do a good action; to avert a catastrophe by her
prayers, or her fears or her good sense" (68). She has
courage, high intelligence and a truly independent spirit,
and even acts as her own lawyer. But hers is not a happy
fate: she is eventually tried for murder. The same year
saw the publication of an extraordinarily popular best
seller, St. Elmo, centered on the career of an ambitious
orphan, Edna. It starts out as a success story closely
resembling that of a man's career; Edna becomes as
successful and as pretentious a writer as Augusta Evans,

the book's author.[24] At one point Edna refuses a proposal
saying "'I am able to earn a home; I do not intend to marry
for one'" (187). But then it becomes a feminine story as
Edna abandons her literary career to become a redeemer of
men, but especially one man, St. Elmo. His early career as
a rake provided racy reading and his recall by the efforts
of Edna to religion and morality offered a soothing
denouement. But more surprising is that the heroine, after
struggling against great odds all her life to achieve
status, is herself adamantly opposed to changes in the
status of women. She accepts with joy the "divinely limited
sphere" of the women (465-66). She sees the movement for
political rights for women as "'this most loathsome of
political leprosies'" (394). The day women got the vote
would be in her opinion

> "the blackest in the annals of humanity, would
> ring the death knell of modern civilization, of
> national prosperity, social morality, and domestic
> happiness, and would consign the race to a night
> of degradation and horror infinitely more appalling
> than a return to primeval barbarism." (395)

Ouida's 1867 Cigarette has already been mentioned, but she
is regarded as a warm-hearted, unsexed freak, hardly
qualifying as a role model for anything.

Jo in Little Women probably had more influence on
ambitious young women than any other fictional character.
She wishes over and over that she were a boy--hardly penis
envy, but mere observation of the greater freedom and more
abundant options available to the male sex in her world.
Her scorn for the limitations of woman's sphere--and the
term is used--is vast (414). Her "dearest wish" is to be
independent (135), and she does achieve this in both
opinions and action. In spite of the sentimentality of the
novel, she is believable and many young women identified
with her.[25] With the exception of the feminist novel,

The Heavenly Twins in 1893 she is the last truly independent
woman in the best sellers until Scarlett O'Hara in 1936.
In 1874 E. P. Roe reports the objections of a woman at being
lifted into a carriage, saying "'I'm not an invalid'" (125),
but she later turns out to be a dictatorial eccentric not
admired by the author. Barbara Cartland in 1934 offers
Lady Caroline who exercises her independence by driving her
own carriage; the result of this is, however, disastrous:
she is abducted. Here as in The Sheik one is led to the
notion that women who take charge of their own locomotion
always risk calamity. Perhaps the reputation of women as
bad drivers is the modern version of the fear of women in
charge of anything that moves. Later in Cartland's Duel of
Hearts the heroine happily submits to her husband because
she wishes "to be mastered" (239).

Scarlett O'Hara exhibits the same kind of independence
as Jo although their characters are quite different.
Scarlett's ruthless ambition reaches its goal, but leaves
bodies scattered in its path. Her cold-blooded, relentless
ambition is like that associated here with masculinity, and
indeed she is sometimes accused of not adequately fulfilling
the feminine nature. On the other hand she fits the
feminine nature defined in these books perfectly in her
manipulation of others. Only Auntie Mame in 1955 manages
to be both independent--indeed original and eccentric--while
at the same time likeable and feminine, but her author
hardly expects her to be taken seriously.

That the position of women in the society was changing
and that there was a movement for women's rights is now and
then acknowledged. Hill's Manual in 1905, offering advice
on how to cope with the manners and mores of America, gives
twelve examples of forms to be used for calling public
meetings, and one is for the calling of a woman's suffrage
convention. The same book uses as an example of oratory a
piece called "Results of Higher Civilization" in which

improvement in the status of women is lauded. Women are
now in front "in spite of ridicule, jealousy and opposition," and have "demonstrated business capacity and
intellectual talent of a high order" (456). And in a
section devoted to "Political Issues on Which People Differ
in Opinion" there is an argument for women's suffrage
suggesting that if women had the vote they would improve
intellectually because they would read more. Their
presence in the political arena would elevate its tone, nor
would voting make them bad mothers any more than it makes
men bad fathers. But Hill's Manual also contains a
description of marriage in which men must represent "the
positive--physical and intellectual, women the negative--
sympathetic, spiritual and affectional" (165). So here,
the curtain of feminism is pulled aside but briefly. Three
studies of society look forward to true equality for women:
Edward Bellamy's Utopian novel Looking Backward (1888) which
became the core of an ephemeral reform movement looking
toward socialism, and the Outline of History (1921) by
H. G. Wells and The Story of Philosophy (1926) by Will
Durant. The latter two were best sellers only over a long
period of time and probably languished as unread prestige
items on many a coffee table.

In This Side of Innocence in 1946 Taylor Caldwell in
what is otherwise a passionate, soap-opera novel uses a
sympathetic character to point out that men have "'imposed
the most tiresome virtues on us, and have called those
virtues "natural" to us.'" Essentially, she continues,
women are "'the most reckless and violent rakes under their
demure manners'" (197). She completely rejects what she
calls "'the foolish belief that females are different from
the other half of humanity'" (38). Women have the same
hearts and emotions and are subject to the "'same tides and
instincts that govern men. . . . They share the identical
passions and longings and hopes.'" But they are

"relegated to the ranks of the sub-human,
dependent on the whims of the masters, denies the
right to dispose of our own lives and climb to
any heights we desire, to live and laugh in self-
made security and dignity. We must please or we
do not eat, or, if we eat, we eat the bread of
charity and of menial work." (173)

1893 saw the publication of the one truly feminist novel,
The Heavenly Twins by an English author, Frances Elizabeth
Clarke McFall, writing under the nom de plume Sarah Grand.
It is an incredibly complex and awkward novel which probably
reached best seller status because of its sensationally
radical attitudes on the subject of women; its radicalism
seemed too extreme to be threatening. Grand denies that
women have any natural limitations as measured against men.
They are denied educational opportunities offered to men,
and then accused of being ignorant; they are denied opportunities to develop their talents and then accused of having
none (13, 17). The main character in the first section of
the novel is a scholar and a person who thinks for herself;
she becomes an ardent advocate of women's rights and women's
liberation. She observes that women are no longer content
to be part of "'the livestock about the place'" (92). When
she marries she refuses her husband sexual intercourse
because of his previous sexual encounters. (A friend of
hers married a man with venereal disease and as a result
both she and her child had become infected and died. Incidentally this is the first time venereal disease is discuss
discussed in these books.) Evadne's husband agrees, if she
will not embarrass him by taking radical stands on issues
of the day. To carry out this arrangement she stifles her
nautral feelings in public and finally in private, cuts
down on her reading and even burns some of her books. From
here on the story of Evadne is as confused as she is, and
her part of the novel ends with the formerly independent

Evadne a psychological cripple who tries suicide several
times. The rest of the novel is the tale of one of the
"heavenly twins"--Angelica, the sister of Diavolo and his
intellectual superior. Angelica is an enthusiastic and
persistent feminist who dresses as a boy in order to have
experiences denied her as a woman. When a male friend
discovers her sex she explains: had she not disguised her
sex she could not have become his friend: "'I have enjoyed
the benefit of free intercourse with your masculine mind
undiluted by your masculine prejudices and proclivities with
regard to my sex'" (451). She avers that she knows "'the
value of man's cant about protecting the weaker sex'" (451);
she scorns the exalted status women are supposed to occupy:
"'There is no room to move on a pedestal'" (458). In her
opinion women lead the "'life of a lap dog'" (317). This
novel is a disaster as literature, but its radical ideology
is still relevant and radical. Many other reform movements
appear in the book: questions of slums and poverty
especially. On women's liberation even the church is
attacked for its hypocrisy when a woman tells a clergyman
that the clergy think of women either as angels or beasts
of burden. She asks if they couldn't try to think of women
simply as human beings (181). Angelica suggests that since
girls are raised by reason, and boys by the stick, there
might be fewer wars if women had more say.

But these few advocates of change are small voices in the
whole. Some make fun of active women and the possibility
of their liberation. Harry Golden, for example, in 1958
ridicules women who go door-to-door soliciting votes for
their candidates, but have no idea what the candidate stands
for.[26] He says he agrees with Cato that women should
influence politics by influencing their husbands (220). In
the same year, in the novel Exodus a woman discussing
equality on a kibbutz in Israel evaluates it so: "'It was
good to live with a purpose. But too much purpose could

destroy womanliness'" (351). Other drastic changes are
predicted as results of the movement for equality: the 1959
Goldfinger is sure that all women will become Lesbians
(269). And in I, the Jury a 1947 Mickey Spillane novel
describes a female murderer: "'You no longer have the social
instinct of a woman--that of being dependent on a man'" as
an explanation of her deed (209). Less dire opposition is
visible when a much admired female character is carefully
dissociated from any such movements as in Owen Wister's
The Virginian in 1902: Molly Stark is emphatically declared
not to be a "New Woman" (101).

That women actually behaved in ways defined as feminine
in these books is probably true. But that such behavior
was a result of qualities bestowed upon them by nature is
an unwarranted assumption both stated and implied in these
books and one might presume in the society that accepted
them. Females were considered as dependent as children,
but without the possibility of growing out of that state.
With so few options open to them they could achieve goals
and esteem only by submission, deceit and manipulation. And
the feminine role, as seen here was self-fulfilling. It
would take an extraordinarily independent woman to defy
conventions so deeply buried and so basic to the social
organization of the times.

In these books there are drastic changes in the presentation of sexual matters both in what is presented and how
it is presented. But what is most fascinating is the
persistence of the image of women as naturally inferior to
men. The cloak of femininity cast over women changes color,
but the warp and woof are essentially the same. Women
appear in these books only in relation to men and take
their meaning from this relationship rather than from any
action of theirs. In 1965 a question from the 1876 Haines
and Yaggy is still relevant:

68

Man is bold--woman is beautiful.
Man is courageous--woman is timid.
Man labors in the field--woman at home.
Man talks to persuade--woman to please.
Man has a daring heart--woman a tender loving one.
Man has power--woman has mercy.
Man has strength--woman love;
While man combats with the enemy, struggles with
   the world,
Woman is waiting to prepare his repast and sweeten
   his existence. (14)

Chapter 4: THE MALE SHEATHED IN MASCULINITY

In turning from the portrait of the female in best
sellers to that of the male, one is inevitably struck anew
with the limitations imposed on women in popular culture.
Men are active in all fields except the home where they are
concerned only with major decisions; their heroism or their
villainy offers vast variety as compared to that of women.
Yet the man is also locked into a particular behavioral box;
it has more ventilation than that of the woman, but it too
provides constraints and limitations. To be a man requires
fitting a pattern of masculinity decreed by society rather
than by nature.

In contrast to the female the male is assumed to be
direct and honest. A woman who doesn't dissimulate is
viewed with surprise and always compared to a man as in
Trilby in 1894: "'Why she's as upright and straight and
honorable as a man!'" (76). According to Hervey Allen in
1933 it is the "masculine sense of honor" bestowed on the
male by nature that preserves him from tattling and eaves-
dropping (203). Charles Reade in 1866 observes that a woman
driven too hard "cajoles", a man driven too hard "hits"
(124). Edison Marshall removes honesty from the realm of
morals in 1947 but keeps it within the male nature, by
noting that although it may not be the best policy, it
"calms a man's nerves" (136).

But the characteristic most universally and firmly
associated with the male in these books is strength, both
physical and psychical. Eggleston in 1871 states that the
first requirement for the Hoosier schoolmaster is not
knowledge or teaching talent but physical strength. He
must be muscular or the students might throw him out: "'It
takes a man to boss this deestrick [sic]'" (3). In

The Shepherd of the Hills by Harold Bell Wright, an author
much concerned with spiritual values, the phrase "best man"
always refers to the physically strong; Wash Gibbs whose
character is not admired but whose feats of strength are,
is described as "'a sure good man!'" Ollie, physically
weak but virtuous is said to be not "'so mighty much of a
man'", but "'clean.'" And one who did not develop this mode
of action because of his education as a priest "had grown
timid and gentle as a woman."[1] The male child who does not
exhibit his strength is inevitably termed "sissy." Not only
must the male develop his muscular strength but he must
exhibit it, and he must never admit to weakness. Whatever
the provocation, as advised in Trilby, it is "unmanly to
cry" (188). For a woman to reveal or confess to weakness
is considered a feminine prerogative, a recognition of the
frailty of the feminine nature. But the male must endure
and prevail and show that he does, whatever the circumstances. Robert Service and Rudyard Kipling offer the same
advice to men: if all goes wrong just "grin" and never let
anyone know you are afraid.[2] Jean Kerr in 1957 revises
Kipling in the light of the common sense allowed women on
this issue: ". . . if you can keep your head when all about
you are losing theirs, it's just possible you haven't
grasped the situation" (13). Only in Uncle Remus' black
folk tales do the meek inherit the earth, and here the weak
are so much weaker than the physically strong that only wit
can save them. Even Jesus is redefined in terms of this
concept of masculinity by Bruce Barton in 1924. He had
"muscles hard as iron" (37), and used these muscles as well
as a whip to overturn tables and drive the moneychangers
from the temple. As Barton explains in the introduction to
The Man Nobody Knows, his motive in writing a biography of
Christ was precisely to demonstrate that Christ's personality was as masculine as that of Daniel, David or Moses,

and did not deserve the meek and "sissified" character
foisted on him by previous biographers.

In the twentieth century another element was added to
the strength of the truly masculine male: he is both brutal
and merciless, close to the animal world. In the wake of
the Alaskan gold rush at the end of the nineteenth century,
best sellers reported enthusiastically on the strenuous
life. In the first decade of the new century (and,
appropriately in the presidency of Theodore Roosevelt) the
harsh environment of the Klondike appeared in the writing
of three of these authors: Jack London, Robert Service and
Rex Beach. It was a primitive and often savage life where
arguments are undertaken by fists not words. And as Rex
Beach points out in The Spoilers in 1905 there is "cruelty
in the strength" of a "man's man" (56, 308). His hero's
favorite sentence is "What I want, I take." In The Sea
Wolf (1904) Wolf Larsen's masculinity is "of the brute"
(127). Even some female novelists recognize this quality.
While she transposes it to a milder climate Florence
Barclay in The Rosary the male nature echoes "the roar of
the lion", "the fierceness of the tiger" in "the primeval
forest" (109). In the Twenties this element became much
more prominent. Sabatini in 1921 reports: ". . . spirited
brutality is the birthright of the male" (34). The title
character in E. M. Hull's The Shiek in the same year is
described as cruel (56), like a tiger, "a graceful, cruel,
merciless beast" (95), ruthless (78), and brutal (57).[3]
Rhett Butler, that model of masculinity in Gone With the
Wind is also a graceful strong ruthless male. Qualities
that used to belong to villains are now assigned to admired
characters and sometimes to heroes. The hard-boiled
gangster, daring and cool and tough is now not only to be
admired, but emulated, the hero of the slums. Studs Lonigan
patterns his behavior and practices his manners (the sneer,
tough-guy talk) on these new urban heroes.[4] As H. L.

Mencken and Eric Partridge observed this decade introduced
a new American term to describe a virile, masterful man--
"he-man." Invented in the United States, it appeared in
Punch in 1960 when they described an American as "one of
their hundred-per-cent he-men."[5] But it was, of course,
Ernest Hemingway who produced the cult of machismo. The man
who has lost faith in all things seeks it in his own masculine strength. The he-man can only reveal his masculinity
by constantly testing himself in struggles with nature, and
woman and participation in sports and bull-running. Faith
in the ability of human beings to solve their problems by
rational means was slowly disappearing in the wake of
World War I, and evidently much of the lost generation hoped
to find itself in this masculine mystique.

From the 1940s on masculine strength was also increasingly exercised in these books by depersonalized sexual
activity. As early as the first decade of the twentieth
century Gene Stratton Porter delicately notes the fierce
temptations that strike a man every few days. Her Harvester
in the book of that name reports that in spite of this it
is possible to keep oneself "clean", but the temptations
are so great that one who succeeds in maintaining purity
has a right to be credited for extraordinary self-control.[6]
By the 1930s sexual activity divorced from affection takes
up much of the fiction. By this time women too are depicted
as sexually active, but sex to them it still not the
essential activity it is to the male, and is usually related
to affection. In nineteenth century novels as well as in
the modern Gothic novels the promiscuity that demeans a
woman, that creates a "bad girl" or "bad woman" is expected
of the male. It is in his nature to "sow his wild oats."[7]
In recent war novels--Mailer, James Jones, etc.--and in
tough detective stories--Chandler, Spillane, etc.--hetero-
sexual activity is prominent indeed, but women are not.
Sex acts are depersonalized to the point where the man

requires an object not a partner. Warmth on the part of
the male is directed not so much to women as to other
males--the male bonding that appears in serious American
literature as well as in popular novels. The woman is a
mere convenience. Irving Stone's Lust for Life in 1934
bestows unique importance on sex when Van Gogh expresses
gratitude to a prostitute: "Lack of love in his life could
bring infinite pain, but it could do him no harm; lack of
sex could dry up the well-springs of his art and kill him."
Van Gogh says to himself: "'Sex lubricates'" (179). The
adolescent Holden Caulfield in Catcher in the Rye in 1951
is troubled because he cannot fill out the male image since
he can't separate affection and sex. He can't get really
sexy with a girl he doesn't like a lot: "'Boy, it really
screws up my sex life something awful'" (140). But he
consoles his masculine ego: "'In my mind [sic] I'm probably
the biggest sex maniac you ever saw'" (62). The novels of
Kyle Onstott in the 1960s are obsessed with sex and its
expression by the male. In Drum in 1962 the size of the
penis (for example, pp. 182, 194, 233) and its activity
with or without a partner seems to be the central subject.
And masculinity is measured by how many times the male can
accomplish coitus in one night; ten is agreed to be the
measure of "the real men" (10, 32).

The sado-masochism surrounding sexual encounters in
twentieth century best sellers has already been discussed
with regard to women.[8] Here it should be noted that sadism
seems to be a by-product of what is said to be the natural
wish of the male to assert his physical superiority.
Masculinity is most easily proved by brutality in sexual
behavior--behavior that asserts without question the greater
strength of the male and his absolute control of the female.
Why this became so prominent in books after 1940 is a
complex problem. The world of the Nazis and of World War II
was an era in which one could hardly escape force and

violence. It is possible that sexual sadism had not
increased in the society that produced and read these books,
but simply that descriptions of such activity were now
acceptable as they had not been before. But it is also
possible that best sellers mirrored their culture by showing
an increase in sexual sadism itself. The assertion of
physical strength was less and less needed as the economy
changed and the machine took over heavy labor; more and more
workers sat at desks, or on a tractor or tended an assembly
line. Although modern warfare was vastly more lethal than
anything in the past, it too was mechanized and depersonalized. It is rare indeed that the individual soldier pits
his strength against another visible human being. So,
while the assertion of physical strength was still an
essential part of masculinity, there was less and less
chance of exercising and displaying it except at sports and
in bed.

In one book sexual activity is viewed as a hindrance to
a successful life. In his 1937 success manual Think and
Grow Rich Napoleon Hill includes a chapter called "The
Mystery of Sex Transmutations." He asks why outstanding
men seldom achieve success before the age of forty, and
concludes that young men have a "tendency to dissipate their
energies through overindulgence in the physical expression
of the emotion of sex." The sex drive is the most powerful
of human forces. If, therefore, the male can sublimate his
sexual energy into making a living, success is assured. He
goes on to say that the most highly sexed males make the
best salesmen; they communicate sex energy to others in tone
of voice, handshake, "vibrations of thought." And he
includes a large and fanciful list of highly sexed men whose
achievements in the world he ascribes to sublimation of the
sex drive: Napoleon, Shakespeare, Elbert Hubbard, Abraham
Lincoln, Robert Burns, Woodrow Wilson, Andrew Jackson and
Caruso. George Orwell in his controlled society of 1984

outlaws sexual intercourse except for reproductive purposes
as a slightly disgusting operation, like having an enema
(66). Orwell's Party would agree then with Hill: sexual
energy must be directed into other channels to maintain a
productive society.

While sex is acknowledged as basic to the male, it also
involves dangers. Venereal disease appears in most novels
after the Twenties. Nineteenth century novels barely hint
at it until The Heavenly Twins in 1893, when the death of a
mother and her child from venereal disease contracted from
the man of the family is the central tragedy. By 1929
Hemingway in A Farewell to Arms notes that clap is expected
by all soldiers: "'It's an industrial accident'" (175), and
is usually blamed on prostitutes. But even more dangerous
to the male is the power sexual attraction necessarily
bestows on the female. While the importance of sex for the
male is constantly stressed, its very importance makes it
a source of danger. Fear is often expressed that the female
as siren may put the male in her power, and since her sex
drive is assumed to be much less strong than that of the
male she can bargain with her sexual attractiveness. In a
curious way, then, the very sex act may deprive the male of
some of his masculinity because it bestows power over him
on a woman.[9]

In all of his relations with women the masculine male is
in charge whether as lover, exploiter or protector. "'No
woman can tell us what to do'" as one character says in 1948
Rampart Street (160), a declaration the reader senses in the
minds of most of the male characters in these novels. The
question of the working wife rarely comes up in these books,
but when it does the husband rekects the notion as demeaning
to himself. Eddie, in Bad Girl states unequivocally "No
wife of his was going to work while he had his health."[10]
The fundamental male, Tarzan, realizes that it is the nature
of the man to care for the woman: "He knew that she was

created to be protected, and he was created to protect her"
(222).

The male as a father is remote from family affairs as
compared to the mother. Running the house is the wife's
chore as earning the family living is his. But in important
issues involving the family the final decision is his. The
Common Sense Book of Baby and Child Care, the 1946 bible for
child-rearing by Dr. Benjamin Spock makes some attempt to
counter this notion by bringing the father into the lives
of his children. He observes that most fathers were brought
up to think the care of babies and children is the job of
the mother alone: "This is the wrong idea. You can be a
warm father and a real man at the same time" (15). His
practical suggestions in this area are, however, mild:
parents should not try to divide chores equally, but the
father might make the formula on Sundays, or now and then
do a 2 A.M. feeding. He should make a reasonable effort,
but shouldn't "force himself beyond his endurance." He
might play fifteen minutes with the child and then say,
now I'm going to read the paper. He had better cut short
his time with the children than to spend the whole day with
them reluctantly or angrily (254). The mother is given no
such option. But Spock at least widens the male role, and
recognizes that such paternal activity need not interfere
with the father's perception of his masculinity.

What roles in the outside world do these books consider
most acceptable for men? Doctors and preachers are present
in many best sellers, if not as central figures inevitably
as casual characters. These two professions are probably
particularly attractive to writers of popular literature
because their popularity with readers is assured. Since
they deal in their various ways with death and salvation,
they appear naturally in dramatic situations the reader is
sure to meet in some form at some point.

Scholars are as rare in these books as preachers and doctors are plentiful. Men are assumed to be rational by nature and women irrational, and intellectuals are always male, but there is no premise that men are intellectuals by nature. Only two books, both published in the 1920s, grant much space to intellectuals and philosophers: H. G. Wells, The Outline of History (1921) and Will Durant, The Story of Philosophy (1926). Durant quotes Voltaire expressing his opinion that Isaac Newton was the greatest benefactor of mankind "'. . . for it is to him who masters our minds by the force of truth, and not to those who enslave them by violence that we owe our reverence'" (227). But this is indeed a minority opinion. Although men are not regarded as naturally given to the arts or the intellectual life, serious endeavors in these fields are clearly the province of the male; women dabble, men create.

Heroes are plentiful in these books especially before the complexities of the modern industrialized world enter best sellers c. 1940, and their hallmark is courage. One notes with interest that the courage assumed by these heroes is rarely the courage of dissent. This is not to say that participants in the American Revolution do not inhabit these books; they do indeed, but rather as founders of the nation, establishers of the Establishment, than as dissenters. Heroes of war combat are more prominant than heroes of principle; this is as true of World War II as of any previous war.

The self-made man appears frequently as a hero. He is not journeying down unpopular pathways; he is fulfilling the pattern of the American Dream. Abraham Lincoln is often presented primarily as a self-made man; in The Crisis in 1900 he is used as an example of the truism that "the greatest men rise from the people" (77). In this book Lincoln appears as a Christ-like figure. He is a "God-sent prophet" (77) who speaks in "homely parables" (144), in

language similar to "the simplicity of the Bible" (155).
And his death as a martyr is compared to that of Jesus
(158).

Heroism of the sort advocated for all men by Emerson and
Thoreau rarely appears; few are willing in best sellers to
stand erect and walk alone. In The Little Minister in 1891
Babbie describes her ideal man as one ready to stand up for
what he believes in if he must defy the world to do so
(211-12). In The Keys of the Kingdom in 1941 the humble
Father Chisholm stands up for what he believes in against
great odds in the missionary field and in spite of opposition from his superiors. Rampart Street in 1948 has a ship
captain who refuses to carry slaves in spite of financial
losses. Perhaps the most independent character in all of
the fiction is Atticus in To Kill a Mockingbird, Harper
Lee's 1960 novel. He tells his children that courage is not
a man with a gun, but a sick old woman licking a drug habit
before she dies (121). He acts on his statement that "'The
one thing that doesn't abide by majority rule is a person's
conscience'" (114) when he sits alone at the jail door
defying would-be lynchers. Non-fiction on the best seller
list is just as seldom concerned with non-conformity. Some
passages in Harry Golden's Only in America in 1958, the
post-McCarthy period, are in agreement with Emerson's "Who
would be a man must be a non-conformist," and indeed Golden
uses the statement. And in 1961 Griffin in Black Like Me
describes in some detail Martin Luther King's doctrine of
passive resistance. But much of the non-fiction is made up
of success manuals which advise the reader to avoid standing
on principle, but to develop techniques for getting along
with people if he (and these manuals are addressed to men)
hopes to become a success. Evidently the individual who
acts bravely in the ordinary vicissitudes of life attracts
the ordinary book buyer, but the individual who stands in
opposition to society is rarely accorded such an audience.

Perhaps serious dissent makes the reader uncomfortable
about his/her own ability to withstand criticism. The
individualism of getting ahead materially is ever present
in these books; the individualism of being different, of
standing up for what you believe is as rare in these books
as it is in life.

The most popular men--popular in the sense of appearing
most often as highly approved central figures in the
novels--are Westerners (frontiersmen and cowboys),
detectives and self-made business men.

The prototypical Westerner was limned in 1902 by Owen
Wister in The Virginian.[11] He is daring, courageous, tough
and cool. He is ingenious, highly intelligent, but by his
own admission, has always been a poor student and still has
only scorn for scholarship. He tells good stories, is given
to pranks and is both shy and amiable. Above all he is pure
in heart, living in harmony with nature, and untainted by
man. He is also physically powerful as he must be to be a
success in the West. The environment sieves out the weak.
As Robert Service points out in his verse of 1907:

> This is the Law of the Yukon, that only the
>   Strong shall thrive;
> That surely the Weak shall perish, and only the
>   Fit survive. (30)

Pride in physical strength runs through all of the Westerns.
Destry in Destry Rides Again in 1930 exercises his strength
"for the pure sake of combat" in itself, not for any prize
it might bring (1). The Virginian has a stern code of
morality for himself and others, and will accept no interference with it even from the law. In one way he is unlike
his successors in Western novels: he is part of a community
and has a warm and continuing relationship with a woman.
The cowboys who succeeded him in popular novels, like the
frontiersmen in the earlier fiction of James Fenimore
Cooper are very private individuals who appear rarely in

society and then only to protect the society against itself.
The Western became a morality play with minor variations on
the theme of a young Lochinvar triumphing over the forces
of evil in a community unable to solve its own problems.
This plot was used over and over by Zane Grey and others,
and was firmly and visibly fixed in the American mind by
thousands of movie versions.

The importance of the Western hero lies not only in his
function of liberating a community from corruption, but in
his personification of the free individual. He is a loner
pure and uncorrupted by the societies that sap the manhood
of other males. He is also free of the past. One
frequently finds in these stories the idea that the West
doesn't care who your ancestors were; you stand on your own
two feet unsupported by tradition of any kind. Yet the
individualism of the cowboy is not the individualism of
dissent; he is essentially a quite conventional man
upholding conventional virtues. He attacks a corrupt
Establishment for not living up to its own values, for
being dishonest. Perhaps the most important freedom of the
Westerner is his freedom from women; he has a warm relationship to his horse, and quite often to other males, but women
are shadowy figures in these tales. His is a "clean" life
and one under his own control. He exerts physical and moral
power in nature and sporadically in society. But society
can make no demands of him as it does of other human beings;
his powers are at his own command. He is uniquely independent; he is part of neither a community nor a family.

The myth of the cowboy must have been irresistibly
attractive to men enmeshed in a machine-ridden society over
which they had little control. The myth developed as most
myths do when its factual basis was extinct; by the 1890s
the frontier had disappeared and the Long Drive was over.
Cattle raising had become a capitalistic enterprise
involving large investments and the cowboy was an ordinary

employee. The Western probably was to the American male
what the Gothic romance was to the twentieth century female.
The persistence of the myth of the cowboy was strikingly
evident in 1979 as evidenced by public reaction to the death
of John Wayne: Congress voted him a medal, records and
cassettes taken from his films proliferated, and expensive
silver plate with his portrait was widely advertised, paeans
of praise poured out of television, radio and the press.
This extraordinary outburst of feeling was not for John
Wayne the actor, but for the cowboy he had played in films
for fifty years--an ideal of the simple, strong, honest
American male effectively holding a society to tried and
true ideals.

Probably the most popular genre of all on the best
seller list was the detective story.[12] The classical
detective story offers not only a plot but a puzzle; the
reader can match his wits against those of the detective
to discover "Who done it?" The solution is usually satisfying because it is clear and neat with all the ends tucked
in. From Edgar Allan Poe, the inventor of the type, to
Ellery Queen the detective is a model of rationality in an
ordered world temporarily deranged by a criminal. These
detectives would agree with Erle Stanley Gardner's Perry
Mason in The Case of the Sulky Girl in 1933: "'A man can
nearly always think his way out of any situation in which
he finds himself'" (7). Emphasis is not on the crime but
on its solution--a game shared by reader and detective. The
function of the detective is to use deductive reasoning to
restore order by identifying the criminal. Such tales
remained popular throughout the period, and are still
perhaps the most widely read form of American fiction.

But in the 1930s the detective took on a quite different
character in a quite different world. Disillusion with
World War I, the gangster-ridden cities of the 1920s and
finally the Great Depression of the 1930s had shaken belief

in the power of reason to order society. For the first
time a number of books describing the slums realistically
appeared on the best seller lists of the 1940s, books by
Shulman, Algren and Motley. The hard-boiled detective who
now surfaced inhabits a tough, irrational world in which
one cannot readily tell the good from the bad guys. His
scene is always an urban slum and even the police are
corrupt. There are no heroes or heroines; most of the
characters are involved in at least petty crime. The story
always centers on the crime rather than its solution.
Violence is everywhere, in the action and in the language.
To define the cold-bloodedness of one character in Farewell
My Lovely in 1940, Raymond Chandler, one of the inventors
of the genre, describes his eyes which ". . . could watch
lions tear a man to pieces and never change, that could
watch a man impaled and screaming in the hot sun with his
eyelids cut off" (117). In Strip for Murder by Richard
Prather there are eight violent deaths all separately
detailed, and innumerable forms of violence by knife, gun,
bomb and other less conventional weapons.[13] In any Mickey
Spillane novel one expects that when Mike Hammer, the
private eye answers a knock at his door, if it's a woman he
will rape her, if a man Hammer will shoot him without even
knowing the name or errand of his victim. Victims of
violence abound in these crime stories, not just the
murderee, but anyone who innocently gets in the way of the
murderer or the private eye.

The private eye is smart-alecky, tough, cynical and
cruel. He must be physically strong and very good with a
gun. Unlike the classical detective of middle or upper-
class background he glories in a sordid world, and fits very
well into the lifestyle of the urban slum. His cases are
never solved by the deductive logic of the classical
detective. Sometimes it seems that his solutions result
rather from accidental confrontations as he messes around

the neighborhood than from any rational process. The
hypotheses of a Sherlock Holmes or a Maigret are totally
absent here. As Spillane's Mike Hammer tells one of his
suspects in the 1947 novel I, the Jury: "'Before I'm done
I may shoot up a lot of snotty punks like you, but you can
bet that one of them will have been the one I was after,
and as for the rest, tough luck'" (28-29).

Both the cowboy and the hard-boiled private eye are
American inventions with little in common ostensibly except
that both were created by male writers. The cowboy is a
man of principle, the private eye a man of greed; the cowboy
is innocent, the private eye streetwise; the cowboy inhabits
the natural world, the private eye a customarily corrupt
city; the cowboy adopts a deferential attitude toward women;
the private eye sees them only as objects. But as one gets
closer a surprising number of similarities emerge. Both
are loners detached from family and community. Neither has
any significant relationships with women: the cowboy is
physically remote from them; the private eye has frequent
physical encounters with women's bodies, but is quite as
remote as the cowboy from women. Apparently women are a
threat to their power and their carefully guarded independence. Sexual activity abounds in tough crime stories,
but as violence; to the tough detective women are only
breasts or genitals. Both cowboy and detective live in
violent worlds, and above all must be equipped to handle
violence. Muscles are useful, but the gun even more so.
Theoretically they use this equipment to protect society,
yet both are above the law. The Westerner may need the
concept of the "higher law" to justify making his own law
in each instance, but the private eye gets by without
feeling a need for justification. Both are vigilantes.
As patterns of masculinity the private eye and the Westerner
reinforce each other. William Ruehlmann in Saint With a Gun

puts it succinctly: "The private eye novel was a Western that took place somewhere else."[14]

Next to these examples of the macho male the most popular and most admired American men throughout the period are self-made business men. These books accept as self-evident truth that the United States offers unique opportunities for the American to succeed in making a comfortable living, and the rags to riches mythology is equally unquestioned.[15] Failure rather than success seems more interesting to such major American writers as Hawthorne, Fitzgerald, Dreiser and Faulkner, but not to the most popular American writers. This dichotomy while more noticeable in the United States may be common to other cultures as well. Somerset Maugham sees it as inevitable and universal: the last sentence of his 1944 novel The Razor's Edge comments: "And however superciliously the highbrows carp, we the public in our heart of hearts all like a success story. . . ." Successful characters find a natural habitat in wish-fulfilling books, and most popular writers must be aware that popular success of their novels is more likely if the novel embodies a story of success. That American culture embodies a mystique of success has been noted by most commentators on the American scene from Tocqueville on. William James' characterization of the American romance with success is widely known: "The exclusive worship of the bitch-goddess SUCCESS [sic] is our national disease." Dwight MacDonald sees it as our major motivating force: the American is "not at all convinced that there is any higher motive for activity than success."[16] Indeed today book ads in American newspapers urge one to buy a particular book not because it is interesting, entertaining, intellectually stimulating, informative or for any other intrinsic reason, but merely because it is a best seller successful in the marketplace. The term "success" in many circles has been limited only to financial success.

In most of these books success is recognized only when it results in material prosperity. There are some exceptions, as Mellors in Lady Chatterley's Lover in 1932. It is, however, mainly clerical characters in best selling novels who are permitted to evaluate success in other than material terms, as in Robert Elsmere (1888), In His Steps (1897), The Shepherd of the Hills (1907), Random Harvest (1941), The Keys of the Kingdom (1941), The Cardinal (1950), and the novels about Christ and those by Lloyd Douglas. In two books the dichotomy between success as a person and success in the world is subject for comment. Will Durant in The Story of Philosophy notes that Spinoza "loved wisdom too much to be a 'successful' man" (172). Doc, a character in John Steinbeck's Cannery Row in 1945 observes: "'The things we admire in men, kindness and generosity, openness, honesty, understanding and feeling are the concomitants of failure in our system. And those traits we detest, sharpness, greed, acquisitiveness, meanness, egotism and self-interest are the traits of success'" (150). In two instances humor is allowed to transform failure in the army into successful books. In See Here, Private Hargrove and No Time for Sergeants two soldiers hopelessly mired in army red tape come out as successful and delightful human beings, probably offering consolation to a public made up of many veterans of World War II.

Not until the 1930s when some books finally paint a realistic picture of poverty in the United States is the American Dream questioned. In the late nineteenth century the reform tracts of Henry George, Edward Bellamy and William Harvey did make the best seller list, but the twentieth century was singularly barren of reform schemes. Now for the first time parts of the United States are shown denying success and even ambition to their inhabitants. John Steinbeck in 1939 introduced Americans to desperate rural poverty; Algren, Motley and Shulman did the same for the urban slum. In the slum one might with luck become a successful criminal or even a private eye, but in these books the environment disallows any kind of achievement. The modern city is not susceptible to rational management, and contrary to the American Dream overwhelms the desire and the possibility of any upward mobility. Its inhabitants are not just products, but prisoners and indeed victims of their habitat. Horatio Alger's Ragged Rick translated from 1867 to 1940 would have remained ragged. This evaluation of city conditions comes rather late to the best sellers--some fifty years after Stephen Crane's Maggie, and it remains a minority report.

Success in America has two components: performance of some task and public recognition of one's achievement. Esteem is quite as important as the work accomplished, and is most easily acquired if the work has concrete, visible results. The perfect medium for the exhibition of such concrete results is, of course, money which allows one to conspicuously consume, relax or acquire power. To fulfill his role in these books as family provider the male must achieve a modicum of success, but the highly successful man--the one who has made lots of money--earns almost heroic status. In E. P. Roe's 1874 novel Opening a Chestnut Burr he describes a young American woman's assessment of her young man: "To the practical mind of this American girl, his success in the vast and complicated transactions of business were as grand as the achievements of any hero" (151). He might have been talking of Ayn Rand whose several best sellers manifest an extraordinary admiration for the over-achieving money-maker. The successful man must concentrate only on making profit and disdain consideration of the social results of his activities. In Atlas Shrugged in 1957 one entrepreneur highly approved by Rand, says that he hopes to be able to afford the price of admission to heaven when he dies. His friend points out it is virtue

and not money that allows entrance to heaven. D'Anconia
responds: "'That's what I mean, James. So I want to be
prepared to claim the greatest virtue of all--that I was a
man who made money'" (96, see also 410-15).

From Horatio Alger on making money is the central pursuit
of most American males, and one highly approved in these
books. It is an undertaking requiring intelligence,
courage, and on occasion, ruthlessness. A few of the early
books warn against too much love of money,[17] but most take
the attitude of Russell Conwell in his 1887 pamphlet Acres
of Diamonds: "I say to you that you ought to get rich, and
it is your duty to get rich," Having money is unimportant,
but making money in a competitive market is a test of
manhood. Again in The Razor's Edge an American declares:
"'Money is nothing to us; it's merely the symbol of
success.'"[18]

These books abound in illustrations of how money is made.
The general assumption in most books is that it comes from
hard work. In the earlier books many express absolute
certainty of a causal connection: "It must lead to wealth
with the same certainty that poverty follows in the train
of idleness and inattention."[19] Most of the earlier books
also consider inherited wealth a disadvantage to a young
man, and indeed advocate hardship as a means to spur the
young man to hard work. Even "Genius, that noblest gift of
God to man, is nourished by poverty," according to Haines
and Yaggy (495, see also 125, 184-85). The Horatio Alger
stories, read widely from 1867 on seemed to illustrate this
point of view; rarely was it noticed that in each book the
major character got his start by a bit of luck and courage
rather than just by hard work. In Ragged Dick, for example,
Dick saves a merchant's son from drowning when he falls off
the ferry, and is rewarded by a job in the merchant's shop
(275). Dick's hard work in the job puts him on the way to
fortune, but without the accident of the job hard work would

have been irrelevant. A character in Harold Robbins'
Never Love a Stranger in 1948 who has worked hard but to
no avail is quite caustic about the Horatio Alger stories:
"'. . . all that Horatio Alger stuff is a lot of crap;
because no matter how hard the Alger hero would work, no
matter how honest he was, no matter how difficult his
struggle, he never got anywhere until he either saved or
married the boss' daughter'" (365). Most of the later books
while still showing the successful business man as a hard
worker, also recognized that luck, political connections,
exploitation of others, bribery and other less savory means
also often played a large if not the most important role in
business success.[20] Earlier books such as Opie Read's 1895
novel The Jucklins and Winston Churchill's 1900 The Crisis
severely criticized exploitation or corruption as the way
to wealth. But just as the gangster became the hero of the
slum, so the ruthless business executive, exploiting nature
and man can now inspire admiration simply for achieving
success by whatever means. Looking back from 1953 to the
1920s, Polly Adler remarks that the credo of that decade
was "Anything which is economically right is morally right"
(5), and ". . . the only unforgivable sin was to be poor"
(74). Ayn Rand in 1957 makes a philosophy of the disregard
of the business executive for social values in the process
of accumulating wealth. One of her executives in Atlas
Shrugged in 1957 states flatly: "'I'm not interested in
helping anybody. I want to make money'" (22).

In a society so centered on success it should occasion
no surprise to find some twenty how-to-be-a-success manuals
among the top best sellers. Some offer advice in specific
fields: Chesser in 1947 on sex, Spock in 1946 on raising
children, Kains in 1935 on how to get out of the Depression
by acquiring and running a farm, Lindlahr in 1940 and Jarvis
in 1958 on diet. But most of the manuals give advice on how
to lead happy and successful lives. The earlier manuals

such as Haines and Yaggy in 1876 and Hill's Manual in 1905
offer the reader reams of practical advice about getting
along in the world, what actions and qualities it rewards,
and how to cultivate these in oneself. These traits turn
out to be the same ones Americans had been taught to develop
in themselves in order to produce a good character: honesty,
diligence, thrift, unselfishness. Virtue need not be its
only reward; a good character leads to success in building
a fortune as well as in building character.

As one might expect the Great Depression of the 1930s
brought on a spate of how-to-be-a-success books. But these
were addressed to people disillusioned with the message of
the old manuals. These victims of the Depression had worked
hard and their fortunes had declined. In 1937 Napoleon Hill
produced a book whose title Think and Grow Rich indicates a
new attitude toward success. He decries the popular belief
that riches come to those who work hard; no, ". . . riches
begin with a state of mind, with definiteness of purpose,
with little or no hard work" (27). He is quite as certain
as the old manuals that ". . . riches are not beyond your
reach, that you can still be what you wish to be, that
money, fame, recognition and happiness can be had by all
who are ready and determined to have these blessings" (16).
But one must work oneself into a "white heat of desire for
money" (37); ". . . we must magnetize our mind with an
intense desire for riches" (29-30). This dynamic wish for
money will then create the plans for acquiring it. Following the earlier positive thinking of Trine in 1897 and
Haddock in 1907, Hill argues that one must put oneself in
harmony with the infinite by using the subconscious which
links the finite power of man to the infinite power of God.
This is to be accomplished by what he calls "self-
suggestion" (50), and he offers a formula for its realization. One must go through six steps, beginning with
deciding exactly how much money you want, and ending with

reading your plan out loud every day. Like Trine and
Haddock (and Coué in the 1920s) you must think only positive
thoughts and constantly tell yourself all is well. Hill
believes that "practically all of the great fortunes began
in the form of compensation for personal services or from
the sale of ideas" (104), rather than from hard work or
knowledge of a process or a product.

Dale Carnegie in his two best sellers, How to Win Friends
and Influence People in 1936 and How to Stop Worrying and
Start Living in 1948 resembles Hill in many ways; his road
to success is also based on positive thinking and self-
manipulation. But Carnegie lays particular stress on
learning how to manipulate others. Most of his illustrations of those who have learned how to influence others are
successful business men such as John D. Rockefeller, Charles
Schwab, Walter Chrysler and Andrew Carnegie. He suggests
that both Schwab and Andrew Carnegie knew less about making
steel than about making others do what they wanted; they
knew "how to handle men and that is what made [them] rich"
(80, see also 35-36, 43). Dale Carnegie's prescription for
success appears fully in chapter 6, entitled "How to Make
People Like You Instantly." He proffers much sensible
advice on good manners, but more advice on how to use other
people to one's own advantage. He recommends such ploys as
getting them to say yes to almost anything immediately so
that they get used to agreeing with you, or letting them
feel an idea you have approved of originated with them
rather than you. Carnegie advocates becoming genuinely
interested in others, but his examples indicate no real
interest, but a mere manifestation of interest (68-69). He
remarks that the highest paid engineers are not necessarily
those best in engineering, but those skilled in human
engineering: self-salesmanship and manipulation of others
(13). When you want help, don't ask for it, but figure out
how you can make the other person want to help you (43).

Success depends not on being useful to society, but on
selling oneself.[21]

One of the most interesting and powerful of the positive
thinkers is Norman Vincent Peale; interesting not for any
originality or subtlety of thought, but in the connections
he makes as a clergyman between success in this world and
the next. The practicality of religion in America has a
long tradition observed by Tocqueville in the 1830s, but
extending back to the Puritans of New England with the idea
that worldly success was a presumptive sign of salvation.
In 1887 Russell Conwell, also a clergyman appeared on the
best seller list with Acres of Diamonds, a pamphlet embodying a speech he had given some 6,000 times. He classifies
the acquisition of wealth as a Christian duty because of the
good one can do with cash. The relationship of financial
success to religion was an old and close one in American
culture. Peale's particular contribution is not simply in
seeing a direct relationship between faith and prosperity
(212), but in urging his readers to use religion to advance
their prosperity. He advocates the use of "prayer power"
for business success (63-64). He advises a vacuum cleaner
salesman to repeat: "If God be for me, then I know that with
God's help, I can sell vacuum cleaners" (119). Like Dale
Carnegie he too is concerned with selling oneself; chapter
15 is entitled "How to Get People to Like You." Like Hill
he recommends constant repetition of particular words to
achieve serenity (23), and like Hill, Carnegie and Maltz he
offers a list of rules for success. As his intellectual
forebears he cites Thomas Jefferson, Emerson, Thoreau and
William James who saw the power man could achieve by putting
himself in touch with the infinite by positive thinking (15,
79, 137, 201, 204). Peale's version of their ideas offers
dubious distinction, and would indeed have surprised these
thinkers. For a clergyman to offer aid to others in
discovering how to become a successful human being is hardly

unusual, but Peale's frequent identification of the
successful human being with the successful business man is
a bit startling. Of the many examples he gives of the
success of positive thinking, forty-two are of successes
made in business.

So the way to success in modern manuals is not production
but salesmanship, mirroring a shift in emphasis in the
economy from production to consumption.

In comparing the status accorded males and females in
these books it is important to note that femininity is said
to be shaped almost entirely by nature, masculinity mainly
by social convention. Nature has ineluctably fashioned
women into irrational, emotional weak creatures able to
operate effectively in a very limited sphere. If these
books mirror attitudes between the sexes in America, it is
no wonder that men consider women "mysterious" and inconsistent. Women would have to be consummate liars and
manipulators to fit this pattern of femininity, and, at the
same time, have the intelligence, self-control and physical
strength to keep house and raise a family. Because woman's
place was assumed to be naturally in the home, if she did
involve herself in a career outside the home, no one was
surprised if she failed, and she for such failure would
collect no appreciable opprobrium.

The male, on the other hand is believed to be innately
strong in muscle, mind and will. He is granted freedom to
choose in which areas he wishes to assert himself, but to
enjoy respect as a man he must exercise these strengths.
He must shoulder a constant burden of self-assertion. He
may do so by the kind of machismo one finds in Hemingway.
But, brought up to believe in the rags to riches mythology,
the American male needed also to prove his manhood by
"getting ahead." In the United States he is not just
expected to support his family, but he is under the
necessity of proving himself by bettering his status. In

another culture he could blame failure on a faulty or corrupt political, economic or social system. But in the United States, the land of opportunity for the common man, failure to make money is a sign of personal inadequacy; one can blame only oneself. While the American Dream stimulated ambition, it probably also spawned an American Nightmare in those who failed for whatever reason. Poverty in America meant not only the ordinary miseries of poverty anywhere but uniquely in the United States a paralyzing kind of frustration and a lowering of self-esteem. The horizons of the male were broader than those of the female but he still had to walk a fenced path.

Chapter 5: HERITAGE, RACE AND RACISM

Americans of the late nineteenth and early twentieth
centuries altered the natural world they inhabited more
drastically and more rapidly than had ever been possible
before, and these changes were reflected in their popular
literature. Did best sellers view human nature as equally
malleable?

The definition of human nature has always been a matter
of fascination to speculative human beings. But surely
never more than in the nineteenth and twentieth centuries.
Central to such speculation is the question: which is more
important to the formation of character, heredity or
environment? Philosophes of the Enlightenment divested man
of innate ideas. To John Locke the human being untrammelled
by heritage is a tabula rasa on which experience writes.
The environment--physical, intellectual, spiritual--creates
the human being. And Hector St. Jean de Crevecoeur's
description of the American shortly before the American
Revolution is a perfect illustration of Locke's theory.
The American he describes is not only bigger, but has more
initiative than his European cousins. He is in all ways
the creature of his new environment.

The nineteenth, the century of the novel, probed
constantly and profoundly into the structure and function-
ing of the human personality. But Locke's blank tablet,
immersed in the racism, nationalism and imperialism of the
new century brought out images on the tablet that seemed
to be ineradicable. The nineteenth century no longer
accepted Enlightenment "man." This abstract man had now
become primarily part of a family, a race, a nationality
with a vast array of inherited traits. Such heritage
created men different from each other not only in physique

but in intellectual ability, character and personality as well, and these differences were assumed to be eternal. The appearance in 1859 of Darwin's hypothesis of evolution by natural selection seemed to give empirical sanction to the overwhelming importance of heredity.

Speculation on the relative importance of heredity and environment is still very much with us, and current controversies involving behaviorism and biopsychology indicate that it flourishes as a matter for dissension that is far from decision. Novels are of necessity heavily populated, and in choosing heroes or villains or in rejecting the possibility of heroism or villainy the author exposes the reader sometimes deliberately and sometimes inadvertently to his/her ideas on human nature. Did the inhabitants of popular novels act with the Emersonian freedom to "stand erect, walk alone and possess the universe"? Or were their options limited by cultural conditioning and/or fixed genetic inheritance? Twentieth century authors had available new tools for their interpretations of personality; the nature of the human being was fitfully illuminated by theorists from Freud to the Behaviorists, and psychology was increasingly accepted as a science.

In a country made up of immigrants getting a new start in life, one might expect popular authors to offer their characters a future relatively free of the past, a personality made rather by environment than heredity. In 1782 Crevecoeur could answer his question "What is this American?" by showing him to be a new man, an Adam created by a new physical and cultural environment. But a century later popular literature ascribed the nature of human beings less to cultural ambiance than to a heritage usually seen as genetically determined. Crevecoeur's question would now seem to call for quite different methods of analysis in an atmosphere of doubt that a "new man" was possible.

Many of these books stress, and most imply that nature
rather than nurture determines human personality. And it
is generally assumed that inheritance involves not merely
biological but intellectual and psychological traits as
well. Individuals are defined with great frequency as being
blessed by "good blood" or cursed by "bad" or "tainted"
blood.[1] Some form of the phrase "blood will tell" appears
in many best sellers, even those of recent publication.[2]
Alcoholism and mental retardation are invariably assumed
to be inherent. But what is startling especially in
twentieth century writers is the great variety of personality traits and behavior ascribed by their authors solely
to heredity: for example: "burning avarice" (1941 Cronin,
127), "wrath" (1912 Grey, 70), "calculating" personality
(1945 Costain, 31-32), "emotional intensity" (1944 Williams,
153), "cupidity" (1908 Rinehart, 297). Darwin himself is
quoted in one novel: "'I am inclined to agree with Francis
Galton in believing that education and environment produce
only a small effect on the mind of anyone, and that most of
our qualities are innate'" (1893 Grand, quotation preceding
Book I). The power of heredity is perhaps best expressed
in A. J. Cronin's 1941 novel The Keys of the Kingdom: "'The
hand of heredity propelled Judy forward without mercy'"
(127). Gene Stratton Porter, one of the most popular
novelists of the early twentieth century ascribes almost
all qualities to heredity: pluck, honesty, warmth.
"'Thistles grow from thistles, and lilies grow other
lilies'" (1904 Freckles, 365). And in The Girl of the
Limberlost in 1909 a sympathetically drawn character states
unequivocably that honest men and liars are born and not
made (229). John Fox, Jr., another very popular writer of
the same generation, even ascribes the settlement of the
West to well chosen genes; a pioneer depicted in The Trail
of the Lonesome Pine (1908) is such "by instinct, inheritance, blood and tradition" (40).

One fascinating use of heredity in these books is the
way many authors relate heredity and class. In a country
that habitually boasted of its classlessness and took pride
in its public school system as a class equalizer, it seems
especially curious that so many of its popular books ascribe
courteous behavior entirely to heritage quite apart from
training. Thoughtfulness, kindness, the good manners of the
upper class, would seem to be inherited rather than learned.
There are a number of instances in which a person who lives
in a most unmannerly environment behaves like a gentleman
or lady; the reader (and sometimes the character itself)
later discovers that he or she comes of noble lineage and
therefore comes by good manners naturally. Angel in
Freckles (1904), for example, discovers Irish nobility in
his ancestry. Ahmed, the hero of The Sheik (1921), is
revealed to the reader and Ahmed's lover as the son of an
English peer. And most importantly, when Tarzan kisses a
lady's locket the author comments:

> It was the hallmark of his aristocratic birth,
> the natural outcropping of many generations of
> fine breeding, an hereditary instinct of gracious-
> ness which a lifetime of uncouth and savage
> training and environment could not eradicate.[3]

Conversely peasant ancestry cannot be hidden by education
or changed circumstances. In the 1942 Vivian Connell novel
The Chinese Room a rich banker is plagued by hands that act
destructively on their own without his direction (39, 75,
79); the author attributes this to his peasant heritage.
What is usually called instinct in these books is always
more powerful than training or education or whatever sort.
London's 1903 Call of the Wild is a hymn to all-powerful
atavistic instincts. Domesticated men and animals are
quickly "decivilized" (48); layers of culture disappear
when the wilderness calls forth the much more powerful
hereditary instinct: "He was older than the days he had

seen and the breaths he had drawn" (141, see also 176). In
The Crisis (1900) when education is suggested as a solution
to the problems of Afro-Americans, Colonel Carvel responds:
"'Education isn't a matter of one generation. No, sir, nor
two, nor three, nor four. But of centuries'" (75). A 1958
compendium of natural foods suggests that health can only
be maintained if one follows the food habits of one's
particular race.[4] In this popular literature then there is
no notion of America as an Eden inhabited by a new Adam
untrammelled by the past. This Adam is the product of
evolution rather than creation; his personality is the
result of the past rather than the present--a past
impossible to escape since it is "in the blood."

One sharp but idiosyncratic disagreement with the
importance of heredity appears in a 1907 how-to-be-a-success
book. Frank Haddock in The Power of the Will puts forward
the assertion that education can actually lead to physical
changes in the brain itself: "The gray matter of our brains
is actually plastic and capable of being fashioned" (IX).
But the importance of the environment in forming lives and
character becomes prominent in these books only with
discussions of the city, and especially of the slum. In
Butterfield-8 in 1934 John O'Hara introduces this point of
view (see esp. pp. 138-39), but it is not until the 1940s
that this interpretation becomes common, and only in those
novels centered on the vice-ridden city. It is as though
Crane's Maggie had finally entered popular fiction.

Even more ubiquitous than family heritage or class
heritage in best sellers is the mythology of racial heri-
tage--a concept with vast social consequences. Biologically
race describes a group who ". . . share a statistically
significant proportion of their genes."[5] But because no
one knows what number of which genes are statistically
significant, and since the vast mixture of people in
historical and pre-historical times rules out any such thing

as a "pure" race, one if left with the idea that although
the concept of race exists, it is doubtful that races do.
Whether races exist or not, however, has little to do with
the importance of the concept of race in human affairs.
It has been a veritable behemoth, much more important in
history than in biology.

One author, H. G. Wells in The Outline of History in 1921
recognizes both the fact and fiction of race. He notes that
all races are "more or less mixed" (110), and carefully
disposes of the notion of ranking mankind by racial
heredity. Only two authors before 1940, Julia Peterkin
(1928) and Pearl Buck (1931), carry this interpretation into
their fiction, specifically drawing differences among people
as cultural clothing covering a common humanity. After 1940
this attitude becomes prevalent; the 1940s produced several
novels more or less centering on that theme by Lillian
Smith, James Michener, Pearl Buck, Irwin Shaw. These
authors may be reacting to the newer studies of race and
racism by Boas, Benedict, Klineberg and others. But even
more important to the popularity such novels achieved was
the American identification of racism with the enemy in
World War II. Sentiments against racism could now be
regarded as not only more acceptable to American society,
but even patriotic. Now and then an author who specifically
disavows racial prejudice in general will none the less
casually use racial stereotypes--as in referring to Orientals as "fanatic little yellow men."[6]

But, let there be no mistake: the mythology of race is
all but universal throughout the period. Potentialities
for good or evil, for success or failure are largely
determined by one's racial heritage. The superiority of
the white race is axiomatically accepted; the term "white"
is a synonym for "good", "just", "honest", as in "That's
damned white of you."[7] To be white is equated with being
clean, as in Graustark in 1901 when a character decides to

take a bath in order to "feel like a white man" once more
(97). Being white may also confer social status: Tarzan's
Jane (1914) makes this differentiation: "They were negroes--
he is a white man--a gentleman" (299). Alexander King who
disavows racial prejudice uses the phrase several times,
"It was damned white of . . ." in his 1958 best seller (190,
294). One curious sentence used in several books to
compliment a Jew is: "You're a white guy, Moishe!"[8]

The origin of races rarely comes up, but when it does
white superiority is evident. Most of these books would
agree comfortably with the American geographer Arnold Henry
Guyot who in 1866 pronounced the white race "the normal or
typical race." Uncle Remus in 1880, discussing the origin
of races, asserts that originally all people were black, but
stepping into a pond would wash one "'nice and w'ite.'" The
nimblest got there first and came out white, but the water
in the pond was soon used up, and late comers remained black
(167). An account of creation addressed to Indians in Zane
Grey's 1906 The Spirit of the Border avers that God created
the white man in his own image, and later sent his son to
"'the chosen tribe, the palefaces.'" And God was so pleased
with the palefaces that he made them wiser and wiser and
masters of the world, assigning them the duty to go forth
and teach the "'ignorant tribes'" (101-102). Uncle Remus
and Zane Grey are agreed that whether the original men were
white or black, the superiority of the whites was assured
from the beginning.

Except for nationalities, subdivisions of the white race
are rarely mentioned as such. But in 1903 John Fox Jr. in
The Little Shepherd of Kingdom Come has a rhapsodic piece
on Anglo-Sazon superiority. He refers to American Anglo-
Saxons as a people chosen by Mother Nature for glory. She
has confined them in the Appalachian mountains with "savage
nature, savage beast and savage man" so that she can keep
them close to herself and strengthen them by their struggles

with a formidable environment (127-28). Many of these books
assume that Anglo-Saxon superiority produced the United
States. Conan Doyle apparently believed that the success
of the Mormons was the direct result of exercising their
Anglo-Saxon tenacity.[9] The American Revolution and its
institutionalization of freedom are often ascribed to such
racial traits. In the last paragraph of his historical
novel Richard Carvel (1899) Winston Churchill's title
character prays that the breach between American and English
Anglo-Saxons will be healed so that together, with their
inborn love of freedom they may "'cleanse the world of
tyranny.'" Jules Verne in 1874 produced the most unusual
racial characteristic for Anglo-Saxons. Their "taste for
symmetry" is so pronounced that it determines their culture,
both material and spiritual: in America everything is done
"'squarely'--cities, houses, and follies" (176). By 1947
Anglo-Saxonism appears more realistically in Irving
Shulman's The Amboy Dukes not as a virtue, but as an unfair
social advantage in American culture; only prosperity
negates the advantage of a WASP background in finding a job
(5).

With the exception of London's Call of the Wild in 1903
those books that mention the subject assume that the progeny
of a racially mixed union will inherit the worst qualities
of both races.[10] Jack London, while a strenuous advocate
of white superiority, allowed certain half-breeds (Eskimo,
Indian, white) both ingenuity and great courage in coping
with the wilderness. But miscegenation is generally decried
Several of the later books explore the problem in depth and
with sympathy; Lilliam Smith's Strange Fruit in 1944 and
James Baldwin's Another Country in 1962 examine with sensitivity what was a basically tragic situation in American
society. "Passing" occurs in Hal Ellson's 1949 novel Duke.
Duke, a young, black gang leader, is well aware that one
must be white to get on in the world; to him there is "a

fence around the world." He watches with approval as a
black girl passes from the black to the Hispanic world (14-
15, 47). Rampart Street a 1948 novel by Everett and Olga
Webber centers on these problems. Raphaelle, a blond slave,
illustrates the American rule that one drop of "inferior"
blood conquers all of the rest of one's sanguine heritage,
and this one is black. (At the end of the novel Raphaelle
discovers that she and another baby were switched in the
cradle, and she is pure white.) However illogical the
superior strength of that one drop of "inferior" blood is
an article of firm belief in most best sellers.

BLACKS

Throughout this period as whites occupy the zenith in
racial rank, so blacks are at the nadir. The status of
blacks is instantly perceptible in diction. The term
"nigger" appears casually in most books that mention blacks,
even those of fairly recent composition.[11] Sometimes, as
in Chandler, it appears in a realistic recreation of
American culture or one of its subcultures; sometimes it
seems to be the author's idea of universally acceptable
nomenclature (compare two 1940 books: Chandler, p. 68 with
Christie, p. 74). But whatever the reason, it is ubiquitous
enough that white readers of best sellers would be likely
to accept it without question in whatever context it
appears. In both Tom Sawyer (1876) and Uncle Remus (1880)
it is used consistently, and there are few instances when
specific objection is made in other novels. In John
O'Hara's Butterfield-8 (1934) Isabel objects to its
application to a black woman on the grounds that she is
"swell enough" to be called colored instead of being
referred to as a nigger. In this case class exempts one
from the term. It is used in one instance (1876 Habberton,
181) as a synonym of the color black, when a child says:
"'I want my shoes made all nigger.'" Although the names of

other races are regularly capitalized, "Negro" rarely
appears in that form. Joel Chandler Harris in 1880 (XIV,
XVI, 15) and Barry Goldwater in 1960 (33, 34, 37) sometimes
capitalize it and sometimes do not. Adult black males are
commonly referred to as "boys." John Griffin recording his
experiences as a white masquerading as a black notes that
in this guise he is always called "boy" by whites. One of
the more interesting pejorative uses of language is in the
employment of dialect. In most novels set in the deep
South only the speech of blacks is written in dialect.[12]
Oddly enough the one exception of this is in the fiction
of Kyle Onstott. Although Mandingo (1957) and Drum (1962)
are sensationally and thoroughly racist, dialect is used
for both black and white when appropriate. The convention
of dialect for blacks alone implies that the standard, the
normal is white and the deviation black; the black out of
incapacity cannot learn normal speech.

Africa, a land of mystery to Americans in the nineteenth
century was being explored both physically and intellectually in the twentieth century. But to the reader of best
sellers it was a mystery throughout the period. Probably
the most influential of the nineteenth century books dealing
with Africa were those by H. Rider Haggard: King Solomon's
Mines in 1886 and She in 1887. A good performance by an
African occasions surprise in Haggard's books; he was "a
good hunter, and, for a native, a very clever man" (King
Solomon's Mines, 255). Blacks are frequently referred to
as "savage", cruel (She, 60, 83), but possessing "remarkable
instincts" (this when one is able to locate a source of
water by the sense of smell, in King Solomon's Mines, 286).
Although they are animalesque they make trustworthy servants
and hard workers (264). One major character in King
Solomon's Mines, a Zulu named Umbopa, is a sort of noble
savage, brave and eloquent, showing that "the race is by
no means devoid of poetic instinct and of intellectual

power" although much given to repetition (277). Umbopa is
clearly an extraordinary black--a token. In comparing white
with African civilization (the many African cultures are
inevitably boiled down to one--"African"), Umbopa observes
the predilection of the white for toys (jewels) and money
(314). But he is also used to promulgate the myth of the
greater value put on human life by European civilization
(336), a curious evaluation in an era that saw the development of modern warfare. Africa is pictured as a land of
witchcraft, punishment without trial, cruelty and cannibal-
ism in contrast to the life-giving rationality of European
civilization. As late as 1940 the idea that Africans don't
mind dying--"they were only natives"--is expressed by both
sympathetic and unsympathetic characters in Agatha
Christie's And Then There Were None (46, 69).

In the twentieth century Haggard's Africa is supplanted
by the Africa of Tarzan. Since Edgar Rice Burroughs
published the first Tarzan book in 1914 at least twenty-five
million copies of the books have been issued, and there are
still twenty-four of them in print. There have been forty
movie versions, many comic books, and a television series
is currently to be seen. Russell Nye estimates that except
for Mickey Mouse, Tarzan is the best known fictional
character in the world.[13] That a book's popularity has
nothing to do with its accuracy is clear as one views
Burroughs' innocence of any knowledge of Africa. The
natives are referred to as "savages" with filed teeth whose
"bestial brutishness" (107) is evident in their features;
all Africans are cannibals (288) who inhabit a jungle filled
with lions as well as true jungle animals. Obviously the
Africa Burroughs produced could not possibly foster any
complex cultures in the past, present or future. It was a
land of savage men and beasts, far down on the scale of
evolution, colorful, but incapable of progress in orderly
society without white guidance. At one point in the story

Burroughs introduces Esmeralda, a black woman raised in Europe as a maid. In many ways she is made a figure of ridicule: she is physically ludicrous, often hysterical (168, 178), superstitious (218) and given to the habitual slaughter of the English language (246, 309). In white civilization the fierce African black translates into the ineffectual, foolish servant.

Indeed blacks living outside of Africa are almost always disguised in this stereotype until books written in the 1940s. They are gullible and superstitious. Only Michener's Tales of the South Pacific (1947) specifically rejects the latter characteristic when he describes two blacks who are caretakers of a cemetery for casualties of World War II in the Pacific. Asked if they don't fear ghosts--and the question itself backs the stereotype--they reply that there are no ghosts here, only heroes (321-22). Hard menial labor is so generally associated with blacks that it becomes part of the language: to do such work, according to Hay in 1884 is "to make a nigger of myself" (20). Yet blacks are almost invariably assumed to be lazy by nature. Their love of music is associated only with spirituals and minstrels. Jazz rarely appears at all and when it does it is regarded rather as a rude interruption than a contribution to American culture. The 1927 Elmer Gantry suggests that "'nigger-songs--hand 'em a jolt'" (163). In Bad Girl, a year later, Dot in a maternity hospital in a Harlem in process of becoming a black ghetto is disturbed by the "'rotten music'" from a neighborhood jazz band (221). Amiability is a quality assigned to blacks by authors as diverse as Jack London, Dale Carnegie and D. H. Lawrence. All laud blacks as house servants. Though they may not be given to hard work, their natural warmth and amiability allow them to fulfill this role with great satisfaction to both white and black. Harold Bell Wright in 1909 expresses it so: "Is there, after all, anything

more beautiful in life than the ministry of such humble
ones whose service is the only expression of their love?"
(138). The convenience to whites to believe in this version
of the nature of the Negro is obvious.

Before 1940 only two of the best sellers treat blacks as
human beings, ethnically different from other groups, but
with the same potentialities as whites. Joel Chandler
Harris in 1880 uncovers black folk lore whose theme is the
triumph of the weak over the strong by carefully concealed
cleverness. Harris also objects to the dialect assigned
to blacks by white writers as an "intolerable representation
of the minstrel songs" (VIII). To Harris the nature of
blacks includes remarkable poetic imagination and humor.
The other writer who accords blacks both dignity and
intelligence is Julia Peterkin in her Scarlet Sister Mary
published in 1928. In other books the stereotype is usually
there in major as well as in casual characters. Readers of
best sellers before the 1940s became so used to the stereotype that a neutral statement is startling: in 1876
Habberton's Helen's Babies contains an illustration of
four children dressed more or less alike and playing
together with the title: "Adolphe's ancestors had evidently
emigrated from Africa" (161). Another exception to the
stereotype is in Mark Twain's Huckleberry Finn in 1884.
Twain, an artist as well as a writer, explores in depth the
complexities in the relationship between Jim and Huck as
Huck tries to reconcile his Southern upbringing with his
conscience.

In the twentieth century the lineaments of the stereotype
of the foolish but lovable black are redrawn with a sinister
quality. The child-like black, a conventional figure in
the writings of George Fitzhugh and other defenders of
slavery, has now become the frightening, animalesque figure
who haunts the novels of Thomas Dixon and the oratory of
white supremacists. Comparisons to various animals become

common. They are: "But one degree above the brute"; "They
have lived like wild beasts in the depths of the jungle
since the days of Ham."[14] A resemblance of blacks to apes,
monkeys, baboons is frequently noted, although in fact the
hairiness and thin lips of these animals would seem to
relate them more closely to whites. Except in Frank Yerby's
The Vixens blacks did nothing to achieve their own freedom
except to terrorize whites in the period of Reconstruction
after the Civil War. Their attacks on whites were not
tactics adopted in a rational process to produce a
particular political end; they were the result of uncontrollable animal passions peculiar by nature to blacks.

By the 1930s the animalesque nature of blacks has been
transmuted from general violence to sexual violence. Black
females of any age are assumed to be more amiable and more
experienced in such matters than whites and therefore more
desirable as sex partners. As James Baldwin observes, all
black women are both with bad reputations in American
culture.[15] But much more prominent especially in novels
from the 1940s on is the sexual prowess of the black male,
an accomplishment both deplored and envied. The physical
equipment of the black male is assumed to be prodigious.
Furthermore he is irresistibly impelled to use it on white
women. James Baldwin sees this attitude as a product of
the white male's fear of sexual superiority of blacks.[16]
Another non-fiction best seller, Jailbait (1949) observes
that although the American myth is that most rapes are
perpetrated by black males on white females, actually in
the rural South which leads the U.S. in the incidence of
rape, it is overwhelmingly white males who rape black
females (108). And John Griffin, a white masquerading as
a black in 1961 found that whites assumed he as a black
was so lacking in moral principles that nothing would offend
him (28).

Two best sellers by Kyle Onstott, Mandingo (1957) and
Drum (1962) are veritable catalogues of graphically
described sex acts involving blacks. Both novels center
around a breeding farm for slaves. Young African males,
told that they will be used as studs, welcome the chance
to become slaves. Their "native savagery" makes them
irresistible to white as well as black women (Drum, 148-51),
however ghastly the consequences. In Mandingo when a white
woman bears a black child the black father is literally
boiled in oil. The sexual acts described in these two
novels in great variety and vast profusion have nothing
whatever to do with affection, but are essentially forms
of violence. The reader soon gets used to the idea that
whenever Onstott allows two characters to meet, especially
if at least one is black there will be some kind of sexual
explosion; such sensationalism unquestionably sold books.

This extended and explicit discussion of black sexuality
from the 1940s on does not necessarily mean that this was a
new white perception of blacks. By the 1940s there was a
new perception of sexuality in American culture which made
explicit and graphic descriptions of sexual acts acceptable
in books sold above the counter. And writing in this mode
almost guaranteed a wide sale. Prodigious and violent
sexuality are then added to the inherent character of blacks
in best sellers.

Slavery is generally envisioned as a cruel institution,
but one that kept blacks happy. Unquestionably Uncle Tom's
Cabin in 1852 had an enormous effect on most later nineteenth century novels. But however important to the anti-
slavery movement, it also upheld racism, as Joel Chandler
Harris pointed out in the preface to the 1895 edition of
Uncle Remus. And, as J. C. Furnas observed Stowe subscribed
to the "A.S.P.C.A. rather than to the Declaration of
Independence."[17] To Harriet Beecher Stowe blacks are by
nature affectionate, careless, and irresponsible with a

passion for the gorgeous and fanciful which "draws on them
the ridicule of the colder and more correct white race"
(202). "If not a dominant and commanding race, they are,
at least, an affectionate, and magnanimous and forgiving
one" (534). She does present Eliza and George as blacks
who cannot accept slavery, and in many ways George is a
militant. But her condescension to blacks is evident even
in George who hopes to bring the glories of Anglo-Saxon
civilization to Africa.

Two extraordinarily popular twentieth century novels
dealing extensively with the slave South are much less
critical of slavery, and movies made of these novels were
quite as popular as the original books. In a 1933 novel
the title character, Anthony Adverse gets rich in the slave
trade and justifies his profession by comparing the position
of the black in the United States to blacks in Africa:
"'They are safer, more comfortable. Even their hardships
are comparative luxuries'" (581). Gone With the Wind in
1936 presents only the domestic slave as stereotypical mammy
who loves and controls the white family. On the whole
slaves appear seldom on this Southern plantation, freeing
the reader from what might be a painful subject. In neither
novel is there a rebellion or a runaway slave. Frank Yerby
in 1946 counters this with a somewhat more realistic picture
of the institution. In one instance an adult slave explains
to a slave child that the whites are stronger than we are;
therefore we must be clever "like a swamp fox"; we must be
polite, think fast, learn to read, write and figure, but
don't let master know (238-39).

Except for Yerby, who is himself black, those authors
who deal with the Civil War and Reconstruction give no
indication that blacks had anything to do with their own
freedom. Chad, the hero of John Fox Jr.'s 1903 novel, The
Little Shepherd of Kingdom Come, is said to have no prejudice, but is horrified to hear that the Union army is about

to enlist black troops. Yerby, in The Vixens, treats such
a reaction with scorn. More typical is the portrayal in
Gone With the Wind (1936) of the slaves' reaction to their
emancipation at the end of the war. The "better class of
them scorning freedom" stay on the plantation, but the field
hands run away taking the master's movable property with
them. Scarlett meditates on how "stupid" they are (654,
639, 407). The black role in Reconstruction is to steal
(656), rape (562, 648, 656, 745), live without work (555,
639), and sit in barefooted ignorance in state legislatures
(904). Schools founded to educate blacks in the period of
Reconstruction are usually regarded as a waste of time and
money because blacks are uneducable.[18] And in most popular
novels, including Gone With the Wind, the South (and the
term always means the white South) is saved only by its
brave young men organized into the Ku Klux Klan and the
Knights of the White Camellia. Only Yerby in The Vixens
in 1947 offers a more realistic picture of the terror these
organizations sponsored (190, 194). He also shows blacks
flocking enthusiastically to the new Reconstruction schools
(210), and whites burning those schools out of fear that
they might become an agency to achieve equality (9). But
most of the books that deal with Reconstruction at all have
accepted the view of the nineteenth century Southerner.

White treatment of blacks comes to be regarded as
mistreatment only by the 1940s. In that decade race
discrimination as an unfair mode of behavior takes many
forms. Sometimes it appears in ancillary incidents as in
the 1954 novel Not as a Stranger by Morton Thompson
describing discriminatory admissions to medical school
(415), or in Raymond Chandler's 1940 Farewell, My Lovely
where the police pay little attention to a crime if the
victim is black (15, 36). But several thoughtful and moving
novels investigate the problem of inequality in depth with
the welter of conflicting emotions and actions these produce

in both whites and blacks. Perhaps the two best are Lillian Smith's <u>Strange Fruit</u> in 1944 and Harper Lee's <u>To Kill a Mockingbird</u> in 1960. Their popularity was probably achieved by their sensational subject matter, but they deserve recognition both for literary quality and for allowing whites to enter the world of discrimination on a new path. Harry Golden, a Jew living in the South, analyzes the problem with old knowledge and new humor in <u>Only in America</u> (1958). In 1961 John Griffin detailed his experiences in <u>Black Like Me</u> while living as a black in the South. This book offers to the white reader a unique opportunity to walk in the shoes of blacks and an uncomfortable and dangerous trip it is.

Politicians on the subject of black equality entered the best seller lists first in Wendell Wilkie's <u>One World</u> in 1943. In the midst of World War II he sees the necessity of doing away with what he calls "imperialism at home" if we expect to fight it abroad. But in 1958 J. Edgar Hoover's <u>Masters of Deceit</u> implied that those who struggled for equal rights were probably Communists and/or Russian agents. And finally Barry Goldwater in <u>The Conscience of a Conservative</u> defended segregated education on the grounds that education is not a civil right and the Constitution permits no interference by the Federal government in education. Although from the same political party the contrast between Willkie and Goldwater is interesting; both books were campaign documents.

Politics appears in particularly interesting conjunction with race in an Irving Wallace novel, <u>The Man</u> published in 1962. Through a series of accidents, Dilman, a black Senator, becomes President of the United States. The novel analyzes the complex reactions of Dilman and the nation to his and their situation. Much of his energy is spent trying to counter the nation's stereotypical view of black character. For example, he feels he cannot marry the woman he

loves because she has a light complexion, nor must he ever
be alone in a room with a white woman. His friend describes
this sensitivity by saying he is constantly afraid of making
"'Negro mistakes in front of your white peers'" (233).
Wallace describes with care the veil between white and black
in America, both the fierceness and the delicacy of race
relations. Most significantly this novel presents an
intelligent and knowledgeable, gentle but independent black;
he is a unique character in best sellers.

The popularity of these few books is heartening. Yet a
study of the best sellers reveals a prejudice of such age
and depth that it can not be wished away soon. In the white
mind Sambo still plays around foolishly, mammy still cleans
the house, and the jungle savage lurks around each urban
corner.

AMERICAN INDIANS

Although American Indians join blacks in their general
inferiority to whites in best sellers, they occupy a
significantly different position. And quite literally. To
white readers of twentieth century best sellers the problem
of the Indian was remote in both time and place. He
belonged to history and to segregated reservations. Nineteenth century Americans lived in an era of Indian warfare,
but it was geographically remote from most of them. And
warfare was a more conventional way of handling a different
culture than the complex problems of integration posed by
blacks.

Like blacks Indians were assumed to be violent by nature,
but theirs was a quite different kind of violence. The
sexual overtones heard in the descriptions of black violence
are absent from descriptions of Indians except in The
Carpetbaggers, Harold Robbins' 1961 novel. Robbins manages
to color everything with sex of a violent sort; in this case
Indians torture an enemy by positioning his genitals on an

ant hill. Whenever Indians enter these books they are portrayed as fierce: in Tom Sawyer Injun Joe slits his enemy's
nostrils--an action that identifies him as an Indian:
"'because white men don't take that sort of revenge'" (411).
Examples of Indian cruelty are innumerable in these books,
always as concomitants of war. At the same time that they
are described as savage, they are also recorded as unemotional and cold.[19] Even as late as 1954 in The Royal Box
by Frances Parkinson Keyes Indians are critical of ordinary
means of killing because "'the guy'd die without suffering'"
(49). Their cruelty is coldly calculated rather than
passionate, and is called out primarily by warfare. In the
1934 Thin Man Hammett cites them as cannibals (62), but this
is the only instance of this particular charge. Peace
negotiations are no deterrent to cruelty; Anya Seton's The
Winthrop Woman in 1958 shows a group of Indians chopping
a captive slowly into small pieces while smoking a peace
pipe (240). Owen Wister's Virginian in 1902 offers the one
dissident opinion in reassuring a frightened Easterner: the
stories about Indian cruelty are exaggerations by newspaper
editors to keep troops in the country so that friends of
the editors can make money supplying the troops (298).
Indian misbehavior enters language with the cliché "wild
Indians" applied to rude, noisy, boisterous children.

The love of gaudy finery is ascribed to Indians as to
blacks. But the squalor, dirt and smell of modern Indian
villages is as frequently mentioned.[20] Rarely is kindness
of any sort ascribed to Indians. Bret Harte's 1870 story
"High-Water Mark" is one of the few instances: Indians
rescue a woman and baby from a flood.

European policy toward Indians rarely rates criticism in
these books. In a story of the American colonies, published
in 1958, Anya Seton's heroine explains Indian warfare as a
natural response to unfair Dutch policies (399). This book
also details the cruelty of the Massachusetts settlers in

their massacre of the Pequot Indians: they sold the captive
Indian women as slaves and exhibited the severed hands of
dead warriors in Boston. Finally her heroine states that
the Indians are no more cruel than the colonists (472). The
1905 edition of Hill's Manual uses as an example of irony a
statement to the effect that the Indians have been benevo-
lently relieved of "vain baubles and the filthy lucre of
this world" so that they can now concentrate on matters
spiritual (62). These are, however, most unusual evaluations. Most of these books would agree with the opinion
expressed by Betty MacDonald in The Egg and I in 1945:
". . . the more I saw of them the more I thought what an
excellent thing it was to take that beautiful country [the
Northwest] away from them" (220). In 1948 in How to Stop
Worrying and Start Living Dale Carnegie dissolves Indian
problems in a miasma of positive thinking when he quotes a
general whom he admires greatly: "'. . . nearly all the
worries and unhappiness of the Indians come from their
imagination and not from reality'" (64).

In 1884 a book devoted primarily to Indian-white relationships was published; it became in Frank Luther Mott's
phrase a "better", but not an all-time "best" seller, and
eventually a very popular movie whose theme song "Ramona"
is still played. The author, Helen Hunt Jackson, had
published four years earlier A Century of Dishonor, a
critical review of U.S. Indian policy. Ramona is a love
story of the marriage of a woman of Latin American descent
to an Indian and their trials living as Indians in a white
country as the whites steal their land. Ramona observes
that Mexicans and Indians kill only for hate or in anger,
but white Americans will commit any crime, even murder, for
money (295, 219). An older woman in the story, from a poor
family that has migrated west from Tennessee is slowly
divested of her prejudice against Indians, a prejudice she
says she imbibed from newspapers and narrations of Indian

massacres of whites (355-58). She is especially tender
toward Ramona and Alessandro. But it should be noted that
her understanding comes from domesticating, from Anglicizing
Indians, by seeing them as exactly like herself, by melting
them in her own pot. This book probably had some influence,
but it could hardly withstand effectively the tremendous
wash of anti-Indian writing in western novels--and the best
seller lists included great quantities of these.

Perhaps the most important if the novelists who wrote at
length on Indians was Zane Grey, the author of many best
sellers, all made into extraordinarily popular movies. Grey
portrays the Indian as possessed of "inherent" nobility--as
he says in The Spirit of the Border in 1906. He is noble
in his pride, honor, love of freedom and hatred of deceit
he so frequently meets in whites. As whites conquer or
steal away Indian land, the Indians' "chivalrous courage,
that sublime inheritance from ancestors who had never known
the paleface foe, degenerated into a savage ferocity" (95).
Indians are easier to kill than to tame. Most of the action
in the novel is of Indian warfare as is the case in many of
Zane Grey's other novels. To Grey the Indians will be
redeemed by religious conversion, a process going on in a
mission settlement called the Village of Peace: "Here . . .
was incontestable proof that the savage nature could be
tamed and civilized" (85). After conversion they settle
down into the ways of white civilization working in shop or
field (91). The superiority of white civilization over that
of the Indians is made quite clear; the future of the noble
savage depends on his acceptance of white civilization--he
must become white in culture if not in color. And the
reward for such conversion will be an abundance of material
goods, as is clearly explained to the Indians by a character
much admired by Grey (104).

So, although Zane Grey seems to exalt the Indian, fundamentally he seems to agree with a statement in James M.

Cain's <u>Serenade</u> in 1937 that "primitive man is not any fine, noble brute at all," and modern man is his superior in all ways (21).

ORIENTALS

In the light of racial attitudes and actions expressed elsewhere in the culture it seemed reasonable to expect strong racial prejudice against Orientals in the best sellers. Early in the twentieth century the racist diatribes of Madison Grant and Lothrop Stoddard, their fears that the superior Nordic race might not survive the proliferation of colored and therefore inferior races were widely known. Even the socialist, Jack London, after the defeat of Russia by Japan was alarmed by the "Yellow Peril" from both inside and outside the United States. Such fears, based on theory, were put into action by the Federal government in the Chinese Exclusion Act of 1882 and the Gentlemen's Agreement with Japan in 1907, both designed to keep out Oriental immigrants. At the same time the Pacific states set up a series of discriminatory acts against Orientals by outlawing alien land ownership and establishing segregated schools. And after the Japanese attack on Pearl Harbor in 1941 such domestic persecutions were spectacularly nationalized by the gathering of West Coast Japanese into concentration camps.

Yet surprisingly in the top best sellers there is relatively little prominence given to Orientals; the yellow peril is, in most books, a pale buff. It may be that both readers and writers of these books were mainly Easterners, and not so acutely aware of Orientals as were inhabitants of the Pacific Coast. By comparison to blacks, Indians and Jews, Orientals appear but rarely as incidental characters. This lack of interest in the top best sellers is, however, more than compensated as far as the Chinese are concerned by two fantastically popular series: Fu Manchu by Sax Rohmer

and Charlie Chan by Earl Derr Biggers. No single one of
these books meets the criterion used to define a best seller
in this study, but their collective numbers and influence
was phenomenal. There were thirteen Fu Manchu books
published from 1913 on, and continuously in print since
that time; most of these appeared first as magazine serials.
After book publication both Fu Manchu and Charlie Chan
haunted the movie screen—forty-four Charlie Chan movies
were made.

The Japanese appear in a much more favorable light than
the Chinese. This may be because the Chinese appear more
often as immigrants to the United States with all of the
problems thereof; the Japanese on the other hand almost
never appear in that guise. Instead they are representatives of a strong coherent nation emulating the virtues of
Western civilization. They are hard workers in the
American sense, working for an accumulation of material
goods in a rapidly industrializing society.[21] That they
make excellent soldiers is noted as early as 1874 by Jules
Verne (139). The novels portraying the Japanese at any
length are novels about World War II where although
brutality is ascribed to them as it always is to the enemy,
their soldiering is greatly admired.[22] Praising Japanese
military prowess at that time could well be popular with an
American audience. The more favorable the foe, the more
heroic the victory, and we did defeat the Japanese in that
war. Michener alone translates Japanese military talents
to Japanese Americans in noting their extraordinary bravery
in the American army; he assumes they were trying to prove
themselves particularly loyal and useful Americans in the
face of prejudice (948).

Equating Japanese with Europeans in character and motives
occurs in few best sellers. H. G. Wells in 1921 argues
against Kipling's white man's burden by pointing out that
most Europeans do not yet realize that Asiatics are as bold,

as vigorous, as generous and as self-sacrificing as Europeans (988). Irwin Shaw in 1948 allows them to share the
faults as well as the virtues of the West by giving the
views of a Japanese-American gardener in California, as he
meditates on Japanese motives at Pearl Harbor: "'Before
England wants, she take. America wants, she take. Now Japan
wants . . . she take'" (182). Uris in 1953 allows his characters to use the language of racial stereotypes "monkey"
(254), "fanatic little yellow men" (365, 381), but he also
allows an intellectual to make the point that they were
civilized "when all good Texans were living in caves" (254).

The only best seller centering entirely on the Japanese
is John Hersey's Hiroshima in 1946, a stunning journalistic
account of the impact of the first atomic bomb attack on
the lives of six citizens of Hiroshima. In each case Hersey
leads the reader from the customary morning routine to the
inevitable individual disasters that accompanied the
explosion. Unlike most best sellers Hiroshima offered no
mythology to comfortably explain disaster, it posed no
"happy problems", it did not paint the Japanese as subhuman
"gooks" or "monkeys" deserving annihilation. It offered
horror, but real horror, not the delightfully frightening
kind so frequently found in popular books. On the contrary
the reader was drawn into the lives of people with whom he/
she could identify as they moved from ordinariness to
despair. Americans were forced by this book to confront
their victims, innocent civilian casualties of American
military action. That it is well written is not enough to
make it a best seller; had good writing been a criterion to
enter the best seller lists, the lists would be small
indeed; yet it went through twenty-five printings in the
twenty years following publication.

On the whole, the Chinese did not fare so well, probably
because the Chinese unlike the Japanese are perceived as
clinging to their own culture rather than adopting the

industrialization of the West. In these books this is a rejection of parts of American culture of which we were particularly proud. Only H. G. Wells in 1921 and Wendell Willkie during World War II foresee a hopeful future for China, but it is a future looking much like the American present. Willkie expects from the Chinese what the Japanese have already produced--the swift industrialization promised by Chiang. By 1958, however, The Ugly American infers a future filled with cruelty and inhumanity as China's direction veers to catching up with the Communist rather than the capitalist world (126, 131). Before Pearl Buck and James Michener join the ranks of best sellers, most books that mention China at all picture Chinese culture as does Hill's Manual in 1905: ". . . they are opposed to European and American civilization, the building of rail- roads, and generally to the Christian religion" (141)--all damning characterizations. Only one book, Thomas Costain's The Black Rose in 1945 mentions the glories of ancient Chinese civilization: the invention of the compass, paper, printing, gunpowder, the telescope. Actually in this story of thirteenth century European travellers in Asia, a certain superiority of Chinese civilization is implied in the comment that the West uses these inventions only to make money. This accusation against the West is most unusual; ordinarily it is the Chinese who are accused of greed for money and sharp business practices. In William Huie's The Revolt of Mamie Stover in 1951 the Chinese are called "the Jews of the Orient"--and that is no compliment.[23]

Chinese Americans appear in a uniformly unfavorable light. The earliest author to characterize the Chinese is Bret Harte. In 1870 he deplored the "vulgar clamor about servile and degraded races" as applied to the Chinese (244- 47). But he was not so tolerant of the Chinese as this would make him appear. His poem "The Heathen Chinee", quoted up and down the land, characterizes the Chinese as unique "for ways that are dark and for tricks that are vain." He shows Ah Sin (a carefully chosen name) winning by cheating at a game of cards he professed not to understand. And when Harte reports a Chinese dramatic performance he thinks it amusing that the hero gets up and walks away after an agonizing death on stage. That none of the audience laughs convinces him not that stage conventions differ, but that the Chinese have no sense of humor (242-43).

Chinese women always appear to be sensitive, highly sexed and gracefully subservient. In The World of Suzie Wong in 1957, the story of a Hong Kong prostitute with a heart of gold, the author observes that Oriental women have retained a femininity lost in the West: they are "dedicated to building up the masculinity" of their men whereas Western women are dedicated to its destruction (102). In Pearl Buck's writing this involves a delicate self-effacement on the part of the female, but in the popular Fu Manchu series Chinese femininity seems to imply a willing acceptance of any exercise of masculine will and power, however painful. At one point Fu Manchu's daughter, exhibiting scars from a merciless beating remarks that in China "women are still treated as women."[24]

Casual twentieth century references to the Chinese living abroad places them inevitably in restaurants or laundries, and always in Chinatown. In Bad Girl in 1928 the proprietor of one such restaurant muses that Americans probably picture China as one big Chinese restaurant (24). Chinese abroad are generally referred to as "mysterious."[25] As drug users they appear as early as 1874 in Jules Verne's Around the World in Eighty Days; Verne blames the British for foisting opium on the Chinese (113). American Chinatowns appear as bend of drug iniquity in most of the books that mention Chinatown at all, whether in New York, London, or San Francisco.[26] In 1955 the title character of Auntie Mame ascribes the popular American picture of the Chinese to the movies which delight in peopling China and Chinatowns with innocent drug victims, slaves subjected to elaborate tortures, and Tong Wars (12). But the best sellers probably contributed to this vision.

The greatest expansion of American consciousness of the Chinese came with the Fu Manchu series starting in the U.S. in 1913. The thirteen books detail innumerable nefarious schemes of Fu Manchu to take control of the world by a combination of science and mysticism. These far-reaching Asiatic conspiracies are surely the yellow peril at its most fearsome. Fu Manchu exhibits an extraordinary disregard for human life; in The Trail of Fu Manchu in 1934 he quotes Paracelsus: "'Light is the fire, the body the fuel'", but interprets it literally and uses human flesh as fuel for a furnace (101, 134-38). His cruelty is not restricted to strangers: he tortures and finally executes his own daughter. Fu Manchu himself is described as: "the Devil's Agent on earth" (15); "the yellow peril incarnate in one man" (1913 The Insidious Dr. Fu Manchu, 17). There are sexual overtones in descriptions of "his evil, wonderful face" (1934 Trail of Fu Manchu, 115) that remind one of Dracula. His bearing is that of a prince, he radiates authority and a great brain shows out of his long green eyes. The series abounds in fake Oriental mysticism. By a combination of chemistry and the occult he can control people by talking to them even when there are no physical means of communication or when they are on different continents. According to his daughter this is an Eastern talent: "'In the East, when we are interested, we know how to get in touch'" (70).

Fu Manchu's virtues and vices transfer easily to the Chinese in general. Both the power and the personality assigned to the Chinese in this series are terrifying indeed. The Insidious Dr. Fu Manchu the first of the series (1913) established the pattern. The Chinese are an "inscrutably mysterious race" (38); "the Oriental mind is cruel and cunning" (80, 183); they commit "strange Oriental horrors" (44), such as infanticide performed on human beings by scorpions (64). The narrator says "'No white man . . . appreciates the unemotional cruelty of the Chinese'"; when they think they are being merciful, "'God help the victims of Chinese mercy!'" (63). The yellow peril is the theme of the series. The almost omnipotent Fu Manchu is trying to turn "the balance which a wise Providence had adjusted between the white and yellow races" (123). The organization he heads is described as "a murderous conspiracy to subject the Western races to domination by the East" (1934 The Trail of Dr. Fu Manchu, 212). In The Wrath of Fu Manchu published in serial form in a magazine in the 1950s Fu Manchu's comspiracy has been updated to the cold war: in order to get U.S. support in his effort to wipe out Communism, he threatens, by reverse alchemy, to de-gold some of the treasure in Fort Knox!

Most of Fu Manchu's activities while world-wide, center in Limehouse, London's Chinatown, easy for Americans to translate into the Chinatown of any American city. Here opium and hashish are daily available, and the ways of the Chinese are indeed seen to bear our Bret Harte's warning. The inhabitants of Limehouse cooperate fully in the schemes of Fu Manchu, and lead secretive lives in a filthy, chaotic environment organized only by their devilish leader. Sax Rohmer, the creator of Fu Manchu, knew as little of China as Edgar Rice Burroughs knew of Africa; neither had even visited the continents whose people they stereotyped. And the public accepted without question their racial myths to explain to themselves their own hostility and cruelty to Negroes and Orientals. Tarzan and Fu Manchu entered American culture at about the same time; they have been in print for sixty-five years and still are. They are so much a part of American culture that even those who somehow

escaped reading either a Tarzan or a Fu Manchu book are
familiar with their names, styles and exploits.

A somewhat different picture emerges from the other
popular twentieth century series centered on the Chinese in
Earl Derr Biggers'. Charlie Chan mysteries. Charlie Chan is
a Chinese detective originally from the Honolulu police
force and now operating in England and the United States.
He is genial and generous. His particular Chineseness is
brought out in his ability to read the human heart as the
core of his success as a detective. Reading the human heart
is an instinctive not a rational process, and while it lacks
the magic of Fu Manchu it is assumed to be a mystical
Oriental ability. Chan himself frequently characterizes
the Chinese as "'psychic people.'"[27] In The Keeper of the
Keys in 1932 he considers it "barbarous" to search the
pockets of a suspect (91). At one point in contrasting
Eastern with American culture he notes the American passion
for results: "'. . . yet the apple-blossom is so much more
beautiful than the dumpling'" (254). That he is of a
philosophical turn of mind seems to be indicated in that he
speaks almost entirely in aphorisms. Like most fictional
American detectives his cooperation with the police sometimes leaves something to be desired. While exhibiting
his infinitely greater skill in solving crimes he usually
cooperates, but in one spectacular instance he disobeys the
law to frustrate the police. When he realizes a faithful
old Chinese servant may be indicted for helping his master
(who is accused of murder) Chan plans and helps to carry
out his escape to China so that he can live out his last
days in peace (122-25). Chan, an educated Chinese, is then
sensitive, and delicate. Other Chinese Americans in these
books are portrayed as inveterate gamblers (205). Chinese
servants in America seem to be very much like black servants
as depicted in best sellers: they may express what seems
like independence in harmless complaints, but their loyalty

to their employers is boundless (35). Unlike Sax Rohmer,
Earl Derr Biggers notes the oppression of Chinese immigrants
in their adopted land (122).

But on the whole malevolent Fu Manchu and benevolent
Charlie Chan both embody the same fake Oriental mysticism.
Both were popular in magazines such as Colliers, This Week,
The Saturday Evening Post, and in movies as well as in books.
Although it is impossible to acquire accurate figures on
comparative sales, apparently Fu Manchu was and remained
more popular than Charlie Chan. Fu Manchu has been continuously in print and is still selling briskly in paperbound
reprints; Charlie Chan is today available only in a rather
expensive English reprint. A comparison of the two produces
solid evidence that lucid writing is not the primary
requirement for books to sell in great numbers. The Chan
series, while not great literature is readable. The Fu
Manchu series is made up indeed of tales of mystery: they
are so badly written than the reader is frequently at a loss
to know what has happened in the story. They offer scientific wonders, the occult, plenty of gore imaginatively
presented, sensational horrors of all sorts, a titanic
struggle between Oriental deviltry and white rationality.
Apparently these were more than adequate substitutes for
intelligibility.

Finally in 1931 the best seller list included a book
about China by an author really knowledgeable about the
country: Pearl Buck, the daughter of missionaries, was
raised in China. Torn by the Depression Americans welcomed
The Good Earth with its tale of poor, simple Chinese
peasants; in a sense it seems like a Chinese version of the
later Grapes of Wrath by John Steinbeck. In both the very
poor struggling with their poverty are inspired by an almost
mystical love of the land. Her portrayal is a sympathetic
one; they are simple, quaint and logical. As with Michener,
Buck shows their differences with American culture, but at

the same time offers the reader a chance to explore and
understand both their differences and their humanity. She
was awarded a Pulitzer prize in 1932 and a Nobel prize in
1938. In 1946 Buck produced another best seller--<u>Pavilion
of Women</u>, about an upper class Chinese woman who dominates
and manipulates her tradition-bound family. She commands
their lives for them until her own liberation through a
non-traditional (and singularly unconvincing) love affair
of her own. Both novels end with the coming of the new,
modern China foretelling the end of the ordered society
Buck so neatly described. Buck's novels are probably less
important as art than as sociology. She is most successful
at portraying not full-blooded individual characters, but
the customs and manners of a civilization. She offers a
useful counterweight to American mythology of the Chinese,
but Fu Manchu is still selling well in the United States
of the 1980s.

JEWS

One of the most pervasive myths in best sellers is that
the Jews are a race. Discrimination and persecution had
always been practiced on the Jews as a religious or cultura'
group insistent on maintaining their own religion and
identity. One could lost one's life, family, property
thereby, but at least theoretically there was the possibility of conversion and consequent assimilation. But by
the late nineteenth century Jews were perceived widely
not merely as a cultural or ethnic or religious group, but
rather as a race with immutable, inherent physical, intellectual and personality characteristics. As with members
of other alleged races the individual Jew is seen to be
genetically endowed with particular potentialities and
genetically limited in others. Unlike other non-Nordic
groups, however, the genetic heritage of the Jews includes
intelligence and industriousness, qualities acknowledged to

be desirable traits. Such characteristics should have made
them particularly acceptable in an America proud of its
public school system and its open road to success for the
hard-working. But instead of encouraging their assimilation
into American society the intelligence and industry of the
Jews made them particularly undesirable. They were too good
at achieving the American brand of success. As John Fox Jr.
puts it in The Trail of the Lonesome Pine in 1908, Jews are
not just intelligent and ambitious; they are "wily" (390).
They were generally assumed to be immoral in the use of
their intelligence and hence sinister over-achievers. They
achieve success in things of this world, but a success
without esteem because inevitably their financial wizardry
is the product of dishonesty and tricky manipulation. Such
Jews appear as casual characters in most of these books.

The intelligence of the Jew is usually modified in these
books by demeaning adjectives. Jewish scholars are narrow-
minded, clever or cunning rather than rational.[28] The word
"cunning" implying chicanery is the most common adjective
applied to Jews. In 1867 Ouida characterizes their contributions to knowledge as "cunning science and the sophistry
of wrong" (125). In The Robe (1942) a Gentile is described:
"'That boy should have been a Jew! . . . He has a keen
mind and is cunning'" (229). That many intellectuals are
Jews is no recommendation to an American audience in favor
of general education but a bit suspicious of scholars.

Physically the Jew is always graced with a large nose.[29]
In Churchill's 1899 Richard Carvel Charles Fox warns that
a certain horse "'. . . has a Jew Nose'" so beware. This
draws the response: ride him with a gold bit and "'he is a
kitten'" (336). Often the face of a Jew is said to exhibit
traces of what is assumed to be Jewish character as in
The Citadel in 1937 where the phrase a "clever Jewish face"
appears (241), or Mutiny on the Bounty in 1932 where "sharp-
faced Jews" are mentioned (16). The life-style of Jews

exclude them from ever being of the world of gentlemen and
ladies; they are fond of flashy clothes and "aggressively
uncouth."[30] Rich Jews are distinguished from rich Gentiles
by an overweening selfishness--they want the best of everything, as it is put in The Silver Chalice in 1952 (138).
Jews, like blacks, are also made figures of derision by
being made to speak in a bastard dialect when all others,
immigrants as well as natives speak standard English. One
idiosyncratic put-down of Jews appears in The Day Christ
Died (1957) by Jim Bishop where it is said that Jews dislike
dogs and in ancient Jerusalem kept them not as pets but only
to guard their shops or houses (35). To a society that
perceives the dog as man's best friend and the possessor of
the particularly masculine virtues of honesty, loyalty,
courage this is criticsm indeed.

On the whole in these books the Jewish religion is
admired as seminal to the major religions of the West, the
source of monotheism as well as the idea that ethics is an
essential part of religion. Nor are the Jews blamed for
Christ's crucifixion except now and then in sentiments
expressed by an unsympathetic character. Oursler in 1949
(265) and Bishop in 1957 (334) point out that Jews were
plagued for centuries for a crime of which they were
innocent: the Jews were fair at Christ's trial, but were
only a kind of grand jury; the Romans convicted him. And
the ancient Hebrews as opposed to modern Jews come out as
human beings in books on that period by Oursler, Bishop and
Lew Wallace. Now and then the ancient Hebrews are criticized as "rich Jews" more concerned with the externals of
religion than are other people.[31] And the Jew's love of
money appears in many guises among the ancient Hebrews. In
1887 She shows the Jews scorning Christ precisely because
he was born to a poor and lowly family whereas they loved
wealth and power (112-13). And Annas, the high priest of
Jerusalem, is shown in both Oursler in 1949 (14) and Bishop

in 1957 (66) not only setting up a market in the temple, but regularly cheating customers in its transactions.

Throughout the period of this study Jews are universally associated with money-grubbing; they use their high intelligence and subtlety to drive a hard bargain, and in most cases, cheat. In almost all books up to the 1940s the Jew is defined by his love of money. Money-lenders are equated with Jews to such an extent that one reads the phrase "go to the Jews" as "go to the money-lenders."[32] In fact one is so used to the identification of Jews with money-lenders that it is a shock when Emma Bovary borrows money from a Gentile. All assume the Jew has no pride or morals where money is concerned. In 1867 Ouida describes a Jew: "Money he loved with an adoration that excluded every other passion" (136; see also Nana in 1880, 225). Even in Ben-Hur a distinction is made between Christ and the Jews on these grounds: "'The Galilean loves honor and the Jew Money'" (442). In Gone With the Wind in 1936 Rhett suspects Scarlett of having some Jewish blood because she is so money-hungry (767). Not only do Jews manipulate money in scurrilous ways, but they also sell inferior, sleazy goods. The Jew manipulates people as customers, and encourages them to buy goods they don't need at high prices.[33] In Paul Leicester Ford's Janice Meredith in 1899 a potential customer for a steel razor is warned that the Jew selling it knows all about "steal" (31-32). Hardheartedness is also assumed to be a Jewish trait. Agatha Christie in 1926 comments that those who try to collect a debt quickly must have "a Semitic strain in their ancestry" (120). In the 1932 Mutiny on the Bounty the suffering of the crew is blamed on a Jew who supplied scanty and poor food; Samuel is described as "a smug, tight-lipped little man, of a Jewish cast of countenance" (39). The phrase "jew me down" is customarily used with no explanation because none is needed.[34]

The evidence of the best sellers would seem to contradict Oscar Handlin's statement that the American stereotype of the Jew "involved no hostility, no negative judgement" until the 1890s.[35] The stereotype of the inherently greedy Jew cultivating his ambitions with his superior manipulative intelligence was common in America long before the large influx of Eastern Jewish immigrants in the 1890s. The books Americans bought in greatest numbers accepted this image of the Jew with its purely negative connotations without question in the second half of the nineteenth century. Immigrants of the 1890s were typed before they set foot on shore.

It should be noted that in some best sellers the Jews' way with money is a threat comparable to the yellow peril, and played an important role in the politics of the 1890s. In 1894 Coin's Financial School, an economic textbook for the Populist Party, assumed that control of gold was the central problem in the plight of the poor farmer. On a map of the world showing the amount of gold held in each country there is an octopus centered over England but with tentacles reaching throughout the world; it is labeled "Rothschilds." The title of the map is "The English Octopus. It Feeds on Nothing but Gold" (215). The Protocols of Zion would be no surprise to the readers of this best seller.

A Roman Singer by F. Marion Crawford in 1883 is the first novel centered on a Jewish character. Benoni, a great violinist is "a pronounced Jewish type" with eyes "long and oriental in shape" and an "unmistakably Semitic nose" (158). He advises his protegés that "'. . . money is the only thing worth having'" because with it one can help others more and help oneself to heaven. Nino, his Gentile protegé, is horrified at such sophistry (163-65). Benoni is intelligent, boastful, "poisoned with evil from his head to his heart" (273), but, as he himself says, he makes a poor sort of villain because he is impulsive as villains should never

be (220). He is a figure of mystery and a paradigm for the
wandering Jew. The author notes the prejudice of the
Germans for those of Jewish faith, and in one sentence
attempts to denationalize Benoni by declaring that although
he happened to be a Jew "his peculiarities would have been
the same had he been a Christian or an American" (259). But
the stereotype is fully realized.

Ekeven years later Du Maurier's Trilby appeared with the
central character Svengali "of Jewish aspect, well-featured
but sinister" (11). Only Svengali's accent is spelled out,
although most of the major characters are also foreigners
in France and must have had accents as well. Svengali walks
"up and down the earth seeking whom he might cheat, betray,
exploit, borrow money from, make brutal fun of, bully if he
dared, cringe to if he must--man, woman, child or dog" (37),
but he is a great musician. One of his students, Honorine
Cohen, who is Jewish is described as having no intelligence
whatever "except about sous and centimes" (39-40). Like
Benoni in Crawford's novel Svengali has peculiar and
mysterious powers in music, and in some other ways as well.
One interesting departure from all other treatments of race
in these books occurs here in the description of the much
admired Little Billee. This handsome, elegant and popular
young man is said to have "a faint suggestion of some
possible remote ancestor--just a tinge of that strong,
sturdy, irrepressible, indomitable, indelible blood" of the
Jew. Jewish blood in "diluted homeopathic doses" is
compared to a Spanish wine (Montijo) which is not meant to
be imbibed pure, but without which sherry cannot keep its
flavor, or to a bulldog strain without a touch of which no
greyhound can be a champion (8). These statements are
unique; in popular literature in general and in best sellers
in particular one drop of inferior flood conquers all--a
marvelous mathematical phenomenon. But unlike most other
"inferior" races Jews had customarily been assigned some

superior qualities (imagination, intelligence) although
these were usually channeled into nefarious ways by the
inherent immorality of the Jews.

Hemingway's 1926 novel The Sun Also Rises was a major
contribution to American literature and at the same time
to anti-Semitism. Robert Cohn. the outsider, is a Jew whose
career in the novel paralleled that of a friend of Hemingway's in life. For whatever reason--personal animus, a
literary need for a character outside the accepted cult,
indigenous anti-Semitism--Cohn fits perfectly the pattern
of the popular image of the Jew, and all of his personal
qualities are referred to his being Jewish. He has a "hard,
Jewish, stubborn streak" (10). "'We'll not let him get
superior and Jewish'" (98), says one Gentile character.
He has a strong sense of "Jewish superiority" (168) and a
"sad Jewish face" (184). He is, of course, rich and an
object of scorn as well as a foil for other characters in
the novel.

Finally in the 1940s there is a visible change in the
attitudes toward Jews. Anti-Semitic patterns are still very
much present. Casual Jewish characters are still kikes,
sheenies, hebes and mockies, but now and then there is a
"white Jew"--a Jew whose behavior does not momentarily
follow the stereotypes.[36] As counterweight the reader is
now sometimes allowed to share the problem of being a Jew
in an anti-Semitic society. As Henry Miller puts it in
Tropic of Cancer in 1961: "For the Jew the world is a cage
filled with wild beasts. The door is locked and he is there
without whip or revolver" (9-10). This new consciousness
of the Jew as victim undoubtedly came from the fact that the
enemy in World War II sponsored an ideology based on the
extermination of the Jews as a race, and, as in all wars,
participants took a new and critical view of ideas associated with the enemy. Such a review released from academic
circles new studies of race by psychologists and anthro-

pologists such as Franz Boas and Otto Klineberg. Furthermore a spate of novels by Jews now appeared: Uris, Shaw,
Mailer, Algren, Robbins produced best selling novels.

Sympathetic Jewish characters appear as early as 1933
in Anthony Adverse when the title character is given a
captain's chair by a Jew. When Adverse accepts the chair
as a gift the Jew comments that he is the first Gentile who
didn't look with suspicion on a gift from a Jew assuming
them all to be Shylocks. And when Adverse recounts the
incident, a lawyer asks him how that could be: "'I thought
he was a Jew'" (900). In 1964 The Man offers an entirely
admirable Jew, a Chicago civil rights lawyer, rational,
generous and sensitive, whose courage protects the black
President at great personal cost to himself. To assign
courage to a Jew is new. Jewish doctors are frequently
casual characters in best sellers and, in most cases are
sympathetically presented. "'Jewish doctors are smarter'"
explains one woman in A Tree Grows in Brooklyn (1943) who,
after ten stillbirths has decided for the first time to
have a doctor preside at her eleventh confinement; she
chooses a Jewish doctor as special insurance (395). Discrimination against Jewish doctors preventing their
promotions or limiting their chances for research is
increasingly remarked. The prominence of Jews in psychiatry
is also noted and indeed, I Never Promised You a Rose Garden
in 1964 produces a much admired psychiatrist who is both
female and Jewish. Now prejudice is decried in many
novels.[37] In these it is only unsympathetic characters who
express anti-Semitic prejudice. Organized anti-Semitism
is treated at some length by Norman Mailer in 1948 and Harry
Golden in 1958 gives an extensive account of the Leo Frank
case. William Shirer in The Rise and Fall of the Third
Reich in 1960, while probably not as widely read as the
novels, offered the reader a formal analysis of the development and practice of Nazi policies.

How do Jews handle discrimination? Golden in 1958 after discussing the lynching of Leo Frank in 1913, fears that some Jews will feel safe only if they conform to the other prejudices of the WASP society in which they live (141). In From Here to Eternity in 1951 Bloom, a Jew, considers the way Jews have handled prejudice and decides that there are two kinds of Jews: (1) Those who would really rather be Gentiles and therefore, toady to Gentiles. (2) Those who would rather remain Jews and hug to themselves their superiority in being God's Chosen People--a status Gentiles cannot aspire to (571). But Bloom finally decides no one likes him for himself and he commit suicide. In The Naked and the Dead in 1948 Goldstein governs every action, every word, by his desire to please Gentiles and make a good impression (451-52). When he is successful he is pleased with himself but also pleased because Gentiles will also be pleased with a Jew. Acceptance in Gentile society can also be achieved by being good in school sports which require qualities not available to the Jewish stereotype. In 1953 Uris in Battle Cry introduces a boy who, taunted all his school life as a Jew, finally wins acceptance by winning the softball championship (287). That Jews have not fought their own persecution is assumed in many books; most ascribe this to Jewish cowardice. A sympathetic character in Dr. Zhivago in 1958, baffled by the unwillingness of the Jews to give up their own identity and accept what he regards as a liberating Christianity calls their intransigence "'voluntary martyrdom'" (105).

Jews, actively fighting back do not appear until Leon Uris' 1958 Exodus, the story of European refugees trying to establish themselves in Israel. In the foreword to this book the author states that all of the clichéd Jewish characters--"the clever business man, the brilliant doctor, the sneaky lawyer, the sulking artist"--who people American popular fiction will be thrown out of this book. The

self-pitying Jew will be replaced in his novel by the
reality of the fighting Jew. And indeed, though they never
achieve three-dimensionality they do appear as fighters,
struggling against what the author calls "fantastic odds."
Equality for them will be possible only if they can
establish their own nation (115). To Uris Exodus is the
story of the "greatest miracle of our times," and the theme
is the suffering and heroism of Jews.

Probably more important than diatribes against prejudice
and discrimination is the experience now offered to the
reader to identify with Jews who cherish their own culture,
but are shown at the same time to have the same basic needs
and desires as those of the reader whatever his/her background. This is especially true of those books showing the
growth of a Jewish child in an anti-Semitic atmosphere.
The most important and moving example is the non-fiction
Diary of Anne Frank. There is also a spate of novels such
as the 1948 Never Love a Stranger by Harold Robbins or the
1964 I Never Promised You a Rose Garden by Joanne Greenberg,
showing what it is like to grow up in an anti-Semitic
community in America. Surely the most engaging picture of
Jews in America comes from the observations of eleven-year-
old Francie Nolan in A Tree Grows in Brooklyn in 1943. In
her Brooklyn neighborhood rye bread is known as "Jew bread"
(27), dill pickles as "penny sheeny pickles" (38), and both
are regarded as delicious additions to a Gentile diet. When
a young Jewish boy is told to stay off a particular street
controlled by Gentile boys, and especially to stay away from
Gentile girls, he is delighted because it indicates that he
is thought man enough to be a danger to girls (15). Francie
is surprised when her mother tells her Christ was a Jew;
she had always considered him a Catholic (9). Francie
meditates on why Jewish women have so many babies and walk
proud whereas pregnant Irish women seem to be ashamed of
their state. She decides it is because any Jewish woman

may be bearing the Messiah whereas an Irish woman knows her
child will be "just another Mick" (9).

By this time in the best sellers there is also an attempt
to combat specifics in the anti-Semitic pattern of the Jew.
In Never Love a Stranger in 1948 Robbins quoted the aunt of
a little Jewish boy who interrupts his attempt to kneel in
the synagogue by saying: "'A Jew does not kneel to his God.
His humility must be of the spirit, not the body'" (75),
refuting the idea that the religion of the Jews is one
largely of externals. In another novel, The Carpetbaggers
in 1961, Robbins creates two equally corrupt businessmen,
Jonas Cord, a Gentile, and Bernie Norman, a Jew, indicating
that business immorality is hardly confined to Jews. John
O'Hara in A Rage to Live in 1949 offers a unique situation
in these books: a Jewish businessman cheated by a Gentile
(107). Auntie Mame in 1955 argues with an anti-Semite,
finally pointing out to him that the very adjectives he
uses against Jews--mean, pushy, avaricious, possessive,
loud, vulgar, bossy--apply more to him than to any Jews
she knows (206-209). In Exodus the stigma of cowardice so
often applied to the Jews is spectacularly refuted. Uris'
picture of agricultural Jews, "a Jewish peasantry" (239),
also counters the image of Jews capable only of business
activities. Irwin Shaw's The Young Lions in 1948 brings
this picture of the heroic fighting Jew nearer home with
Noah, an American Jew who tries to enlist in the army the
day after Pearl Harbor. In the army he is blamed as a Jew
for anything that goes wrong. He is exposed to all kinds
of anti-Semitic propaganda, even the Protocols of Zion and
discrimination of all sorts. In response he feels he must
behave in certain ways to refute such propaganda as in
fighting ten men in the barracks over a stolen ten dollar
bill. He is portrayed as a warm and courageous human being,
and finally a hero to his country, a far cry from the
cowardly Jew. Indeed he feels that the fact that he is

Jewish requires him to show more courage than anyone else,
precisely to refute the stereotype; he is forced to become
a martyr.

This shift in the 1940s is quite pronounced. There are
more Jewish characters in the novels now that the cities
are more commonly used as the setting for novels. Reactions
to Hitler unquestionably produced readers more sophisticated
on the question of the Jews, anti-Semitism, discrimination
and persecution. World War II provided receptive ground
to the new scientific studies of the concept of race.

But one should beware of being too sanguine. In the
library copy of From Here to Eternity used in this study,
a reader had written in ink "dirty" above the word "Jew"
(495 and 571) and "kike" (666). Perhaps the most pertinent
comment on the essentially narcissistic American attitude
toward race discrimination appears in Joseph Heller's
Catch-22 in 1961 when an Indian chief explains his feelings
about race: "'Racial prejudice is a terrible thing. . . .
It's a terrible thing to treat a decent, loyal Indian like
a nigger, kike, wop or spic'" (45).

Chapter 6. NATIONAL CHARACTER

Another mythic concept quite as powerful and certainly
as pervasive in the modern world as race is the idea of
nationality, and, as employed in the late nineteenth and
the twentieth century the two are quite closely related.
Nationality is modern, an invention of the late eighteenth
century. The word itself was evidently new to nineteenth
century America: an 1828 Reader, popular in American
elementary schools explained: "'Nationality' is used by
some writers in America, but is a new word and not to be
found in the dictionaries."[1] Like race it is an extraordinarily useful myth to explain and/or justify actions of
a group within a state as well as actions of a nation-state.
Both imperialism and national liberation are rationalized
in terms of the necessary and proper behavior of a national
group. Nationality has been instrumental in providing a
morally acceptable explanation for exploitation both at home
and abroad. In the United States particularly, nationalism
(loyalty to the nationality) has been employed at least as
often to justify internal as well as external policies.
Here the part is substituted for the whole as one group
declares its social and political program to be uniquely
"American" and decries the program of its opponents as
"un-American." Since the founding of the country Americans
with their varied immigrant backgrounds have been engaged
in a constant identity crisis. Crevecoeur's eighteenth
century query "What is an American?" still absorbs American
consciousness and curiosity.
    When group action calls for it a nationality can be
created by exploiting historical fact or fiction as a common
denominator uniting the group. A common language, historical
experience, religion, territory, race have been so used, and

nationalities have in fact been based on each of these.
Yet no single one is necessary to create a nationality.
The single necessary element seems to be the desire to
create a nationality; as Hans Kohn puts it: "Nationality
is formed by the decision to form a nationality."[2] Any
criteria acceptable and important to the group can be used
as the founding ideology. Once founded the nationality
demands the paramount loyalty of its members and supersedes
in importance to the individual the many other groups to
which he or she belongs. Disloyalty to the nationality is
the worst of crimes in the modern world on a par with heres
in the medieval world, as Carlton Hayes has pointed out.
It may be more important than loyalty to the state as
Kirsten Flagstad discovered dramatically when she returned
and gave at least tacit support to her native Norway then
under the domination of the Nazis; she was reviled as being
loyal to the Norwegian state but disloyal to the Norwegian
nation.

   Nationality, then, does not exist in nature, but this is
not to say that it does not exist in fact. By the end of
the nineteenth century race and nationality were generally
believed in the western world to be the most significant
ways of classifying human beings.

   And nature was enlisted as an invaluable aid in unifying
a national group by ascribing to its members an inherited
national character. That different cultures have distinctive life styles at a given period may be true, but their
definition is a slippery business indeed. Cultures change,
and what is regarded as idiosyncratic in one era may be
radically revised in another. The seventeenth century
British with their many revolutions were generally regarded
as fickle and unstable. By the nineteenth century the
French were assigned these same characteristics because of
the vagaries of their series of revolutions at the end of
the eighteenth century, while the British were now regarded

as stolid shopkeepers. Germans in the early nineteenth
century were perceived as intellectuals and philosophers
incapable of action in the practical world. Their rapid
industrialization and their success in war near the end of
that century challenged this evaluation materially. The
Germany of Bismarck and later that of Hitler produced quite
different manifestations of character than the Germany of
Schelling and Hegel. If then there is such a thing as
national character it is surely ephemeral--the creature not
of heritage but of historical circumstance.

An even more important caveat, however, is that national
character has no valid application to the individual.
Setting up a national character always involves substituting
the part for the whole. The only specific thing all members
of a nationality have in common is the wish to be part of a
nationality. Nationalities consist of individuals with
diverse interests: which is French: the Parisian or the
peasant? Is there a typical American, an American temperament, an American character? Is he a Henry Ford, a Eugene
Debs, a Ralph Waldo Emerson, a Jefferson? Is she an Alcott,
a Schlafly, a Steinem, a Stanton, a Marilyn Monroe or an
Eleanor Roosevelt? Is it a successful industrialist, a
tenant farmer, a Bowery bum? Does he/she live in New York
City, California, Appalachia? Of what religion? Of what
class? From what ethnic background? A nationality is an
infinitely complex conglomeration of individuals and any
definition that imputes specific qualities to individual
members of a nationality inevitably excludes vast numbers
who consider themselves of that nationality.

Yet in the face of such ambiguities specific national
characteristics have been assigned to every nationality and
assumed by the late nineteenth century to be inherited by
each individual in the group, thereby bestowing immutable
identity on the nationality. Nationality in popular literature had become a subdivision of race. And it is largely

in this guise that the people of other nations appear in
American best sellers.

THE SCOTS

In nineteenth century best sellers the Scots come out
very well indeed: they are intelligent, they are the
proprietors of a public school system, they work hard and
are usually successful. They are careful with money; they
are rigidly moral and profoundly religious with a Calvinism
(although it is rarely identified as such in these books)
to match that of seventeenth century American Puritans.
These latter qualities are so well accepted in the early
twentieth century that Will Durant can characterize Immanuel
Kant as "the uncanny Scot of Koenigsburg" because he so
strongly believes in duty for duty's sake. In fact the
Scots in these books sound much like what the Americans
thought themselves to be.

There is an unusual cluster of books by Scotch writers
published here in the 1890s: Barrie's The Little Minister
in 1891 and A Window in Thrums in 1892, and MacLaren's
Beside the Bonnie Brier Bush in 1894. That so small a
country should produce three best sellers in one decade in
the United States is extraordinary. At Mott points out this
is probably because the international copyright law was
easily avoided at the time and American publishers could
offer very cheap pirated reprint editions. But these books
also have in common the kind of Scotland they present to
their readers. As in Lorna Doone in 1874, these books of
the 1890s describe a simple, rural society romantically,
sentimentally and nostalgically. Villages are prominent
and cities do not exist in these pages. The ways of rural
Scottish folk appear in casual characters in other books as
well. They are the only people whose folk songs and folk
dances are mentioned in books that do not center on their
culture.[3] It is an honest, warm, virtuous and idyllic
society.

To the American of the 1890s, beset by new and appalling problems stemming from the industrial revolution, what an appeal this must have made! The decade exhibited vast discontent in the United States: the Homestead strike, the Pullman strike, both attended with violence, a severe depression, farmers so beleaguered that they formed the Populist Party and ran their own candidate for the Presidency of the United States. Nostalgia for a less complicated time must have made these novels of Scotland especially attractive. It is also germane that the readers of these best sellers were brought up on schoolbooks that admired the Scots only less than the Americans.[4] The authors of nineteenth century schoolbooks were mostly from New England and saw the virtues they admired in their own region mirrored in the Scots.

The twentieth century, while not unfriendly to the Scots, does not celebrate them so enthusiastically. Stories centered in Scotland disappear from best seller lists, and fewer casual Scottish characters appear. Their morality is still stressed even in 1929 when Ernest Hemingway notes that Cathy, his heroine, is a Scot and the Scots are a moral people (246). They still work hard, but their carefulness in saving money now becomes meanness, stinginess.[5] In Gone With the Wind in 1936 Rhett, aware of Scarlett's money hunger, asks: "'Are you sure you haven't some Scotch or perhaps Jewish blood as well as Irish?'" (767, 49). Perhaps this reflects the shift in American culture from a producing to a consuming economy; the 1920s replaced Benjamin Franklin's adages on saving money to those urging one to keep up with the Joneses. As conspicuous consumption became more and more esteemed, the Scots became less so.

THE ENGLISH

The English not only inhabit many of America's best selling novels but many of the American best sellers in the second half of the nineteenth century were written by English authors. Not until 1891 was an effective international copyright law enforced, and the decline in reprints of foreign publications was noticeable thereafter. Before this time foreign books abounded on the best seller lists because, among other factors they could be pirated and reprinted cheaply. And among such foreign reprints British books had the further advantage of a language common to Britain and the United States.

Dickens was, of course, popular here before the period of this study as well as during it. Then in 1866 came Charles Reade's Griffith Gaunt or, Jealousy. In spite of a plot as complex as that of a comic opera it could hardly avoid popularity: it includes bigamy, the sinister influence of a Catholic priest, a female rake and an illegitimate child. Furthermore it had the incredible luck to be attacked as "an indecent publication" by a New York periodical.[6] Reade sued the magazine, and in the course of the trial half of the novel was read to the jury. He won the case, was awarded only 6¢ in damages but invaluable publicity. The popularity of this novel ensured that of his next, A Terrible Temptation in 1871. It too is about a bored British aristocracy given to unconventional sexual activity, and was quite as sensational as Griffith Gaunt. It was also attacked by the press as "'the most indecent book that has lately issued from the press . . . a mass of brothel garbage served by a narrator of vice.'"[7] Reade's earlier novels, concerned with social reform never achieved popularity in America comparable to these delineations of a decadent, sexually immoral aristocracy. Although the British upper classes rarely appear in quite so abandoned a form after this, they remain a favorite subject in those books that deal with British culture for the next fifty years.[8] Marie Corelli's Thelma introduces a country girl as the bride of an upper class Englishman. The chapter

describing her debut into English society is called "The
Land of Mockery." She is appalled by the emptiness of upper
class marriages, by the boredom of the upper class, by their
insincerity and willingness to make fun of those not born
into their exclusive society. Winston Churchill's
historical novel Richard Carvel in 1899 portrays English
society in much the same way; its "luxury and laxity" make
rakes of its young men (291-92). Churchill contrasts this
specifically with what is to him a simple, constructive
America. And in those books where such specific contrast
is not made, this picture of a debauched English upper class
was likely to enhance American pride in what they considered
to be their own classlessness. The book that finally tidied
up the British upper class in American popular culture was
the 1924 Jeeves by P. G. Wodehouse. Bertie, Jeeves' master
is not debauched or wicked, but merely stupid and foolish.
Without the constant aid of his butler Jeeves he is utterly
helpless even in his own restricted world.

The inherent qualities assigned to the British are
surprisingly consistent. The tone set in the early novels
is carried throughout the period. Except for the aristocracy they are believed to be slow, calm and stolid. In
Jules Verne's Around the World in Eighty Days (1874) one of
the voyagers complains of the slow English boat: "'Oh these
English! If this was an American craft we should blow up,
perhaps, but we should at all events go faster!'" (105).
Passepartout, being as he says of a lively nature, finds it
necessary to serve in an English house now and then "'to
find repose'" (8). This stolidity, this reserve is as
firmly fixed in the modern best seller as in the early
ones.[9] In Taylor Caldwell's This Side of Innocence in 1946
British choice in food and drink--beef and heavy Port--are
regarded as consonant with the sluggish British personality.
This is contrasted to the combination of the sparkling wines
of Latin countries and their "sparkling literature, grace

in living and in art" (358). Elinor Glyn in Three Weeks in
1907 commenting on a young Englishman central to her romanc
observes that the English are so stolid they have no sense
of romance (57, 142). While it may do them out of sentimental feelings, some authors consider this quality the
basis of their natural ability to endure: ". . . the least
drop of English blood is worth the best of any other, when
it comes to lasting out."[10] Their endurance produces
bravery in battle, and sometimes even gallantry, although
the latter never appears when they are fighting the
Americans. In Oppenheim's The Great Impersonation appearin
just after World War I, they take foolish chances in
warfare, but under any circumstances they are always both
unflappable and heroic. In books that deal with World War
II their ability to endure the incessant bombings of their
civilian population is often pointed out in both fiction an
non-fiction. To be English is to be outwardly calm at all
times--a very private person always maintaining one's
dignity. In 1932 D. H. Lawrence notes: ". . . the quiet,
self-contained assurances of the English, no loose edges"
(289), a life-style with which Morris West concurs in The
Devil's Advocate in 1959 (16). Colonel Nicholson in the
1954 Bridge Over the River Kwai uses his "ponderous dignity
as a mark of superiority and a weapon as well (10). The
American conviction that the British lack a sense of humor
comes out in only one book, David Harum in 1898 (249), a
book that abounds in rustic American humor. The adjective
"clean" much in use at the turn of the century to describe
what seems to be a combination of honesty, neatness and
asexuality is applied to the British by several authors.[11]

Two other qualities universally assigned to the British
in these books are an inborn sense of justice and a love of
freedom. For American readers these qualities presented an
ambiguous situation: why then was there an American
revolution against a political system set up by a nation

with such admirable political instincts? In these books
the anomaly is resolved by the explanation that British
oppression after 1763 was a temporary British aberration.
Winston Churchill in 1899 places the onus on George III who
"is alone to blame for that hatred of race against race
which already has done so much evil" (449). Another
historical novel, Janice Meredith published in the same
year offers a British evaluation: "'We forgot 'twas our own
whelps grown strong, we sought to subjugate'" (503). In
the historical novels American victory in the American
Revolution was merely a case of the inborn traits of the
British nationality coming out in their children. By the
second half of the nineteenth century the importance of
genetic heritage by race and nationality shifted the British
into a new position with American writers and readers of
best sellers, most of whom were probably of British descent.
However badly the British might have behaved toward the
Americans in the Revolution and the War of 1812, they are
now reclaimed as the source of American justice, freedom
and honor. In Janice Meredith a character is asked if the
British beat the Americans in the Revolution. The response:
"'No. . . . 'Tis the old spirit of England that has
conquered as it ever will . . .'" (502). And at the end of
Richard Carvel the author, Winston Churchill, hopes that
England and America can forget the Revolution, and together
"cleanse the world of tyranny" (536). On the whole the
British are liked as stodgy parents whose children have
inherited their best qualities.

But also by the late nineteenth century the British
appear in these books as imperialists using their industrial
and commercial success at home to develop economic and
political power of an unprecedented kind throughout the
modern world. The only book in which the United States
appears as the victim of modern British power is in a kind
of economic textbook used in the Populist political

campaigns of the 1890s: Coin's Financial School by William
Harvey in 1894. Here England through the Rothschilds or
the Rothschilds through England have gotten control of the
gold of the world to the detriment of Americans in general
and the American farmer in particular. One drawing in the
book (183) shows a cow with an American farmer feeding it,
a New Yorker milking it, and finally the milk being
delivered to England. Harvey points out that where
England's material interests and sense of humanity come
into conflict, England becomes the enemy of human liberty
(222). But this is the only case where British profits
harm American interests. As settlers the British are
superb; as conquerors they are no better than other nations
who are noted for tyranny at home as well as abroad. In
1874 Jules Verne shows the awful and far-reaching effects
of the British introduction of opium to China (113). He
is also severely critical of British despotism in governing
India. Two English writers, Arthur Conan Doyle in 1890 and
Willkie Collins in 1868 illustrate a bifurcated British
honor: to steal a jewel from an English person is shameful,
but the jewels of an Indian Rajah are fair game.

Certainly the major exposition of British imperialism
in the nineteenth century comes from the extraordinarily
popular writings of Rudyard Kipling whom H. G. Wells calls
"a Prussianizing Englishman" (1012). Kipling's celebrations
of British expansion might well cancel out the unfavorable
views expressed by the few critical best sellers; they were
read by the same generation. That they happened to be
published here just before the 1891 copyright law gave them
an advantage, but their appeal to the spirit of adventure
and sentimentality would probably have found a wide American
audience anyway. That they happened to be published at this
time is important for another reason: they were read by the
generation that sparked our first imperialist ventures.
American conquest of the Philippines would seem like a

glorious expedition of liberation to readers already
intoxicated by Kipling.

From the end of the nineteenth century to the 1930s
British imperialist ventures played no role in American
best sellers. Most of the best selling authors of that
period--Owen Wister, John Fox Jr., Gene Stratton Porter,
Zane Grey, Harold Bell Wright--were Americans concerned
primarily with the American scene.

But the Depression and the rise of Fascism produced a
more critical attitude toward the national acquisition of
wealth and territory. In 1933 the title character of
Anthony Adverse writes in a letter from England that the
English are so obsessed with wealth that "'A man of sterling
character' exhausts all compliments here" (915). Criticism
of the attitudes of the British toward the other cultures
they encounter and dominate becomes quite common. Little
sister Hsia in Pearl Buck's Pavilion of Women in 1946, for
example, is a narrow-minded missionary incapable of understanding any other human being let along one of a different
culture. In Mutiny on the Bounty in 1932 the English
rationalize their reluctance to learn any but the English
language by explaining that if English were spoken slowly
and loudly anyone even "a stupid foreigner" could understand
it (108). But British criticism of British policies is also
set down when a British ship's doctor wonders if the term
"savages" applied by the British to natives of the South
Seas couldn't more justly be applied to the British (240).
In Random Harvest in 1941 James Hilton contrasts British
politeness at home with the disrespect they show abroad by
quoting a sign put up by the British in Shanghai "'No dogs
or Chinese allowed'" (171). In Goudge's Green Dolphin
Street in 1944 Marianne, an unsympathetic character, tries
to set up a little England in the New Zealand forest. She
feels she can liberate the Maori from their inferior culture
by making them over in her own image.

As the British Empire begins to loosen up with World
War II, Wendell Willkie's One World in 1943 observes this
with approval and foresees a quite different future. But
at the same time he finds British officers currently
stationed abroad visualizing a future straight out of
Kipling (15). Exodus in 1958 is severely critical of
British actions toward Jewish refugees trying to escape
European persecution by escaping to Palestine. One Jew
reports happily to a British major that the British are
losing their empire piece by piece (11). From World War II
on the British are pictured in general as despising and
brutalizing the natives of any land they occupy, and
limiting their inherent sense of honor and justice to
Europeans. But this new criticism of imperialism is not
confined to a criticism of British imperialism but includes
all imperialisms even that of the Americans. One interesting prediction of the future appears in Random Harvest
written in the midst of Nazi peril in 1941. A sympathetic
character, observing British racism and tyranny abroad,
meditates on the future and fantasizes that however bad
the British system may be the world has never known "sweeter
masters"; a cowed and brutalized world of the future may
one day look back on British imperialism as a golden age
(171).

On the whole the British come out rather well, offering
to their American descendants a heritage of rationality,
courage, courtesy combined with stolidity, and sound
political sense. And in the historical novels Americans
could take comfort in the notion that British aberrations
such as class consciousness and the political oppression
visited on the Americans at the time of the American
Revolution could be cleansed from British immigrants by the
pure air of the American Eden.

THE IRISH

Of all immigrants from the British Isles the Irish are
least favorably and most often portrayed. Their Catholicism
cancels any favorable emendations they might have received
from their neighbors in Europe. In the best sellers the
religion of the Irish is rarely mentioned, but anyone
identified as Irish would certainly be read as Catholic in
the United States, and such identification was clearly
pejorative. The only admired individuals of Irish descent
in the whole period are Freckles, the title character in
Gene Stratton Porter's 1904 novel of that name, and
President John F. Kennedy in Theodore White's 1962 The
Making of the President. Freckles' Irishness is constantly
referred to throughout the book, but the author is careful
to detach him from Catholicism--he is Episcopalian (150),[12]
probably the only non-Catholic Irish person in the whole
century of popular novels. Freckles is advised to be proud
of being Irish; he is told that if Ireland had fertile soil
the Irish would probably lead the world (208-209). Two
desirable qualities sometimes assigned to the Irish are wit
and imagination. Of the nineteenth century books read by
the generations that faced the problem of massive Irish
immigration from the 1840s on only Robert Elsmere (1888) by
Mrs. Humphrey Ward presents a pleasant picture of the Irish
and that novel was written by an Englishwoman.

The twentieth century American novel is no more complimentary to the Irish than the nineteenth century one.
Several indicate that the Irish work hard,[13] but they are
rarely seen to be successful. The only self-made fictional
Irishman appears in Henry M. Robinson's 1950 novel The
Cardinal; he is a stern and prudish man who has traversed
the legendary American road from rags to riches. Apart from
this the Irish are universally portrayed as poor, their
women as servants. In 1867 Alger reports one Irishman so
poor but so imaginative that he invents spectacles for his

horse so the horse will think shavings are food. The
deception is successful, but of limited value: the horse
eats the shavings, but dies of starvation (177).

The only arena in which the Irish are shown to have
continuing success is in politics. There are as many Irish
policemen in the best sellers as in reality. Their success
in city politics is succinctly expressed by Huie in 1951 in
his description of New York City: "The Jews own it, the
Irish run it . . ." (74). But it is well to keep in mind
that success in municipal politics was a petty and indeed
often corrupt and sordid business, hardly to the credit of
the Irish. Finally in an Irving Wallace novel, The Man in
1964 an Irish politician comes into the national scene, and
he is both successful and likeable (39). In non-fiction
Dale Carnegie in 1936 introduces his readers to two real-
life self-made national politicians of Irish background:
Patrick J. O'Haire who becomes successful after he manages
to get over being a "belligerent Irishman", and Jim Farley
whose "Irish geniality" is a natural in politics (78, 113).
And in 1962 Theodore White makes Irish politicians
respectable by exposing the reader to the Kennedy family--
a family of brilliant triumphs in both the financial and
political worlds; they carefully sustain their ethnic
background but put it through Harvard.

During this whole period one predilection assumed to be
assigned by nature to the Irish is an uncontrollable love
of alcoholic beverages. There are abundant examples of
drunken Irishmen. Although they work hard they remain poor
because they cannot resist spending their hard-earned money
on drink. Irish women, almost always named Bridget, find
drink as irresistible as do Irish men. Alcohol not only
dilutes their wages, but produces belligerence and tangles
with the law.[14] This irresistible attraction to liquor is
not limited to the poor and uneducated. Trilby's Irish
father "a gentleman and scholar" is also an alcoholic. It

is assumed to be an Irish national characteristic so
powerful that it cancels out opportunities offered to the
Irish immigrant by the American environment.

Prejudice and discrimination against the Irish is
mentioned critically in few books. In E. P. Roe's Barriers
Burned Away in 1872 a man looking for a job is told by a
storekeeper: "'Ours is not the work for Paddies'" (34).
The pre-Civil War Nativist movement with its physical and
psychological attacks on the Irish appears in a 1941
novel.[15] In Butterfield-8 O'Hara records a long conversation between a WASP woman and a man of Irish descent annoyed
with her use of privilege. She points out that his family,
like hers, is well-to-do and has sent him to good schools.
His response: "'. . . but I am a Mick. Still a Mick. We're
not Americans. We're Micks'" (58-60). Three years earlier
Studs Lonigan notes that prize-fighters who are "'dagos,
wops, sheenies'" are now taking Hibernian names (98); the
older immigration had now achieved some degree of respectability on the backs of the new.

In general, respectability is consistently denied the
Irish; they are usually referred to in terms of derogation.
As in the case of blacks and Jews they are made to speak
with a thick accent when other immigrants are not. The
brogue is meant to be laughed at. And indeed as they appear
in these books the Irish are meant to be laughed at. While
they are as disreputable as blacks, Chinese and Jews they
are not objects of fear. While the power of their church
may be seen at times as sinister, they are not, because it
is not in their nature to be so. They may be, in fact,
their own worst enemies. By nature the Irish are genial
but short-tempered, hard-working but feckless and eternally
bound to the bottle.

THE FRENCH

In these hundred years of best sellers the French maintain essentially the same character. They are described as lively and emotional, but lightly so without the heavy passions that distinguish the Italians. They love to talk, but according to Kipling in 1891 they talk "of much more than they will ever accomplish" (133; see also 1947 Roberts, 59). They may be logical but, since they consider only trivial subjects, their talent for logic is not as important as it might be. Superficiality is universally regarded as a French characteristic; Marie Corelli in 1887 refers to the "feather-light mind" of the French (106). French absorption with fashion is much remarked from Little Women on. They love baubles even in furniture. Churchill in 1899 describes "French baubles of tables and chairs" (71-72). In 1947 Roberts reports that the head of the French fleet when about to land in Haiti at the beginning of the nineteenth century set up elaborate French furnishings on deck--carpets, upholstered chairs as well as people garbed in silk and pearls (135). Sometimes French style is used as a foil for what is seen as the honest, rustic American style as when John Fox Jr. in 1903 notes with pleasure the presence at an Appalachian party of the simple banjo instead of the "French fiddler's bows and scrapings" (51).

French politesse is also frequently remarked. The forma courtesies they offer, however, in contrast to the dignifie politeness of the British are made to seem wholly artificia if not hypocritical. They know how to make "pretty phrases."[16] This contrast is made specific in Little Women when Laury tries to kiss Amy's hand in farewell, and Amy responds: "'I'd rather have a hearty English handshake than all the sentimental salutations in France'" (356). Churchill in 1899 (205) and Glyn in 1907 (140-44) point out that to be regarded as a gentleman or lady one must know th

French language or at least use French phrases. The French
are preeminent in matters of manners, but lacking in matters
of morals.

As Halevy puts it in 1882 Paris, "a universal and international city" is also the world's capital of vice (73, 10),
and this is a unanimous opinion. Even in Trilby, centering
on artists who enjoy and need the easy Parisian atmosphere,
Paris is called "the most corrupt city on earth" (91), yet
the book itself shows no corruption at all, but rather a
delightful innocence. One might wonder how the American,
well acquainted with the immorality of political corruption from the Grant regime throughout the period could place
Paris above Washington or New York as the most wicked city
in the world. But quite clearly "immorality", "wickedness",
"vice" all refer only to one form of immorality--sexual
deviation from the conventions of the day. The substitution
of this part for the whole was so generally accepted in
American English that it became a convention of the language
and is still so used. The reader of Faulkner's Sanctuary
in 1931 knows quite well what is meant when the Madame of
a brothel evicts an employee saying" "'I ain't going to have
my house turned into no French joint'" (184). Curiously,
in contrast to the British who are often described as a
"clean" race (honest, direct, asexual), the term is
pointedly denied the French in The Foxes of Harrow in 1946:
"Apart from their own persons, the French were not a cleanly
race" (184). All French women in Paris are suspect, and the
influence of the wicked city even affects such visitors as
Gunter who reports that a girl from Ohio who moves to Paris
takes her beauty but leaves her virtue behind. (Virtue in
unmarried women refers of course only to chastity.)[17] In
1888 Corelli comments on a French woman who is a perfectly
happy wife, "one of those rare exceptions", a French woman
exclusively in love with her own husband (53). Sexual
immorality is identified with the French through the 1960s.[18]

When a book of Maupassant's short stories became a best
seller in the United States in 1889, it was used as proof
of French salacity. That this book became a best seller
should have said something to Americans about themselves.
While ostensibly unwilling to accept pornography, the
suspicion of pornography in an imported book was enough in
itself to create best-sellerdom.

As American sexual morality changes, there are changes
in sexual attitudes in best sellers, but the French still
maintain their preeminence and virtuosity in this field.
In 1928 Bad Girl (and notice the title), when an unmarried
couple are feeling guilty about sleeping together because
most people consider it wrong, the young man consoles his
woman by observing that perhaps in France it would not be
considered wrong (56). And in Fannie Hurst's Back Street
in 1931 when Walter proposes that he and Ray share an
apartment, he tells her that he wants her to feel as a
French woman would feel (159). Edison Marshall in Yankee
Pasha in 1947 distinguishes the French for respecting and
wanting carnal as well as spiritual love "as the due of
marriage" (77). And Huie in 1951 states that the French
nation treats its whores well: they are expected to marry
and their husbands are considered fortunate (221). In the
later books when it is permissible to mention V.D. it is
identified as a French disease.

This "freedom and tolerance, . . . easy acceptance of
life" ascribed to the "French character" becomes a positive
quality in only two books which extol the French for
creating a congenial habitat for the civilized person.[19]
Torres' Women's Barracks in 1950 is unique in breaking down
the stereotype of France as the home of loose sexual morals
by noting another France, a France alien to the usual image
in popular books, a France of close-knit, ordered and
carefully preserved families (10). Torres also introduces
two French women who behave in what readers of best sellers

would consider a most un-French way by clinging to chastity.

French political behavior is often criticized and compared unfavorably to the British and the American. The Crisis in 1900 compares the American and French Revolutions: "Heads are not so cheap in our Anglo-Saxon countries; passions not so fierce and incontrollable" (353). Even Zane Grey in 1906 calls French settlers in America "savages", "depraved vagabonds" (55, 201, 239). And in books of the 1950s and 1960s the French in Southeast Asia are regarded as untrustworthy and hated by all, Communists and anti-Communists alike.[20] The atmosphere created by both World Wars, however, offers some chance for rehabilitation of the French even when discussing things other than the wars themselves. Tarzan presents a most complimentary picture of French soldiers and sailors (261, 303-306). Willkie shows a proud and principled DeGaulle in 1943 (23) and Irwin Shaw in 1948 shows both the French bravely defending the French nation and collaborators attacking it. Finally he offers this evaluation by an American officer of the French as the most annoying people in the world--"'. . . chauvinistic, scornful, reasonable, independent and great'" (608).

France is acknowledged as an intellectual center in Coin's Financial School in 1894 "the cradle of science" (221). But the scientific ability of the French is downgraded by Doyle in 1890 in The Sign of the Four: their "quick intuition" is useful, but they do not have the wide range of exact knowledge necessary for accurate scientific work (124). France is often acknowledged as a center for the arts. The Paris of Trilby in 1894 is certainly a focal point for the arts, yet at the same time Du Maurier is severely critical of French evaluations of their own art. They consider themselves superior to the English in literature, art and music but they exalt Zola, Loti and Maupassant "these three immortal French writers of light

books" (138). The reputation of the French in literature
is turned into notoriety by several best sellers of the
1890s. A character in Mrs. Humphrey Ward's 1888 novel,
Robert Elsmere reacts to a French farce: "'How they do reve
in mud!'" (174). Another English novelist sees France as
"'the literary sewer' that streams . . . throughout the
world," a literary sewer that is a conduit for women shown
in "gross impropriety of conduct."[21]

Thus French superficiality and immorality are seen an
national characteristics that determine and limit the
French intellectually and aesthetically.

THE GERMANS

Like the British and in contrast to the French, Germans
are treated with respect throughout the period. The
adjectives most often applied to them are sober, stolid,
solid, methodical; they are also said by Churchill in 1900
to have a temperament inherited from "Teutonic ancestors"
(65). Only Crawford in 1883 endows them with imagination.
They make excellent immigrants and citizens because they
work hard, and are thrifty, thorough, respectable and clean
In best sellers published before World War II they appear
mainly as immigrants or persons of German ancestry in the
United States, and always in a favorable light. That one
of the most admired women in all of these best sellers, Jo
in Little Women, marries a German immigrant is recommendation enough. That he is a professor is perhaps significant
but it is interesting that Germans as scholars appear in
only two books: Will Durant's The Story of Philosophy in
1926, and the earlier Robert Elsmere, an 1888 novel avers
that "Half the great names of modern thought" are in a
bookcase of German books (196, 314). But the intellectual
life is not particularly prominent or sanctioned in these
best sellers. In books written shortly after World War I
the good qualities of the Germans are still there, but in

two instances they are also seen as a positive danger to
the world,[22] and World War II intensifies this vision. Now
besides exhibiting bourgeois virtues they are seen as "a
war-like race."[23] Shirer in 1960 in The Rise and Fall of
the Third Reich spells out what he describes as "the
calculated butchery of human life and the human spirit
outdid all the savage oppressions of the previous ages" (5).
Hitler found "in the German people, as a mysterious Providence and centuries of experience had molded them up to that
time, a natural instrument . . ." (5-6). Nazi horrors are
depicted in passing in many books, but unquestionably the
Diary of Anne Frank published here in 1952 gave to most
readers an unforgettable chance to identify with the victims
of Nazi Germany. The zenith of the human spirit is visible
in Anne, and the nadir in the Germans of the time. That
human nature and not just the nature of the Germans could
produce Nazism is not considered in these books.

On the whole what are described as inherent characteristics are quite similar in the English and the Germans, and
a common racial background is assumed. But Germans are also
believed to have other urges that temper these qualities in
the later books. The Devil's Advocate in 1959 finds "a
grossness in them and a violence that was released by liquor
and big speeches and the need to assert themselves" (256).
They are still regarded as hard-working, methodical and
excellent soldiers, but under the Nazis Nordic efficiency
becomes German ruthlessness.

THE ITALIANS

In Little Women an Italian is described as having
"'handsome black eyes and pretty manners,'" with the added
comment "'Italians are always nice'" (49). But at about
the same time, Mark Twain in Innocents Abroad is appalled
by what he sees in Italy, particularly the coexistence of
terrible poverty among the people with the extraordinary

wealth of the churches. Nor is he impressed with their
art especially when he observes that the great painters of
the Renaissance painted tyrants as admirable and indeed
heroic figures. Not even Venice came up to his expectations: it was dirty, and even the songs of the gondoliers
were dull. He often draws a sharp and detailed contrast
between conditions in the United States and in Europe much
to the disrepute of Italians in particular. He considers
the source of Italian problems to be not merely a deficiency
in government but in the character of the people. Unlike
their Pompeian ancestors, modern Italians are both lazy and
ignorant and content to be so. His reaction to beggars
clustered around the Duomo in Florence is: "Oh sons of
classic Italy,--is the spirit of enterprise, of self-
reliance, of noble endeavor, utterly dead within ye? Curse
your indolent worthlessness, why don't you rob your church?"
(I-266). Neapolitans he finds particularly offensive; they
love cheap miracles and expect two cents every time they
bow to you (II-18). Much the same observations are made
in 1959 in The Devil's Advocate. The contrast between
prosperity and poverty is still vast, but the population
will give money freely to canonize a saint, but not to pay
those who teach their children (21, 47-49).

Besides this fecklessness Italians are usually shown as
prone to violence. They are full of easy affection and warm
family feelings. But these approved attitudes in the case
of the Italians seem to be mere by-products of their "hot
blood."[24] Louis Beretti's family, in the book of that name
in 1929 is frightened of him "because they knew he loved
them with the devouring, vengeful jealous love of their hot
blood" (19). They are usually described as passionate, an
adjective D. H. Lawrence refuses to apply to the Italians
in the 1932 Lady Chatterly's Lover because "passion has deep
reserves. They [the Italians] are easily moved, and often
affectionate, but they rarely have any abiding passion of

any sort" (308). To Hemingway in _Farewell to Arms_ in 1929
they are: "'All fire and smoke and nothing inside'" (66).
However shallow Italian feelings may be there seems to be
general agreement that they require melodramatic expression.
The very popular 1929 novel _The Magnificent Obsession_
applies this to an Italian surgeon: ". . . by race and
temperament cordial toward the grand opera aspects of the
situation" (317). Such emotional equipment also leads to
easy sexual dalliance without commitment as the Boston
iceman in Irwin Shaw's _The Young Lions_ in 1948: he claims
to have fourteen women on his ice route in love with him
(532). Whether Italian feelings are easy to arouse and
allay, however, Italians are assumed to be capable of savage
revenge. A Maupassant story popular here after 1889 about
an Italian vendetta describes a Sardinian woman training a
dog to tear a mannequin apart so that he can repeat the act
on her son's murderer (114-20). Lindsey in 1932 expresses
the general opinion in describing Italians as "a nasty
vengeful lot" (54).

Apart from violence stemming from individual relationships, from the 1940s Italians often appear as bootleggers,
proprietors of illegal gambling establishments and engaged
in other occupations that almost inevitably lead to violence.
They are assumed to be the natural leaders of organized
crime, whether Black Hand, Mafia or just organized
rackets.[25] This is particularly true in detective stories
laid in the United States. Harry Golden is alone in being
critical of the bad press the Italians invariably get. He
says there are no more Italians than other ethnic groups in
the rackets, and wonders why the Italians don't protest; in
1958 when Golden's book came out they hadn't (152).

It seems astonishing that the Italians would not be
redeemed by their prowess in the arts. But in very few
instances are Italian accomplishments in this field
mentioned. In Stone's 1961 biography of Michelangelo the

subject is, of course, treated at length and with respect,
but in casual references in most best sellers the attitude
is often similar to that of Mark Twain who preferred copies
of Italian paintings to the originals. Rosamund Marshall
in 1946 discusses an Italian sculptor only in terms of his
foppishness (18, 20). Costain in 1945 applies the old theme
of the superficiality of Italian emotions to their architecture when he complains that the beauty of Venice is "all
on the surface" (350). Shellabarger in 1947 gives adequate
attention to the glories of Renaissance Venice, but also
thinks it remarkable for its arrogance (18). And, as one
might expect Italian music is usually shown to be super-
ficial and full of cheap tricks with Rossini designated in
James Cain's Serenade by a sympathetic character as "'that
most unspeakable wop of all.'"[26] German composers are often
used as a foil for the lighter Italians. Only in Anthony
Adverse does a sympathetic character appreciate Italian
culture: ". . . a return to Italy must ever be to every
civilized European a home-coming," but this opinion is
unique (703).

Americans of Italian descent appear in these books in
two guises, either as criminals in the rackets or as
inhabitants of dismal urban slums. In both cases they are
victims, but almost willing ones, of the city.[27] Like the
Irish their Catholicism does nothing for their prestige in
the United States. And like other "inferior races" and all
immigrant groups new to the United States they are given
widely used derogatory nicknames. "Wop" appears first in
the 1920s and is ubiquitous from that time on. "Dago" is
also applied to the Italians, and Burdick in 1956 uses both
and "ginny" as well (95, 101).

From these books Italian national character would hardly
seem to be a desirable ingredient in the American melting
pot.

LATIN AMERICANS

Latin Americans occupy a unique place in the North
American consciousness as they do on the American continent.
Until the 1930s the idea of "liberating" Latin America from
her Catholicism and her economic backwardness was popular
in some official circles as well as in some of the public's
opinion. This was to be accomplished by economic rather
than military conquest, although United States marines were
not unfamiliar with Central America in the early twentieth
century. The relationship of the United States to Latin
America, so often characterized as that of a big brother,
could be more accurately described as that of a step-brother
with no genetic relationship and occupying a different
apartment in the same house. North Americans tended to
look on South Americans not as Guatemalans, Argentinians or
Venezuelans, but as Latin Americans, heirs to an Iberian
personality and therefore very much alike.

In best sellers two virtues are invariably associated
with Iberians: pride (although this is sometimes so extreme
as to be a fault) and courtesy. Thornton Wilder in 1928
uses the sentence: "That's not Spanish of you" to mean
that's not courteous of you (102). But until well into the
twentieth century the Spanish, especially those settled in
North America, are sadly demeaned. Only Ramona in 1884
showed Spanish Americans as ordinary human beings with a
viable culture. In the late nineteenth century so favorable
a view was unusual in popular American books; jingoism
expanded both financial and military dominance over much of
Central America. That the Spanish should be supplanted in
America by the Yankees is unquestioned in most nineteenth
century books, and that they will be is regarded as
inevitable. Since such conquest is a result of the natural
superiority of the Anglos to the Spanish this process is
necessary for world progress, as Harold Bell Wright maintains in The Winning of Barbara Worth in 1911 (290). The

two cultures cannot co-exist according to Bret Harte: "The shriek of the locomotive discords with the Angelus bell" (238). Only Thornton Wilder (in 1928) discusses the glories of Spanish American culture.

Like the Italians, the Spanish and Portuguese in both Europe and America are assumed to have a "Latin" nature that embraces laziness, violence, vengefulness, superstition, loyalty to a venal clergy, dishonesty and unreliability.[28] Violence is accepted as part of the Spanish nature even by writers who admire Spain and the Spanish. In 1928 Hemingway introduced Americans to the Spanish pursuit of macho in The Sun Also Rises. In James Cain's Serenade in the course of an argument about the value of Mexican civilization, a ship captain points out that true beauty is necessarily accompanied with terror--as in the works of Beethoven, the sea and Mexico (123). The demeaning of the Latin Americans is also accomplished by language. They are spoken of as "greasers", "spicks", "gooks."[29] Even Auntie Mame, usually extraordinarily tolerant, refers to them as "spics" in 1958 (93).

A more favorable view surfaces in some books in the 1950s. John D. MacDonald in The Damned describes the terrible poverty of the Mexicans, but also its accompaniment "love and contentment, a quiet peace of the soul" (69). The book begins and ends with a poor Mexican ferryman whose life seems simple, but happy and constructive by comparison to that of the mean, competitive and unhappy Americans. Edna Ferber's Giant in 1952 uses discrimination against Mexicans as a major theme; she shows them being excluded from various places, hired only as servants, and even kept out of a celebration of the exploits of their own conquistadors (61, 152, 334). A final indignity is visited upon a Mexican-American who, although awarded the Medal of Honor for heroic action in World War II is refused burial by a Texas funeral director. Characters sympathetic to the plight of the

Mexicans point out that the whole of Texas was built on their backs, and that the English-Americans were once as much "foreigners" as the Mexicans are now (415, 320, 358). At about the same time Uris in Battle Cry portrays another Latin American war hero who, in the course of his army service, discovers for the first time in his life that he can walk with impunity into a restaurant with a white man; this occurs, of course, not in the United States but in New Zealand. There he finds himself regarded as an American for the first time. He is aware that his experience is shared by blacks as well.[30]

This more sympathetic tone in speaking of Latin Americans may be a retarded reflection some twenty years later in best sellers of Franklin Roosevelt's Good Neighbor policy, but reinforced by a post-World War II reevaluation of imperialism in all of its guises. It should however be noted that although the problems of the Latin Americans are viewed more sympathetically from the 1950s on, the estimate of inherent Latin American character does not change appreciably.

NORTH AMERICA: THE UNITED STATES

When Americans are characterized as a nationality, they are shown in most of these books as a people uniquely blessed: they live in a land that offers freedom to expand and develop their own capabilities to an extent impossible elsewhere. Sometimes the very size of the country is said to encourage both physical and psychological growth in its people. In Florence Barclay's novel, The Rosary in 1910 a "nerve doctor" advises an English patient to go to the United States "'to see a few big things'" such as Niagara and skyscrapers. "'And then, . . . the great-souled, large-hearted, rapid-minded people of America'" will restore you "'to enthusiasm with their bigness . . .'" (131-32). Taylor Caldwell in 1946 sees the American mind "affected by the vast skies and great plains and immense vistas of the new

country" (369). Americans, they assume, have been granted
an Eden, an Eden they chose for themselves by the act of
migrating to America. And their own act of choice has made
them a Chosen People; the Puritan identification of
themselves as the new Chosen People of God is secularized
and extended to all Americans. The American is not called
to respond to a theological challenge, but to a moral one.
Every man is free to try his mettle in a contest with nature
where the prize--material prosperity--is equally available
to all. Success may no longer be a presumptive sign of
membership in the Heavenly Elect, but it is a sign of
character which is rewarded by money and esteem. The
special function of the United States is to bring this
possibility to the humble of the world.

That this is the primary mission of America is unquestioned in all but a few books, and is presented with
greatest fervor just after World War II. Frank Yerby in
The Foxes of Harrow has a character express it thus:
"'. . . 'tis the last best hope of men. Never upon earth
has the poor man, the commoner, had such freedom; never has
there been so much respect for the essential dignity of
mankind.'" Taylor Caldwell sees it as a cosmic experiment
and returns the matter to God: "'It is an experiment
conducted by God to discover whether man has come of age,
whether he is mature enough to order his own destiny,
whether he had acquired sufficient greatness of heart to
succor other men. Here is the hope of the ages. Here is
the dream of the prophets.'"[31]

Two books, a decade later, question the outcome of the
experiment, and see it resulting only in a selfish materialism. In Advise and Consent by Allen Drury in 1959 this
passage appears: "The great age of the Shoddy came upon
America after the war; and Everybody Wants His became the
guiding principle of far too many [sic]." But Drury is not
wholly pessimistic because he hopes the "innate decency and

good will" of the Americans will retrieve this situation
(483-84). Henry Miller in Tropic of Cancer in 1961 sees
only decline: "Whatever there is of value in America
Whitman has expressed, and there is nothing more to be said.
. . . The future belongs to the Machine, to the robots"
(239-40). "America is the very incarnation of doom. She
will drag the whole world down to the bottomless pit" (94).
But Miller, regarded as both eccentric and pornographic,
would be unlikely to persuade his readers of the validity
of his social criticism; they might in fact consider him
part of the problem.

What then is this American? The qualities assigned to
an American nationality describe what sounds like a younger,
more spontaneous version of their stereotype of the
Englishman. Americans as heirs of British character are
just, honest, fair, brave, enterprising and "clean-minded"
(as Edgar Guest puts it in 1916). Although free blacks,
the Irish, the Italians, Jews and other newer immigrants,
and the inhabitants of the slums began to appear in best
sellers around 1940, they could hardly qualify as part of
the American nationality as defined in these books. They
substitute a part for the whole by allowing successful men
of Northern European descent (preferably English, Scottish
or German) to bestow their ideas, life-style and even their
names on the American nation. For example, in Hill's Manual
in 1905, a guidebook to success, the sample letters to be
copied by ambitious Americans applying for jobs, writing
letters of recommendation, etc., use only English names.
There is one exception, Bridget Mallory, whose name appears
in a letter refusing to recommend her because she is
dishonest and addicted to liquor (92). Morris West in
The Devil's Advocate notes that the Americans are, like the
English, sentimental and tough, but younger and richer.[32]
Americans are not melted together in a pot in which all
contribute equally to the resulting brew; nor are they

168

tossed in a salad of separate but equal parts; they make
up a stew whose flavor comes from only a few of its
ingredients, threatened by other indigestible components.

American youthfulness and energy are constantly remarked.
A European woman in The Rosary in 1910 observes of an
American woman: "'. . . she is not middle-aged, because she
is an American, and no American is ever middle-aged.'"
Americans are usually represented as enterprising and hard-
working. Mark Twain in 1869 suggests that it might be
better if Americans worked less hard and learned how to
relax. This is a position reiterated by Henry Miller when
he remarks that American ambition allows status to every
man whereas in Europe ". . . every man is potentially a
zero"; but in Europe everyone lives in the present", and
"life is sweet." The combination of youth and hard work
makes Americans daring and almost too energetic. In Around
the World in Eighty Days Jules Verne suggests that a
dangerous experiment in crossing a shaky bridge over the
rapids of a river is "a little too American." And in
Microbe Hunters Pasteur, frantically collecting equipment
is compared to ". . . an American about to build a sky-
scraper in six weeks"; later in the book he is described as
". . . the so typical misplaced American that he really
was."[33]

Several less admired American traits sometimes appear.
The American inclined toward nothing but material success
comes up often. From Horatio Alger to Ayn Rand this is a
much admired quality and one regarded as the basis for
American prosperity. It makes a neutral appearance in
Around the World in Eighty Days as a quality everyone would
recognize as an American peculiarity. The ship captain
comments as Fogg gloats over the amount of money he will win
should be get to Liverpool on time: "'Captain Fogg, you've
got something of the Yankee about you'" (223). But some
writers, especially Europeans, view this American

idiosyncracy with contempt. In <u>Thelma</u> by Marie Corelli a
Scandinavian asks rhetorically: "'. . . is not its confessed
watchword "the Almighty Dollar"?'" Later in the same novel
an extended discussion refers to the "dollar-encrusted
Americans", "rich and vulgar Yankees" who measure all by
riches.[34] Salesmanship is often shown to be endemic in the
United States; even in philosophy. Durant in 1926 considers
William James American in both voice and phrase because
". . . there is something that smacks of salesmanship" in
his work (552, 564). Americans are also shown putting value
on things only according to how much money they must pay for
it: in James Cain's <u>Serenade</u> in 1937 a bordello charges the
high price of five dollars because if it charged less it
would not attract American customers who undervalue bargains
(37-40). In <u>The World of Suzie Wong</u> in 1957 an Englishman
feeling himself to be overcharged responds: "'What do you
take me for--a Yankee? I'm not. I'm English'" (38). In
<u>The Razor's Edge</u> Maugham allows an American to counter the
European charge that Americans care only for money: "'Money
is nothing to us; it's merely the symbol of success. We are
the greatest idealists in the world'" (313). And Golden in
1958 reinforces this idea by observing that success in
America is not in having but in making money: "In our
society self-esteem comes with the acquisition of wealth"
(129). Whatever the reason given, however, a passion for
money is assumed to be a central part of the American
character.

Americans are usually limned as simple, honest, kind if
unmannerly; one can see the adumbration of Uncle Sam in this
picture. American hypocrisy on the subject of class is
often decried. In <u>Barriers Burned Away</u> in 1872, a character
observes that Americans are so class conscious that they
treat the poor as servants "'. . . and there is often a
marvelously wide margin between your boasted equality and
the reality'" (164). Many books in the first fifty years,

and most of those by Europeans, bear tales of wealthy
Americans who buy their way into European aristocracy by
marrying off their daughters to impecunious members of the
nobility.[35] In a best-selling sociological study of
American society in 1959 Vance Packard confirmed the
American dichotomy on this issue: while Americans have a
classless society as both creed and dream, they are actually
obsessed with status. He concluded that at the time of his
writing Holland, England and Denmark had a more open class
system than the United States (5-10).

Regional subdivisions of the American nationality are
made in those books concerned with such regional problems
as the Civil War or the movement west. In those books that
deal specifically with North-South hostility the myth that
the South was settled only by the British upper class and
the North by the less well bred is perpetuated, and these
regional differences are usually assumed to be inbred rather
than environmental. While all Americans are pictured as
hard-working and money-grubbing, these qualities are said
to appear in most extreme form in New England. In The Foxes
of Harrow in 1946 a Southern woman advises a young man:
"'Don't talk like a Yankee, Stephen. There are other things
in the world besides money'" (240). New Englanders work
hard and save not to enjoy the wealth they accumulate, but
to provide for the future. The New Englander is sometimes
almost excessively moral, reserved and austere, and lacks
the easy grace of the Southerner. He is brave and strong
and cannot hide his scorn of weakness.[36]

The Southerner, on the other hand, while as brave as his
Northern cousin, is also remarkable for his kindliness,
courteousness and hospitality. Like his northern counter-
part he is a man of principle, but more generous in material
things as well as in his evaluation of others. In books
about the Civil War and Reconstruction the suffering and
patient endurance of the former slaveholders is carefully

delineated.[37] Always when "the Southerner" is mentioned
it is the upper class white male the author is talking
about. Mark Twain in 1883 sees the South as living in the
past in a "grotesque chivalry" that keeps alive "a maudlin
Middle Age romanticism that is hurtful" (179). He points
out that Southern authors, except for Cable and Joel
Chandler Harris are carrying on the tradition established
when the South adopted Sir Walter Scott for their own.
While most Southern authors have deserted this tradition,
Southern best-selling authors have not.

The West (when referred to as "the West" these authors
are not indicating a specific geographical section, but
essentially a moving frontier) is the nursery of American
national character. The Westerner has the New England
qualities of energy, thrift, hard work and ingenuity; he
also has the easy manners, generosity and daring of the
South. But he lives in a land where above all things he
must stand on his own two feet. The only standard of the
West according to Harold Bell Wright in The Winning of
Barbara Worth is one's answer to the question: "What can I
do?" (115). "Every man has a chance here no matter what
his past has been: you see we don't care what a man has been
or what his fathers were; we accept him for what he can do"
(128). According to Busch in 1944, in the West "Success was
not won by soft measures. . . . The weaklings died by the
way and the cowards had never started" (10-11). The West
is a testing ground for manhood. "For it was a man's world,
without law and order, without gentleness, without ease.
It was savage, dramatic and thrilling."[38] The reader of
these books encounters the world of business in the West
only in Prather in 1951 and Ferber in 1952. The West is
for adventurers and settlers not business men. And from
1900 on in the best sellers its principal inhabitant is the
cowboy.

So, in these books the American nationality is created from Northern European genes tested in an environment that allows opportunity to every man to raise his status.

Obviously representatives of most national and ethnic groups appear somewhere, at least briefly in one or another of these books; one might identify all Arabs with the shrouded, romantic figure in The Sheik, or all Russians with those in Cold War books, busily engaged in a world-wide conspiracy less arcane, but quite as sinister as that of Fu Manchu. But this chapter is limited to those ethnic groups who appear in a substantial number of best sellers.

In the world of best sellers the persistence of racial and national characterizations is nothing less than astonishing; for any group the characteristics assumed to be inherent in individuals within the group changed hardly at all in spite of great changes in the real world. Although a quality may be perverted as with Scottish thrift or German efficiency the characteristic is still essentially and recognizably there. One might think the post World War II stress on human and civil rights as well as the emergence of the Third World would have been enough to change the lineaments of most of these stereotypes. But although some of the more recent books specifically attack ethnic discrimination, most of the books perpetuate the same old ethnic stereotypes. And indeed in some books, such as those by Kyle Onstott, such ethnic identities are central. To the reader these national characteristics, attached both to central and peripheral characters, constantly reiterated, might seem not only inherent but eternal.

That heritage should be assigned so important a function in individual personality would seem to belie the idea of the immigrant as the New Adam in a New Eden. Far from the freedom of Eden this Eve and Adam are the bearers of the heavy weight of an inescapable past in individual, racial and ethnic heritage.

PART II: MIND AND SPIRIT

Chapter 7: RELIGION: THIS WORLD AND THE NEXT

In the century 1865-1965 religious institutions and their
theologies met more severe and diverse challenges than ever
before in Judaic or Christian history. Fascinated by
questions of change and development the nineteenth century
spawned many theories of evolution before Darwin, but none
that carried the shock effect of The Origin of Species in
1859 or The Descent of Man in 1871. Darwin's hypothesis
posited a non-teleological evolution with unexplained
variations, variations that occurred, as he said, "for
reasons inherent in the embryo." The process of natural
selection had nothing to do with morality or purposefulness,
but merely the ability of the variation to physically
survive. Chance rather than divine plan seemed to rule the
world. Darwin apparently displaced the Garden of Eden with
a nature red in tooth and claw, inhabited by human beings
who were the product not of divine creation, but of an
evolutionary process. Furthermore Darwin's work appeared
with an overwhelming abundance of empirical evidence--not
easy for the nineteenth century or indeed the twentieth to
question. And at the same time the nineteenth century was
finding remnants of early animals and man that long
antedated Bishop Ussher's accepted date of 4004 B.C. as the
year of God's creation of the world. Lyell's earlier work
in geology prepared the ground and the bones of Neanderthal
man came to light at about the time of the publication of
Darwin's Origin of Species. Was man created in the image
of God or was he a mere descendant of the animal kingdom?
Intellectuals and many theologians made their peace with
these apparent contradictions by the 1880s. But in spite
of such activists as Asa Gray, the Harvard botanist who
announced proudly to Darwin that he would "baptize" the

theory, popular culture continued to see the issue as a
troubling enigma and the Scopes trial still echoes in
Fundamentalist circles to this day.

Another intellectual adventure disconcerting to established churches was the Higher Criticism in which scholars
examined the Bible as an historical document rather than a
record of divine revelation. Philology, anthropology and
science contemporary with Darwin dealt some sharp blows to
literal interpretations of the Bible, and the comparative
study of religious thought found parts of Christian
mythology, such as the Virgin birth, the flood, in religions
outside the Judaic-Christian tradition. These problems were
likely at first to disconcert the clergy rather than their
congregations, although Washington Gladden's book Who Wrote
the Bible? in 1891 was widely read in the United States at
the turn of the century.

The general American population, however, was probably
less concerned with theology and more with social attitudes
of the church in the late nineteenth century. The new
industrial city with its visible and extensive slums had
developed in a world very much alive to theoretical questions of liberty and equality stemming from the American
and French Revolutions. The succeeding century spawned
innumerable theories of social reform; it was the nineteenth
century that "discovered poverty" (in Robert Bremner's
phrase), that began to speculate on the subject of economic
equality. In such an atmosphere, in such a society what is
the function of the church: to help relieve the miseries of
the poor? to help sweeten the character of the wealthy by
exercising charity? to awaken the conscience of the well-to-
do? to encourage the poor to political action? to console
and persuade them to be content with their lot? Is social
conscience as important as individual conscience? Or,
should the church ignore the whole issue and concentrate
instead on saving individual souls?

Best sellers centering on a religious theme are scattered throughout the period. Of all the best sellers published between 1865 and 1900, 10.2% are primarily religious; this drops to 8.8% between 1900 and 1940, but recovers to 9.5% in 1940-1965. Evidently the Depression did not turn readers' tastes to religion; that decade had not a single best seller with a religious theme. On the other hand the era of World War II produced a veritable flood of religious books that continued into the next decade.

One might make the easy assumption that a generation involved in war and preoccupied with death in various guises would inevitably turn to religion. But how then could one explain the post-World War I period? John Fox Jr. and Harold Bell Wright were still being read, but the books on religion produced in the 1920s, except for The Magnificent Obsession in 1929, were hardly of a consoling nature. Bruce Barton transformed Jesus into a successful business man and Sinclair Lewis' Elmer Gantry used religion as a business rather than a faith. Perhaps radio, television and movies made the devastation of World War II more immediate and more frightening, and rendered the consolations of religion more attractive.

But in novels not primarily about religion one is conscious of a steadily increasing rate of secularization as the period advances. This is evident even in language. Secularization now allows the casual use of the Lord's name in exclamation rather than in prayer. This is clear in the differences in translation of Nana from the 1880 version to that of 1972. The exclamation translated as "good heavens" in 1880 (64), becomes "Christ" in 1972 (69); "Do be quiet" in 1880 (67) becomes "Shut up, for God's sake" in 1972 (62); "upon my life" in 1880 (75) becomes "Christ" in 1972 (71). This is not to say that cursing was unknown in the nineteenth century--Bret Harte in 1870 notes that use of the term "God" at a christening was ". . . the first time that the name of the Deity had been uttered otherwise than profanely in the camp" (11). But the genteel tradition of language in literature precluded the representation of actual speech. During the next seventy years, however, taking the Lord's name in vain had evidently become more and more respectable even in print.

Religion was still a noticeable element in the intellectual climate of all novels until the 1920s. In 1867 Horatio Alger is careful to have Ragged Dick become a faithful attendant at Sunday school. In 1951 Salinger's Holden Caulfield is absorbed in finding himself, but his search is hardly centered on religion. He does admit that he likes Jesus, but not "'the other stuff in the Bible'" (99). Marjorie Morningstar in 1955, although strictly observant of Jewish laws and active in Jewish organizations is still much more absorbed in things of this world than the world of the spirit.

Many of the early novels almost routinely offer redemption as one of their themes. Redemption supplied a particularly promising subject for a potential best seller because it allowed the author to put before the reader a book both racy and pure, both prurient and moral. The sensation of 1866, St. Elmo, by Augusta Evans, reveals Edna, an innocent, ambitious, pious orphan girl both attracted and repelled by a rude, cynical, arrogant roué. His good features are "blotted by dissipation and blackened and distorted by the baleful fires of a fierce passionate nature and a restless, powerful and unhallowed intellect" (50). Theirs is a stormy relationship with many of the same thrills as The Sheik in 1921. The respectability and redemption necessary to the fulfillment of their love comes about by a religious conversion of the handsome but wicked St. Elmo. Both of E. P. Roe's best-selling novels, Barriers Burned Away in 1872 and Opening a Chestnut Burr in 1874, are novels of redemption saturated with religion. In Barriers

Burned Away the great Chicago fire incinerates the heroine's
religious scepticism. Christina had viewed Christianity as
a superstition increasingly ignored by its adherents to the
point where the cross "'is dwindling to a mere pretty
ornament'" (176). She is converted when she sees how faith
supports people in a life-endangering situation because
death has no fears for them (436-43).

Indeed the function of religion to comfort and console
in the face of death plays a large and a curious role in the
early books. Authors brought up in the United States often
present death as a happy occasion of rebirth into a land
closely resembling the United States but more serene.
Holden in 1900 refers to heaven as very like a neighbor's
farm, but without death, quarrels or hard winters.[1]

The definitive nineteenth century description of heaven
appears in two best sellers, both by Elizabeth Stuart
Phelps: _The Gates Ajar_ in 1868 and _Beyond the Gates_ in 1883
(the gates in the title are, of course, the pearly gates).
In both books she provides her readers with a geographical
and sociological survey of a heaven that is physically and
spiritually comfortable, sociable and cozy. In the first
book a young woman mourning the death of her brother in the
Civil War, is appalled when the deacon of her church tells
her that her brother in heaven has no feeling left for her
because now all of his affections are centered on God. Her
aunt auggests that Protestants, visualizing a heaven that
is purely spiritual, have gone too far in recoiling from
the materialism of the Catholic church (110). Heaven is
not limited to spirit; we will all have bodies in heaven,
new ones, exactly patterned after the old, but in better
condition. Grey-haired Aunt Winifred thinks of the future
happily: "'Well, when I am in Heaven, I shall have my pretty
brown hair again'" (131). The senses are fully operative
in heaven: the rain is scented, the landscape pleases the
eye, the birds enchant the ear, one gets hungry and is

happily appeased by tasty food. Nor is heaven an idle place; everyone works busily (88). The American used to working hard to get ahead will feel quite at home in Phelps' heaven. All have duties and perform useful services, or they may further their education by taking courses, using the library and attending concerts (some conducted by Beethoven). Material things too expensive on earth will, in some cases, be provided in heaven. A girl who on earth longed in vain for a piano her family could not afford, is guaranteed one in heaven (152). A boy who loves machinery is assured he will be able to enjoy it in heaven as well (186). All in all one can see with such prospects how the still popular euphemism "sleep" easily replaced the word "death" in the vocabulary of optimistic Americans; this was a sleep filled with soothing dreams.

Several European writers of books popular in the United States criticized such visions of heaven. George Du Maurier in 1894 described it as "'a bliss so futile, so idle and so tame that we couldn't stand it for a week'" (154). In Marie Corelli's Thelma in 1887 the Scandinavian father of the heroine characterizes the Christian heaven as suitable only for "'girls and babies'"; Valhalla is the place for men (67). In his discussion of the historical Jesus, H. G. Wells explains one of the differences between Jesus and his followers who thought of salvation in terms of a magical ascension to heaven: "Few of them understood that the renunciation of the self is its own reward, that it is itself the Kingdom of Heaven" (510). Dr. Zhivago in 1958 tells a dying woman that there is no resurrection of the body after death; there wouldn't be room. She rose from the dead when she was born, and immortality is in her own consciousness when communicated to others (60). This subject, so common in the earlier books, appears rarely in the later ones. Only the evangelist Billy Graham in Peace with God offers extended discussion of heaven and hell, and while he is not as specific as Phelps his heaven is closely related to hers. It will be a place of beauty where we will be reunited with friends and family. At the resurrection the body will be raised to join the soul in spite of cremation or decay. God can bring all of its original chemicals back together and reconstitute the body. Addressing an audience enamored of science he uses the second law of thermodynamics to back up this point: "Scientists have already proved that no chemicals disappear from the earth" (81).

Conflicts between science and religion play a minor role in all of these novels except Robert Elsmere by Mrs. Humphrey Ward in 1888. In St. Elmo in 1966 there is a casual and approving reference to the idea that the earth has been peopled for just 6,000 years (43). And in Little Women Prof. Bhaer offers a spirited defense of "'The old beliefs. . . . God was not a blind force and immortality was not a pretty fable but a blessed fact'" (304-305). At about the same time, however, Bret Harte's story of a school oral examination is both more specific and pro-science. When asked if the sun and earth always move as the scientists say, a student denies this by citing the Biblical story of Joshua commanding the sun to stand still. But another student, Mliss, says firmly: "'It's a damned lie. I don't believe it.'" Harte's comment is that her response shocked all but the teacher whose respect for Mliss was already vast (170-71). In 1894 Trilby introduces Darwin's doctrine when Billee says one's choice must be between the Pope and Darwin. He chooses Darwin because if God created man in one day and he fell the next, God did not make him well, and how can one say this of an omnipotent God. A parson who meets Billee carrying a copy of The Origin of Species and defending its doctrine banishes him from his sight calling Billee a thief for "'. . . trying to rob me of my Saviour [sic].'" In his account of Billee's choice

of science over religion, Du Maurier interjects the
statement that the tale is set in the early 1860s before
religion made up its mind to meet science halfway (153-58).
Gene Stratton Porter in 1911 takes the pathway popular among
many churches: evolution is the creation and is God's "'plan
steadily unfolding'" according to the Harvester (312). With
his usual optimism in The Outline of History H. G. Wells
concludes that there is no real antagonism between science
and religion. What religion declared by "inspiration and
insight" history and science display as reasonable and
demonstrable (507). Paul de Kruif in his biographies of
scientists included in The Microbe Hunters (1926) indicates
that all of the scientists but Metchnikoff, an atheist of
Russian-Jewish background, accepted God as Creator. He
juxtaposes this to his observation of the current fashion
of questioning religious dogma (27). In This Side of
Innocence by Taylor Caldwell in 1946, a novel quite uncon-
cerned with religion, a sympathetic character suggests a
reversal of this trend, a reaction among scientists to the
new materialism. At the moment they are intoxicated with
Darwin and Huxley, but they will probably rediscover God
(202).

The book that centers on the conflict between science
and religion is Robert Elsmere (1888), the intellectual and
spiritual journey of a young clergyman from the established
church of England to the rejection of all Christian churches
and Christian theology. Elsmere struggles to retain his
faith in the face of the Higher Criticism, historical
relativism and the natural sciences. He sees Jesus as a
great soul, but not a god; he can no longer accept either
his incarnation or resurrection. He agrees with a friend
who characterizes Christianity as "'the passionate
acceptance of an exquisite fairy-tale'" (182). In the end
he discards Christian theology, but remains enthusiastically
devoted to Christian ethics. He finally leaves the ministry

and founds "The New Brotherhood of Christ" to put Christ's
ethics in practice in the slums of England. The book was
evidently a sensation both in England and the United States,
although one wonders how the ordinary reader could find
his/her way through many of the theological arguments.

That religion should win out in the struggle with science
is a universal hope, and not only because religion is the
instrument for universal salvation. In Of Human Bondage in
1915, Renan's Life of Jesus, a biography of Jesus as a
figure of history rather than divinity, is discussed (135).
A man who doesn't believe in God is asked how he can sit by
while his children are taught things he doesn't believe to
be true. He responds: "'If they're beautiful, I don't much
mind if they're not true.'" Besides its beauty, religion
adds prestige to good moral behavior: "'A man is more likely
to be a good man if he has learned goodness through the love
of God than through a perusal of Herbert Spencer'" (538-39).
Earlier books express much the same idea, but put it in
terms of how religion helps to subdue the "brutal passions",
and holds "the lower and baser" part of man's nature in
subjection.[2] The most spectacular illustration is in the
1896 novel Quo Vadis by Henryk Sienkiewicz. The triumph of
Christianity over paganism is the conquest of a depraved
and unstable society by responsible and moral people. The
book could hardly avoid becoming a best seller: it is a
veritable catalogue of gore and violent sex. Lions tear
apart and eat Christians, virgins are raped in the arena
(and everywhere else), bowels are torn out, hundreds are
crucified, Rome is lit by human torches before the general
conflagration. Thirty-seven of its four hundred forty-seven
pages offer nothing but sensational sex and blood. This was
the first of the best sellers to describe explicit sensual
pleasures, and all under the moral aegis of the triumph of
Christianity! Back in the realm of rationality Durant
quotes the Deist Voltaire who thinks it best for most people

to believe in immortality: "'If God did not exist, it would be necessary to invent him'" (264). Not only does religion act as a social curb, but it is frequently shown as a source of personal happiness and consolation. In Strange Woman in 1941, one of the characters approved by the author says he thinks of God as an older brother, friendly, understanding and always available to help. Nineteenth century books often observe that religion helps to keep order in society by reconciling people to their lot in life however miserable it may be; when religion carries the message "be content" it helps to produce if not a happier population at least a more submissive one.[3]

In the 1950s and 1960s several books are quite as certai as those of the nineteenth century that a stable and orderl democratic society rests on religion, and specifically the Christian religion. Theodore White in 1962 in The Making of the President notes that although Christianity does not assure a democratic state, there has never been a democracy that lasted any length of time "outside Christian influ- ences" for "without the quality of mercy and forgiveness, there is only logic and reason to guide a state, and these guarantee no freedom to any man" (237-38). J. Edgar Hoover in 1958 uses religion to sanctify the struggle against Communism; ". . . atheism was the first step toward communism" (26). He details the case history of a nice young man who becomes ripe for conversion to Communism when he loses his religious faith in high school; the final step is taken when he reads the Communist Manifesto in college (106). Marx's declaration of war on religion began "a war that was to become the cornerstone of Communist philosophy" (14-15; see also 321,324-25). To J. Edgar Hoover atheism inevitably breeds Communism. Thus religion in these books is regarded as of great practical value in producing what their authors consider a good society.

In general atheists and agnostics are given neutral
treatment only by H. G. Wells and Will Durant. They appear
rarely in the novels and unfavorably in all but one case.
A. J. Cronin's The Keys of the Kingdom in 1941, a book by a
Catholic and about Catholic missionaries describes an
atheist most sympathetically. Of his religious beliefs
Dr. Tulloch merely says "'I inherited a most satisfying
atheism'" (129). His atheism is not a private affair (he
is said to be an open adherent of Ingersoll), nor does he
trumpet it about, but he is severely critical of Christian
magic: he demonstrates that the stigmata exhibited by a
woman are hysterical rather than miraculous in origin, and
comments cynically: "'If she steers clear of the asylum,
she'll probably be canonized'" (131). He is angered by the
disparity between the attention church members give to so-
called miracles while ignoring child labor in the mills.
Dr. Tulloch is as devoted to helping humanity as his devout
Catholic friend, Father Chisholm, and far more than most of
the Catholic clergy who appear in this book. Father
Chisholm says of him that God believes in him although he
doesn't believe in God. He assures the dying Dr. Tulloch
that he will be most welcome in heaven; Christ was, like
Tulloch, a free-thinker (212-15). This is a unique position
in these books.

Until the middle of the twentieth century all of the best
sellers were written by Christians. Those authors who wrote
fictionalized biographies of Jesus, or, as in the case of
H. G. Wells, an account of the historical Jesus tended to
limn him in the image of their own ideals. The first of
these, Ben-Hur in 1880, a melodramatic moral tale in which
the villains come to grief and the heroes to glory, was a
runaway best seller and still is. Jesus is described as
delicate, kind, gentle and benign. His mission is not to be
king of the Jews on earth, but to offer life after death to
all of the virtuous. As the author points out through an

admired character this grants compensation particularly to the poor (452-57). One of the more curious parts of the characterization of Christ is assigning this Middle Eastern Jew blue eyes and yellowish-brown hair (130), coloring that still persisted in Fulton Oursler's 1949 biography The Greatest Story Ever Told, and indeed Oursler lightens his beard to "golden" (98). The racist atmosphere of the late nineteenth and twentieth centuries evidently required that so great a personage must come from Northern European ancestry.[4] H. G. Wells in 1921 explains that he will treat Christ as a man not a god because he is writing history not theology. He rejects Christian mythology of the virgin birth, the star guiding the Magi and any other supernatural elements, and he points out their similarities to magical elements in other religions (513). Essentially Wells separates Jesus from Christianity; Jesus did not talk of himself as God, nor of a Trinity, nor of sacraments. "All that is most characteristically Christian in worship and usage he ignored" (499). Wells sees Jesus as a great hero who preached not of salvation after death but the rebirth of the human soul on earth by renunciation of self. He set up no temples and no altars; he was a teacher rather than a priest. And Wells, himself a socialist, sees Jesus as a socialist, a "great revolutionist", the first to attack the concept of private property (886; see also 502-503).

Another popular book about Jesus was written by Bruce Barton, an advertising executive. The Man Nobody Knows was published in 1924 and is a marvelously representative produ product of the 1920s. He wrote the book, as he says, to contradict the image of Jesus as humble, lowly and a "kill-joy." His revision reveals Jesus as an extraordinarily successful executive who forged an organization that "conquered the world" by the use of modern business methods Barton recreates Jesus as a very clever public relations ma akin to those of the 1920s who invented the high pressure

advertising of today. Far from the humble gentle man of
Ben-Hur this is an aggressive go-getter, and "the most
popular dinner guest in Jerusalem" who sells himself as one
might sell a product. Far from the socialist of The Outline
of History this Jesus is an upholder of the business world
of the United States, a pillar of the Establishment.

The Robe by Lloyd Douglas pictures Jesus as brave,
serene, self-assured and, as the Roman soldiers observed
at the crucifixion, no coward (108). Here he is a savior
cast in a character likely to appeal to people at war as
the Americans were when the book was published. He is also
described as a lover of beauty, children and dogs (241).
(Dogs are considered the domestic animals appropriate for
the divine Jesus: dogs are symbols of manhood; cats usually
appear as symbols of womanhood.) Douglas also offers magic
in the peace that descends on anyone who touches a robe
worn by Christ. In The Greatest Story Ever Told Fulton
Oursler describes Jesus in familiar terms as the boy next
door. Jesus appears as a toddler playing with his toys
(75). Oursler endows him with a quality highly regarded
in the United States--he is friendly and has "unbounded
charm" (107). That he sometimes found the religious
services of the time "prolonged and tiresome" adds another
common touch (79). And in the post-War world of 1949
Oursler stresses the universality of Christ's appeal:
Christ would speak to all and make of many people one world.

Jim Bishop's dramatic account of Christ's last twenty-
four hours in The Day Christ Died in 1957 has Christ
speaking only the words given him in the four gospels.
(The apostles tend to sound like bewildered boys in the
speech and thoughts he assigns to them.) Bishop, to give
his readers the immediacy of a journalistic account,
describes Jesus as mortal man, not especially brace in
facing death (132), and bowed down by physical agony as his
body "began to throb with pain" (262). He is a man of the

people who must be opposed by the Jewish upper class. The
Jewish leaders had already perverted their covenant with
God by debasing religion into a matter only of externals
(35-36, 298). It is they--the Jewish upper class who
condemned Christ; "the people didn't" (31, 90). Like
Oursler he offers the immediacy of good journalism, but
with little sense of history. Both fictionalize at length,
and, aware of the American romance with the empirical, pile
detail on detail with little regard for organization or
relevance. One of Bishop's paragraphs should illustrate
this; it succeeds a paragraph on sheep and shepherds:

> Jewish friends showed their esteem for each
> other by always walking hand in hand. No one ever
> slept in the dark, a lamp was always burning in
> the family sleeping quarters. Bread was never
> cut; it was broken in wedge shape so that it could
> be used as a spoon for dinner and was dipped into
> a common dish. (55)

While some Christian clergy are portrayed as Christ-like
figures, there are also many examples of clergy who hardly
follow in his steps. Protestant and Catholic clergy,
however, are discredited for rather different reasons.
When an author is critical of Roman Catholic clergy, he
usually depicts them as being more concerned with political
and economic power, than with the spiritual or physical
well-being of their parishioners. The Prince of Foxes by
Samuel Shellabarger in 1947 discloses Roman Catholic
officials hip-deep in Italian politics and in avid pursuit
of economic power.[5] This also translates from European
power politics to the parish priest: Father Monaghan in
The Cardinal in 1950 is nicknamed "Dollar Bill" because he
is always after money (56). In The Bridge of San Luis Rey
Thornton Wilder lists a priest's schedule of charges: "two
measures of meal for a fairly good absolution and five
measures for a really effective one" (178).

Disapproved Protestant clergy or active laymen on the
other hand usually appear as bigots, hypocrites or prudes.[6]
The fervent Miss Clack in Wilkie Collins' The Moonstone in
1868 perhaps best represents all of the qualities associated
with perverted Protestantism. She spends most of her time
distributing tracts; her religion even gives her the courage
to tip a cab driver with a pamphlet (235). Collins lists
the titles of her favorite tracts: "Satan in the Hair-Brush,"
"Satan Behind the Looking Glass," "Satan Under the Tea-
Table," "Satan Among the Sofa Cushions" (244). She claims
to represent true Christianity; "'. . . we are the only
people who are always right'" (249).

Incidentally while the clergy are, of course, male, there
is substantial agreement that their sermons are designed for
female listeners. Christian congregations are made up
largely of females whose more emotional and spiritual nature
requires religion.[7] Ouida in 1867 (393) and Maugham in 1915
(538) see religious activity as most proper for women and
children, and Onstott's plantation owner thinks religion
primarily designed for women (141) and slaves (260) in
Mandingo. Harold Bell Wright in his 1909 novel The Calling
of Dan Matthews faces this issue. Dan is surprised when he
realizes Nurse Farwell is not a church member. She ascribes
his reaction to the fact that she is female, and asks if she
hasn't as much right to paganism as he (98). In the
ambiance of these books designating Christianity primarily
for females hardly adds to the prestige of the church.

Missionary activity evokes ambivalence on the part of
many of these best selling writers. There are some humane,
tolerant and self-denying missionaries.[8] But others are so
intolerant that the culture they are trying to convert
remains opaque to them and they are guilty of gross offenses
to their hosts. Pearl Buck's Pavilion of Women discloses a
particularly unpleasant example in Little Sister Hsia.
Missionary activity itself is sometimes criticized as a

process preparing the way for imperialism, far from the path of Christ. In The Keys of the Kingdom in 1941 an upper class Chinese remarks: "'You missionaries walk in with your gospel and walk off with our land.'"[9] Except for Mark Twain, criticism of missionary activity as such comes only with World War II when the issues of racism and imperialism were being intensively reexamined. One book The Green Berets in 1965 has high praise for the political activities of Christian missionaries who are shown as effective agents in fighting Communism (225).

Throughout the period best sellers agree that Christ bestowed on Christianity a major social mission--to help the poor and unfortunate. There is sometimes severe criticism of clergy who refuse this responsibility as in the case of hard-shelled Baptists in Eggleston's The Hoosier Schoolmaster in 1871 who expel a member for starting a Sunday school and joining a temperance society (97). In 1876 Haines and Yaggy imply that the social mission of the church is limited to the fact that the church "is the only place on this side of the grave designed for the rich and the poor to meet together in equal prostration before God" (341). Only H. G. Wells sees Christ's teaching as leading inevitably to socialism. But several books present devout individuals who sacrifice all thought of personal comfort to work in the slums for the poor.[10] There is also criticism of the hypocrisy of well-to-do churchgoers and clergy who offer the glories of heaven to the poor in exchange for their acceptance of earthly misery.[11] The sharpest recognition of this problem occurs in a dialogue in The Calling of Dan Matthews in 1909, a dialogue already referred to. Dan, the minister, and Nurse Farwell discuss the problem of a poor woman who has attempted suicide. Nurse Farwell, claiming to be a Christian though not a church member, berates Dan and the church he represents: "'Your ministry is a matter of schools and theories, of

doctrines and beliefs. This is a matter of life'" (164).
When Dan confesses that he hadn't known about the problem,
she responds that it is his business to know--the business
of the church: "'The religion of Christ is so far forgotten
that it never enters into any thought of the church at all'"
(98). To her the church has only one duty: "'Man serves
God only by serving man. There can be no ministry but the
ministry of man to man'" (103). At the end of the novel
Dan leaves the ministry. The relationship between religion
and an equitable society is put another way by Edward
Bellamy in his Utopian novel Looking Backward in 1888 when
he points out how much easier it is to believe in God in a
just society than in one of poverty and oppression.

The 1890s with their fearsome social problems and
conflicts produced two best sellers, one a pamphlet, the
other a book, that dramatized the social mission of Christ
to an extraordinary degree. The Other Wise Man in 1895 is
the tale of a fourth Magi who is thirty-three years late in
getting to the scene of Christ's birth because he is
constantly diverted from his pilgrimage to help others.
Finally he uses his last jewel to ransom a girl sold into
slavery; this is the jewel he had hoped to use to buy
Christ's freedom from crucifixion. The moral of the tale
is that like this Wise Man, the Christian must let nothing
interfere with his duty to help others. And in 1897 came
one of the most popular novels of all--In His Steps by the
Congregational minister Charles Sheldon. A down and out
stranger stumbles into a Protestant church in the middle of
a service and queries the congregation "'What do you
Christians mean by following the steps of Jesus?'" The
minister, shocked by what the query reveals of the relationship of his church to current social questions, asks
for volunteers to pledge for one year not to do anything
without first asking themselves "What would Jesus do?", and
following exactly the path revealed by an honest answer.[12]

The results are revolutionary: the newspaper stops printing detailed accounts of crimes, stories of prize-fights, advertisements for liquor and tobacco. There are to be no slangy, sensational headlines (this at the very moment when Hearst and Pulitzer were vying with each other by promoting yellow journalism in their competition for circulation). All political issues are to be discussed not from the point of view of political parties, but of right and wrong. To free the Sabbath for worship Sunday editions of the paper are dropped. An aspiring opera singer trades in this role for the much less well paid one of gospel singer; every profession and occupation is shocked into new and drastically revised perceptions and behavior. That each must act as Christ did is dramatized in a watchman's song:

> Must Jesus bear the cross alone
> And all the world go free?
> No, there's a cross for everyone, .
> And there's a cross for me. (196)

While this prescription roused the conscience of the Christian, and emphasizes his/her social responsibilities, like a patent medicine it failed to analyze the complexities of the disease. And the answers to the basic question "What would Jesus do?" about the ills of a newly industrialized society have been various indeed.

Of the many religions that appear in these books those centered in the East attract least attention.[13] Mohammedanism enters in scattered and usually unfavorable references. Haines and Yaggy in 1876 declare: "Mahomet still lives in his practical and disastrous influence in the East" (505). This is not very different from the 1947 opinion of Kenneth Roberts that religion is the Arabs' greatest curse because they occupy themselves with it to the exclusion of everything else (340). In 1921 H. G. Wells is more tolerant. While he is critical of Mohammed himself calling him "vain, lustful and egotistical," and not in a class with Jesus,

Gautama or Mani, nonetheless he grants Islam noble attributes in spite of stemming from a less than sublime founder.
He sees no social oppression in countries dominated by
Mohammedanism; although there are slaves, they are provided
with the same food and clothes as others, and human
relations between free and slave are kindly (577-81).
Napoleon Hill in Think and Grow Rich in 1937 presents a
wholly favorable view when he uses Mohammed as an example
of the importance of persistence in acquiring power. He
quotes at length a Herald Tribune book review by Thomas
Sugrue. Sugrue points out that Mohammed was not intending
to start a new religion, but inviting Christians and Jews
to join hands in one united faith. Had they accepted
"'Islam would have conquered the world.'" But "'They would
not even accept Mohammed's innovation of humane warfare.'"
The latter contradiction in terms is explained to the
satisfaction of Sugrue and Hill by the contrast in behavior
of the armies of Islam with those of the Christian
crusaders. When they entered Jerusalem the Christians
killed every Moslem there, whereas the Moslems killed no
one because of his/her faith. Sugrue also observed that
the Christians accepted "'one Moslem idea--the place of
learning, the university'" (164-66).

Religions of the Far East fare well when they appear at
all, as in the novels of Pearl Buck. In Lost Horizons in
1933 Shangri-La is inspired by a religion whose basic tenet
is moderation in all things and whose tolerance is illustrated by the comment of one inhabitant: "'. . . it is
possible that many religions are moderately true'" (99).
The stress in Eastern religions on contemplation and the
pursuit of wisdom is emphasized. The appeal of the
spiritualism of the East is of great importance in the life
of a major character in Maugham's novel of 1944 The Razor's
Edge. Larry finds it increasingly difficult to accept some
of the basic dogma of Christianity: (1) that God created

the world for his own glorification; (2) that one must ask
God the father for one's daily bread when earthly fathers
do not have to be asked; (3) why should God want to be
praised constantly? (4) the constant Christian preoccupa-
tion with sin. If the evil in men is the result of
heredity and environment, they cannot help sinning, so how
can God condemn them? (5) why did the good, all-powerful
God create sin at all? (282-84). After a long spiritual
hegira Larry finds in the East a religion with the one
essential doctrine--that God is within you. Kahlil Gibran
in The Prophet in 1926 brought much the same message, one
still very popular among young people. Although nineteenth
century American intellectuals were much interested in
Eastern philosophy and religion, this interest evidently
did not extend to the general reading public. Young people
of the mid-twentieth century uncertain of their complex
culture and their place in it have become increasingly
interested in Eastern religions as they search for their
own spiritual peace.

Christianity appears in many guises in these books. The
two made-in-America sects--Christian Science and the Church
of Latter Day Saints--come out very badly every time they
appear. Christian Science, invented in the late nineteenth
century appears for example in a casual remark in
Steinbeck's Cannery Row in 1945: half the girls in the
whore house are said to be Christian Scientists (17). The
1964 biography of Jean Harlow blames her death on her
mother's espousal of Christian Science which kept the
actress from medical attention. The lack of interest in
Christian Science apparently does not indicate a lack of
interest in its basic philosophy because two best sellers
at the turn of the century were upholders of the mind power
central to Christian Science: Ralph Waldo Trine's In Tune
with the Infinite in 1897 and The Power of the Will by Frank
Haddock in 1907. These books grew out of the New Thought

Movement, but rather than swelling the ranks of the
religious helped usher in the later success-through-mind-
power books as the success manuals turned from advising
hard work to personality expansion as the way to get ahead.
They are intellectual ancestors of Dale Carnegie, Napoleon
Hill and Norman Vincent Peale.

The other made-in-America theology, and it is more
prominent than Christian Science in these books, is
Mormonism--the Church of Latter Day Saints. The only
sympathetic mention of this sect occurs in Around the World
in Eighty Days by Jules Verne in 1874; a Mormon Elder
informs the travellers in a lecture that many Mormons have
been martyred in America, and that there will be more (173-
75). But in the two novels in which Mormons play a major
role in the plot they are shown as sinister, brutal and
immoral. Arthur Conan Doyle's first published story,
A Study in Scarlet appeared in England in 1887 and in the
United States in 1890. In this tale Brigham Young, leading
a veritable army of Mormons across the desert, comes across
a man and a little girl about to die of starvation and
dehydration. Young will save them only if they will
convert: "'We shall have no wolves in the fold.'"[14] After
conversion they live in the Mormon community and discover
that no individual freedom is permitted, and that Mormon
persecution of heretics is worse than it was under the
Spanish Inquisition. A secret society, the Avenging Angels,
that seems to be "omniscient and omnipotent and yet . . .
neither seen nor heard" enforces the dictates of the church.
Men suddenly vanish after disagreeing with the Elders of
the church. "A rash word or a hasty act was followed by
annihilation and yet none knew what the nature might be of
this terrible power which was suspended over them."[15] When
the female population is insufficient for Mormon purposes
suddenly "fresh women appeared in the harems of the Elders--
women who pined and wept, and bore upon their faces the

traces of an inextinguishable horror" (63). Ferrier
himself succumbs when he supports his daughter's opposition
to marrying a Mormon, and both die.

The other extensive treatment of the Mormons is in a
most popular Western by Zane Grey--Riders of the Purple Sage
in 1912. As in Doyle's book sinister bands of male Mormons
ride through the West kidnapping women to be used in "'the
last unspeakable crime'" as one character puts it (213).
They are also said to "'do absolutely any deed to go on
building up the power and wealth of the church, Their
Empire'" (20). Interestingly enough later versions of
these two tales considerably tone down their attacks on the
Mormons. In the case of A Study in Scarlet the Modern
Library edition edited by Christopher Morley eliminates
five chapters on Mormonism because the editor considers
them innacurate and tedious. And the movie made in 1925
of Riders of the Purple Sage starring Tom Mix is still
about kidnapping women, but Mormons are not mentioned; the
kidnappers are now simple outlaws. The Mormons' carefully
regulated practice of polygamy, translated into sexual
freedom for males, was certain to make the book sell; it
had that unbeatable combination of prurience finally
conquered by morality. One would like to think this change
in attitude toward the Mormons reflected a growth in
religious toleration in the United States, but it probably
merely mirrored the growing secularization of the twentieth
century, and the prosperity of the Mormons in Utah. And by
the 1920s sexual adventure had chosen other paths, and the
Mormons, who had repudiated polygamy when Utah entered the
Union in 1891, were now a firmly settled and powerful group
in the country.

Until the 1940s Roman Catholicism appears in many of
these books as a religion of foreigners and one inimical to
American culture. Only three nineteenth century authors,
two English and one French, allow Catholicism, the dignity

ordinarily accorded to Protestants. In 1866 <u>Griffith Gaunt</u>, a novel of some sophistication by Charles Reade, details the disastrous effects of anti-Catholic prejudice. The story involves a marriage between an urbane and indifferent Protestant and a devout Roman Catholic. The husband seems less concerned with his wife's Catholicism than with her increasing piety, but finds it acceptable in these terms: "An ugly saint is an unmixed calamity to jolly fellows; but to be lord and master, and possessor of a beautiful saint, was not without its piquant charm" (199). Throughout, it is the wife who is the admirable character, and, indeed, acts heroically in the face of her husband's jealousy and finally bigamy. In 1882 Ludovic Halévy published <u>The Abbé Constantin</u>--a gentle love story of a wealthy American girl who marries a European. Everyone, including the Abbé, curé of the French village where the couple live, is virtuous and Catholics and Protestants get along well together. The Abbé's warmth contrasts with what he fears as the "'frigid utterances'" of Protestant pastors who are expected in the village now that the castle has been sold to Protestants. The Abbé is reassured when the Protestants turn out to be Americans with both the wealth and desire to restore the castle and establish a cooperative and amiable relationship with the Abbé. The book is a quiet one, but one that probably attracted American readers because it was one of the few European novels that gave a favorable picture of Americans. Then in 1887 Marie Corelli's <u>Thelma</u> shows dramatically and at some length the anti-Catholic prejudice present in English society in the late nineteenth century. The novel presents a most unattractive Protestant clergyman who turns to convert the heroine. The Rev. Dyceworthy is bigoted, ruthless and dishonest. He plans to rape Thelma so that the man she loves will refuse to marry her. He assumes that because she is Roman Catholic she is "'hopelessly damned'" (37). His attempts at conversion involve vivid descriptions of the horrors of hell; to which she responds: if hell is so terrible then one surely needs the Roman Catholic religion which at least provides purgatory (128). One character in the story blames the Reformation on Luther's being "'tempted by a pretty woman'" (40). Catholicism is viewed favorably in only these three books before the 1940s when a Catholic Renaissance occurred in American best sellers.

The more typical view of Catholicism is that established by Mark Twain especially when reporting on his European travels in Innocents Abroad. He is scornful of most of what he sees of the Roman Catholic church: the numerous pieces of the "true cross" revered in innumerable churches he calls "Jesuit humbuggery" (I-41, 63, 310). He makes fun of Catholic altars as "gilt gimcracks and gingerbread" (I-42). He contrasts the wealth of the church with the terrible poverty he sees in the Papal States (I-270). He lists the priority given by Catholics to holy people: (1) the Virgin Mary (2) the Deity (3) Peter (4) canonized Popes and martyrs, and finally (5) Christ as an infant (II-11). Eventually, after accepting the hospitality of a monastery he apologizes by saying: "I have been educated to enmity toward everything that is Catholic, and sometimes in consequence of this, I find it much easier to discover Catholic faults than Catholic merits" (II-349). But he is still critical in Life on the Mississippi in 1883 when discussing the planting of what he terms the "confiscation cross" by French missionaries in New France; the French went on to conquer America "while the priest consecrated the robbery with a hymn" (12).

Lorna Doone in 1874 is full of such terms as "bloody Papists" (197), "murdering Papishers" (19). John Ridd distinguishes between Catholics and Protestants by observing: "'Papists burn Protestants in the flesh; and Protestants burn Papists in effigy'" (342). Contempt for

Roman Catholicism and Roman Catholics is consistently and casually expressed by admired characters in the novels.[16] In <u>Janice Meredith</u> by Paul Leicester Ford in 1899 the villagers tar and feather an effigy of the Pope (52), and use the phrase "vile Jesuit" as a term of opprobrium for someone with whom they disagree although he is not necessarily either a Jesuit or a Catholic.

Then for the first time, at the end of the Twenties two books realistically portraying youth at the mercy of an urban environment, center around Catholic families whose hope for their children lies in the efficacy of the church. Louis Beretti in 1929 never misses church while pursuing a life of crime; in fact, he robs an express company at night, but goes to church on his way home. Studs Lonigan in 1932 is carefully brought up by his devout mother to be a priest, and attends a parochial school. These Irish parents are quite as pious as the Italian Beretti family. But hypocrisy on the part of the parents as well as the church is pointed out by both Donald Henderson Clarke and James T. Farrell. In <u>Studs Lonigan</u> the children complain that the principal of the parochial school is "'as bad as a kike'" because he is constantly asking for money (42). Both boys, Beretti from the slums and Studs from a lower middle class family on the make in the city, come to sad and futile ends. Although Studs' family is not poor, Farrell characterized him as living in "spiritual poverty." The parents cling to the church as a counterweight to a decadent society: "'There's nothing like the church to keep one straight'" (49). In both books the church is depicted as ineffective, but not deliberately evil as it had appeared in so many earlier novels.

By 1943 when <u>A Tree Grows in Brooklyn</u> was published, the public was evidently ready to accept a more kindly view of Catholic family life. The book is just as full of Catholic home rituals as the last two; for example, Francie Nolan's grandmother sprinkles holy water in their new apartment in case a Protestant had lived there or a Catholic had died there before receiving absolution. But this is a heart-warming novel full of nostalgia and seen through the fresh eyes of a small girl.

In the 1940s and 1950s, in the midst of a veritable flood of religious books came an outpouring of best sellers centered on Catholic theology and the Catholic church, and written by Catholics. The Keys of the Kingdom by A. J. Cronin in 1941 is the story of a Scottish priest, Father Francis Chisholm, a missionary in China. He is an humble man whose religion requires him to devote himself to the poor and the sick. He is loved by the people to whom he ministers but not by the church hierarchy. Previous missionaries had produced many more conversions than had Father Francis, but these were only "rice Christians"—those who accepted conversion not because they believed, but for the material benefits that would be given them. To Francis heaven was not in the sky, but in "the hollow of your hand" (7). He is also remarkably tolerant, asserting that salvation is available to any good person whatever his religious creed. When the book was reviewed by The Catholic World in August, 1941 it was scorned as a piece of propaganda on the futility of organized religion. Whether this had the same results as banning a book in Boston is hard to say. But it became a Book-of-the-Month selection and was widely read.

The next year another favorable view of Catholicism was published in The Song of Bernadette by Franz Werfel. Werfel, a Jew escaping Hitler, was sheltered for several weeks at Lourdes until he got a visa. Here he learned of Bernadette and vowed to write her story. With a good deal of objectivity he details the reaction of various groups in the town to the alleged miracle. The recognition of Bernadette is seen as a triumph of the poor and lowly. In

came Fulton Oursler's The Greatest Story Ever Told and in
1950 The Cardinal by Henry Morton Robinson. The latter is
the story of the success of a young priest. Father Stephen,
unlike Father Francis never names mistakes. He is highly
intelligent, an excellent diplomat and well versed in and
committed to Catholic theology. Readers of other faiths,
while caught up in this story, might be put off by the
emphasis on Catholic doctrine and practices, as when a
mother is chosen to die so that her baby can be born.

Six years later the biography of a female member of the
regular Catholic clergy appeared in The Nun's Story by
Kathryn Hulme. For seventeen years she fights a losing
battle to bury her own individuality ("singularity"). As
a student she is told to flunk an examination in a subject
she knows well. She tries hard to achieve total self-
control. "Custody of the eyes," for example, is necessary
in the strict order to which she belongs. She is stunned
by the realization that never again will she have any
privacy. Finally, after working in the Underground in
World War II, she realizes she cannot subdue herself to the
total obedience without question demanded of a nun, and she
leaves the order. The extraordinary thing about this story
is that neither Gabrielle nor the church is shown as a
failure. The reader can follow and respect both the logic
of the rules of the order and the problems encountered by
those facing a lifetime of such rigid conformity.

In 1959 Morris West in The Devil's Advocate offers yet
another favorable view of Catholic clergy--this time in a
kind of religious detective story. Monsignor Blaise
Meredith is assigned to examine critically the credentials
of a potential saint; Monsignor Meredith is the Devil's
advocate. Again here Catholic doctrine is made both visible
and comprehensible.

The nascence of Catholic books in best seller lists from
1940 on is startling. Up to this time readers of popular

books were introduced to the Catholic religion surrounded
by an aura of both scorn and fear, and probably the two
were related. It should be said at once that this is also
the period when Jews were for the first time depicted
sympathetically: Shaw, Uris, Golden, Shirer.[17] Since these
books came after a war in which the enemy of the United
States stridently and ruthlessly promoted anti-Semitism and
the destruction of the Jews, one would expect a more
receptive attitude to develop toward Jews in the United
States. Was this surge in popularity of Catholic books a
mere spin-off from the reexamination of the Jews? Probably
the acceptance of both Catholic and Jew as Americans came
from quite different sources. Up to the mid-1940s
Protestants ranked above Catholics in income, occupation
and education; but this situation began to shift in that
decade.[18] The floods of new Catholic immigrants from
Southern and Eastern Europe had provided a large supply of
people employed in menial and poorly paid jobs. Catholics
were associated in the minds of the verbal Protestant
Establishment with attitudes and qualities the middle class
likes to think keep the poor in poverty: lack of ambition
and intelligence, drunkenness, slothfulness, etc. But
passage of laws restricting immigration in the 1920s altered
this situation conspicuously. Furthermore by this time many
of the older immigrants had moved up into the middle class.
Also in the 1930s the Irish were prominent in the labor
union movement; Ahlstrom estimates that they made up two-
thirds of American union membership in that period. Theirs
was a conservative union movement that took a firm stand
against Communism and in favor of middle class values. By
the 1940s the Catholics were regarded at last as Americans
with political and economic power and clout; evidently to be
middle class is to be American. The nomination of Al Smith
for the presidency was an obvious sign of some change in the
status of Catholics in American consciousness although the

campaign was marred by vicious anti-Catholic attacks and
he lost the election. Yet by comparison to the Jews
Catholics were much nearer acceptance; there had never been
an attempt to nominate a Jew for the presidency. The
election of John F. Kennedy in 1960 seemed like a final
acceptance of Catholics as Americans.

The Fundamentalist preacher of camp meetings and urban
revivals appears in many novels, but rarely favorably.[19]
In Duel in the Sun, Busch's 1944 version of the West of
1880, the toughness of the Western hero appears in an
evangelist who preaches in a gambling house, and knocks
out anyone who disagrees (78). Erskine Caldwell's novels
of the 1930s with their tragic-comic poor whites of the
South are full of evangelical religion, but their version
is one in which God's actions can be used to excuse human
behavior. In Tobacco Road Sister Bessie talks to God cozily
as one might to a favorite relative, and scolds him for
tempting good folks to steal: "'Ain't no sense in your
letting a man just keep on doing a sinful thing all the
time'" (61). Jeeter Lester says God's giving Ellie May a
hare lip "'was just meanness on his part.'" But Bessie
thinks perhaps God did it just to save her pure body from
wicked men, especially from Jeeter, her Pa (70). God's
omniscience is questioned by Bessie: she thinks it better
to talk over her problems as a married woman with another
married woman rather than God, since the other woman would
know more about it than God (61-63). The Rev. James Casy
in Grapes of Wrath is a revivalist treated with both realism
and sympathy. He gets "the call", preaches but backslides
periodically. In the latter state he confides to his friend
Tom: he "'got a lot of sinful idears--but they seem kinda
sensible'" (27). Then he decides that perhaps sin and
virtue do not exist, and that he loves people but not Jesus
because he doesn't know Jesus, and perhaps the holy spirit
is really the human spirit (32-33). Later he gets the call

again when he hears of farmers pushed off the land (76).
For a revivalist to be concerned with social issues as well
as individual salvation is unusual but the combination was
perhaps natural in the era of the Depression.

The most extended and critical account of an evangelical
preacher is that of Elmer Gantry in 1927. Sinclair Lewis'
Gantry is a hypocrite from his first sermon; his attraction
to preaching comes from the sense of power in exercising
control over his hearers and in the money to be made in
preaching. Lewis' critical eye examines not just a
revivalist preacher, but the more conventional religious
institutions of the day. Elmer's education, for example,
is described so: "He had in fact got everything from the
church and Sunday school, except, perhaps, any longing
whatever for decency and kindness and reason" (28). The
vision of Jesus preached by the fictional Gantry is as much
of the 1920s as that advocated by the actual Bruce Barton
whose Christ was an advertising executive. At one point
Gantry sees Christ as a Rotarian (359), but essentially he
visualizes Christ as a strong man not unlike the football
heroes of the 1920s (40-45).

Harry Golden, writing in 1958, notes a change in
revivalist preaching. The old evangelists are unable to
compete with the more sophisticated ones heard and seen on
television, and the evangelicals are, like their audiences,
becoming middle class (109).

In 1953 Billy Graham, one of this new breed of revival-
ists, spectacularly successful on television, produced a
best selling book, Peace with God. The Bible shows what
"natural science seems so unwilling to admit" that "nature
reveals both a creator and a corrupter," God and Satan who
are at war in the world and in us (50). The Bible must be
taken literally; it is the source of historical as well as
theological truth. The story of Creation is not a myth:
"The Bible tells us exactly what happened in the beginning.

The first man was no cave-dweller--no gibbering,
grunting, growling creature of the forest--trying
to subdue the perils of the jungle and the beasts
of the field. Adam was created full grown with
every mental and physical faculty developed. (43-44)
Chapter Sixteen on the social obligations of the Christian
hallows the myths of middle class America. Only Christian
nations provide a humane society: they have outlawed child
labor, slavery, and exalted the position of women. He makes
it sound as though Christianity were correcting the faults
of some other cultures rather than its own. While observing
that life is cheap in the non-Christian world he urges
Americans whatever the issues, to fight and die for their
country if asked, and to do so gladly "as unto God" (191).
His ideas of social justice seem to be limited to support
of the Community Chest, Red Cross, the Salvation Army,
Rotary, Kiwanis and the Lions Club, and he notes: "Lots of
pagan religions never had a service club" (198). The race
question (this was the year before the Brown decision) will
be solved when all are "born again": "The closer the people
of all races get to Christ and His Cross, the closer they
will get to one another." The "woman's role is to love and
help and reassure her husband in every way she can" while
he provides for her and "her children." The employer should
be just and the employee must work as hard as he can "as
unto work done for God, and not merely for men." Graham
confirms the fears of the middle and upper classes that they
are being milked by the undeserving poor when he warns that
many Christians take "spiritual pride in being poverty-
stricken" and do nothing to get out of that state,
attributing their condition to the will of God. He makes
all of the poor sound like characters in an Erskine Caldwell
novel. Like J. Edgar Hoover, Graham believes religion to
be the main enemy of Communism. He suggests that one of
the signs of the second coming of Christ in the Bible

(Ezekiel: 38-39)--great armies marching against the Lord--
may be the legions of The U.S.S.R. All in all then this
advisor to many American presidents accompanies his
Fundamentalist religious creed with a simplistic and
heartily conservative social philosophy.

Religious books popular in the United States often
involve a formula, a gimmick, a simple technique to unite
the human being with the deity. As we have seen, In His
Steps proposed that everyone should ask herself/himself
"What would Jesus do?" when facing any decision and direct
all actions down that pathway. Lloyd Douglas in The Robe
in 1942 allows salvation by magic when Marcellus touched
the robe worn by Christ to his crucifixion. But the most
popular technique outlined in best sellers comes from mind
power. The first of these books to carry this message was
Corelli's A Romance of Two Worlds in 1888, a tale both wild
and vague combining mysticism with pseudo-science. The
heroine plugs into what Corelli calls the "Electric
Radiance" of God. She names electricity the wonder of the
age, but avers that "human electricity," emanating from God
has been neglected as a source of spiritual power. She is
the only Catholic writer to write in this vein. The publication of the book was timely indeed; it appeared in the
United States when the New Thought movement was becoming
popular with its emphasis on the vast spiritual power
embodied in the divinity within each person. It was an
extraordinarily optimistic movement; evil and pain could be
eliminated by developing inner resources. Christian Science
was one branch of the movement.

But as the theory of mind power germinated it began to
stress personal fulfillment by achieving power on earth
rather than salvation in heaven. The techniques offered in
best sellers for tapping God's power become techniques for
getting ahead in the world. God appears as a device to
serve man. He is important not because he offers spiritual

redemption and eternal salvation, but because he is the source of power for fulfillment in the finite world. As we have seen, religion is generally regarded as important to man because it is useful in producing social order. Hill's Manual of 1905 in an essay on nineteenth century progress ascribes American progress to "the essential principles of Christianity . . . the foundation of all right living and the cornerstone of society and social order" (288). But the mind power movement goes far beyond this, and asks that each person use God to advance himself by positive thinking. It is a curious movement to invade Christianity; it seems to secularize God. Sin and evil disappear along with humility and self-abnegation. One wonders what happened to the Sermon on the Mount.

Ralph Waldo Trine's essay, In Tune with the Infinite, came out the same year (1897) as In His Steps and could not at first match the popularity of the novel. Trine urges the reader to come into harmony with God and His universe: "to come into the possession of unknown riches, into the realization of undreamed powers" (Preface). "Ideas have occult power . . ." (181). While he cautions against hoarding wealth, he urges spiritual power to achieve wealth.

> If one holds himself in the thought of povery,
> he will be poor, and the chances are that he will
> remain in poverty. If he holds himself, whatever
> present conditions may be, continually in the
> thought of prosperity, he sets into operation
> forces that will sooner or later bring him into
> prosperous conditions. (176)

He becomes a magnet for prosperity (178). One senses in this book on religion a foretaste of Dale Carnegie, Napoleon Hill and Norman Vincent Peale.

In Elmer Gantry in 1927 Sinclair Lewis satirizes such forms of New Thought when Gantry, involved in the movement, takes courses in Mysticism, Love, and one called

"Prosperity" (229). Lewis' description of Gantry's version
of New Thought seems more like a description of reality
than satire in the light of the future course of Positive
Thinking.

In 1929 Lloyd Douglas published his extraordinarily
popular novel The Magnificent Obsession. Dr. Hudson, a
surgeon, dies when an inhalator cannot be used to save his
life because it is being used to save the life of a rich,
spoiled idle young man who has been injured in an automobile
accident. Feeling guilty that he has been spared at the
cost of so useful a man as Dr. Hudson, young Merrick decides
to try to replace him by becoming a doctor himself. Unex-
pectedly he finds the doctor's diary and discovers that Dr.
Hudson believed he had the power to do anything he liked:
"'All you have to do is follow the rule! There's a formula
you know'" (128). The formula from the Bible becomes a
magnificant obsession and changes Dr. Hudson's life. It
involves building up your own personality by going into
other personalities and helping them secretly (136). Again
pseudo-science is involved and the talk of Volta and Faraday
reminds one of Marie Corelli's "Electric Radiance." The
formula enabling one to be a success in any field is to
shut oneself up in a closet and say to God: "'I have
fulfilled all the conditions required of me for receiving
power! I am ready to have it! I want it! [sic]'" (141),
and miraculously one gets it, and cannot fail in any
profession. Merrick, who had thought of the Bible as "a
jumble of soporific platitudes, floating about in a solution
of Jewish superstitions" used as a "numbing narcotic to dull
the . . . sense of wanting what they couldn't have," now
sees it as a useful compendium with a "scientific thesis"
(184-85). Now Merrick reads the Bible as science not
ethics, and points out that we must show "how religion is
a science" (296). Again this spiritual power is guaranteed
to make one a success in any field.

The current version of this train of religious thought
is found in the writings of another Protestant minister,
Norman Vincent Peale, author of The Power of Positive
Thinking in 1952. As with his predecessors there is no
room for evil or tragedy in his philosophy; one controls
one's own destiny. According to his introduction the
purpose of the book is: "to suggest techniques and to give
examples which demonstrate that you do not need to be
defeated by anything. . . . This book teaches you how to
'will' not to be [defeated]." Like Douglas he sees religion
as an "exact science": ". . . religious faith is not
something piously stuffy but is a scientific procedure for
successful living" (60, see also 220). He too offers
specific formulae such as repeating ten times a day: "I can
do all things through Christ which strengtheneth me," and
he gives ten rules for success all involving suppression of
negative thoughts and concentration on the positive (16).
Four of these center on the power God gives the individual.
At one time, he says, he "acquiesced in the silly idea that
there is no relationship between faith and prosperity . . ."
(212), but most of the examples he uses of those who have
made a success by positive thinking have made it in
business. The endless tales of success in this world and
its untrammelled optimism make the book a compendium of the
American Dream. Religion is designed not to sweeten one's
character but to enhance one's personality and popularity
so thay one can get ahead. God is a means to an end, an
earthly, a material end. One becomes a success not by using
the old virtues of thrift, hard work, persistence to produce
something, but by becoming a more attractive personality.
Instead of self-denial, devotion to one's fellow human
beings and to God, one is to be absorbed in self-development;
one is to exalt oneself by positive thinking. One praises
oneself rather than God, and guilt and therefore redemption
are left by the wayside.

Peale calls on Emerson and Thoreau as his predecessors
and inspiration. But it is a bastard version of Transcendentalism, and a contradiction in terms since the aim of
Peale's transcendence is mainly a material one. Emerson's
Transcendentalism remains transcendent; in uniting with the
Oversoul one achieves spiritual fulfillment and the
independence to stand up for moral principles. To Emerson
a successful man is a non-conformist; to Peale a successful
man is one who gets along with his colleagues. (One of
Peale's chapters is entitled "How to Get People to Like
You.") Both Emerson and Peale would have the individual
unite with the infinite power of God, and both are incurable
optimists, but there the resemblance ends. Their aims are
polar opposites.

Economics and religion have always had a close and
curious relationship in the history of the United States.
The Puritans regarded success in this world as a presumptive
sign of salvation. Making money or winning an election
would not achieve salvation but might indicate that one was
already predestined by God to that blessed state. Success
in this world, then, was likely to be accompanied not only
with the esteem given the man successful in his profession,
but the approbation awarded to a member of a divinely
appointed elite. Virtues advocated by Protestantism (the
hymn "Work for the Night Is Coming" comes to mind) were
virtues that might well help one to success in this land of
opportunity. But the church taught that such virtues are
to be practiced to show forth the glory of God rather than
to achieve earthly glory for oneself. Now religion is to
be used to accomplish worldly goals. God becomes a conduit
to worldly success, and it seems entirely appropriate that
apart from his ministry, Norman Vincent Peale is chairman of
the Horatio Alger Association (1982).

That Christian ministers could advocate tapping divine
power for the self-cultivation that produces worldly

accomplishments and goods is astonishing when one considers
the circumstances and teachings of the man they considered
their divine preceptor. His life was lived among the poor;
his particular concern was for the unfortunate and lowly.
He cautioned against the accumulation of earthly goods:
"'Do not lay up for yourselves treasures on earth, but lay
up for yourself treasures in heaven'" (Matthew 6:19), and
"'You cannot serve God and Mammon'" (Matthew 6:24). If it
is the meek who are to inherit the earth, one wonders about
the future of the Positive Thinker.

Apart from the Positive Thinkers there are other best
sellers that equate religion with business. As early as
1887 in Acres of Diamonds Russell Conwell, like Peale a
Protestant clergyman, observes: ". . . to get money honestly
is to preach the gospel." And, as we have seen, the advertising man Bruce Barton transforms Christ into a business
man very like himself. This reincarnation is countered by
Aldous Huxley's satirical deification of a business man--
Henry Ford--in Brave New World. In his nightmare Utopia,
six centuries hence, time is measured not by A.D. but by
A.F.; one swears "by Ford" rather than "by God"; the sign
of the cross becomes the sign of T (for Tin Lizzie). Huxley
burlesques the horrors of his projected technocracy and its
religion. But Huxley's satire of the worship of business
becomes Ayn Rand's theology. In Rand's novel Atlas Shrugged
in 1957 Dagny Taggart enjoys walking through the concourse
of the Taggart terminal; it looks to her like a temple, and
to look at the statue of her ancestor who founded the
railroad "was the only form of prayer she knew" (59).
D'Anconia, an admired business executive, claims to possess
"'the greatest virtue of all--that I was a man who made
money'" (96). One character, frowned on by the heroes and
heroines of the book, urges them to be humble, do good to
others, reject materialism and cultivate unselfishness
(264). To equate morality with living for others is

heretical to John Galt (1055) and other admired characters:
"'. . . achievement of your happiness is the only moral
[sic] purpose of your life'" (1059). The last sentence of
the book describes Galt in a dramatic moment: "He raised
his hand and over the desolate earth he traced in space the
sign of the dollar." To Rand the "Almighty Dollar" is the
Almighty.

Most of the issues that faced the church in this period
hardly enter best sellers at all. As we have seen, the
effort to reconcile science and religion in a post-Darwinian
period appears seriously only in Robert Elsmere and H. G.
Wells. The Higher Criticism appears only in the latter.
The social mission of the church is supported in only a few
books throughout the period, although a major criticism of
the clergy is their failure to do more for the poor.

If one hears the testimony of best sellers one must
conclude that religion in the United States is distinctive
in several ways. Until the 1940s Catholics and Jews when
they appear at all are shown in a most unfavorable light,
subversive not only of Protestantism but of Americanism.
Not until the middle of the twentieth century as Catholics
moved up into the middle class in great numbers was the WASP
Establishment challenged in popular books, but the relation
of religion to ethnicity continued some of the old anti-
Catholic stereotypes in spite of the election of John
Kennedy. Books favorable to Jews also began to appear in
the 1940s and Jewish writers now became popular. But since
Jews were identified rather as a race than a religious or
ethnic group they still seemed far from the kind of acceptance that allowed a Catholic to become president in 1960.
Nevertheless the shift in popularity of Catholic and Jewish
writers was a dramatic one; they could be seen now by a wide
public not as monsters, slobs, subversives but as ordinary
people with a viable theology.

The religion of the WASP that dominate best sellers for most of the century had some rather strange features which one might designate as materializing the spirit. In the 1930s Tocqueville observed a situation that interested other foreign visitors:

> . . . the American preachers are constantly referring to the earth, and it is only with great difficulty that they can divert their attention from it. . . . It is often difficult to ascertain from their discourses whether the principal object of religion is to procure eternal felicity in the other world or prosperity in this.

This kind of ambivalence is evident in the popular writings of the Protestant clergy. They not only visualize God in the image of man, but God's dwelling place--heaven--in the image of the United States, particularly New England.

In the Protestant books secularization increases in various ways. In the post-Civil War period God was present in all novels, even those not primarily concerned with religion; a century later there is very little mention of religion. And in the books with religious themes the concept of God changes in significant ways. The divinity of the nineteenth century books is omniscient, omnipotent, august, a Creator whose existence is accepted quite apart from human beings. Man's duty is to serve God. By mid-twentieth century, however, God seems to exist mainly to serve man: to assure him peace of mind, a stable society and prosperity. God is not only portrayed in the image of man, but he is almost wholly secularized. In the previous century one called on God to give one the strength to conquer pride, selfishness, laziness, sinfulness. According to the Protestant Ethic such virtues would be rewarded in this world and the next. But the God of mid-twentieth century books is called on not to strengthen one in the virtues espoused by Christ and Christianity, but to help enlarge one's ego, to develop the pride and self-centeredness of Positive Thinking, to become a pleasing personality. The old virtues had served as economy geared primarily to production; the new ones seemed functional to an economy geared to distribution. To be a good salesman one must be liked rather than admired. The religion of the Positive Thinkers demeans God by limiting his power to helping man to success rather than to virtue. Perhaps the mid-twentieth century ego was so enfeebled by the depersonalized world it inhabited that divine succor of the ego rather than the character was essential. In any case redemption in these books is identical with worldly success. In matters of religion these best sellers seem more responsive to what was happening to the economy than to the major religious and spiritual issues of the day. God is created as a business man, business is deified, and God's importance lies primarily in the aid he offers human beings to make them better salespersons.

Chapter 8:   SCHOLARSHIP AND THE ARTS

SCHOLARSHIP

Intellectuals who delight in the play of ideas are less than prominent in best-selling novels. Serious and interesting discussions occupy some of the dialogue in both of Maugham's novels, and the life of the intellect is obviously a strenuous and exciting one for Captain Nemo with his extensive library and art collection.[1] But the American West, business and crime--the settings of most of the fictional heroes--produced intelligence but no intellectuals, and indeed, many, like the Virginian in the book of that name specifically disavowed intellectualism. Intellectual prowess rarely appears among these fictional characters, and when it does, is hardly a matter of celebration: one of the most intellectual of all, described as a "bookworm" and given to long discussions of literature and philosophy is a person admirable in no other way and not meant to be so--Jack London's Wolf Larsen, the Sea Wolf of 1904. The writers of these books may themselves enjoy working their own minds but they assume their readers as readers won't.

There is, however, one genre of best sellers in which the plot revolves around use of the mind--the classical detective story. The archetype of the detective who has extraordinary reasoning powers applied to solving difficult and sometimes devilish puzzles is of course Sherlock Holmes who appeared in American bookstores in the 1890s. While both Holmes and his readers enjoy his marvelous feats of deductive reasoning, Holmes himself deliberately limits both the methods and the areas in which he permits his mind to work. As explained in A Study in Scarlet in 1890, Holmes

believed the mind has limited space, so he deliberately
avoided increasing his knowledge of subjects he believed
irrelevant to his work to ensure room enough for material
he considered necessary. He admits to knowing nothing of
contemporary literature, philosophy or politics. He is
unfamiliar with Copernican theory, nor can be identify
Carlyle (36). To preserve his genius at deductive
reasoning then, he must restrict his acquisition of
knowledge to quite narrow limits.

While the clear head of the classical detective is
admired, the scholar rarely achieves a major role in these
novels. One wonders if most of the authors would agree
with H. Rider Haggard in She in 1887 pointing to a child
who was bright but no scholar: "He had not the dullness
necessary to that result" (18), and dullness would hardly
sell books. But not all best-selling authors agree with
Billy Graham that the Bible "contains all the knowledge man
needs" (26). Sometimes the accoutrements of scholarship--
a large library, a university degree--are accorded major
characters, as the narrator of Mutiny on the Bounty or the
title character in Anthony Adverse, but the reader's
interest centers on exploits quite unrelated to such
possessions. Professional scholars appear sympathetically
in three nineteenth century novels, all, as it happens, by
women. Two of these, describing female scholars would be
unlikely to add to the prestige of either women or scholars
In 1866 St. Elmo's Edna is a professional intellectual, but
a more tiresome or pedantic one would be hard to imagine,
although she is much admired by her creator, Augusta Evans.
Evadne in The Heavenly Twins in 1893 is a serious scholar
trying to discover things for herself. But she becomes
locked in an emotional bind, and finally burns her books.
In the end she is an intellectual cripple. Another late
nineteenth century novel, Robert Elsmere by Mrs. Humphrey
Ward in 1888, introduces us to a scholar as scholar. The

title character, a clergyman at odds with himself over philosophical and theological questions, is absorbed for much of his life in serious study. As one concerned with the social mission of the church he worries now and then about "'that absorbing and overgrown life of the intellect which blights the heart and chills the senses'" (260). But he also states unequivocally: "'The decisive events of the world take place in the intellect'" [sic]. Probably the most sympathetic and sensitive view appears in four chapters of Beside the Bonnie Brier Bush by Ian MacLaren in 1894. These chapters are devoted to the life and death of a gentle young man from a humble family in Scotland; he becomes a scholar at great and finally mortal cost. Most of the scholarship that appears in the novels has to do with natural science as in Wilkie Collins The Moonstone (1868), Jules Verne Twenty Thousand Leagues Under the Sea (1870), Robert Louis Stevenson Dr. Jekyll and Mr. Hyde (1886), Ellery Queen The Dutch Shoe Mystery (1931) with a scientist as murderer, Thomas Costain, The Black Rose (1945).

The twentieth century also accepted as best sellers a number of non-fiction accounts of scholarly investigations. Will Durant and H. G. Wells offered popular examinations and evaluations of history. But other best sellers involving serious research are all in the realm of science: in 1926 Paul de Kruif's The Microbe Hunters, in 1950 the adventurous Kon-Tiki by Thor Heyerdahl, in 1941 the poetic The Sea Around Us by Rachel Carson. But psychology was the favorite field (and still is). Along with the do-it-yourself psychology manuals offering advice based primarily on the author's intuition, came a number of books beginning in the 1940s based on serious research in the field: Benjamin Spock (1946) and Ilg and Ames (1955) on child-rearing; Chesser (1947) and Geddes and Currie (1954) on love and sex; Vance Packard on public opinion and public behavior (1957, 1959). In most of these scholarship served the reader in a practical way, and best sellerdom was assured.

Throughout the period the reader was now and then warned by the authors of best sellers of the unpopularity of scholars among the bigoted or ignorant. Betty MacDonald describes attitudes of the author's neighbors in a rural community in the North West where reading was regarded as "a sign of laziness, boastfulness and general degradation." Two books reveal the particular hazards of being an intellectual in the United States in the McCarthy period. Auntie Mame in the 1955 book of that title contrasts intellectuals with business men, and concludes that while the former are humane the latter are bigoted, reactionary, hate Jews, blacks and Franklin Delano Roosevelt, and make the life of the scholar a dangerous one. And in that book this is an indictment. Harry Golden in 1958 defends intellectuals under attack in that atmosphere and decries book-burning as "the crime of crimes" (292, see also 178-80).

But many authors through sentiments expressed by sympathetic characters in their novels aver or imply that scholarship is not good for scholars, and may indeed be dangerous to life and limb. In Ragged Dick in 1867 Horatio Alger comments on a death: "Perhaps he had devoted too much time to study, for he was not naturally robust" (224). In 1900 Holden who admires poets and scholars at times assumes that the pursuit of the book may limit people in other pursuits: he gives the example of a man unable to aim his gun properly in a hunt: "'Killin' an' book learnin' don't often go together'" (175-76). In She in 1887 Cambridge students are described as "fossils" with the warning that one petrifies if one follows such a path too long (59). In Of Human Bondage an Englishman visiting Harvard observes that it is full of "bloodless men without Passion" (128). And in Black Rock in 1898 an American visiting British

scholars comments on the triviality of their lives: they
"'potter away their lives among theories living and dead
and end up by producing a book!'" (237). In Tarzan of the
Apes a professor appears only as stereotype; he is
"impractical" and "absent-minded" (175). Even the hard-
headed Madame Wu in Pearl Buck's 1946 novel Pavilion of
Women observes her father-in-law to be gentle and shy "as
too many books make a man" (40). Two books ascribe to
scholarship a detelerious effect on sexual activity: Amber
of the 1944 novel Forever Amber acquires a third husband
who is impotent; she implies that he got that way because
of his intellectuality. This would seem to illustrate the
caveat of Eugene Chesser in Love Without Fear that writers
and artists who are absorbed in their work are often too
exhausted for sexual intercourse, and may become impotent
(125). Finally J. Edgar Hoover in 1958 expresses great
fear of learning. He gives a number of examples of college
students converted to Communism by reading the Communist
Manifesto in college assignments (106, 108, 112, 113, 118).
"In particular the Communists have made an appeal to the
so-called intellectuals. The seduction of many intellectuals over the years by the Party stands as a disgrace.
Thinking men and women, trained to analyze critically, all
too often have been duped" (112). He shares Billy Graham's
evaluation of the Bible as the most effective counterweight
to such sinister influences, and suggests a program of daily
Bible reading. To portray scholarship as injurious to one's
physical, emotional and political health might even please
readers of popular books. Here they found a ready rationalization for avoiding a career ostensibly requiring both
intelligence and self-discipline.

Nineteenth century best sellers are much more certain of
the importance of general education to the individual and
the society than those of the twentieth century, perhaps
because they were being read by people whose world had only

recently established public schools. That the United States had established public schools was usually a matter of great pride to the nineteenth century American--a national contribution to world progress. Augusta Evans in 1866 sees education as a bulwark against "'. . . ignorance, superstition and intolerance . . . the red-handed Huns that ravage society, immolating the pioneer of progress upon the shrine of prejudice'" (93). In 1876 Haines and Yaggy see education as a means to greater prosperity for both the individual and his society; they observe that the educated mechanic is more profitable for his employer than the uneducated man (142). MacLaren in 1894 suggested a reason for having public schools that was most likely to appeal to Americans: public education "melts class" (475). H. G. Wells had vast respect for education. He blames the decline of the Roman Empire on the lack of general schooling which gave government to the rich (467). He also praises the Catholic Church for inadvertently opening the prospect of modern education in Europe by its system of schools designed at the time by the Church for "the subjugation of minds" (707).

Two twentieth century books saw "book-learning" as a useful aid in ordinary life, helping one to cope with personal problems. In his 1935 book on how to be a successful farmer, M. G. Kains addresses a Depression-ridden generation desperately seeking ways of supporting themselves He notes with pleasure "'Book farming' formerly a term of contempt" is now accepted although it doesn't replace experience and observation (12). A character in Kenneth Roberts' Lydia Bailey in 1947 illustrates Kains' point of learning how to become a successful farmer through study, to the astonishment of the community.

But many twentieth century best sellers challenge the value of education. Few would go so far as Lindsay in his 1932 novel The Cautious Amorist: "There's no doubt that

education destroys whatever intelligence the people have"
(75), but many approach it. Kipling in one of his 1890
ballads called "Arithmetic on the Frontier" points out that
£2,000 of education is no help on the battlefield (75-77).
And the young soldiers of All Quiet on the Western Front
in 1929 bitterly blame their presence on the battlefield
in a devastating and useless war on "all that rubbish they
learned in school" (9, see also 18, 84-85). Gene Stratton
Porter's girl of the Limberlost, Elnora, collects moths to
pay for her education which is to be a "means of escape"
from drudgery. When she loses them by accident, she is
persuaded by a Harvard graduate not to bother with further
formal education. She has gained more from the "School of
Experience" (302) than she ever could from school; as a
graduate of the "School of Hard Knocks" (355) she is
advised to concentrate on practical experience. She is
even cautioned to avoid books in her field. Dale Carnegie
in 1936 assures his readers that ". . . personality and the
ability to talk" are infinitely more important than education (3). And he gives many examples of self-made business
leaders who had little schooling. In his later best seller
of 1948 How to Stop Worrying and Start Living he defines
his own position as a practical man by stating in the
introduction: "So this book didn't come out of an ivory
tower." Napoleon Hill in his success manual Think and Grow
Rich backs up Carnegie by adding more examples of the
successful-uneducated to those adduced by the latter.
Norman Vincent Peale points out that the student who gets
A's in school may get C's in life.[3] Finally Ayn Rand is as
firm on this as on many subjects having to do with success.
One of her favorite characters in Atlas Shrugged in 1957 is
a successful business man who scorns books for experience
(95), and one of her least favorite characters, an intellectual, comes from a college-bred family despising the
practical education involved in a business career (537).

Thus the successful business man, a paradigm for the
successful man, achieves his goals with very little aid
from formal education.

At the other end of the economic scale Gullah blacks in
the South had a particular distrust of education according
to Julia Peterkin in her 1928 novel Scarlet Sister Mary.
To them book learning "takes peoples' minds off more
important things." When Keepsie wants to go to school,
Scarlet Sister Mary expresses her fears of what "'book
reading might do to him.'" She associates schooling with
whites, and whites have not only established schools, but
have also invented many dangerous things such as the machine
that accidentally cut off Keepsie's leg (196-97). As a
white institution then, the school is suspect.

From the 1940s on, as more and more books are concerned
with the industrial city, its slums and its children,
disillusion with American teachers, children and the schools
where they meet becomes general. Although parents, especially mothers (as in Louis Beretti and Studs Lonigan) still
believe in the school, the urban school in the pages of
these books is no longer a tool to help one climb the social
ladder or adjust to middle-class culture. To the children
in Louis Beretti in 1929: "School was a hostile institution
always." Cops and teachers are in the same category; they
are the enemy and the urban child is advised to fool them
if he can (7, 22). Studs Lonigan, like Beretti, regards
school as a "jail house" (3). Slum children, imprisoned in
school for part of the day, acquire their education in the
streets in fighting, robbing and other ordinary street
activities. Furthermore, the education of the streets
spills over into the school so that the school experience
itself is a brutalizing one. The school system is blamed
for overcrowding and for promoting the students whether they
meet the standards of the school or not, and for inadequate
teachers.[4] Even the amiable Private Hargrove in 1942

revives the old canard: "Who can does; who can't teaches"
(1). The 1943 A Tree Grows in Brooklyn offers an explanation for ineffective teaching in the public schools: since
female teachers were not allowed to marry, most "were women
made neurotic by starved love instincts" (137). But even
a dedicated teacher is lost in the system; all he/she
learned of pedagogy is irrelevant in the modern public
school. In their own education teachers are taught how to
deal with an unruly child, but not with a whole classroom
of them.[5] The picture emerging from the best sellers of
the 1940s and 1950s is of an urban school system taken over
by a decadent society, one unable to enforce its own laws.
Two books even point out that students must now buy protection in the school as well as in the streets.[6]

Bel Kaufman in Up the Down Staircase in 1964 singles out
an infinitely complex and tyrannical bureaucracy running
the schools by multiplying rules that have nothing to do
with education. A few teachers are inspired but most have
given up. The problem, according to one teacher who has
not given up "'is not unreachable kids, but unteachable
teachers'" (117, 58). When treated as individuals with a
dignity missing from their lives in and out of school, most
students respond, but are shocked to discover a teacher who
actually cares about them.

That scholars are viewed in popular books as irrelevant
to a healthy society is hardly surprising. Education is
almost always evaluated in practical terms, and judged
valuable to the individual and society in the degree to
which it contributes to material success. The public
school, until the 1940s, fits this image, but the scholar
does not. After 1940 many of the best sellers face their
readers with the deterioration of the schools along with
the surrounding city. Instead of acting as a bulwark to an
orderly society, the school has been engulfed by the social
disintegration of the community, and rescue can come only

from a general social reform. In their evaluation of the
urban school, best sellers may have been offering their
readers an unaccustomed taste of a depressing reality.

THE ARTS: THE WRITTEN WORD

To explore these best selling books as literature is
beyond the design of this author. As noted earlier the
inclusion of a book on the list of best sellers had nothing
to do with the quality of the writing. This is not to say
that well-written books are prevented by that fact from
becoming best sellers, but their popularity comes from other
qualities attractive to popular taste. Some of the best and
worst written books climbed on the lists for much the same
reasons. With vast differences in the art of writing,
Nabakov on the one hand and E. M. Hull on the other offered
erotica; Wilkie Collins on the one hand and Sax Rohmer on
the other offered mystery; both Ian MacLaren and Chic Sale
offered nostalgia (Sale spiced his with scatology). When
the reader of best sellers met art in these books, it was
pure serendipity.

Whatever their own literary gifts, many of these writers
submit their own literary criticisms to their readers in
the form of opinions of favored characters on what is "good"
literature. The writers most frequently and approvingly
mentioned are English and American. While not all would go
as far as Harry Golden who in 1958 called Shakespeare "the
greatest brain ever encased in a human skull" (172), he and
Dickens are more often mentioned with approval that any
others although Scott runs a close third in the first fifty
years of these best sellers. Byron, Shelley and Keats are
also conspicuous. Contemporary writers do not appear at all
until 1915 when Maugham in Of Human Bondage includes extensive discussions of Oscar Wilde, Walter Pater, Mallarmé and
Ibsen (117-18, 124). Maugham reports his desertion of the
Romantics and Victorians in favor of Realism and Symbolism.

In a few books Zola and Flaubert are praised for their dramatic revelations of human suffering.[7] But Thelma, in the 1887 novel of the same name, talks of Victor Hugo as the Shakespeare of France and agrees with the opinion of a friend that the popularity of Zola is an indication of a drastic decline in public taste: "'. . . what would it avail to write as grandly as Shakespeare or Scott, when society clamors for Zola and others of his school'" (124, 288). The great Russian novels of the nineteenth century are hardly mentioned at all until the end of the period (War and Peace and Anna Karenina were best sellers here, but not in the terms used in this study, since it took them fifty years to achieve that status). It is interesting that apart from these rare examples best sellers completely disregard serious contemporary writers. The century of this study (1865-1965) was one of original innovative writing, of new directions as different as Realism, Naturalism, Symbolism. Perhaps some of the authors of best sellers were unconscious of movements disturbing the literary world; others, aware of the serious writing going on in their society, evidently did not want to startle readers with references to new literary and philosophical movements. One might rock the boat with sexual play, but avant garde art might sink the ship and drown potential buyers of a book the author hoped would be popular. Serious contemporary writing is often controversial, and, on the whole, conservatism rules the literary tastes of these books.

Of American writers, Emerson is most popular. Poe, judged one must assume, as many nineteenth century American critics judged writers--by the virtues and vices ascribed to the author rather than his/her written work--is mentioned only in novels written by Europeans. Whitman appears only in the diatribes of an English novelist, Marie Corelli (who also castigated Zola). The heroine of Thelma in 1887 is surprised that anyone enjoys "the commonplace sentence

writing of Walt Whitman" (302). A writer she admires is
appalled that some English circles regard Whitman as
". . . the new Socrates. . . . That any
reasonable Englishman with such names as Shakespeare, Byron, Keats and Shelley to keep the
glory of their country warm, should for one
moment consider Walt Whitman a poet! [sic] Ye
Gods!"
When asked if Walt Whitman is an American, the writer
responds: "'An American whom the sensible portion of America
rejects. . . . His chief recommendation is that he writes
blatantly concerning commonplaces--regardless of musical
rhythm'" (445). Hawthorne, Melville, Thoreau, Henry James,
T. S. Eliot and other major writers are conspicuous by their
absence both on the best seller list and in best sellers.

In nineteenth century best sellers there is much discussion of the social responsibility of the writer. Inevitably
this leads these writers of popular novels to consider in
particular the social role of popular fiction, and here they
could write from their own experience. What does make a
book sell? What should make a book sell? What is the
author's responsibility to his/her public?

Professional writers as characters in two novels of the
1860s come to grips with these issues in their own careers.
Edna, the pedantic heroine of St. Elmo believes the writer
of popular fiction has a holy mission: ". . . all books
should be to a certain extent didactic, wandering like
evangels among the people, and making some man, woman or
child happier, or wiser, or better--more patient or more
hopeful--by their utterances" (169). Her editor scoffs at
this view, and warns her that a novel written with such high
moral purpose will not sell. He suggests that she misappre-
hends "'the spirit of the age; people read novels merely to
be amused not educated.'" Since novels reflect rather than
mould a culture they must suit popular taste to be accepted

(370). But Edna refuses his advice and is vindicated when her book comes out; although the critics pan it the public loves it (444-45). In the novel Edna, the fictional author, and her public meet on a plane of high moral suasion. But applied to.the actual novel one could legitimately doubt that the story of Edna derived its popularity from its high moral tone; while it did describe the reform of a rake, the rake before his reform provided splendid opportunities for hints and descriptions of sensational immorality.

On the other hand Jo in Little Women enjoys reading sensational novels such as the major best seller of 1850, The Wide, Wide World by Susan Warner. And while reading the stories of "Mrs. S.L.A.N.G. Northbury" (a thin disguise for the actual Mrs. E.D.E.N. Southworth) Jo decides she could do as well and starts writing and selling stories of this sort. Alcott, the author of Little Women, comments: ". . . for in those dark ages, even all-perfect Americans read rubbish" (298). Jo's editor, like Edna's encourages her in her pursuit of a wide audience: "'People want to be amused, not preached at you know. Morals don't sell nowadays'" (300). (The author again interjects here to point out that this was not quite a correct statement.) So Jo continues to follow the path of Mrs. Northbury with exciting stories of the exotic: bandits, gypsies, nuns, all in foreign settings. Then at a literary evening she is disillusioned to discover that serious poets and writers at the party do not talk literature, but behave like ordinary people. A man she admires (and later marries), Professor Bhaer, derides a sensational periodical pointing out that it is bad for young people. Jo observes that respectable people read it, and Bhaer counters: there is a demand for whiskey but respectable people don't sell it. She finally comes around to his point of view and gives up writing trash (303-307). In both St. Elmo and Little Women literature is perceived as being of two kinds: morally bad and morally good. Naturally both heroines support the latter, while their editors and publishers prefer novels involving questionable morals because they sell better. In neither case are novels to be judged on their literary quality.

In an essay entitled "On Reading" (162-70) Haines and Yaggy in 1876 carry out this theme stressing the dangers involved in reading books "which present false pictures of human life." The indiscriminate reading of novels "can have horrendous effects on the incautious reader." A man will end up "nerveless, inane and a nuisance." To save his manhood parents and friends should "snatch from his hand the book that relaxes and effeminates him. . . ." For a woman the results may not be worse, but they are described in harrowing detail. She:

> will be unfitted for the duties of wife, mother, sister, daughter. There she is, hair disheveled, countenance vacant, cheeks pale, hands trembling, bursting into tears at midnight over the fate of some unfortunate lover; in the daytime, when she ought to be busy, staring by the half-hour at nothing; biting her fingernails to the quick.

Furthermore, the "bad" book is more influential than the "good." The essayist asks the reader who has read, he assumes, both good and bad books, "Which stuck to you? The Bad! . . . You cannot afford to read a bad book, however good you are." (This is reminiscent of the one drop of "inferior" blood in racist literature that always conquers all of the other "superior" drops.)

> Alas, if through curiosity, as many do, you pry into an evil book, your curiosity is as dangerous as that of the man who should take a torch into a gunpowder mill merely to see whether it would really blow up or not.

Immoral books are particularly injurious to the female whose virtue requires constant protection. The effects of such

literature as Madame Bovary are well known. Mr. Barnes in
Gunter's 1887 novel is disturbed to discover the woman he
admires, "his divinity" reading a novel by Ouida, although
as a male he considers it permissible reading for himself
(55). The feminist novel The Heavenly Twins, however,
refers several times to Ouida with approbation, probably
because she often rejects the feminine stereotype that
riddles these popular books.

Charles Sheldon's In His Steps carries his Christian
crusade into literary criticism. One of his characters is
a writer of popular books with "no purpose except to amuse."
His books are not immoral, but, on the other hand, are not
positively Christian. He writes for money and fame "what
nearly every writer wrote for" (173). And he doesn't join
the crusade that affects so many other professionals in the
town--to do only what Christ would do. As a result Jaspar
Chase is a social success, but loses the woman he loves,
and is finally covered with remorse at the failure of his
character.

In The Wild Palms in 1939 William Faulkner offers an
amusing anecdote of the influence of popular literature.
He introduces a gullible but angry convict whose rage is
directed not at the police or lawyers but at the writers of
dime novels "who he believed had led him into his present
predicament." He had saved and studied them for several
years and used them as guides believing in their "stamp of
verisimilitude and authenticity" (23). But their information was wrong, and he was misguided to jail.

Twentieth century popular writers are no longer critical
of ephemeral literature on moral grounds. Sometimes
characters in their novels read best selling books happily.
In 1931 Fannie Hurst describes the reading list of a
successful business woman, and it is much like this one:
She, Ben-Hur, Ramona, Robert Elsmere, and Under Two Flags
(Ouida).[8] William Brinkley in his 1956 tales of the naval

war in the Pacific during World War II, <u>Don't Go Near the</u>
<u>Water</u>, acknowledges the overweening influence of popular
literature on the Public Relations branch of the U.S. Navy.
A P.R. man for the U.S. Navy invites Edgar Rice Burroughs
rather than a naval expert to witness naval operations of
his unit because in his opinion the American people will put
more faith in Tarzan's word than in any official dispatch
(10).

But sensational best sellers are sometimes disparaged in
recent best sellers for literary rather than the moral
qualities deplored by nineteenth century writers. Sometimes
the books are viewed as the province of children seeking a
thrill. Young Francie in <u>A Tree Grows in Brooklyn</u> in 1943
is reading right through the books in her Brooklyn branch
library starting with the authors whose names begin with
"A". She can't wait to get to the "C's" and "Corelli" (40).
Part of Francie's delight stems from escape into an exciting
and glamorous world. When she writes stories about her own
life for school assignments, the teacher gives her a C
instead of an A on the grounds that poverty, starvation and
drunkenness are not fit subjects to write about; drunks
belong in jails not stories (289). Betty MacDonald, the
author of the autobiographical, <u>The Egg and I</u> in 1945 is
distressed at the contents of the local bookstall in a
neighborhood acknowledged to be unliterary: <u>The Sheik</u>,
Elinor Glyn, Zane Grey, Kathleen Norris, F. Marion Crawford.
Edna Ferber in <u>Giant</u> in 1952 describes the reactions of a
well-read Eastern woman to the literary tastes of Texas.
Used to reading Proust, Gide, Carlyle she is saddened to
find the bookshelves of her husband's ranch stocked only
with <u>Girl of the Limberlost</u> and <u>The Sheik</u> along with <u>The</u>
<u>Cattleman's Gazette</u> (66). In <u>Please Don't Eat the Daisies</u>
in 1957 Jean Kerr satirizes both Mickey Spillane (117 ff.)
and Francoise Sagan (131 ff.). And in <u>Return to Peyton</u>
<u>Place</u> in 1959 by Grace Metalious, Allison makes a career of

writing books so sensational that her publisher asks her to
cut out some of the gore. Her book is said to outdo even
Tobacco Road in sex (85) although she denies it is pornography (102). While pleased with the success of her novel
which is sold with the same techniques used to sell soap,
she considers publishing a dirty business (100). By
contrast to her success in the marketplace, the man she
loves writes four novels liked by critics, but not by the
public.

While both male and female authors must have been equally
aware of the poor literary quality of such novels, the
authors who turn a critical eye on sensational romantic
novels--Smith, MacDonald, Ferber, Kerr, Metalious--are all
women. Since so much of this literature was addressed to
women and read by women perhaps female authors were more
aware of their deficiencies: the image of women in the
sentimental, romantic novel was of the feminized stereotype--
the polar opposite of themselves and the women they projected into their books.

Book publishing as a function of business rather than
literature appears in Hill's Think and Grow Rich in 1937.
The same advertising techniques used to sell any consumer
product are highly lauded when applied to the book business.
Hill describes what is to him a fine example of the use of
imagination by a publisher of low cost books when faced by
a book that isn't selling. The publisher simply ripped off
the cover, and changed the title without changing the book
in any way (99).

The two Utopias in reverse, Aldous Huxley's Brave New
World in 1932 and George Orwell's 1984 in 1949 harness both
language and literature to political service. By performing
the function of an opiate they contribute to the nightmare
social order in both novels. Art flees the written word; as
in Huxley:

"You've got to choose between happiness and what
people used to call high art. We've sacrificed the
high art. We have the feelies and the scent organ
instead." (150)
Sensation has replaced emotion.

In literature then a clear distinction is drawn, albeit
on different grounds in the nineteenth and twentieth centuries, between high art and popular art in these popular
books. Mark Twain alone seemed to inhabit both worlds.
Perhaps this is a sharper distinction than would be drawn
in other countries. The American literary artists' sense
of alienation from his culture has been remarked many times,
a sense of alienation frequently marked by the physical
alienation of voluntary exile. Perhaps the very breadth
of the reading public in the United States, extended by
public education beyond that of most other countries until
quite recently, ensured such division. While the literate
public expanded, the public for literature as art did not.
Most of these new readers had neither the leisure nor the
education to cope with the demands of high art. Reading
offered escape rather than confrontation. They sought a
Harold Robbins rather than a Henry James, a Dale Carnegie
rather than an Edmund Wilson.

THE VISUAL ARTS

Although there are several novels centered on the lives
of artists, the visual arts are much less prominent than
either music or literature. Casual references to painting,
sculpture and architecture are rare in books other than
those whose central character is a professional artist.

Mark Twain's comments on European painting and sculpture
are peculiarly American, justifying his title Innocents
Abroad. He is aware of this and he confesses that he has
been more impressed by Europeans' railroads and turnpikes
than their art, because his judgment of engineering is based

on knowledge, his judgment of art is not (I-262). He prefers the statuary of the Genoa cemetery with all of its sentimentality to the classical statuary in Italian galleries (I-168). In the Louvre he criticizes the "cringing spirit" of the artists revealed to him in their paintings of great men; he speaks of their "nauseous adulation of princely patrons," and uses Rubens as a prime example (I-131). His art criticism is more relevant to democracy than to art. The American predilection for the new is evident in his preference for new copies of old art: "Maybe the originals were handsome when they were new, but they are not now." And he makes fun of visitors awed by old paintings (I-190).

E. P. Roe in his novel Barriers Burned Away in 1872 portrays sympathetically a young artist to whom "Nature had given . . . a deep, earnest love of the beautiful, and a keen perception of it" (75). The author praises those liberal American citizens who set up a prize to encourage art in the United States. Clearly, however, their endeavors are rather for the social good than for the sake of art. When the young man is presented with the prize the president of the organization offers as a wish for his future: "'May your brush ever continue to be employed in the presentation of such noble elevating thoughts'" (390-91).

Another peculiarly American comment is from Charles W. Gordon (writing in 1898 under the name Ralph Connor), a Canadian minister and missionary in the North West. The narrator, an aspiring artist, becomes an illustrator as a practical solution to the problem of earning a living. At the end of the book he gives up art entirely and Mrs. Mavor, a sympathetic friend, comments: "'I knew you would not long be content with the making of pictures, which the world does not really need, and would join your friends in the dear West, making lives that the world needs so sorely!'" (240). Again the socially useful, and, in this case, art is not

considered admissible to that category, outweighs all other
human functions.

As late as 1958 American rejection of art as art is shown
in the autobiography of Alexander King, Mine Enemy Grows
Older. King, himself an artist, points out that the French
are no more artistic than the Americans, but the climate of
American opinion rejects art whereas the French welcome not
only Picasso, but minor artists as well. As a painter the
author's style was similar to that of George Grosz: "But in
the good old sentimental U.S.A. [sic] my stuff was
definitely freakish" (91).

Hill's Manual that 1905 guide to success in all aspects
of life, offers strict guides to the artist, explaining
exactly what is beautiful and therefore what he/she must
paint. Four essentials make up the essence of this formula:

1. Any object "to present a pleasing appearance to the
   eye, should have a base of sufficient size and
   breadth to support the same. Nature is full of
   examples."

2. ". . . all that is beautiful in nature is made up of
   curved lines" as is the human countenance.

3. Contrast is as vital in art as in nature: ". . . a
   bouquet of flowers is beautiful in proportion to the
   many colors that adorn it, and the strong contrast
   of those colors."

4. In architecture buildings should have "striking pro-
   jections."

Although our paintings cannot be as good as the "real
grandeur of the works of nature," yet the function of the
artist is to imitate nature (26-27, 176, 484-85).

Such guidance may be preferable to that offered by Art
Linkletter in 1957 recounting interviews he had with
children on his television program. When a small boy says
that he hopes to grow up to be an artist and draw bugs,
Linkletter asks if that is the "prettiest thing" he can

think to draw. When another child says he also wants to
be an artist, in order to draw Marilyn Monroe or Jane
Russell, Linkletter responds with approval, "'It's a good
choice'" (19-21). To be an artist, then, is to be a master
of prettiness.

In the visual arts as well as in literature conservatism
dominates in these books; in most instances where art
enters the novels, the reader is not presented with the art
of his generation. In the first fifty years of this century
of best sellers, when Impressionism, Post-Impressionism,
Pointillism, Cubism were agitating the art world, and
leading artists away from copying nature and from teaching
moral lessons, there is no hint in the books read by these
generations of any such movements. Of their contemporaries
Holman Hunt, Burne-Jones, Rosetti and Millais, hardly
painterly radicals, appear in only two novels.[9] New
movements in the arts enter these books about half a century
late. Irving Stone's Lust for Life, a biography of Van Gogh
offers the first discussion of Impressionist and Post-
Impressionist painters, and that book was published in 1934.
In 1961 Henry Miller discusses modern art, and is especially
taken with Matisse (162-63). But contemporary painters of
the mid-twentieth century appear first in 1942 in the novel
The Chinese Room by Vivian Connell. Here Henry Moore,
Picasso, Miro and Barbara Hepworth are discussed. Steinbeck
in Cannery Row in 1945 mentions Dali, Picasso and Grosz.

In two novels the conservatism of the art establishment
is criticized. Kipling's artist, Dick in The Light That
Failed in 1891 defines popular taste in the arts as essentially conservative: "'Give 'em what they know, and when
you've done it once do it again'." When he paints a
soldier, disheveled and oozing blood no one wants it, but
when he cleans it up and makes it less realistically violent
and brutal, he is paid twice as much as he expected (57-58,
136). Ayn Rand's novel The Fountainhead in 1943, the tale

of a gifted and highly individualistic architect named
Roark, centers on the quarrel between an innovator and the
traditionalists of the architecture Establishment. Roark
declares that he wants to be an architect not an archeolo-
gist (17); he uses highly sophisticated engineering
techniques to construct buildings relevant to their function, site and material available. But when he discovers
a housing project he designed is not being built according
to his directions, he bombs the bastard version. Here
conformity to the past is seen as deserving violence.

Three post World War II books refer to the political
judgment of art in the modern world, akin to the moral
judgment of art in the nineteenth century, but in each case
disapproved by the author. Irwin Shaw in his novel of
World War II in 1948 refers to the Nazi ban on abstract art
as "decadent" (87). Auntie Mame, in 1958 notes the characterization of modern art as "atheist art" and "Bolshevik
barbarism" by someone she dislikes; she is very fond of
modern trends of art in all fields (44). And J. Edgar
Hoover who, one suspects, would approve more highly of the
style of "Socialist Realism" than of any modern trends,
accuses the Soviets of using art as a weapon in the class
struggle: in the U.S.S.R. "Art doesn't exist for art's sake"
(168).

Whatever these books have to say about the arts, they
are as one on the subject of the personality and character
of artists: whatever the value of the artist's work, as a
person he doesn't contribute to society, and may even be a
disruptive force. Only Roark in The Fountainhead is disruptive for ideological reasons; artists in all of the other
books throughout the century are disruptive by nature.
Du Maurier's presentation of the life of the artist in
Trilby in 1891 seems to be the one exception; Du Maurier
describes a gentle, humane, whimsical group of artists
living happily in Paris. But in Of Human Bondage Maugham's

Philip, after reading La Vie de Boheme comments on the art
world as described in that book (and he might have been
commenting on Trilby). Philip is at first delighted with
the picture of good-humored starvation, picturesque squalor,
moving bathos and a sordid love shined up with romanticism.
Only later does he realize its unreality, "the utter worthlessness as artists or human beings of that gay procession"
(166-68).

The artist is believed to be eccentric by nature. As
Corelli puts it in A Romance of Two Worlds in 1888, he needs
imagination and an emotional and spiritual nature, but he
doesn't need or have common sense (67). Little Billee in
Trilby is emotional, over-excitable, a cry-baby, but: "It
was all part of his genius, and also a part of his charm"
(188). Lloyd Douglas in The Magnificent Obsession in 1929
describes public acceptance of the eccentric nature of the
artist by saying he has "permission to be eccentric" (128).
And in Lust for Life in 1934 Van Gogh is told by a doctor
after he leaves the mental hospital that he has never been
normal: "'Normal men don't create works of art,'" and "'The
strain of art breaks every artist in time'."[10]

The concentration of the artist on his work to the
exclusion of anything else is illustrated by a character in
Of Human Bondage. He must devote himself to his work even
if his family starves (300). The relationship between
sexuality and art is stressed in recent books. Chesser's
1947 sex manual points out that the artist who throws
himself into his work has no energy left for sex (51, 125).
Richard Mason's novel The World of Suzie Wong in 1957 sees
a more direct but essentially similar relationship: "The
creative impulse had its roots in sexuality" (21). And in
Lust for Life (1934) Van Gogh and Gauguin agree it is best
to have sex without love; one must put one's emotions into
one's painting (313). Conventional morality is irrelevant
to the artist.[11]

In popular books, then, the artist will violate moral and social conventions whether society recognizes his right to do so or not; it is his nature. When artists are mentioned, in no part of the period would the reader be made aware of current movements and controversies in the arts. As in so many other fields the best sellers seem to be about half a century behind what was going on in their society.

MUSIC

Of all the arts, music is by far the most popular in best sellers; it appears more frequently and is discussed more fully than other media. Throughout the period there is general agreement that music has a more powerful effect on human beings than any other art--a statement attributed to Schopenhauer by Durant. This power comes from the heart: in Barriers Burned Away in 1872, E. P. Roe contrasts two singers: one is highly trained but is vastly inferior to the other because the latter works in "the sphere of the true artist who can touch and sway the popular heart . . ." (189). Sherlock Holmes, himself an amateur violinist, maintains that according to Darwin music belonged to man long before speech, and we remember those early days in our souls (67). Therefore music is the most expressive of the arts. In The Prince of Foxes by Samuel Shellabarger in 1947 this is illustrated when a painter describes a woman as too beautiful to be painted; her beauty can only be adequately expressed in music rather than in words or paint.[12]

Of all musical instruments the human voice is most important because God made it, and it is capable of the most subtle as well as the most powerful expressions of the human spirit. According to Haines and Yaggy every song soothes and uplifts (484-86). Those novels centered on singers picture the singer as the high priest of the emotions; he/she frees them and endows them with redeeming power.

The knowledge of music and the discipline and hard work
required of a professional singer are unimportant, indeed
invisible in these books. All the singer needs is a
passionate nature. In F. Marion Crawford's 1883 novel
A Roman Singer Nino's singing teacher considers the exercise
of his passionate nature more important than any other
preparation for the concert stage: "'. . . in order to be a
great artist, Nino must be in love always'" (40). And in
Trilby musical genius is imparted to the title character not
by natural talent or study, but by hypnosis. Always a bit
of magic adheres to singing in these books. The plot of
The Rosary in 1910 (and the title is taken from the title
of a popular song) stems from the emotional power of music.
The heroine thrills her audience by her passionate singing
of this song and wins for herself thereby the love of the
hero. As has been said before, the profession of the singer
is assigned in most of these novels to women when other
professions are not. There are only two professional male
singers, but fourteen women--more than in nursing or
teaching. Singing comes naturally to women because it is
assumed they are given to the spontaneous expression of
emotion unhindered by reason.

With so much emphasis on the human voice one would expect
opera to be prominent, but it is not, perhaps because it
would be hard to visualize operatic singing as the pure
spontaneous expression of the soul. James M. Cain's 1937
novel Serenade introduces a twentieth century male singer
who recovers dramatically from a strained throat to become
an opera star. But opera as art hardly enters this novel.
Its plot is as complex as a nineteenth century Italian opera
with the added ingredient of the meaningless mayhem of a
tough detective story. Two novels--Hemingway's A Farewell
to Arms and· Hervey Allen's Anthony Adverse offer serious
discussions of opera incidental to the stories. Herman Wouk
in The Caine Mutiny in 1951 suggests that an American who

likes opera is a snob; enjoying opera is "a mark of higher
breeding unless you were Italian" (15).
Next to the voice, strings are the favorite instruments
of these books and violin playing is particularly extolled
throughout the period. Like the human voice is too produces
an emotional utterance. The tone of the violin described
by Crawford in A Roman Singer is a copy of the human voice,
albeit an extraordinary human voice: "sweet as love that is
strong as death, sobbing great sobs of a terrible death-sonç
and screaming in the outrageous frenzy of a furious foe's
wailing their cries of misery" (156).
Not only does the musical taste favor certain instruments, but also certain kinds of music, particularly the
sentimental. Haines and Yaggy in 1876 reporting a concert
by Jenny Lind manage to describe with rationality her
singing of Beethoven and Handel to twenty thousand listeners
at Castle Garden. But then, she thinks of home, forgets
Beethoven and Handel and sings Home Sweet Home as tears gush
from the eyes of the audience and "Howard Payne triumphed
over the great masters of song" (49). In a poem entitled
"Real Singing" Edgar Guest in 1916 observes that one can
praise opera and Caruso, but no music brings such joy as the
singing of children. In the Christian novel In His Steps,
Rachel refuses to join a travelling opera company because
Christ would never use a talent to make money (56-57).
Making this choice condemns her to singing sentimental
gospel hymns rather than musically more interesting opera,
lieder or sacred music. She devotes herself to singing
simple hymns for the poor. The author comments:

> Ah! What were the flippant, perfumed critical
> audiences in concern halls compared with this
> dirty, drunken, impure, besotted mass of humanity
> that trembled and wept and grew strangely, sadly
> thoughtful under the touch of the divine ministry
> of this beautiful young woman! (82)

As with all of the artists in American best sellers the
social usefulness of the musician is often questioned. In
Little Women in 1868 Laurie's grandfather says: "'His music
isn't bad, but I hope he will do as well in more important
things'" (47). Even Crawford's A Roman Singer offers a
sympathetic character who rejects a musical career on the
grounds that "'The mind is better than the throat'" (28).
Indeed Nino, the hero of the book, finds it necessary to bow
to public opinion by posing as a professor of literature
instead of a singer, because being a professor has more
social prestige (38). But in the end the sentiment of a
violinist is accepted: "'. . . art is real, true, and
enduring; medicine in sickness and food in famine; wings to
the feet of youth and a staff for the steps of old age'"
(159). The question of the importance of music comes up
again in Robert Elsmere in 1888. Catherine is troubled by
the time and energy her friend Rose lavishes on her violin
playing:

> "How was it lawful for the Christian to spend
> the few short years of the earthly combat in any
> pursuit, however noble and exquisite, which merely
> aimed at the gratification of the senses, and
> implied in the pursuer the emphasizing rather than
> the surrender of self?"

She is answered by Robert Elsmere, the cleric who increasingly devotes himself to social service. Pure beauty has a
function in life. God gave the talent to bring joy to the
drab lives of city workers--superior to the "brutalizing
joys of the workman" (83).

As in literature and painting very little attention is
given to art contemporaneous to the best seller. Mrs.
Humphrey Ward in 1888 allows her characters to be familiar
with Brahms, Wagner, Rubenstein--she calls them "passionate
voices of the noblest moderns" (176). Wagner is also
mentioned in The Heavenly Twins in 1893 (371), and in 1898

Black Rock. In the latter a sympathetic character tells of
"adoring Wagner" (61). Another novelist who is clearly
aware of major movements in contemporaneous music is Patrick
Dennis, creator of Auntie Mame. She loves non-objective art
in general, and is fond of Bartok and Hindemith. These are
the only notices of serious contemporary composers.

Ayn Rand in Atlas Shrugged in 1957 faces the issue head-
on with conclusions as usual, both startling and conservative. Richard Halley writes melody "at a time when no one
wrote melody any longer" (13). But his music although out
of tune with the world of the composer is exactly in tune
with popular culture. Trainmen whistle his music, and
though lambasted by critics who say "'Our age has outgrown
that stuff'" (67), his opera is a success. Then he
disappears from the world of music and reappears as a
business man saying he'd give three dozen modern artists
for one real business man:

> That sacred fire which is said to burn within
> musicians and poets--what do they suppose moves
> an industrialist to defy the whole world for the
> sake of his new metal, as the inventors of the
> airplane, the builders of railroads, the discoverers
> of new germs or new continents have done through
> all the ages? (783)

Apparently in Rand's opinion for true fulfillment the
artists must find art in business.

Modern popular music--ragtime and jazz--are subjects of
discussion in a few novels. Ragtime is viewed with approval
when first mentioned in Robert Service's The Spell of the
Yukon . . . in 1907 (57), and The Rosary in 1910. In the
latter it is played along with Beethoven by the hero (330).
Auntie Mame is a fan of Bessie Smith. But several voices
deplore jazz. Grave Livingston Hill in 1908 ascribes jazz
to a city slicker: "for this man was master of nothing but
having a good time."[13] Lloyd Douglas in 1929 describes a

young man who leaves college for "the profession of bouncing
and writhing and puffing himself purple every night from one
until two in the front row of a dance orchestra" (95-96).
This new music he disparages as "lately imported, duty-free,
from the head waters of the Congo . . ." (154).

Other performance media--cinema, the theater, and
television--are surprisingly rare, and dance never appears
at all. Two of the biographiers are of movie actresses,
Lillian Roth (an autobiography) in 1954 and Jean Harlow in
1964, and Harold Robbins' novel, The Carpetbaggers in 1961,
is, in part, a thinly disguised biography of Harlow. Here
the emphasis is on complex personalities and on the movie
industry as industry engaged in selling its personalities
and by cut-throat competition. The only general comment of
the relationship of cinema to the society is in James Jones'
novel of 1951 From Here to Eternity. Prew ascribes his
belief in fighting for the underdog to films he grew up
with:

> He had learned it, not from The Home, or The
> School, or The Church, but from that fourth and
> other great molder of social conscience, The
> Movies [sic].

In the 1930s they "had not yet degenerated into commercial
imitations of themselves" (275). Almost all of the best-
selling novels have been made into movies at least once, yet
film plays almost no role, not even casual mention in the
novels.

PART III: THE INDIVIDUAL AND SOCIETY

Chapter 9:   POVERTY, WEALTH AND THE AMERICAN DREAM

The most trenchant description of American attitudes to
poverty (and perhaps to sin) is summed up in the pronounce-
ment of a character in Vera Caspary's novel Bedelia in 1945:
"'Most people would rather confess to sin than poverty
. . .'" (19). In the best sellers poverty is decried not
for its deprivations or its lack of physical comforts, but
for the disesteem that inevitably accompanies it in the
United States.

Yet in some nineteenth century books poverty is endowed
with two valuable assets: it builds character, and it offers
the most effective training in techniques necessary to
graduate from poverty to sufficiency or even affluence.
After characterizing poor boys as "lucky" (45), Haines and
Yaggy go on to present such plaudits to poverty as: "Poverty
. . . is oftener a blessing to a young man than prosperity
. . ." (184); "A smooth sea never made a skillful mariner"
(531); "Men are frequently like tea--the real strength and
goodness is not properly drawn out of them till they have
been a short time in hot water" (544); "The ripest fruit
grows on the roughest wall" (594). Such sentiments are not
limited to how-to-be-a-success-in-life manuals, but appear
often in late nineteenth century novels. In Little Women
Mrs. March lectures her family frequently on the usefulness
of poverty to develop character: it keeps us from "ennui and
mischief", and permits the great satisfaction to be gained
from hard work.[1] (It should be noted that the much-
discussed poverty of the March family like that of the
Paget family in Kathleen Norris' 1911 novel Mother is of a
quite genteel sort--each family, poor though they consider
themselves to be, has a servant). That Jesus was poor and
preached especially to the poor sanctifies poverty in all

books offering fictional biographical accounts of the life
of Jesus from Ben-Hur in 1880 through the books by Charles
Sheldon, Lloyd Douglas, Fulton Oursler, Billy Graham and
Jim Bishop. Ralph Waldo Trine in 1897, however, while
assuring his readers they can escape poverty by hard work,
ridicules this notion: "The old and somewhat prevalent idea
of godliness in poverty has absolutely no basis for its
existence and the sooner we get away from it the better"
(177).

Some early twentieth century books indicate that one can
be content though poor; Edgar Guest suggests one can be rich
in smiles though poor in material goods.[2] But the quintes-
sence of this idea is in Mrs. Wiggs of the Cabbage Patch in
1901. Its author observes: "The sum and substance of her
philosophy lay in keeping the dust off her rose-colored
spectacles" (3-4). Mrs. Wiggs constantly counts her
blessings and poverty is one of them. Her almost farcical
optimism appears throughout this book; its first sentence
(spoken by Mrs. Wiggs) sets the tone: "'My, but it's nice
an' cold this mornin'! The thermometer's done fell up to
zero!'." While contentment with poverty is preached in
these fifty years, the conclusion is not that one should be
content to remain in poverty; while one should not rail
against it, one should enjoy the lessons it allows and
spend one's energy escaping it.

Until the Depression of the 1930s descriptions of the
miseries inflicted by poverty are always of the poor outside
the United States written by Europeans (or in one case a
Canadian): Kipling, Barrie, Hope, MacLaren and Maugham. To
be poor in countries other than the United States is clearly
not one's own fault, and American readers could be expected
to read sympathetically and at length about the afflictions
of those who did not have the good fortune to live in the
land of opportunity. Apparently not until well into the
twentieth century were Americans willing to accept the fact

of poverty in the United States. Late nineteenth century
books had described the slums of Chicago and New York (as
in Stephen Crane's Maggie), but these books did not attain
great popularity at the time. Urban slums first appeared
on best seller lists with Louis Beretti in 1929 by Donald
Henderson Clarke, and then, as the United States was
engulfed by the Depression, in great numbers of books
thereafter. Rural poverty gained celebrity with Erskine
Caldwell's two novels, Tobacco Road in 1932 and God's Little
Acre in 1933, and finally with The Grapes of Wrath by John
Steinbeck in 1939. In this last conditions are do bad that
a man paroled from prison steals a car in order to return
to prison where at least one is fed regularly (36). The
Depression aroused a new interest in poverty on the part of
Americans, some facing it for the first time, and unemployment provided more time to read books borrowed from the
library.

Do the poor differ from other classes only in having less
money and less material goods? Most associate sufficient
mores particular to the poor to create a veritable culture
of poverty. Many agree with William Harvey in Coin's
Financial School in 1894 that poverty breeds materialism
and selfishness:

> The conditions of life are so hard that indi-
> vidual selfishness is the only thing consistent
> with the instinct of self preservation; all public
> spirit, all generous emotions, all the noble
> aspirations of men are shrivelling up and dis-
> appearing . . .

as poverty grows (91). Philip in Of Human Bondage in 1915
learns how little "there was in common between the poor and
the classes above them" (701). "Lack of money made a man
petty and grasping; it distorted his character and caused
him to view the world from a vulgar angle; when you had to
consider every penny, money became of grotesque importance;

you needed a competence to rate it at its proper value"
(717). Franz Werfel in 1942 concurs: "Not wealth but
poverty is the last refuge of materialism. Need and want
are condemned to overestimate the value of common material
things" (258). And Morris West in The Devil's Advocate in
1959 carries this sentiment over into politics: "Hunger has
no loyalties"; the allegiance of the poor is always to the
strong (283). Erskine Caldwell's novels are comprehensive
catalogues of a culture created by long-term poverty--a
culture that rejects many of the fundamental doctrines
predominating in American society such as working hard and
taking care of one's children. Self-indulgence rules the
Lester family. Steinbeck's more sentimental The Grapes of
Wrath sharply contradicts this view of the materialism and
selfishness of the poor. Here poverty unifies the Okies in
their desperate trek to California; they become a family,
a community united by adversity. They share the little they
have even when depriving themselves, and unselfish community
self-government naturally develops. Ma Joad believes
passionately: "'If you're in trouble or hurt or need--go to
poor people. They are the only ones who help'" (513).

The poor must also develop diverse talents unnecessary
to the rich. Barbara Cartland in 1934 invents a character
who was born poor, inherited money and is now rich and
bored. When poor, he says, "'I had to make myself into an
entertaining companion so that I paid for my supper. . . .'"
But the rich need not be entertaining and "'are just rich
and devilish dull'" (116). Werfel cites talents the poor
must develop for such things as telling time without a
watch: "Without dial or bell they know what hour has struck,
for the poor are always afraid of being late" (15).

They also differ from other classes in the strength,
expression and direction of their emotions. In The Moonstone by Wilkie Collins in 1868 one character notes the
emotional repression required of the poor:

"People in high life have all the luxuries to
themselves--among others the luxury of indulging
their feelings. People in low life have no such
privileges. Necessity which spares our betters,
has no pity on us. We learn to put our feelings
back into ourselves, and to jog on with our duties
as patiently as may be. I don't complain of this.
I only notice it." (174)
When a woman accuses common laborers of being dirty and
ignorant, in The Robe by Lloyd Douglas in 1942, Marcellus
responds--yes they are, because they despise themselves
(469). Douglas equates their poverty to failure as human
beings, an attitude particularly understandable to Americans
brought up on the myth of the American Dream. And repressed
anger at their own inability to rise from poverty could be
deflected from themselves to others. In describing a
protest meeting of the unemployed at Columbus Circle at the
time of the Depression, Harold Robbins in Never Love a
Stranger shows the transformation of their anger into bitter
resentment at the government of the United States, Jews,
blacks, Catholics, unions and scabs (232). Rage at what
they perceive as their own failure is expressed as indiscriminate bigotry.

Poverty also creates particular attitudes toward the
medical profession. In A Window in Thrums in 1892 James
Barrie explains why the poor avoid doctors: because the poor
can only afford to go to the doctor when desperately sick,
consulting a doctor is a clear sign of imminent death (37).
Erich Remarque in 1929 notes that just as the poor are less
free to express themselves and their emotions in general,
so they are less free in medical situations. A poor man is
afraid to speak frankly to a doctor, to ask, for example,
how much an operation for cancer would cost him for fear the
surgeon might take offense (199). According to the narrator
the information one could expect in answer to such a

question is replaced in the poor by uninformed worry. In
Morton Thompson's novel about doctors, Not as a Stranger in
1954, Dr. Fletcher points out that the great enemy of the
doctor isn't cancer but poverty:

> ". . . that's your disease. That's your prime
> foe. Poverty. That's where the stress is. That's
> the enemy humanity's battling against every con-
> scious moment, that's the stress that's stacked
> against every cell. The pressure never lets up.
> And the weakest cells give."

And when an operation is necessary the poor patient cannot
afford it (367).

The pride of the poor shown in these books often leads
them to a symbolic rejection of their state and to attempts
to ape the upper classes. In The Little Minister in 1891
the neighbors delicately pull down their shades when a woman
is being taken to the poorhouse; thus they spare her humiliation.[3] Even a bit of conspicuous consumption may be used
to disguise their state from themselves: in A Tree Grows in
Brooklyn Francie's mother always pours out a cup of coffee
for her daughter although she knows Francie doesn't drink
coffee. It makes them feel rich to be able to waste something.[4] In The Group by Mary McCarthy in 1963 poor mothers
do not want to nurse their babies because bottle-feeding is
much more popular among the upper classes, and therefore
"socially superior" (253). To maintain self-respect the
poor sometimes hide in the mores of the better-off and
imitate whatever of this life-style they can afford.

A much more realistic picture of poverty and the poor
emerges with the Depression of the 1930s. As we have
already seen some books now locate poverty in the United
States. And it is a new kind of poverty: one does not
escape it by hard work, or social reform or even by good
luck. The poor described in a number of books in the 1940s
have given up; their poverty is so pervasive that escape is

hopeless, and they have become apathetic or criminal. One can see this in the books by Chandler, Algren, Motley, Shulman, Ellson, Barnard and even in the sentimentalized slums of Damon Runyon. In several books juveniles inhabiting the slums are heard to mutter what is surely the greatest of American heresies: "'Only dumb bastards want to work!'" (Louis Beretti, 37); "'Only suckers work!'" (Knock on Any Door, 191). Clearly Mrs. Wiggs is dead.

But in most of the novels throughout the period an American passion for work is either implied or explicitly stated, and poverty is the outward and visible sign of an inner inadequacy. With few exceptions poverty is produced by laziness. In 1887 Rev. Russell Conwell in Acres of Diamonds points out that the poor are poor by their own or another's fault. He allows a few exceptions deserving of our sympathy: "God's poor"--widows, orphans and the disabled who cannot help themselves, but "Let us remember there is not a poor person in the United States who was not made poor by his own shortcomings or by the shortcomings of someone else. It is all wrong to be poor anyhow." Ayn Rand in The Fountainhead in 1943 is equally firm on the aberrant character of the American poor. One character in the novel, while spending two weeks living in the slums is shocked by the extravagance of the poor as well as their reluctance to take a job (145). Only the defective American dislikes work. Vance Packard finds the cult of work deeply embedded in the American character in his sociological analysis of American society in 1957--a book that was itself a best-seller.

The concept of work in American popular fiction is particular and limited: it is always assumed to be unpleasant, and it is important not for the thing produced but for the money one is paid for the production. There are a few exceptions: Michelangelo and Van Gogh in Irving Stone's fictionalized biographies of those two artists find their

work its own reward. And the heroes and heroines of Ayn
Rand, although handsomely paid, were artists of their kind.
But most of the inhabitants of these novels, like most
Americans in an industrialized society, did not expect work
to be as interesting as its financial rewards. Industrialization provided work that was physically easier, but
boring, tedious and entirely out of the control of the
worker. One should not expect to have the pleasure of the
craftsman or the professional in creating a good or exciting
result. One works to make a living and to get rich. Gene
Stratton Porter in 1911 scorns the man who tries to make his
work pleasant by using a wheel-plow pulled by three horses
and with a canopy to protect him from the sun. This is a
man who "thinks he's working" (74). In Lost Horizons in 1933
when a woman brought up in Western civilization is asked if
the would like to be a missionary in Shangri-La, she rejects
the proposal because "'. . . there's no good in doing a thing
because you like it'" (99-100). Work is not simply an ex-
penditure of effort, but using effort in something one does
not enjoy. Work is expected to be unpleasant, but must be
undertaken to build character as well as to earn money. To
the worker the end products are character and money. Robert
Wilder in Written on the Wind in 1946 notes that people fall
apart when they don't have to earn a living. To have money
enough to escape work is disastrous: "'Money is a damned bad
thing'" (32)--a sentiment frequently echoed in these books.

In only four novels do questions arise over this concept
of work. In Eben Holden in 1900 an admired poet says:
"'Toil an' slave an' scrimp, an' save--that's 'bout all we
think av 'n this country'" (101). He also comments that
although he is poor, and he may be lazy, he has gotten more
out of life than most: "'And someday God will honor me far
above them'." A friend observes "'. . . anyone that picks
him up for a fool 'll find him a counterfeit'." Shangri-La
in Lost Horizons posits a successful society in which

meditation is the finest work in which one can engage. In
Maugham's The Razor's Edge in 1944 Larry agrees that the
harder we work in industry the richer we will be in material
things, but material things do not interest him. As in Lost
Horizons he is captured by the contemplative life of Eastern
religions, and finds it possible to ignore the advice of
friends who urge him: "'Be a man, Larry, and do a man's
work'" (81). Taylor Caldwell's This Side of Innocence in
1946 records extended arguments between two brothers.
Jerome, who has no respect for money as a symbol of human
time and effort, thinks Americans should be taught that man
cannot live by bread alone, and that he should do the
necessary work as quickly as possible to have time to savor
the wonders of the world (65). His brother Alfred maintains
"'Man was made for work and civilization is the result of
work'" (206). Jerome points out that it was the Athenians,
lovers of joy and beauty who created the arts, not the
Spartans. He hates "'the killers' of joy and gaiety and
the Gospel-Shouters of 'Work'." With sophisticated
machinery we should all have to work only a few hours a day.
Otherwise if we go on with the "'myth of work for its own
sake'" we will be producing "'mountains of foolish trinkets
and luxuries,'" and no one will be happy (405-406). But
these are lonely voices.

While the motive of workers to work remains much the same
throughout the period, their reactions to the conditions of
their work goes through a change with the onset of the
Depression of the 1930s. In the early period working conditions in all but a very few books appear to be pleasant,
and whatever they are the worker is expected to accept them
without protest; indeed bad conditions may build character.
Haines and Yaggy in 1876 offer an idyllic description of the
Lowell Mills, but the Lowell Mills before the great expansion of the labor force by the Irish migration, and before
the Depression of 1837 which drastically impaired labor

conditions. Without dating their description or noting the
ephemeral nature of those conditions Haines and Yaggy populate the Lowell plants with healthy, happy operatives,
former farm girls whose leisure time is devoted to music
and literature (143).

John Hay's book The Breadwinners, published anonymously
in 1884, is the first and the last until well into·the
twentieth century to center on the organization and activities of a labor union. He describes the union as composed
of the "laziest and most incapable workmen in the town."
As the room fills for a union meeting "it seemed like a
roll-call of shirks" (82). The union organizers are wild-
eyed radical villains, anti-Christian, prone to violence
and leading the union for their own venal purposes rather
than for any sort of principle. The "proper" attitude of
the worker toward his employer was set out in Elbert
Hubbard's Message to Garcia in 1899. He compares a worker
in industry to a soldier ordered to deliver a message to a
general. He must ask no questions, but offer blind obedienc
instantly whatever the demands of his employer. Hubbard
scorns what he sees as "much maudlin sympathy for the
'down-trodden denizen of the sweat-shop' and 'the homeless
wanderer searching for honest employment'." Actually it
is the employer who is to be pitied for the slipshod work
foisted on the employer by most workers. The man who
complains of his boss really has "an insane suspicion that
his employer is oppressing, or intending to oppress him."
No wonder employers were so happy to underwrite the publication of this pamphlet. The New York Central Railroad
alone published millions of copies.

Two books offer some sympathy to the embattled worker.
The Little Minister in 1891 describes miserable labor
conditions and violence between guards and strikers (25-60,
113). But the two chief characters are divided in their
sympathies. Hill's Manual . . ., first published at the

time of the 1873 depression still maintains in its 1905 edition some pro-labor material. As a manual on how to conduct one's public life it offers the reader forms to be copied for use on special occasions. Among those for calling a public meeting is one for calling a meeting of mechanics to discuss the eight hour day (417). One example of public speeches is entitled "A Plea in Behalf of the Eight Hour Day" (462; see also 466, 485-87). Labor relations are hardly a favorite subject for popular novels. One would not expect serious studies of factory labor in best sellers, yet the drama of the strikes at Homestead, Pullman, the Lawrence textile strike, and even the Triangle fire were dramatic enough to find their way into popular novels. But they did not.

Not until the Depression of the 1930s do labor conditions and labor organizations to change those conditions get a sympathetic hearing in the best sellers. This is certainly not escape literature. While Dale Carnegie and Napoleon Hill still insist that all one needs to avoid labor confrontations is a friendly manner, many of the best sellers are more realistic. As part of his fictionalized biography of Van Gogh, Irving Stone introduces his readers to terrible conditions in the Belgian coal mines. Erskine Caldwell's God's Little Acre in 1933 centers around the reactions of a labor organization to a lockout at a mill. Here the A. F. of L. is criticized as being too conservative. When the more radical local union takes over there is violence and the workers' organization falls apart. Unions are favorably presented in most books where they appear at all from that time on. Red-baiting of unions and union leaders is described as an unfair tactic in several books of this period.[5] But J. Edgar Hoover sternly warns in Masters of Deceit (1958) of Red infiltration into labor unions; as masters of deceit the Reds, in his opinion, have been quite successful in the labor movement (110, 215).

258

Unfavorable pictures of unions from the late 1950s tend to
portray them as attached to underworld figures and contributors to organized crime.[6]

In spite of the enormous growth of white collar jobs
when distribution became as important as production and
gigantic corporations multiplied, office workers are
conspicuously absent from the novels. The invention of the
typewriter in the late nineteenth century put increasing
numbers of women behind desks. Yet office workers appear
first only in 1928 in Vina Delmar's Bad Girl where the main
female character works behind a desk; here the office is
merely incidental to the story. The only novel employing
the office as major setting is Rona Jaffe's 1958 The Best
of Everything about three young women in an office typing
pool. She paints a rosy picture indeed of office life and
relations between employer and employee. Evidently offices
were hardly seen as centers of romance, and probably office
workers themselves in choosing their own leisure reading
preferred to identify with the heroes and heroines of long
ago, or far away in either geography or class.

Three nineteenth century authors--Henry George, Edward
Bellamy and William Harvey--entered best seller lists with
books describing radical programs designed to provide
economic equality by social planning, and each of these
books became the Bible for a comprehensive reform movement.
George points out that the eighteenth century had expected
scientific progress to end poverty and produce a society in
which:

> Youth no longer stunted and starved, age no longer
> harried by avarice; the child at play with the
> tiger; the man with the muck-rake drinking in the
> glory of the stars. (4)

Instead economic progress and poverty have gone hand in hand
hand; where one finds the greatest progress there one finds
the greatest poverty. To eliminate this George would tax

away unearned increment in the value of land, using the
revenue for social programs. Edward Bellamy in his Utopian
novel Looking Backward, 2000-1887 outlines a society which
has eliminated poverty and equalized work by nationalizing
the means of production. William H. Harvey in Coin's
Financial School, an 1894 Populist tract, faults the gold
standard for poverty in the United States, and warns
Americans: "A financial trust has control of your money,
and with it, is robbing you of your property" (233). The
book is illustrated with cartoons of bloated plutocrats,
one of them with his hair growing in the shape of horns
(156, 85). In this book the cause of poverty is conspiracy,
a conspiracy of financial manipulators. All three of these
authors are optimistic that poverty can be eliminated if
their programs are followed.

One is struck by the fact that in twenty-five years the
late nineteenth century accepted three books advocating
social planning so enthusiastically that they became best
sellers, whereas in the twentieth century not a single book
advocating the elimination of poverty by government action
achieved this status. In the two Utopian novels that did
become twentieth century best sellers, Aldous Huxley's
Brave New World and George Orwell's 1984, nightmare
societies result from attempts at social planning. All are
ostensibly equal, but the individual is lost. The political
and economic fantasies of the nineteenth and twentieth
centuries seem to lead in opposite directions. The most
radical social theories apart from Huxley's and Orwell's
satires are in the novels of Ayn Rand in the 1950s and Barry
Goldwater's own social philosophy as outlined in The Conscience of a Conservative in 1960. Both wish to return to
a thorough-going laissez-faire. H. G. Wells alone in the
twentieth century managed to get on the best seller list in
spite of his advocacy of socialism, and Wendell Willkie's
One World in 1943 suggests that the elimination of poverty

will help all, not just the poor, although he offers no
specific method to accomplish this end (29). But these two
books talk of poverty only incidentally, and were hardly
likely to counter effectively the powerful messages of
Huxley, Orwell and Rand.

The difference between the first fifty years and the last
fifty years is an intriguing problem. The Depression of
the 1930s evidently made Americans eager to read about
poverty in America for the first time, and it appears in
some form in most novels. But although the twentieth
century offered as many serious reformers as the nineteenth
and more actual reform programs (Woodrow Wilson, Franklin
Delano Roosevelt) such material did not find its way into
the most popular reading. Perhaps the poverty Americans
were finally willing to recognize seemed so drastic as to
be beyond repair. Perhaps having specific programs in
effect for coping with the situation however inadequately
made it less interesting to read about. The America that
accepted Henry George, Edward Bellamy and William Harvey
was one singularly free of actual governmental reform
policies. The only major pieces of economic legislation in
the last thirty years of the nineteenth century were the
establishment of the Interstate Commerce Commission and the
Sherman Anti-Trust Act, although Finley Peter Dunne could
describe the latter with a fair degree of accuracy so: "What
was a stone wall to the layman, was a triumphal arch to the
lawyer." Yet reform movements abounded. The popularity of
these books came from the reform impetus of the nineteenth
century and undoubtedly contributed to its fruition in
Woodrow Wilson's domestic program, the New Freedom. The
New Deal, on the other hand, produced economic and social
policies but not best sellers. Undoubtedly the existence
of the Soviet Union and the development of American paranoia
about the Soviet Union brought such books as Brave New
World, 1984, the novels of Ayn Rand, the conscience of

Barry Goldwater and J. Edgar Hoover to the fore. I would
hesitate to suggest as a universal truth that books critical
of general government policies find places on best seller
lists more easily than books supportive of those policies,
nevertheless this would seem to be the case in these two
periods. Both lists represented reform, but in diametri-
cally opposed directions.

WEALTH

Lady Chatterly in D. H. Lawrence's 1932 novel meditates:
"Money and so-called love are civilized society's two great
manias and money a long way first" (110). Money is the first
necessity: "'Money you have to have. You needn't really
have anything else. . . . All the rest you can get along
without, at a pinch. But not money'" (70). Its importance
is not confined to stories of aristocrats, tycoons and the
poor. Even Tarzan finally realizes how essential it is:
"'Without money I must die'" (361).

The power of wealth is often a matter of comment as well
as a major part of the plot of many novels. Wealth can buy
sex, law, government as well as greater physical comfort.[7]
Wealth also provides psychic comfort because it liberates:
"'A rich man can do anything he feels like'."[8] Esteem
automatically attends the wealthy, and, indeed an action
that would bring disesteem to those less well endowed finan-
cially is accepted by the community with equanimity if done
by the rich. A character in Oppenheim's The Great Impersonation in 1920 observes of a wealthy man that he will be
forgiven anything, even murder (28).

The wealthy, perhaps because of their greater opportunities for adventure, intrigue and power, populate most of
these popular novels. The possessors of wealth are divided
into two classes: those who have inherited money and those
who have made it by their own efforts. Distinctions between
these two categories are universal in the novels throughout

the period. The lives of old wealth are empty; according
to Evans in 1866 they are "'poor, gilded moths of fashion
and folly'" (121). Marie Corelli in 1887 recounts the
experiences of a simple Norwegian farmer's daughter after
she marries into the British aristocracy. She is shocked
at their "'world of intrigue and folly--a world of infidel-
ity and falsehood'" (206). Along with many other authors
at the turn of the century Corelli ascribes to them the
"society laugh"--one empty of both spontaneity and mirth.[9]
Aristocrats are not only insincere and hypocritical, but
may trifle with the law.[10] In most books rudeness and even
cruelty come naturally to those of old wealth, and such
behavior is both expected and tolerated by the public. In
The Bramble Bush by Mergendahl in 1958 the town drunk is
accepted by the community because he comes from one of the
town's older families (80). A character in Barbara Cartland's The Runaway Heart in 1961 points out that aristocrats
are habitually rude: "'And they're entitled to be'" (57).
Betteredge, the butler in The Moonstone (1868), has his own
interpretation of such qualities in his betters: "'Gentle-
folks in general have a very awkward rock ahead in life--
the rock ahead of their own idleness'." In their search
for something to do they usually take to what in his opinion
is "'some nasty pursuit'." To this he ascribes the interest
of the aristocracy in scientific research: they take to
spoiling something or torturing something--like catching,
pinning and studying bugs--something of which he highly
disapproves (54). A more famous butler, P. G. Wodehouse's
Jeeves in 1924 considers Bertie, his employer, pleasant and
amiable but not noted for intelligence, and, indeed, something of a fool. When Jeeves is on vacation Bertie is
unable to cope with the world.

To be born into a rich family is shown to be sheer
disaster; the children of old wealth are always "spoiled":
lazy, arrogant, idle, and given to drink, gambling and

dissipation. There is general agreement with Rudolph in
The Prisoner of Zenda: "'Good families are generally worse
than others'."[11] In this context the term "good" always
refers to long-established families of old wealth.

In the earlier books the extravagance and extraordinary
wastefulness of both old and new rich are frequently mentioned, and with scorn. An older woman in Gene Stratton
Porter's The Harvester in 1911 expresses contempt for those
who buy fancy things only because the neighbors are doing
so. One family purchases a "steam vehicle" although
operating it frightens them. But since the neighbors have
one they feel possession of such a machine is essential to
maintain neighborhood respectability (370-71). Characters
in two books in the nineteen thirties tie aesthetic values
to money. In Studs Lonigan in 1932 the chair must be
beautiful because it cost one hundred dollars (50), and in
Serenade one can discover who is the greatest painter in
the world by finding out whose paintings sell at the highest
price (183). Mirroring the market economy, books published
in the 1950s and 1960s abound in examples of conspicuous
consumption, many of them particularly ostentatious and even
bizarre. In Edna Ferber's 1952 novel of Texas one rich
Texan defends his purchase of an airplane: "'Nowadays a
fella without an airplane has got no rating, might as well
be a Mexican'" (22). Lillian Roth's 1954 autobiography
describes her own version of ostentation in outfitting her
car: upholstered in lamb, handles of fourteen carat gold,
and a chauffeur's outfit to match the upholstery. And in
Duchess Hotspur in 1946 the ballroom is lined with ermine
tails (59). While most of the examples of conspicuous
consumption are not approved by their authors, one wonders
why Wallace in The Man in 1964 mentions several times the
"platinum watch" worn by a secretary (17, 21). In The
Hidden Persuaders, Vance Packard's best selling analysis of
American mores in 1957 observes our penchant for purchasing

for prestige rather than beauty or utility; the efficiency
of a car's motor is irrelevant to most American car owners,
but its extravagance in size, cost, upkeep makes it
desirable (52).

Relations between rich and poor are curiously ambiguous,
and sometimes in these books contradictory. The rich have
a primary obligation to give charity to the poor, but the
poor are cautioned not to accept charity. They should earn
their own living. Thus the virtues rich and poor are
constantly urged to cultivate are in direct opposition to
each other. Elnora, the poor but honest girl of the
Limberlost in 1909, when offered clothes she really needs,
rejects them saying: "'People have no right to wear things
they cannot afford, have they?'"[12] Philanthropy should be
directed to the "deserving" poor--widows, orphans and those
truly incapable of earning money. The one exception to
this notion is in The Leavenworth Case in 1878 when a young
woman advocates the right of all the poor to be fed, if for
any reason they cannot feed themselves. She lives in an
isolated area near a railroad, and is asked if she isn't
afraid of being overrun "'with worthless beings, whose only
trade is to take all they can get without giving in
return?'" She responds: "'The only luxury I have is to
feed the poor'." But her questioner continues, asking if
she thinks she should feed the idle poor? "'They are still
the poor'" she replies (303).

With the exception of Henry George, Edward Bellamy,
William Harvey and H. G. Wells, none of these books suggest
that the wealthy should work for the elimination of poverty.
Even Charles Sheldon whose book commended the radical
reforms that would follow if all lived as Christ did,
favored the "intelligent unselfishness" of charity rather
than any attempt to do away with poverty (97). That part
of the social gospel movement advocating social planning to
achieve greater economic equality--George Herron, Washington

Gladden and others--did not make it to the best seller list. On the question of charity Ayn Rand again takes an extreme position. She disapproves of philanthropy as support for the lazy and unproductive. It is selfishness not philanthropy that achieves production and progress. A defender of the idea that wealth must be administered as a trust for the poor is described with contempt in Atlas Shrugged in 1957. He has "the gawkiness of a lout," is made up of pale, soft flesh, is "obstinate and drained" and most damning of all, his railroad is failing (7-10, 46, 99). An admired character is one "'who robs the thieving poor and gives back to the productive rich'" (576). In both of her best selling novels she sees unselfishness "destroying the world."

While inherited wealth is no blessing, the wealth that accrues through one's own efforts confers vast benefits on the individual and his/her society. Hill's Manual . . . in 1905 assures its readers: "It is not the possession, but the acquisition of wealth, that gives happiness" (111). Robert Wilder's Written on the Wind in 1946 includes a tale of two boys who steal empty bottles from a bottling works to turn them in for money. The point of the story of that they enjoy this money much more than the allowances given them by their families, because they made it themselves (22). Ill-gotten gains these may be, but they represent action and accomplishment and therefore produce self-esteem. Rev. Russell Conwell in Acres of Diamonds firmly advises his readers: "I say to you that you ought to get rich, and it is your duty to get rich" because money is power and one can do much good with it. Furthermore to achieve wealth is testimony of good character. Most of the rich are honest, ". . . that is why they are rich"--people trust them with their money.[13] Polly Adler in 1953 entitles one chapter "Everybody Ought to Be Rich," a title taken from an interview of John J. Raskob published in the Ladies Home Journal for August, 1929. He points out, she notes, "'Anyone not only can be rich, but ought to be rich'." But one must make it oneself (143). Ayn Rand in Atlas Shrugged in 1957 believes making money to be the basis of ethics: "'The words "to make money" hold the essence of human morality. . . . money is the root of all good'" (414). Polly Adler equates this money ethic with the 1920s in the United States when the credo was "Anything which is economically right is morally right" (5). Rand adds another virtue to the self-made man in Atlas Shrugged: he is the truly creative artist of the modern age. "'Wealth is the product of man's capacity to think'" (411). This attitude must have been prevalent enough apart from Rand for Harry Golden in 1958 to feel it necessary to point out that the most creative scientists--Copernicus, Galileo, Newton, and Einstein--never met a payroll (202).

In many twentieth century books Christianity blesses the self-made business man. Bruce Barton, as we have seen, treats Jesus as a poor boy who made good: "Stripped of all dogma this is the grandest achievement story of all!" (9). He transcribes the statement attributed to Jesus--"the man who loses his life shall find it"--to business: the way to succeed in business is to bury oneself in the matter at hand without asking questions about salary, title or promotions (166-67). Lloyd Douglas in 1942 does not go so far, but he does allow an admired character to comment that thoughtless people misunderstood Christ's attitude toward business and toward charity. Christ really approved of business, and disapproved of the wealthy distributing all of their goods to the poor (276). One wonders what happened to the biblical warning of the difficulties a rich man would face in trying to enter heaven.

The American love of money is so all-pervasive that it is regarded as a national characteristic. European authors of American best sellers as different as Jules Verne,

Halevy, Corelli, Maugham, P. G. Wodehouse, A. J. Cronin,
and Agatha Christie all use as stock characters the rich
American tossing his/her money around. These are not
admirable characters; their arrogance is often conspicuous
as in the American millionaire in The Rosary in 1910 who
will only climb the pyramids when the natives "'have the
sense to put an elevator up the center'" (133-34). Corelli
in 1887 believes the American not only has a passion for
money, but is not ashamed to admit it: "'. . . is not its
[the U.S.] confessed watchword 'the almight Dollar?' [sic]"
(107). And indeed American writers are quite as frank as
their European counterparts but more forgiving on the
subject of the American love of money and the sharp business
practices they use to get it. The coming of the United
States government or its citizens to any part of the world
means the coming of commercialism. In Anthony Adverse in
1933 a friend of the title character in New Orleans is
appalled at the Louisiana Purchase. "'Now we are going to
have floods of democrats, oratory, humbug, Protestant
anarchy and the world and man for sale at the river mouth'"
(1082). A European who seems to have an overweening desire
for money is often referred to as a Yankee.[14] Most of the
books show rich Americans squandering their wealth, enjoying
their ability to consume, but two point out that Americans
like money not for what they can buy with it, but, as Golden
puts it in 1958, because in the United States its acquisition brings self-esteem (138). Maugham in The Razor's Edge
in 1944 shapes it even more sharply: "'We care nothing for
it. . . . Money is nothing to us; it's merely the symbol
of success'" (313). It should occasion no surprise that the
religion satirized in Brave New World, the worship of
business and money has an American tycoon as god--"Our
Ford." Years are dated "AF" (after Ford) instead of AD
with the beginning year, the year of the introduction of
the Model T. One swears by saying "Ford." People wear a

golden "T" instead of a cross. In Huxley's parody the
successful business man has replaced God.

Many of the more recent books, fiction and non-fiction,
are about business men. According to Polly Adler, John J.
Raskob pointed out that wealth is not achieved by saving
money, but by financial manipulations in the course of.
business. Most of the examples of "positive thinkers" in
manuals on the subject are business men; for example in
Maxwell Maltz' Psycho-Cybernetics in 1960 some twenty-one
business men are used to illustrate the successful use of
mind power. In translating Christ's success in saving souls
to making money Barton sanctifies modern business techniques
by ascribing them to Jesus; Jesus was, he assures us, the
first great advertising executive. Ruthlessness is often
assumed to be necessary to success in business; Scarlett
O'Hara uses convict lease labor. And in the same novel,
Rhett Butler has no compunctions that his running the
blockade in the Civil War hurts the cause of the South; his
actions are purely for profit not patriotism he avers, and:
"'. . . there is just as much money to be made out of the
wreckage of a civilization as from the upbuilding of one'"
(193). Harold Robbins in 1961 introduces many successful
business men--crude, arrogant, unscrupulous, but great
successes in business. Ruthlessness is acceptable if it
succeeds in collecting capital. Business is assumed to be
the center of the executive's life. In Keyes' Dinner at
Antoine's in 1948 a millionaire builds a mammoth palace for
his prospective bride, but tells her the fact that he
confided to her some of his business secrets is "'a lot
bigger compliment . . . a glimpse of what passes for my
soul'" (222-23). In 1937 Napoleon Hill in his manual for
success in business, Think and Grow Rich offers paeans of
praise to capitalism as vital to the progress of the United
States and all of mankind. To him:

The capitalists are the brains of civilization,
because they supply the entire fabric of which all
education, enlightenment and human progress con-
sists. They are motivated by the desire to build,
construct, achieve, tender useful service, earn
profits, accumulate riches. And, because they
render service without which there could be no
civilization, they put themselves in the way of
great riches.
Yet in spite of their contributions to society they are
castigated by evil men: "These are the same men to whom
radicals, racketeers, dishonest politicians and grafting
labor leaders refer as 'the predatory interests,' or 'Wall
Street'" (134-35). Rand agrees with Hill's evaluation of
the critics of business in Atlas Shrugged: "Miles Mulligan
had once been the richest and, consequently, the most
denounced man in the country" (315). Criticism of these
heroes of modern industrial society is engendered only by
jealousy and envy rather than their own misbehavior. The
self-made man is not only an example of industrial success,
but a hero of the modern world; he creates progress.
    Identifying industrial progress with the progress of the
human race is unquestioned in almost all books. The socialists H. G. Wells and Edward Bellamy are quite as enthusiastic about science, engineering and industrial progress as
Ayn Rand. Bellamy's Utopia envisions a future offering as
many conveniences invented and produced by a triumphant
industrialism as any business man might wish, but spread
more equitably through society. Other reformers--Henry
George and William Harvey--also see a more sophisticated
industrialization benefiting all classes by offering greater
efficiency and more leisure to all. Very few question the
notion that increased mechanization will lead to the
greatest happiness of the greatest number. But with the
depression of the 1930s two novels bring the whole civili-

zation into question. In 1932 Huxley's Brave New World
offered a totally industrialized and totally unlivable
world, one that controlled mind as well as material production. And in 1933 Lost Horizons pictured the timeless,
non-industrial, non-competitive society of Shangri-La.
This world, dominated by Eastern mysticism, is isolated
from the Western world where man is busy destroying beauty
and peace. Only: "'. . . when the strong have devoured
each other, the Christian ethic may at last be fulfilled,
and the meek shall inherit the earth'" (145). The only
piece of Western industry they have preserved is modern
plumbing. Western visitors are startled to find that while
the whole outside world is in a state of dissolution with
revolutions, wars, stock-market crash, inner and outer
peace rule Shangri-La. A few novels after this note
industrial depredations of nature. In The Grapes of Wrath
in 1939 agribusiness is responsible not only for depleting
nature, but for depriving the land of the fostering care of
the farmer (316). In 1942 Werfel is appalled at how
business has taken the beauty and spirituality out of
Lourdes and its miracle with plaster saints, and other
souvenirs. James Hilton, author of Lost Horizons, in
Random Harvest in 1941 introduces an industrialist guilt-
ridden by the thought that the way his family became rich is
"'the opposite of the way to make England strong'." Life
has deteriorated "'ever since Englishmen were more interested in the price of things on the market than what they
could grow in their own gardens'."[15]

One novel compares and contrasts the social ethics of
various business men. The frontispiece for Harold Bell
Wright's novel The Winning of Barbara Worth is a poem:

Give fools their gold and knaves their power
Let fortune's bubbles rise and fall,
Who sows a field, or trains a flower,
Or plants a tree, is more than all.

A major theme of the novel is the struggle in developing the West between the capitalist interested only in his own profit and one interested in everyone's profits. To Jeff Worth business need not be sordid and grasping but "the expression of the master passion that in all ages had wrought in the making of the race" (158, 178). The money he made was not as important to him as the work itself. Capitalism is necessary and good. In defending a particular business venture he points out that capitalists "'are simply promoting this scheme in the only way possible to start it, and the people will share the results. . . . They wouldn't have anything without the Company'" (196-97). Another admired character explains to the protesting heroine: You say men shouldn't be driven by desire for gain, but "'So far as I can see, it is this same desire for gain that has driven men into doing every really great thing that has ever been done'" (240). Capitalism is the source of all progress, but not all capitalists are humane, and some do terrible things in the name of "Good Business" (a phrase Wright uses sarcastically some seventeen times). Only the South is shown to be nervous over advancing industrialization. While Scarlett O'Hara and Rhett Butler happily and successfully embrace business, Ashley fears if the North wins the Civil War, the South may adopt the "'money-making activities, acquisitiveness and commercialism of that section'" (212).

The myth of the United States as the land where every man can go from rags to riches pervades most of these books. This idea was widely popularized by a misread Horatio Alger. Alger heroes usually start from rags but go to a competency rather than riches. The legend that grew up around Alger has his heroes achieving success by nothing but their own hard work. In fact, his heroes usually found the pathway to success by fortuitous accident: saving the daughter of a bank president from a runaway horse, or, as in Ragged Dick, saving the son of a business man from drowning after he fell off a boat. Given a job or some other advantage as a reward by the wealthy benefactor, the hero's hard work from then on produced success. Incidentally Ragged Dick of the 1867 story reappears in <u>Little Lord Fauntleroy</u> by Frances Hodgson Burnett in 1886, playing the same role. Again he is favored because on the streets of New York he once helped the little boy who later became Lord Fauntleroy. The Alger message could have been: helping others will lead to your own success, but this is not the lesson popularly drawn from his tales.

Riches instead of mere competency are added to the myth in most books until economic realism enters best sellers in the 1930s and 1940s. In this long period it is assumed not just that one can get rich by hard work, but in the United States one cannot avoid getting rich if one works hard. Haines and Yaggy in 1876 assure their readers: "It [hard work] must lead to wealth, with the same certainty that poverty follows in the train of idleness and inattention." Hard work is "an unfailing source of temporal properity" (246). To start life ragged is a great advantage: "Genius, that noblest gift of God to man, is nourished by poverty" (495). Although best sellers discover American poverty in the Depression of the 1930s, the rags to riches myth persists alongside the tales of hopeless poverty. The method of achieving wealth was often redefined; "working hard" in Dale Carnegie and Napoleon Hill now became working with one's personality rather than with material things. But this new method of self-improvement was quite as sure to produce wealth by one's own efforts as the old one. In 1952 Norman Vincent Peale is still saying "For a man to have lived in poverty when all the time right on his doorstep is gold, indicates an unintelligent approach to life" (80). The United States is unique in that "unlimited opportunity is given to any boy in the United States of America" (211).

The widespread acceptance of the rags-to-riches myth in the United States had consequences of quite diverse sorts. Undoubtedly it encouraged people to exert themselves, believing that in this country hard work was inevitably rewarded. Optimism and greater productivity were natural results. But the psychological effects of failure were surely more devastating than in countries where one was not constantly bombarded with the idea that in this land one could not help but become rich if one worked hard enough. If one remained poor in Europe, one could blame the system; if one remained poor in the United States, one could blame only oneself. In Tropic of Cancer in 1961 Henry Miller asserts that he would much prefer to be poor in Europe than in the United States (69). This may help to explain differences in political action and political parties in Europe and the United States. The poor European, unlikely to climb the ladder of economic success, had two choices: he could migrate to America, or he could try to change the system by political action--he could join a Socialist or Social Democratic party. But the poverty-stricken American imbued with the idea that the United States offered equal opportunity to all, would see little value in joining a party devoted to long-range basic political changes. It wasn't the economic and social status quo that needed changing, but his own character. A political movement designed to eliminate poverty would seem irrelevant. Political movements organized to make basic changes in the society failed to flourish here as they did in Europe; they were temporary (as the Populist Movement), local (as the Farmer-Labor Party) or small (as the Socialist and Communist Parties).

Class, as illustrated in the best sellers, is a complex concept in the United States. The position of blacks is clear throughout the period; they are put in the position of a caste, low on the social scale by inheritance. In a society that offered unusual opportunities for economic and

political advancement for white males, one might except
less emphasis on class among whites than in other countries.
And Americans fondly celebrated American culture as classless, particularly in popular literature. As Mrs. Trollope
pointed out in the 1830s servants resented being called
servants, and insisted on "the girl" or "the hired hand,"
or some other euphemism.[16] Social and political equality
are assumed in the comment of an American in George Barr
McCutcheon's Graustark in 1901: "'. . . every born American
may become ruler of the greatest nation in the world--the
United States. . . . In my land you will find the poor man
climbing the highest pinnacle, side by side with the rich
man'" (385). Owen Wister in 1902 presents a novel view of
American classlessness with hints of Jeffersonianism:
America is divided into two classes--"the quality and the
equality." The Declaration of Independence acknowledged
"the eternal inequality of man [sic]." For by it we
abolished a "cut-and-dried aristocracy" and decreed "that
every man should henceforth have equal liberty to find his
own level. . . . 'Let the best man win whoever he is' that
is America's word. That is true democracy. And true
democracy and true aristocracy are one and the same thing"
(147).

At the same time many of the novels of the first fifty
years of this study refer, often with sarcasm, to the
American penchant for titles. Evans in 1866: "'What a
commentary on Republican Americans that we are so dazzled
by the glitter of a title!'"[17] Archibald Gunter's 1887
tale Mr. Barnes of New York takes his title character on a
European trip and makes a particular and personal point of
Mr. Barnes' worship of titles. When he discovers his rival
for the hand of Enid is an English lord, he comments:
"'. . . it's lucky she's an English girl; if Enid Anstruther
came from my side of the water I shouldn't have a chance in
a thousand'" (101). In E. P. Roe's 1872 novel Barriers

Burned Away an English woman points up American ambiguity
on classlessness: "'. . . you Americans are sometimes
wonderfully inconsistent and there is often a marvelously
wide margin between your boasted equality and the reality'"
(164).

Class for whites and caste for blacks in the South is
generally accepted. Uncle Remus in 1880 refers to "white
trash" as well as to class differences between domestic
slaves and field hands (132-33). John Fox Jr. in The Little
Shepherd of Kingdom Come considers "poor white trash" to
come by their trashiness by inheritance, "worthless descendants of the servile and sometimes criminal class who might
have traced their origin back to the slums of London.
. . ."[18] In 1883 Mark Twain includes in Life on the
Mississippi a diatribe against Walter Scott for his influence on Southern class notions: it was Scott who "created
rank and caste down there, and also reverence for rank and
caste, and pride and pleasure in them. . . ." He introduced:

> . . . silliness and emptiness, sham grandeurs,
> sham gauds, and sham chivalries of a brainless
> and worthless long-vanished society. He did
> measureless harm; more real and lasting harm,
> perhaps, than any other individual that ever
> wrote. (200)

In a country with no history of a legally established
aristocracy and with unusual opportunities to rise in
society, how does one become upper class? As delineated
in these books, climbing the economic ladder does not
guarantee being considered socially elite. Neither making
money nor having money assures one of a position in the
upper classes although it may eventually help to put one's
descendants there. The financial requirement to be upper
class is old money. One should come from a founding family
with economic competency established long ago in the

community. Such a family has had money or property in the past although it may not have it now.

If class status in the United States is dependent on old wealth, an ethnic and/or racial element enters the question of social position. In many of these books natural heritage--breeding--is the major factor in establishing class; it is "in the blood," and ancestors are at least as important as the current generation in determining class status.[19] In a land of immigrants whose settlers migrated mainly from northern Europe for two hundred years, WASPS would inevitably make up most of the upper class. Later immigrants, different in ethnic origin from the early settlers appeared on a scene already preempted by white Anglo-Saxons. Except in extraordinary circumstances Southern and Eastern Europeans, coming in great numbers at the end of the nineteenth century and Latin Americans in mid-twentieth century, were not considered upper class no matter how much money they made. As Catholics or Jews they were viewed with deep suspicion that began to soften only with the 1940s. But even more significant was the idea that they were ethnically, racially different and inferior. One might change one's religion, but could hardly change one's race, however much native ethnicity one might deny in order to assimilate effectively. Ironically then, in a country that proudly vaunted classlessness as part of the American Dream, class became caste. As we have seen, caste was used to condemn blacks, whatever their accomplishments, to being lower class. But it was also used to keep the new immigrants depressed. It was a modified caste system because their background was less visible than that of the black population--a name change, for example, would help the white immigrant. Nonetheless in a society brought up on the idea that everyone in the United States had an equal chance to climb the social ladder, one was limited not just by actual difficulties of the journey from rags to riches,

but by an almost ineradicable origin. Vance Packard was
probably justified in deciding that however un-American
Americans assumed social class to be, England, Holland and
Denmark have a more open class system than the United
States.[20]

With the Depression a new perception of poverty briefly
disturbed the American Dream, but it was an interruption
rather than an awakening. Middle class Americans clung to
the myth that they inhabited a land of equal opportunity
and were part of a classless society. Such myths conveniently provided justification for their own self-esteem and
derogation of those who continued to live in an ever more
visible poverty. They assumed that the poor are poor
because of their own inadequacies. Furthermore their actual
perceptions of class were rooted in their belief in ethnic
heritage. While they used the myth of classlessness to
claim their achievements as results of their own talents
rather than any class advantage, they saw the failures of
the poor as an inevitable result of bad character emerging
from bad genes. Class consciousness was not only present
in American thought, but particularly persistent because it
rested so largely on ethnicity. Belief in these myths of
success were also useful to the middle and upper classes in
freeing them from feelings of guilt about the miseries of
others or worrying about social reform. The enormously
complex economic and social patterns of the United States
in the twentieth century called forth on the best seller
list not plans for redress of grievances for the poor, but
a return to the pure laissez-faire of a long-ago simpler
America. Clearly the dominant point of view is that of a
middle class in a business community.

And what of the poor? Those who are unable to rise out
of poverty are left to meditate on their failure as a defect
of character. They can blame only themselves in this land
of opportunity. In the richest country in the world the

American Dream had become: every one for himself and a
deserved poverty for the hindmost.

Chapter 10: LAW AND ORDER

Since an account of sensational activities sells more
books than an ordinary slice of life--and breaking the law
is usually more spectacular than keeping the law--one should
expect more crime in popular books than in life. But,
besides exciting criminal activity what one also finds in
American best sellers is a general acceptance of the idea
of the impotence of government and approval of the actions
of ordinary citizens who take the law into their own hands.
Exercising or expanding government power is frowned on, but
expanding the power of individuals to take over the functions of government is viewed with approbation. Cowboys,
frontiersmen, Southern whites, gangsters, tough private
detectives and even some detectives in the classical
detective story break the law with community approbation
ostensibly to preserve their own version of public order.
The twentieth century American reader immersed in best
sellers would be forced to conclude that the preservation
of order in the United States requires a wholesale disregard
for law. On the whole the American culture viewed through
its best selling books was a vigilante society.

Maintaining law and order in the United States offers
particular problems because, while Americans think of
themselves as an orderly peaceful people their history is
one embodying much violence. As Hofstadter puts it: the
United States has a history but not a tradition of
violence.[1] Apart from wars American violence has not been
of a revolutionary nature, and rarely ideological; it has
been essentially conservative. It usually develops from
economic and ethnic competition to maintain status. Until
the late 1960s most of it was directed by the established
classes against the rising expectations and economic success

of various minorities: Catholics, Jews, blacks, Orientals, abolitionists, labor unionists, nesters. Most Americans have been brought up to believe that theirs is a peculiarly safe, non-violent society by comparison to the rest of the world. Such sentiments are expressed in many best sellers. In his historical novel of 1900, The Crisis, Winston Churchill compares the American to the French Revolution, and concludes that in the United States "Heads are not so cheap" (353). This is put in racial terms when whites are compared to Orientals or Africans. The "Occidental concept of the value of human life" will not allow you to kill unless you are sure the enemy is going to kill you.[2] But many authors of best sellers who are not themselves American characterize us as particularly violent: Ouida, Jules Verne, W. Somerset Maugham, Morris West.[3] Of American authors only Mark Twain considers violence an American characteristic, but in Life on the Mississippi in 1883 he also notes a consistent American unwillingness to recognize this element in their character (179).

Many books remark the singular passion of the American for the gun. In western novels as well as in those dealing with urban violence the gun becomes an extension of the male, a substitute penis producing excitement, power and violence. Urban juveniles imbibe this attitude early in the city streets. The ease in purchasing a gun is observed, and, if they cannot buy guns, as William Barnard points out in 1949 "with the technical ingenuity characteristic of American youngsters . . ." they-make them (92). In 1947 in The Amboy Dukes by Irving Shulman a gun is made in a school manual training course. Success with a gun always leads to social success. In The Grapes of Wrath in 1939 a young man gains significant status in his community as it becomes known that he has killed a man. In fact even his brother's reputation is enhanced simply by the relationship (114). One takes pride in having survived a gunfight whatever the issues involved in the quarrel. A scar from such a battle has the prestige of a medal and must be constantly displayed as a sign of manhood, as Busch reveals in Duel in the Sun in 1944 (33). Always the aggressor is male, it is a man who holds the gun. Furthermore the books involving most violence--the Westerns, novels of war and of tough detectives--are all by men.

As in the popular literature of other countries individual violence is common. Reading about it offers vicarious thrills without danger. It may also help rationalize the violence of the reader's own feelings while at the same time allowing self-congratulation at his own self-control. As we have seen, sex was equated with violence in most of the twentieth century books and gratuitous gore abounds from Quo Vadis on. Even Joel Chandler Harris' Uncle Remus is full of brutality. At one point Brer Rabbit takes a package of what he calls "good beef" to Mrs. Fox, but warns her not to open the box until she is ready to eat it; the box contains her husband's head (171).

Individual violence on the frontier whether in Appalachia, the Far West or Alaska is a favorite subject in books by Jack London, Rex Beach and Zane Grey. Violence in urban streets becomes a major subject in the late 1940s. Nearly every book from then on becomes almost a catalogue of violence. Peyton Place, for example, offers suicide, incest, murder, automobile accidents, forest fires as well as sexual violence. In these books the use of violence is not consigned exclusively to villains, but it is limited to the male sex. Indeed successful violent action with or without a gun is often equated specifically or by implication with the achievement of manhood. In so competitive a society where individual success is the index of both value and virtue one should not be surprised at the prevalence of violence. And in the depersonalized twentieth century city achieving notoriety may be the only practical way for the young male to be noticed--"to be somebody."

This chapter will consider the treatment in best sellers of attempts to control violence and maintain domestic order, international order, and finally the lawless order of the vigilante.

DOMESTIC ORDER

Government and its practitioners are not prominent in best sellers until the 1950s. After the Civil War when political corruption was widespread and well-known, several major American writers wrote popular political novels: in 1873 Mark Twain and Charles Dudley Warner produced The Gilded Age, and in 1880 Henry Adams brought out Democracy (anonymously). These were popular novels although not best sellers, but they are the only ones centered on the workings of government to be published here until after World War II.

The Post-War world was a dangerous one, a world of only two major powers facing each other and an atom bomb. The Cold War between the United States and the Union of Soviet Socialist Republics was fought not only beyond our borders but on the domestic front as well. With the establishment of the U.S.S.R. many Americans felt they faced an ideo- logical rival for the allegiance of the common people, and attempted to prevent subversion by self-purification. Americans were to be catalogued either as loyal or "un- American"--a marvelously elastic term; it could be made to cover anything the group making up the definition wished to include. After World War II Americans saw the U.S.S.R. not only as an ideological rival but as a rival for world power, and the fear of subversion reached hysterical heights. The 1950s began with the conviction of Alger Hiss, the trial of Communist Party leaders under the Smith Act, passage of the Subversive Activities Control Act (McCarran Act) as well as many state and federal investigations of the loyalty of government employees. And in 1954 came the Senate hearings chaired and dominated by Senator Joseph McCarthy.

Also beginning in 1950 the press was full of Senator Estes Kefauver's Special Investigating Committee examining the relationship between organized crime and political corruption. Committees of this sort were hardly new, but by this time many Americans spent a great deal of time watching television, and Congressional investigations were new in people's living rooms. Both the Kefauver and McCarthy hearings were televised, and the melodramatic atmosphere of these hearings allowed them to compete with the ever popular soap operas for the public's attention. The political importance of television was made sharply evident with the Nixon-Kennedy debates during the presidential election of 1960. The American public was now more exposed to information on government procedures than ever before.

The casual reader was now ready therefore for John F. Kennedy's study of Senators in Profiles in Courage in 1956 and for Allen Drury's novel Advise and Consent in 1959 describing the machinations of the Senate over the appointment of a new Secretary of State with a radical left past. And in the 1960s fuelled by the Bay of Pigs, the Cuba Crisis, Vietnam, the Civil Rights movement, and the assassinations of Medgar Evers, John F. Kennedy, Robert Kennedy, Malcolm X, and Martin Luther King Jr., Americans were evidently willing to read more about politics. The best seller list was enlarged in this direction by including Barry Goldwater's exposition of his political philosophy in Conscience of a Conservative in 1960, Seven Days in May in 1962, a novel by Fletcher Knebel and Charles Bailey of an attempted military coup in the United States, Theodore White's analysis of the presidential election of 1960 in The Making of a President (1962), the 1964 account of John F. Kennedy's death in Four Days in 1964, and finally

The Man, a 1964 novel by Irving Wallace detailing the
responses of officials and the public to the accidental
ascension of a black Senator to the presidency.

In casual references to American politics and politicians
earlier books were more respectful and less realistic. One
exception occurs in St. Elmo published in 1866 in the midst
of the problems of Reconstruction and widespread corruption;
this book avers that "statesmen were almost extinct in
America," replaced by politicians who "raved and ranted"
(464). Although the American presidency was occupied by a
singularly undistinguished lot (except for Grover Cleveland)
from Abraham Lincoln to Theodore Roosevelt, this is an
attitude unseen again in best sellers until the 1950s. In
George Barr McCutcheon's Graustark in 1901 a European character tells an American that in her country there is no
politics because the head of state, the king, is so by
birth. The American responds by describing the presidency:

"Do they know that it is to rule because they
have won the right and not because they were born
to it? . . . All men are equal in the beginning
in our land. The man who wins the highest gift
that can be bestowed by seventy millions of
people is the man who has brains and not title
as birthright." (68, 385)

Little Lord Fauntleroy appealing to a younger audience in
1886 invests the president with both intellect and good
character: "'When a man is very good and knows a great deal
he is elected president'" (34).

Contrast this with the president in Allen Drury's Advise
and Consent in 1959; he is highly intelligent, a very smart
politician, but crafty and unscrupulous. Or with the
realistic asssessments of actual American presidents by
Theodore White in 1962. He shows Lyndon Johnson to be
astute but provincial and not vested with dignity (131-34).
His analysis of Nixon while describing him as "a man of

major talent" (65), nonetheless portrays one quite capable
of the actions that would later require his resignation.
The popularity of such assessments of American presidents
may have come partly from the decline in hero-worship in
the culture, but must also have derived from the greater
exposure to both visual and auditory sources in the era of
television. Most Americans, for example, had seen Lyndon
Johnson displaying his surgical scar to television cameras.

In this new ambiance Vance Packard in The Hidden
Persuaders in 1957 discusses at some length the application
of merchandising techniques to the election of American
presidents. He points out that although the manipulative
approach to politics is as old as man, it has reached a new
level today when advertisers sell the president as they
would sell any other product. He describes Nixon himself
as having the advertising man's approach to achieving and
occupying public office; he will move from one policy to
another depending on whether he things he can sell it to
the public at large or to those with political power.
Packard's analysis was preceded the year before by Eugene
Burdick's novel The Ninth Wave in which the same techniques
were used to nominate a governor.

1964 introduced two presidents, one fictional and one
actual, with admirable qualities. In Four Days John Kennedy
is termed a president who made politics "a respectable
profession" for the first time in thirty years (66). But
since the book is the account of the assassination of a
president shortly after it happened this book is unique and
Kennedy is naturally a hero as well as a martyr. In the
same year Irving Wallace produced The Man, a novel in which
the president pro tem of the Senate, a black, inherits the
presidency by a series of accidents. Dilman, the president,
a sensitive intelligent man, walks carefully on an ill-
defined road between race prejudice and his own fears of
race prejudice. He recalls a ditty from childhood:

> Nigger and white man
> Playin' Seven Up
> Nigger win de money--
> Skeered to pick 'em up. (253)

He is impeached on trumped up charges, but not convicted.
He is depicted not as a hero, but as a man of courage torn
by doubts but still capable of action; his was a profile in
courage.

Of all politicians Senators are the subject of more best
sellers than any other officials--all in the 1950s and
1960s. In an unheroic age they appear as in Elmer Gantry
in 1927: "He was born to be a Senator. He never said anything important, and he always said it sonorously" (1).
Kennedy's Profiles in Courage while extolling certain
Senators keeps them human-size. In each instance of
political courage in this book what is at stake is a
political career rather than a basic moral principle. In
the Foreword Allan Nevins makes a distinction between "true
courage and fanatic courage." "True courage" is the courage
of a senator opposing the opinion of his constituents on
ordinary political questions rather than the "fanatic"
courage of an abolitionist standing for a basic principle.
John Quincy Adams, for example, is assigned "true courage"
for supporting the embargo to which his constituents were
adamantly opposed, rather than for his courage later in
introducing to the Congress a series of abolitionist bills,
bills opposed by most Americans as well as Congress.
Throughout Kennedy stresses the point that compromise is
essential and that there are "few if any issues where all
the truth and all the right and all the angels are one one
side" (5).

Corrupt Senators appear often as in Don't Go Near the
Water by William Brinkley in 1956 (74) and The Ugly American
by William J. Lederer and Eugene L. Burdick in 1958 (239ff.).
A sinister Senator attempting a coup to take over the U.S.

government for the military is a major figure in Seven Days
in May by Fletcher Knebel and Charles Bailey in 1962. The
most extended picture of the Senate and Senators is in
Allen Drury's Advise and Consent in 1959. The experience
of the author as a Washington newspaperman is evident in
his detailed account of large, small and trivial Senate
activities and interchanges. The Senate appears as a tight
little club of men always "bargaining between men's ideals
and their ambitions" (39). Actually ideals are visible in
only two Senators and profiles in courage are rare indeed.
They seem more concerned with their reputations among each
other than with their representation of political principles
or their constituents. They are ordinary people full of
foibles different from most of their constituents only in
having more ambition and more political intelligence.

In keeping with this downgrading of American officials
there is an attitude of disillusionment in many of these
books toward the American government in general. In a
conversation among American soldiers in From Here to
Eternity in 1951 Prew responds to a statement that everyone
in the United States has rights by saying: "'That's the
Constitution. Nobody believes that anymore'." His friend
counters with "'They all believe it. They just don't do
it. But they believe it. No one has any rights except
those he can grab and take away from others'."[4]

The activities of politicians in the Watergate scandal
of the 1970s should have been something less than a surprise
to the readers of best-selling fiction.

A few books mention the importance of law to orderly
orderly society. In 1958 Robert Traver in Anatomy of a
Murder declares that law is what keeps society from becoming
"a snarling jungle" (63). To James Michener in Hawaii in
1959 law "directs the ongoing of society. It is rooted in
the past, determines the present and protects the future"
(663). But the readers of most novels throughout the period

would come up from these sources with the impression that
law in the United States is unproductive because enforcement
is singularly ineffective. From reading these books one
would assume that the police are customarily lazy, stupid,
scared, bigoted, brutal and corrupt. Even in the early
books the reputation of the police is low. In 1869 Mark
Twain in Innocents Abroad notes that in Pompeii a soldier
was caught by the ashes of Vesuvius still standing on duty
because his warrior instinct forbade him to flee the
volcano: "Had he been a policeman he would have stayed
also--because he would have been asleep" (II-41). And in
Barriers Burned Away by E. P. Roe in 1872 a policeman,
asked to aid a citizen who has been robbed of five dollars,
says he cannot; to interfere with such men as the thief
would be too dangerous (42). In American detective stories,
even in the classical detective story, the successful
detective is the private detective or lawyer (as in the
case of Perry Mason) rather than an official charged with
enforcement of the law. And the private detective works
apart from and even in opposition to the police (this
contrasts sharply with their cooperation in most English
detective stories). Here the police are shown to be
incapable of the rational thought that might solve crimes.
In the tough guy detective stories (an American invention
of the 1920s) the police are as brutal and corrupt as the
criminals or even the hard-boiled private eye.

From the 1930s the urban scene is the locale of a great
many novels and it is crime and criminals who haunt these
books. Far from protecting the community the police are
part of the problem. Policemen appear to be routinely
brutal and often in league with law-breakers.[5] In The
Grapes of Wrath in 1939 the California police are in league
with landowners and there is no way migrant workers can get
justice from either their employers or the law. Two books
point out the double standard of white police in their

relations to blacks and whites. Raymond Chandler observes
that if a crime involves blacks as victims cops aren't
interested, and do nothing (15, 92). And in Another Country
James Baldwin in 1962 illustrates the brutality visited
gratuitously on blacks by white policemen (6-7).

Two books suggest that an exaggerated worship of the law
produces criminality when it tries to regulate liquor,
prostitution or any popular product or activity. In 1959
Goldfinger sees law as the "crystallized prejudices of the
community" (159) and when these prejudices see fit to outlaw
a popular product--as heroin in Britain--"Prohibition is
the trigger of crime" (11). Polly Adler in her 1953 autobiography as madame of a brothel quotes Harold Laski on the
relationship of too great respect for the law and lawlessness in the United States. The Puritan effect to control
everything, he says, produced too many laws restricting
activities the community will not relinquish such as
drinking and prostitution. Thus respect for law breeds
disrespect for its enforcement (41).

Consistently then in American best sellers throughout
the period the police are viewed with contempt. They are
disparaged by their authors and shown as faced with scorn
and derision by the community dependent on them for protection. They are not only denied heroic status, which
surely many earned, but they break the law as much as the
criminals they deal with. They are as brutal as these
criminals but have less power than those who make their
living outside the law. If these books mirror society then
the enforcers of law are breakers of law with less stature
in the community than the criminal. If the ideas in these
books influence their readers, the police will be held in
disdain by the American public.

POLITICAL THEORY

Political theory is even less popular than politicians
in best sellers; the former is considered boring, the latter
unsavory. Mrs. Miniver in 1940 expresses an attitude common
to many when she confesses herself weary of the exchange of
political ideas (237). As we have seen, the late nineteenth
century produced three best sellers that looked hopefully
toward economic and political reform: Progress and Poverty
in 1879, Bellamy's Utopia in 1888 and Coin's Financial
School in 1894. But most twentieth century comments on
political creeds reverberate with disillusion over the idea
that human beings are rational enough to govern themselves
under any system. They lived in a world that had spawned
two world wars, a world in which savagery combined with
modern efficiency to produce Nazism in what was regarded as
a most rational and civilized society; it became the century
of the refugee. Only H. G. Wells in 1921, just after the
end of World War I manages to examine irrational society
with his own extraordinary rationalism. He realizes that
". . . men do not act upon theories," but only when they see
a real danger or a practical necessity (835). To him the
major political issue since the American and French revolutions is the problem of the poor (822). He remarks the
increasing destructiveness of war, the increasing inter-
dependence of nations, the need for world health control
because of increased mobility. World government and international law are essential to the continuation of the human
race, and if the idea of nationality is not subordinated
humanity will perish (1,091-92). His enjoyment of ideas
allows him to regard the pursuit of these ideals as a great
adventure, but he also states: "There is no Millennium"
(891). Although different from Wells in almost everything
else Wendell Willkie in 1943 in the midst of the next world
war also advocates world government as a necessity for the
survival of the human race.

The one book of non-fiction specifically devoted to political theory among the twentieth century best sellers is Barry Goldwater's The Conscience of a Conservative in 1960. In the Foreword he expresses his belief that young people yearn for a return to conservatism. The major problem in any age is how to make order coexist with individual freedom, and "In our day order is pretty well taken care of" (14). What he hopes for in the future is a restoration of the individual freedom missing, he thinks, since the presidency of the Democrat Franklin Roosevelt "when that party was captured by the Socialist ideologues in and about the labor movement" (24). Goldwater is more accurately termed a reactionary than a conservative since what he wishes to conserve predates this century's legislation and culture. He is appalled by the graduated income tax since its aim is equalitarianism--". . . an objective that does violence to the Charter of the Republic and the laws of Nature. . . . We are all equal in the eyes of God but we are equal in no other respect [sic]" (62). He ascribes his political principles to the nature of man and "the truths God has revealed about His Creation," and puts them on a par with the Golden Rule, the Ten Commandments and Aristotle's Politics (Foreword). As we have seen the other major political writer of the twentieth century best sellers is Ayn Rand who espouses in fiction a doctrine similar to Goldwater's. She mixes her political doctrine--that government's only power should be to protect life and property from physical violence--so successfully with drama and romance that her two best sellers, one in 1943 and one in 1957 were both best sellers and are still read extensively. Altruism must play no role in government she states unequivocally: "'Every major horror of history was committed in the name of an altruistic motive'" (741). She also seems to condone violence if it supports one of her principles. In The Fountainhead in 1943 her hero, Roark, bombs a housing

project he designed because the builder has not followed
carefully enough his architectural plans. In best sellers
since World War II the American Right is much more prominent
than the Left in political theory.

Socialism, Communism and communism appear more often
than Fascism. Socialism is advocated in two books: in H. G.
Wells' Outline of History as we have seen, and in Edward
Bellamy's 1888 novel Looking Backward. Bellamy contrasts
the logic, equity and order of a socialist state with the
miseries and disorder of American capitalism of 1887. Now
and then socialists appear as casual but sympathetic
characters as in Hemingway's Farewell to Arms in 1929,
Thomas Heggen's Mr. Roberts in 1946, Patrick Dennis' Around
the World with Auntie Mame in 1958, and in Alexander King's
autobiography in the same year. King describes growing up
in the Lower East Side of New York City where all of the
intelligent young people hung out at the Fourteenth St.
Socialist headquarters. But he also describes the socialist
writings of Jack London and Upton Sinclair as the products
of "willful dogooders" who wrote "biased, didactic" books
(58-67). The term "do-gooder", a characterization that
confers both innocence and foolishness, is applied by Mary
McCarthy in 1963 to Norman Thomas, head of the American
Socialist Party. She portrays much of the American Left as
adopting the stance of do-gooder either as a rebellion
against more conservative parents (15-16) or as radical
chic (106). Socialists then appear to be pushed into their
political stance as a response to personal problems rather
than by a rational choice.

Sometimes socialists or communists appear as victims,
conveniently used to take the blame for any anti-social
activity although they actually had no connection to the
event. This red-herring technique is revealed as early as
1890 by Arthur Conan Doyle in A Study in Scarlet when
"RACHE" (revenge) is written in blood on the wall to suggest

that the perpetrators are Socialists. The newspapers accept
the suggestion without question although Holmes points out
that it is only a diversionary technique. From the 1930s on
in American novels many authors point out that all one has
to do to disgrace one active in social reform is to start a
rumor that he/she is a socialist or communist.[6] In all but
one of these the author is obviously opposed to the red-
herring plan. But in The Ugly American in 1958 the authors
applaud the machinations of Father Finian, a Jesuit who
views Communism as a religion rivalling Christianity for
adherents. He fights it by publishing clever propaganda
sheets, one purporting to come from Stalin and the Communists, another containing a spurious article by Marx
condemning the stupidity and backwardness of peasants and
justifying their slaughter (55ff.). The common use of the
terms socialist or communist as terms of opprobrium in the
United States is made evident in The Grapes of Wrath in 1939
when Steinbeck reports the embattled land-owner's definition
of communism: "'A red is any son-of-a-bitch that wants
thirty cents an hour when we're payin' twenty-five!'" (407).
And in The Young Lions in 1948 one soldier describes
another: "'Whitacre is a Communist from New York. . . .
He's crazy about Roosevelt'" (460). These writers are
reporting what they see and hear in America.

But a more common attitude is evidenced by authors who
express scorn for socialism and communism in their writing.
Both are assumed to lead inevitably to Russian Communism and Russian control. James M. Cain's Serenade in
1937 rejects Mexican socialism (46, 248), but since Cain is
contemptuous of so many ideas and institutions this may not
be particularly significant. Aldous Huxley and George
Orwell create monstrous societies out of socialism. Orwell
in 1984 points out that each variant of socialism that
appeared after 1900 gave up a bit more of the original
socialist aim of establishing liberty and equality until

1984 when the Party projected a society institutionalizing
in the name of socialism a system quite the opposite of the
original (204).

Most books of the 1950s, in the era of the Cold War explicitly reject socialism and Communism because their authors
identify them with the U.S.S.R. The actual Billy Graham and
the fictitious Father Finian in The Ugly American equate
Communism with the Devil. Both The Ugly American and The
Devil's Advocate (1959) see Communism as a religion with a
faith, ritual, and the zealous adherents of a religion, and
assume peaceful coexistence between Communism and traditional
religions to be impossible. Le Carré in his 1964 novel of
espionage has a sympathetic character contrast the Christian
view of the sanctity of human life with the ruthless view
of a Communist agent in East Germany (144). Several books
present individual communists as despicable human beings
with contempt for the human race.[7] Le Carré shows Communist
agents willing to bomb a crowded restaurant on the grounds
that individual rights have no standing against the rights
of the whole which will best be served in this case by ter-
rorism (132). He also introduces an anti-Semitic East German
Communist (233). Goldwater in defining his political philosophy in 1960 is so appalled by Communism that he opposes
the United Nations, any test ban treaty, any disarmament
policies, and cultural exchanges with the U.S.S.R.; we must
win the Cold War (86, 106, 118) whatever its relation to a
hot one. It is interesting to contrast Goldwater's view that
socialists subordinate "all other considerations to man's
material well being" (9-10) with Mellors in Lady Chatterley's
Lover in 1932. Mellors thinks both capitalism and Bolshevism
are killing off "'the human thing and worshipping the
mechanical thing'" (256). To him Bolshevism and capitalism
are equally guilty of making machines of men (41).

By far the most vitriolic on this subject is J. Edgar
Hoover who published Masters of Deceit in 1958; this book

came with the prestige of his office as head of the F.B.I.
He too sees the Cold War against Communism and the U.S.S.R.
as a religious war and asserts that Marx's call for a war
against religion was "the cornerstone of communist philosophy" (14-15). ". . . Atheism was the first step toward
Communism," but this atheism set up an evil religion (26,
106); Chapter 23 is entitled: "Communism--a False Religion."
In his history of the American Communist Party he indicates
that it sought power after the establishment of the U.S.S.R.
by subverting our instutitions and traditions, and was made
up mainly of foreigners (55). The Abraham Lincoln Brigade
of Americans who volunteered to fight with the Loyalists in
the Spanish Civil War was not interested in the Spanish
Republic, but only in advancing Bolshevism, and used any
tactics including sex to recruit (72). He asserts firmly:
"Communists are not Americans [sic]" (102). He urges all
citizens to get involved in the struggle against Communism
in the United States; report any information you might have
about the Communist conspiracy (310). He does suggest that
you not confuse dissent with disloyalty, but the program he
assigns to the Party would make such confusion likely:
defend academic freedom, stop the prosecution of Communists,
curtail defense, repeal the draft, outlaw the atomic bomb
and use parades for propaganda for all of these goals (199,
239). He pictures Communists as Sax Rohmer pictured Fu
Manchu: omniscient, omnipotent devils, "barbarians in modern
dress" (99, 103). This is an attitude common to all books
dealing with conflicts with the U.S.S.R. or Communists in
East Asia. The Green Berets, The Ugly Americans as well as
Goldwater and Hoover assign almost superhuman intelligence,
intuition and cleverness to Communists wherever they are.

The American government in these books appears as a
government of men (and weak men at that) rather than a
government of laws. Nor is it good at its fundamental
task--keeping order and enforcing laws. Yet the American

government is highly approved when a specific opinion is vouchsafed. But change in the direction of more government, especially in the direction of more government control is highly disapproved.

WAR AND INTERNATIONAL ORDER

The shift from Rudyard Kipling's Barrack Room Ballads in 1890 to Joseph Heller's Catch-22 in 1961 is an upheaval of earthquake proportions in attitudes toward war. In the first fifty years of this study novels often extol the beauties of war whatever the issues that caused the war. In Kipling's The Light That Failed in 1891, for example, Dick, an artist, loves war because it inspires his painting (165, 226). He looks forward to a sojourn in South America where, he believes, there is always the possibility of war, and he is delighted at the "glorious certainty of war" in the Sudan at any moment (237). War is not prettied up here--there is lots of gore as in the description of a soldier hacked in two--but it offers an opportunity for heroism. Issues involved in the breakdown of international order are never examined. But war in many of these early books offers a chance to find one's manhood in courage and the exercise of force. Oppenheim in The Great Impersonation in 1920 allows one of his older characters to say regret-fully: "'A war in my younger days . . . might have made a man of me'" (7). War is regarded not just as a developer of the manhood of the individual male but of the manhood of a nation. In 1905 Hill's Manual . . ., meditates on the Spanish-American War: "The War developed a type of solid Americanism, and it thrilled us with the knowledge that the type was a heroic one" (140). And in the rest of the book history is dealt with as a series of glorious battles (see pp. 357-68).

Stephen Crane's The Red Badge of Courage in 1895 for the first time depicts modern depersonalized war where the glory of whites-of-the-eyes combat has been replaced by battles dependent on remote machines, where the soldier never sees the enemy and spends most of his time slogging through mud or sitting waiting at the side of the road. The youth who had thrilled to stories of heroic battles realizes in the actual war that this was fantasy (7). A dead soldier on the battlefield doesn't look like a hero or a martyr, but an ordinary mortal whose foot protrudes from a worn out shoe (22). Veterans of the Civil War recognized Crane's war as a realistic picture of their war, although Crane himself had never seen military action at the time he wrote the book.

Novels of World War I continue in this vein with the horrors of war now divorced from heroism. Two books in 1929 set the tone that predominates through World War II. Erich Maria Remarque's All Quiet on the Western Front describes the reactions of young German soldiers to World War I. Those not physically destroyed are psychically devastated and without glory. They had been taught that one's greatest duty is to one's country, but in the war began to see that "death throes are stronger" (12). Hemingway's A Farewell to Arms in the same year took much the same point of view: war has no glory and "The sacrifices were like the stockyard of Chicago if nothing was done with the meat except to bury it" (185).

But World War I appears in relatively few books, its causes cloudy and obscured by diplomacy. Immediately after the war H. G. Wells uses it to preach the necessity to end war forever. He describes the progress of civilization from the ancient Romans with their human sacrifices, gladiators, "organization of murder as a sport" when "the conscience of mankind was weaker and less intelligent than now" (422-23). But conscience and intelligence evidently do not extend to modern war which has "become a universal disaster, blind and monstrously destructive; it bombs the

baby in the cradle and sinks the food-ships that cater for
the non-combatant to the neutral" (VI). His usual optimism
allows him to see a fearless future with international order
restored along with general prosperity, and nationalism
destroyed by cosmopolitanism. Only H. G. Wells and Wendell
Willkie look forward to permanent peace under the aegis of
an international organization. But such hopes fade after
World War II. In 1946 Taylor Caldwell in This Side of
Innocence speaks scornfully of those who expect things to
be better after a war; this is said during every war and
disillusion always follows (156).

A flood of books about World War II began coming out in
the late 1940s maintaining much the same tenor as those of
World War I. One small new element that recurs often is a
humorous but critical look at foolish rules rigidly enforced
by the army bureaucracy as in See Here, Private Hargrove in
1942 and No Time for Sergeants in 1954. The rules of the
armed forces are taken into paranoid hands in Herman Wouk's
The Caine Mutiny in 1951 and Pierre Boulle's The Bridge
Over the River Kwai in 1954. A major change from earlier
books came in the more graphic description of wounds and
death in combat. As we have seen, accounts of sexual
activities involved much more explicit and frank descriptions of physical details; relations between the sexes had
become little more than their physical contact described in
great detail. Much the same happens in war novels with full
physical particulars of wounds and death on the battlefield
minutely detailed. In fact the reader may become thoroughly
familiar with each drop of blood, invasion of maggots, and
other physical minutiae, but miss much of its effects on the
wounded man. Stephen Crane's realism has been lost in
sensationalism.

Such realism in describing gore as well as in reactions
of men to the army and to combat, as in Mailer's The Naked
and the Dead, wiped out nineteenth century patriotic

shibboleths. In Mr. Roberts in 1946 it is suggested that
we talk not of "'our honored dead'" but of "'poor dead
bastards'" (166). Heroes fought in other wars but not in
this. Finally Heller's Catch-22, outrageous, hilarious
and tragic points out the fundamental absurdity of war as
it recounts Yossarian's struggle to stay alive by avoiding
combat. This book added its title to the English language.
It should be noted however that it became a best seller only
a decade after its 1961 publication when it found a sharper
context in opposition to the war in Vietnam.

In contrast to World War I whose issues were cloudy,
World War II is regarded in books in which it appears as
inevitable and our participation thoroughly justified.
Willkie in 1943 sees World War I as having no clear purpose
whereas World War II is a crusade against evil. His title
for Chapter 12 is "This Is a War of Liberation." Fascism
is full-fleshed in three books: The Young Lions, a novel by
Irwin Shaw in 1948, The Diary of a Young Girl by Anne Frank
in 1952 and the full scale study The Rise and Fall of the
Third Reich by William Shirer in 1960. Anne Frank's diary
probably had more popular impact than the others because
as book, play and movie it gave the reader a chance to
identify with a particularly appealing and tragic victim of
the Nazis. Books about World War II began appearing while
the war was going on, but Fascism and Nazism are rarely
described; usually they are identified only as the political
doctrine of the enemy.

By the 1960s new issues justified war in these novels.
Leon Uris restores heroism in what he regards as a just war,
and in some the Cold War seems to restore respectability to
hot war. In The Green Berets in 1965 whatever the United
States does to curb communism serves "the cause of freedom
around the world" (332, 21). This is a sentiment shared by
The Ugly American. While the latter faults the United
States for its arrogance and naïveté in sending representa-

tives to other nations without knowledge of the culture or
even the language, nonetheless it accepts without question
the necessity to fight the Communists wherever they are.

The only specifically pacifist books in the whole
spectrum of best sellers are those by H. G. Wells and
Edward Bellamy. In the Utopian society described by
Bellamy in 1888 conscription is used not for war but for an
equitable distribution of the work load required for a
sound economy. Several books suggest that war is inevitable
because fighting is a natural instinct. Tarzan, his creator
observes, unlike other animals kills for pleasure as well
as for food or in self-defense (122). In Jack London's
The Call of the Wild "blood lust" is a human instinct (74).
Although Rhett Butler in Gone with the Wind thinks all wars
are in reality "'money squabbles'", he is certain that wars
will always be fought because fighting is part of the nature
of the male; men love war even more than they love women
(231, 261). In the feminist novel The Heavenly Twins in
1893 Angelica suggests that the cause of war may be that
boys are raised by the stick; girls, raised more gently,
are less likely to use force to solve a problem, but they
are not in charge of governments.

Readers of war novels of the 1950s and early 1960s might
well wonder whether the war in Vietnam was worth it,
although they would be torn between facing the disasters
of war or abandoning the world to the U.S.S.R. and
Communism.

And the holocaust of future atomic war was evident in
John Hersey's 1946 report of the immediate and long-range
agony of the Japanese people after the bomb was dropped on
Hiroshima. Nevil Shute's 1957 novel On the Beach foretells
the end of life on earth after an atomic war.

War in these books is not attractive, but inevitable.

LAWLESS ORDER

Unquestionably the most interesting and pervasive form
of public order to appear in these books is lawless order--
the vigilanteism characteristic of the United States.
Private citizens, using or threatening violence, mete out
their own version of justice outside the law, ostensibly as
a means of protecting society. This behavior is not the
policy of ordinary criminals nor of revolutionary groups,
but of established classes protecting the status quo. Such
vigilantes have the support of the community; they are
considered primary protectors of decent society; they are
guardians of morality as well as social stability and are
held in high esteem. Their rationalization for these
actions give them respect and honor: they break the law for
the good of humanity.

Evidently this peculiarly American institution developed
on the moving frontier, when frontiersmen and settlers
moves west faster than the United States government and
some substitute for law enforcement was necessary. (In
Canada and in other parts of America where government
arrived before settlers, such a system did not evolve.)
But after law enforcement agencies were established both
the spirit and activities of the vigilantes continued from
the colonial period to the present. In the best sellers
these practices are noted and respected although Harold Bell
Wright in 1907 describes a vigilante committee perverting
its protective purpose by robbing banks (272-73). Various
forms and geographical locations of vigilante action appear
in these books. In fact the West (and all of what is now
the United States was at one time in history a frontier)
protected the nester and the cattle industry from economic
incursions and from each other, and guarded older settlers
from new ethnic groups brought in to perform some economic
function such as building the railroads. The white South
protected itself from the newly freed blacks and carpet-

baggers through the Knights of the White Camellias and the
Ku Klux Klan. In 1915 the KKK was reconstituted with a
program designed to protect society from blacks, Catholics,
Jews, birth control, the League of Nations, labor organizers
and their versions of general "immorality." With this
platform it moved north. It acquired such supporters in
the North as Sinclair Lewis' Elmer Gantry (365). Most such
groups inhabited rural areas although the Ku Klux Klan
burned crosses in cities as well in the 1920s and 1930s.
According to best sellers cities developed their own
versions of lawless order with urban gangs, and tough
private eyes. Even the detective in the classical detective
story, although loath to use violence, often operated
outside the law; Erle Stanley Gardner's Perry Mason is
willing to catch criminals by fair or foul means as he
makes clear in The Case of the Sulky Girl in 1933 (299-30).

In these books the only criticisms of vigilante groups
center on the KKK. The first is by Arthur Conan Doyle in
"The Five Orange Pips" in 1892 in which he discusses the
"outrages" of "this terrible secret society" in terrorizing
blacks (128). And the fact that Elmer Gantry believes in
the later KKK is in itself a criticism by Sinclair Lewis.
But apart from these two books the KKK is let alone, and is
indeed accepted on its own terms in one of the most popular
books--Gone With the Wind in 1936. As the civil rights
movement develops, criticism becomes more general in books
by Lillian Smith, John Griffin and black writers such as
James Baldwin and Frank Yerby. The latter in The Vixens in
1947 suggests that the poor whites "still too enraptured
by the mystical brotherhood of whiteness to comprehend
democracy" are persuaded by rich and powerful whites to
crush blacks. As a result they burn the schoolhouses of
black children leaving "the earth spattered with their blood
and brains" (9, 306). The most moving protest against mob
action is the brave defense Atticus puts up against

potential lynchers in Harper Lee's <u>To Kill a Mockingbird</u> in
1960. He is clearly a hero--a rational moral man willing
to stand up for his principles although he is endangering
his life and limb. But such heroes of individual moral
decision are few.

In the first decade of the twentieth century (appropriately during Theodore Roosevelt's presidency), several books
explicitly explain and defend vigilante action. <u>The
Virginian</u> by Owen Wister in 1902 offers the most extensive
vindication. Molly, a schoolteacher from the East, is
horrified to find her Western pupils playing "lynch the
rustler" at school recess (425). The narrator injects the
notion that one cannot be absolute about the law: should
one disobey a trespassing sign to prevent a murder? In a
subsequent discussion with a judge who has defended a recent
lynching of cattle thieves, Molly asks if he favors lynching
in general. His response: "'Of burning Southern negroes in
public, no, of hanging cattle-thieves in private, yes.'"
And he sees no likeness in principle between these:

> "I consider the burning a proof that the South
> is semi-barbarous and the hanging a proof that
> Wyoming is determined to become civilized. We
> do not torture our criminals when we lynch them.
> We do not invite spectators to enjoy their death
> agony. We put no such hideous disgrace upon the
> United States. We execute our criminals by the
> swiftest means and in the quietest way."

Molly points out that the principle is the same--both are
in defiance of the law; in both citizens take law into their
own hands. The judge's response is that both courts and
Constitution have their source in ordinary citizens. And
lately juries have been too lenient. So such mob action
"'. . . so far from being a <u>defiance</u> of the law, it is an
<u>assertion</u> of it [sic]'" (431-36). In another incident Molly
objects when the Virginian and his enemy Trampas are about

to have a shootout to settle their quarrel. The Virginian answers: there is no way out "'. . . save the ancient, eternal way between man and man. It is only the great mediocrity that goes to law in these personal matters'" (463). So manhood as well as social order are dependent on direct action.

John Fox Jr., writing of the Kentucky mountains in The Trail of the Lonesome Pine, declares that the volunteers who keep order are the "vanguards of civilization" (98). He also notes that since they own stills to make illegal alcoholic beverages, they avoid officers of the law (140). This forces them to keep their own order. Furthermore mountaineers find it hard to understand abstract regard for law and order; they think only of their own immediate interests.

A sympathetic character in Zane Grey's The Spirit of the Border in 1906 argues that one must take one's own revenge: "'A frontiersman must take his choice of succumbing or cutting his way through flesh and blood. Blood will be spilled; if not yours, then your foe's . . .'" (200).

Rex Beach writing of the Yukon in this period sees the coming of law to the frontier as the coming of injustice; "spoilers" (and that is the title of the book) take over and exploit the land and its people under the law. The basic theme of the book is conflict between a legal code recently brought to the area and the moral code preserved by volunteers. An admired character regrets the coming of law to the Yukon because it puts too much power into too few hands instead of in "'our courage and our Colts'" (30). He applies this to himself: "'I've been beyond the law for years and I want to stay there, where life is just what it was intended to be--a survival of the fittest'" (31). He is also fond of saying, and he is quoted many times, "'What I want, I take'." Another much quoted sentence in this book is a saying said to be popular in the region: "'There's never a law of God or man runs north of Fifty-Three'."

All novels of the West and most of the South present some vigilante action; social order is identified with the status quo which they assume can be maintained only by vigilante violence. After Prohibition city gangs asserted a kind of order, defining and enforcing their own geographic and economic turf. But this is significantly different from vigilanteism. Its acceptance by the community is based on fear as shown in Louis Beretti in 1929 when a teacher urges students to report to the police the hiding place of certain escaped convicts in their neighborhoods. The children are shocked and respond: do you want us to get bumped off? (7-8). Even in Damon Runyon's almost amiable view of city gangs, associating with gangs is healthy, associating with cops is dangerous to life and limb (120). The gangster is feared but he is also admired for his power, toughness, and even at times for his cruelty. In Butter-field-8 in 1935 James Cagney is applauded for depicting "America's ideal gangster" (59, 42, 55). But unlike a vigilante the gangster is of lower class origin, and his power rests on fear rather than the higher moral law claimed by the vigilante.

In city novels the maintenance of social order is also claimed by the tough detective. Like the gangster his origins are in the urban working class: his methods—violence of all kinds, including torture—are similar to those of the gangster. In Strip for Murder by Richard Prather in 1955 the detective is involved in eight violent deaths and twelve other instances of violent actions. The hard-boiled detective is cynical and tough, but in one important way he differs from the gangster. He sees the law as ineffective in protecting the community, and so sets himself up as the champion of a morality defined by himself. Mickey Spillane, an enormously popular writer, defines the

role of his private eye in I, the Jury (note the title).
When Mike Hammer, the hard-boiled detective, looks for a
killer he does it in these terms:

> "And, by Christ, I'm not letting the killer go
> through the tedious process of the law. You know
> what happens, damn it. They get the best lawyer
> there is and screw up the whole thing and wind up
> a hero." (11)

Juries are cold and impartial: "'But this time I'm the law
and I'm not going to be cold and impartial'" (11). Cops are
always inept (42-43); legal trials offer too many loopholes
(23). In talking to a suspect he declares if he finds the
man who murdered his friend he will kill him: "'Even if I
can't prove it, he dies anyway. In fact I don't even have
to be convinced too strongly'" (28). The tough detective
is a new kind of hero--messy, irrational, accustomed to
breaking the law, but offering his own justice in a world
out of control.

Why are Americans in their popular literature so prone
to admire individuals and groups operating outside the law?
The only instance of a criminal admired for his actions in
a European novel that reached the best seller lists in
America is Tom Faggus in Lorna Doone. He is another version
of Robin Hood, stealing from the rich to give to the poor.
He is generous and kind, but it is never said that he is
morally justified. But these American novels invoke a
"higher law" that defines and enforces what the community,
and theoretically, God, sees as the good of society even if
the law doesn't. This higher law negates statute law
because it springs naturally from the basic moral nature
of man.

Surely one of the reasons the American uses this concept
so freely to justify illegality was that he saw himself as
freer, more moral and closer to an innocent nature than
other people--a new Adam in a new Eden.[8] He is uniquely

emancipated from the past and therefore in a condition to decide issues on the basis of his natural moral sense. He is freed from the Old World not only by geography but by his own sense of moral mission, a mission embarked on at emigration. R. W. B. Lewis quotes an editorial in the 1839 Democratic Review describing the American as endowed with a "'clear conscience unsullied by the past'."[9] To Thomas Jefferson this meant that no generation has a right to bind the next; each should reevaluate and remake the laws by which which they will be governed. While tradition could be flaunted and laws changed to accord with new circumstances, it would always be a society ordered by law.

But according to the evidence of best sellers--and they seem to illustrate the conclusions of recent studies of the history of violence in the United States--both individuals and communities frequently took it upon themselves to decide what is justice quite apart from the laws, theirs or those of a previous generation. In executing their version of extra-legal justice, they rationalized their actions by referring to a "higher law" which in their view upheld a more fundamental morality than that of statute law. As we have seen vigilanteism developed for the ordering of society on the frontier when settlement moved faster to new land than did government. When government finally did move in, however, vigilante order did not disappear but remained sometimes as adjunct and sometimes as rival to law enforcement. In most of the United States but especially in the South both during and after slavery blacks were customarily denied proper legal procedures and kept in what whites considered proper order by private and usually violent action. Sporadically many disadvantaged groups came to feel the heavy hand of vigilante action. Until the 1960s social violence in the United States was designed not by those challenging the status quo, but by those defending the status quo. American vigilantes came from the Establishment.

308

It seems curious that a country so proud of its political institutions should at the same time accept without question so much disregard of those institutions. This ambivalence is unremarked but quite clear in the most popular American books.

Chapter 11: WHAT BEST SELLERS SOLD, 1865-1965

When one purchases a book for entertainment one also buys inadvertently a compendium of social values and conventions. Best sellers of this period weave a complex pattern of myths that bring order into a confusing world and a pattern of mores that allow a comfortable and unquestioning adjustment to the myths. The most popular books offer middle class readers and those aspiring to that status satisfying and often flattering visions of their hopes, experiences and circumstances. The myths present readers with values they are expected to accept axiomatically; the mores offer approved ways of behavior to live up to the myths.

It is no surprise to find that one myth accepted in these books throughout the period distinguished the United States from all other countries as the land where, if he tries, every man can go from rags to riches, and no one need live in poverty. That there was greater social mobility in the United States than in most other countries was a fact. But it was also a fact that almost all of those who achieved wealth started from a solid middle class background. However descriptive it might have been of an earlier America the equality of economic opportunity implied in this myth hardly described conditions in the burgeoning slums of the post Civil War period. The myth was nonetheless as important as the fact, and became itself a fact of popular culture, probably helping to produce heartening hope as well as higher levels of productivity.

Although improving one's lot remained a consistent aim in books throughout the period, the means to this end underwent a major change in the 1930s. Up to that time the reader was assured that hard work would guarantee financial success: Horatio Alger's Ragged Dick in the 1860s shed his rags by so doing. But the writers of popular how-to manuals in the 1930s were addressing an audience mired in the poverty of the Great Depression despite hard work. They suggest, therefore, that hard work is irrelevant, that money comes from "positive thinking." The title of one of the most popular of this genre--and the book is still read widely--is Think and Grow Rich (1937) by Napoleon Hill. To get on the path to wealth one must train one's personality to manipulate others. This suggested change in tactics is consonant with a shift in the American economy from emphasis on production to distribution and service. The myth is still in place but the mores have changed.

That one's major aim in life should be the accumulation of money by whatever means is not questioned. The possession of money is relatively unimportant, but making money, by whatever means, is essential to self-esteem and is seen as both a duty and a sign of virtue. The ability to buy more material goods and to lead a more comfortable life is mere serendipity: the essential reason for acquiring money is to prove oneself by the process of earning it. For the modern male, and it is he who is addressed on this issue, it is a major test of manhood. If one's efforts have been futile the personal and social consequences are far-reaching. Because the United States is the land of opportunity for all, the failure to escape poverty indicates not just a lack of talent in making money but a defective character. To be poor as a child may offer advantages in that it trains the child to work hard to get out of that state. But Americans who remain poor as adults suffer not only the deprivations that ensue anywhere in the world but they experience also a particular shame and humiliation. Whatever other virtues they may have, they are missing a virtue expected in the United States where poverty is incompatible with self-respect.

The social consequences of this myth are important in
actual American politics. If the system already provides
an opportunity for all to get ahead, then major reforms
such as those taken by other industrialized nations in the
direction of social planning are irrelevant. If you don't
get ahead in the United States it must be your own fault
not the fault of a defective economic and political system.
Middle class Americans tend to regard the poor who accept
aid from government as either lazy bums or welfare cheats.
Perhaps this is also why the United States has never
developed a strong socialist party with political clout.
Twentieth century best sellers clearly reflect this lack of
interest in social reform. Apart from H. G. Wells the only
reforms suggested are reactionary--to rescind social
planning instituted in Roosevelt's New Deal or even in
Wilson's New Freedom.

Either stated or implied in these books throughout the
period is the conviction that the United States is the land
where the individual can best realize himself. But best
sellers are not describing the individualist defending his/
her own particular opinions and beliefs if they differ from
those of the community. As we have seen, this kind of
individualist is rare in these books. Apparently the man
who fails in worldly pursuits--and this individualist is
likely to find himself in this position--whatever else he
may achieve, is less interesting to the authors of American
best sellers than he/she is to our major writers. These
popular books illustrate the point made so well by
Tocqueville and Carl Becker that American individualism is
the right to get ahead rather than the right to be different. And indeed the individualism required for socially
acceptable achievement may act as a curb on the individualism of being independent. To be accepted, to be promoted
one must accept the conventions of society and be one of the
group. One must do what others do not because what they do

is most productive or morally right but because it is
accepted mores. The common use of the concept "best
sellers" in advertising books is an application of this
notion: one should buy a particular book not because of
its literary or philosophical quality, or even because it's
a good read, but only because it is popular. Mass production extends to more than material goods, and one must be
like everyone else. The French architect Le Corbusier
expresses it best in a drawing in his book When the Cathe-
drals Were White: it is a picture of an American community
like Levittown where each house, sturdy and comfortable, is
an exact copy of every other house; he labels it "the
American Dream."

But the idea that everyone can get ahead in the United
States is seriously infringed by the myths about human
nature that pervade these books: character, personality and
intelligence are biologically determined by sex, race and
nationality. If this is so then an environment offering
equality of opportunity will make a difference only to those
endowed by nature with the ability to take advantage of such
opportunity; these fortunate ones are white males of
northern European ancestry.

The persistence of racial stereotypes through the period
is startling. As we have seen, Occidentals are depicted
as intelligent, energetic and enterprising; Africans as
lazy, stupid and prone to extraordinary sexual exploits;
Orientals as sneaky and sinister; Jews, translated in these
books from a religious ethnic group to a race, as cowardly,
endowed with high intelligence, but intelligence always used
for nefarious purposes. Such qualities are believed to
inhere in every member of each race, and because they are
inherent they are also immutable. World War II, fought
against an enemy that boasted of its racism, softened this
enough to permit Lillian Smith's novel Strange Fruit in 1944
to become the first best seller to portray the brutality and

tragedy of race prejudice. But Strange Fruit stood alone
on the best seller list for almost two decades. Americans
were apparently unwilling to buy such books in quantities
large enough to make them best sellers until the civil
rights movement of the 1950s and 1960s educated or at least
made them aware of the problem, so that they were willing
to buy John Howard Griffin's Black Like Me, James Baldwin's
Another Country, and Irving Wallace's The Man. It should
be kept in mind, however, that these books were accompanied
on the best seller lists by two books by Kyle Onstott
embodying and even enhancing the old stereotypes. And in
casual references in other books the stereotype of the black
was drawn with the same old lines.

Jews as well as blacks also benefited in popular literature from the fact that the enemy in World War II was racist
and specifically anti-Semitic. The three novels centered
on the Jews in the 1940s--The Young Lions by Irwin Shaw in
1948 and the two novels of Leon Uris--portray them as brave
and selflessly idealistic, but again, casual characters in
other books at the same time maintain the old stereotype.

Nationality in best sellers appears as a subdivision of
race with an inherent national character defining the group.
In each case national as well as racial qualities determine
the goals an individual can attain. They provide avenues
of achievement and block others. The superiority of the
white race and of northern European nationalities--espe-
cially British, German and their American descendents--is
unquestioned. Such superiority even affects the language
of these books. (One is to feel complimented when commended
by the statement "That's white of you.") These racial and
national myths must have been both comforting and uplifting
to the middle class American reader because they vindicated
long established American policies, at home and abroad.
They explained and justified treating other races and
nationalities as less than human and provided an immutable

natural superiority to explain the right of the white
northern European to dominate the multi-national society
found in the United States. The durability as well as the
universality of these stereotypes makes one wonder if racism
and national chauvinism can ever be eradicated even if other
convenient spacegoats are invented.

Another kind of heritage--sex--also defines and limits
the potentialities of individuals who appear in these books.
The female is irrepressibly emotional, incapable of serious
thought, physically and psychically frail. Her choices in
life are few. Because of her nature the mores of the
society confine her to the home, helping husband and
children. Manuals on how to be a success are addressed only
to men. In fiction throughout the whole hundred years with
few exceptions the authors, male and female, accepted the
subordinate role of women. One of the favorite plots
presents a woman of an independent turn of mind subdued by
a strong man, properly playing the role of the domineering
male. This offers the possibility of sensational melodrama
before the woman subsides happily into her socially accepted
place. These stories are scattered throughout the period:
Edna in St. Elmo in 1866; Diana in The Sheik in 1921;
Marjorie Morningstar in Wouk's 1955 novel. In the whole
century of novels a mere handful allow a woman to maintain
an independent spirit without succumbing to the stereotype:
Jo in Little Women in 1868; Angelica in The Heavenly Twins
in 1893; Scarlett O'Hara in Gone With the Wind in 1936, and
Auntie Mame in 1958. All but the last were the products of
women writers.

In these books nature endows men much more abundantly;
they are capable of thought and action in all fields except
child-bearing. The male is limited not by a lack of ability
or opportunity but by two absolute requirements: he must be
physically strong and must exercise that strength even to
the point of brutality, and he must be an economic success.

Whatever other talents he may have are insignificant should he not live up to the stereotype of the ideal male. He must be careful not to let the so-called "feminine virtues" of thoughtfulness, warmth, sensitivity interfere with machismo. Sadism in depicting both sexes increases a great deal in books published from the 1920s on. Perhaps since the economy required less physical strength and even warfare was mechanized, the male in order to fulfill the concept of "he-man" had to find other avenues for the practice of physical power. Whether this increase in violence was a fact of their society or not, readers of popular fiction were evidently happy to read about it.

Relationships between the sexes change in what appear to be sensational ways in the twentieth century. The language describing sexual relations becomes specific and graphic, and indeed it seems as though the relationship of men to women is nothing but a relationship of the sense organs. But as one examines this change closely it is less dramatic: the woman's role is still primarily to serve the male, but emphasis has shifted from domestic to sexual service. Again it is well to remember that vast numbers of sentimental romances with only the gentlest hints of sexual confrontation were being read at the same time (although not necessarily by the same people), but the role of the woman was fundamentally similar--this woman too was in service to the man.

Another myth that permeates these books is the identification of industrial progress with the progress of the human race. In all books in which the question is relevant particular pride is expressed in the industrial achievements of the United States; even European authors tout American ingenuity and mechanical engineering. But there is also ambivalence here: God's gift to European-Americans--the new Chosen People--of un unspoiled beneficent nature is being rapidly changed by the exercise of America's talent for

industrial production. The farmer is absolved from guilt
in changing nature because he does so by using the laws of
God and nature and by coddling God's gift. And as America
becomes more industrial, nostalgia for what is euphemis-
tically described as the simple life of the farmer remains
strong. In a country rapidly becoming urbanized readers of
best sellers were often offered escape into what was presented as a simpler and more honest past. Only Steinbeck
observes and deplores the application of the machine to
farming and the development of agribusiness.

The city is regarded with distaste and distrust throughout; it breeds misery and devastates both nature and people.
In the earlier books the city tempts its inhabitants to
sexual and financial vice as they try their fortunes. Some
books, published after the Great Depression of the 1930s
portray the hopelessness of a subculture of poverty residing
in urban slums. Whatever the specific accusations, the city
is not a healthy environment either physically or morally.

The myths are various, but whether true or false, they
explain a complicated world in a simple and usually soothing
way. They not only offer happy endings but justify the
reader's own attitudes and actions. To treat races and
nationalities other than one's own as inferior seems natural
and morally justified. To abdicate personal judgment in
favor of popular positions, to equate the pursuit of money
with the pursuit of happiness are acceptable attitudes. To
confine women to a narrow path is not only comfortable but
orthodox. The books are also reassuring in their promise
that one can get ahead by one's own efforts whether by hard
work or by developing an attractive personality.

To me the most striking impression of these best sellers
is their strange combination of sensationalism and conservatism. No one is sure what makes a book a best seller, but
sensationalism seems necessary to give a novel such status
although the kind of melodrama that appeals in one era may

not in another. In the period 1865-1965 biography had
nothing like the popularity it has since achieved: only a
handful made it to the best seller lists, and three of
these were sensational--two of actresses and one the madame
of a whore-house. One would expect the new theories of
Freud and of behaviorism agitating the burgeoning field of
psychology in early twentieth century America to create a
popular interest in biography, but this was not the case.
Because of the centrality of sex to Freudian psychology one
would expect his theories and bastard versions thereof to
set off a popular flood of sensational life studies. But
this did not happen until the 1970s, another illustration
of the half century retardation in popular literature. The
decade of the 1970s has been enchanted with tales of the
supernatural, monsters, the disastrous results of scientific
experimentation, and of natural disaster. John Sutherland's
study of the best sellers of the 1970s describes the introduction in many books (such as The Omen, The Shining, The
Exorcist) as a character missing in earlier best sellers--
the child possessed by the devil. Perhaps the appearance
of a demonic child offered consolation to the readers of the
1970s who were surprised and disappointed at the results of
their own efforts at child rearing following the rational
methods proposed by that earlier best seller by Dr. Benjamin
Spock. But the hundred years of this study exhibited no
such interest; the supernatural in these books centers on
God and religious institutions. Sex and violence account
for most of the sensationalism, and they are everpresent.

The essential conservatism of these books is profound.
Stereotypes of races, nationalities and the sexes persist
throughout the whole period. Intellectual changes and
changes in the mores penetrate the best seller list very
slowly--in many cases only after half a century. Darwinism,
Freud and new movements in the arts took about that length
of time to appear significantly in the novels. The

Realist's conception of nature as neither benign nor malign
but merely neutral in human affairs intrudes, and rarely at
that, only in mid-twentieth century. As we have seen,
changes in sexual attitudes are radical in language and in
graphic descriptions of sex acts, but relationships between
the sexes remain much the same. Political conservatism
increases significantly between the nineteenth and twentieth
centuries. In a few nineteenth century books socialism
appears as a benevolent system. But in the twentieth
century, particularly after the Russian Revolution socialism
becomes anathema. Books centered on political ideology were
all conservative or, more accurately, reactionary, looking
back to the nineteenth century.

Mores of the past often appear in these books as though
they were contemporaneous, and current practices and beliefs
are often conspicuously absent from books about the present.
The cowboy didn't inhabit best seller lists until he had
become legend, twenty years after the disappearance of the
Long Drive. When the cattle industry became big business
and the cowboy was extinct he became one of the most popular
heroes in the best selling novels. Nor are these Westerns
usually identified as part of the past. The invention of
the typewriter in the late nineteenth century put women in
great numbers in clerical positions but women office workers
do not appear in these books until the late 1920s--half a
century later. The urban slum, common at the end of the
nineteenth century in the United States and described by
major American writers in the 1890s does not become the
setting for best sellers until mid-twentieth century when
the Depression made it an acceptable subject.

If best sellers are an index to culture then the 1940s
marked a major shift in the ways Americans viewed their
world. The conservatism enshrined on the best seller list
was displaced by the appearance of books about slums devoid
of the American Dream (Algren, Motley, Shulman, Barnard,

Ellson), of books allowing Catholics and Jews respectability
(Cronin, Werfel, Shaw, followed in the 1950s by West and
Uris), of books decrying the denial of dignity, a decent
standard of living and even life itself to blacks (Lillian
Smith followed in the 1960s by James Baldwin, John Griffin
and Harper Lee). There is even a variant in the character
of the spy from the always clever and macho James Bond to
Le Carré's spy who came in from the cold in the 1960s, a
rather ordinary man who gets tired and makes mistakes.

That greater realism entered the best sellers in this
period should hardly occasion surprise. Within fifteen
years Americans and indeed the world had lived through a
combination of catastrophes--the Great Depression, the rise
of Nazism and World War II. To the middle class American
poverty was no longer a remote, earned condition, but one
that might overwhelm one's family and friends at any time
through no fault of one's own. The War also entered middle
class homes with shortages of consumer goods, rationing, but
especially with the draft of young men. It was a disturbed
and disturbing world and evidently Americans were willing
to read serious analyses of the human condition hoping to
find answers. At the same time unemployment allowed more
time for reading. And the revolution in American publishing
that produced cheap paper-bound books began with the
establishment of Pocket Books in 1939. Cheap reprints of
hard-bound books now became available.

One should keep in mind, however, that the most popular
authors were not writing serious critiques of society;
authors such as Erle Stanley Gardner, Harold Robbins, Mickey
Spillane sold millions more than those who tried to make the
reader face his world. They wrote to please potential
buyers; they might startle, but they must never offend their
readers. They are satisfying because they tell you what you
want to think you know already. They accept and illustrate
what they consider the conventions of a culture, and offer

temporary escape from a brutal world with their romances,
westerns, detective stories and sexual adventures. The
helplessness of the individual in a depersonalized world
could be forgotten in fantasy.

How much American readers absorbed of the social values
of their best sellers it is, of course, impossible to say.
But relaxed readers in a less than critical mood may well
accept without questioning notions they would quarrel with
in their real world. They may use fictional characters as
role models. Not that the ordinary reader would act out
the violence he met in a book; as Jimmy Walker, mayor of
New York City in the 1920s put it--no woman was ever raped
by a book. But constantly exposed to violence in recrea-
tional reading, the reader might find it not only thrilling
but acceptable.

One often finds in these books a central theme, and the
reader might well be forewarned of this before choosing a
book by its title, the reputation of the author, advertisements for the book, reviews, or the advice of friends. When
buying a book by Mickey Spillane one would expect violence,
when buying Gone With the Wind one would expect the point of
view of white plantation society toward the Civil War and
Reconstruction, in buying a novel by Harold Robbins one
would expect lots of sexual activities. But in these same
books one would also meet other social attitudes subordinate
or even irrelevant to the main theme and introduced often
by casual characters. Many if not most of these notions
were accepted axiomatically by the author and transferred
perhaps subliminally to the reader. If racial stereotypes
are a central focus, as in novels involving slavery, the
reader may begin to debate the issue with his/her conscience.
But frequent casual encounters with racial stereotypes
ancillary to the tale may disarm the reader into unconscious
absorption. This study has been concerned with such casual
encounters as well as the central issues. Reiterated in

movies, television, radio, newspapers, periodicals and popular songs as well as books such social attitudes may sink deeply into the national consciousness. No one knows now much the myths of popular culture influence the populace. The one thing we are sure of about popular culture is that it is popular, and whatever its influence it is a pervasive world impossible to escape.

ACKNOWLEDGMENTS

Many New York City libraries and their staffs have been
helpful, and indeed essential to this study: the Columbia
University Library, the New York Public Library, The
Mercantile Library. Mark Piel, formerly head of the Finch
College library, and now director of The Society Library
has been especially helpful. Nineteenth and early twentieth
century best sellers were easy to find, but locating the
more recent ones was often almost impossible. Still basking
in the status of best seller, they were often "borrowed"
permanently from libraries. In one case only a careful
watch by the staff of donations to the New York City Bryn
Mawr bookshop produced a copy of a book absent from library
shelves though not from card catalogues.

For careful critical review of all sections of this manu-
script I am deeply indebted to David Lowenthal of the
University of London and Susan J. Turner, Professor Emeritus
of American Literature at Vassar College. While they cannot
be held responsible for my conclusions, their comments were
truly re-views and invaluable to this investigation.

May I also express my gratitude to the National Endowment
for the Humanities and to Clotilda Brokaw; without their aid
this project would have been impossible.

And finally profound gratitude to my husband, Robert Elson,
whose aid in all areas was vital as I revisited my own
Cloudland.

NOTES

Chapter 1

1. The following studies of American best sellers have been invaluable: Alice Payne Hackett, *70 Years of Best Sellers, 1895-1965* (New York: R. R. Bowker and Co., 1967); Alice Payne Hackett and James Henry Burke, *80 Years of Best Sellers* (New York: R. R. Bowker and Co., 1977); James D. Hart, *The Popular Book: A History of American Literary Taste* (New York: Oxford University Press, 1950); Frank Luther Mott, *Golden Multitudes: The Story of Best Sellers in the United States* (New York: The Macmillan Co., 1947). Also stimulating and useful is: Henry Nash Smith, *Democracy and the Novel: Popular Hesitance to Classic American Writers* (New York: Oxford University Press, 1978).

2. John G. Cawelti, *Adventure, Mystery and Romance: Formula Stories in Art and Popular Culture* (Chicago: University of Chicago Press, 1976).

3. Leo Lowenthal, *Literature, Popular Culture and Society* (Englewood Cliffs, NJ: Prentice-Hall, Inc., 1961), 11. See also Hart, 280-82.

4. Henry Nash Smith, 106-107; see also Mott, 149 ff. and Hart, 150 ff.

5. "Book Ends," *The New York Times Book Review,* July 4, 1976.

6. The year 1948 saw the publication of *The Young Lions* by Irwin Shaw in which Jews appear as ordinary human beings subject to the same kinds of problems as the rest of the world.

7. Mrs. Emma D. E. N. Southworth, *Self-Raised, or From the Depths* (New York: F. M. Lupton Co., 1884). Originally published serially, 1863-64. Jacqueline Susann, *The Valley of the Dolls* (New York: Bernard Geis Associates, 1966).

8. Q. D. Leavis, *Fiction and the Reading Public* (New York: Russell and Russell, 1965), 51, 59.

9. Michael Wood, *America in the Movies* (New York: Basic Books, Inc., 1975), 18.

324

Chapter 2

On the relationship of Americans to their environment see:
Hans Huth, *Nature and the American* (Lincoln: University of
Nebraska Press, 1972); R. W. B. Lewis, *The American Adam*
(Chicago: University of Chicago Press, 1955); David Lowen
Lowenthal and Martyn J. Bowden, eds., *Geographies of the
Mind* (New York: Oxford University Press, 1976); Leo Marx,
The Machine in the Garden (New York: Oxford University
Press, 1964); Roderick Nash, *Wilderness and the American
Mind* (New Haven, CT: Yale University Press, 1973); David W.
Noble, *The Eternal Adam and the New World Garden* (New York:
Braziller, 1968); Henry Nash Smith, *Virgin Land: The
American West as Symbol and Myth* (Cambridge: Harvard
University Press, 1950).

1. 1888 Hall Caine, *The Deemster*, 167; 1887 H. Rider
   Haggard, *She*, 154.

2. 1866 Augusta J. Evans, *St. Elmo*, 30; 1907 Harold Bell
   Wright, *The Shepherd of the Hills*, 165.

3. 1887 Marie Corelli, *Thelma, a Society Novel*, 173.

4. 1908 Grace Livingston Hill, *Marcia Schuyler*, 159-61;
   1944 Ben Ames Williams, *Leave Her to Heaven*, 13; see
   also: 1931 Pearl Buck, *The Good Earth*, 188; Anne Frank,
   The Diary of a Young Girl, 140-41, 222 (1965, originally
   1952).

5. 1887 Marie Corelli, *Thelma*, 107; 1909 Harold Bell
   Wright, *The Calling of Dan Matthews*, 30.

6. 1940 Victor Lindlahr, *You Are What You Eat*; 1946
   Benjamin Spock, *The Common Sense Book of Baby and Child
   Care*; 1958 D. C. Jarvis, *Folk Medicine: A Vermont
   Doctor's Guide to Good Health*. That the author of the
   latter is a Vermont doctor is important to the popularity of the book; had he been from New York City his
   habitat would probably not appear so prominently.

7. 1903 Jack London, *The Call of the Wild*, 25, 92, 47.

8. 1909 Gene Stratton Porter, *A Girl of the Limberlost*,
   293. One might expect a revival of the works of Porter
   in the light of the health food and nature cults of the
   present.

9. 1888 Hall Caine, *The Deemster*, 232; 1895 Stephen Crane,
   The Red Badge of Courage, 34.

325

10. 1906 Zane Grey, *The Spirit of the Border,* 30.

11. 1911 Harold Bell Wright, *The Winning of Barbara Worth,* 115, 129, 131.

12. 1907 Harold Bell Wright, *The Shepherd of the Hills,* 347.

13. 1900 Winston Churchill, *The Crisis,* 214; see also: Thomas E. Hill, *Hill's Manual of Social and Business Forms* (1905, originally 1873), 471.

14. 1946 Taylor Caldwell, *This Side of Innocence,* 102, 297-98, 354-55, 357.

15. 1908 John Fox Jr., *The Trail of the Lonesome Pine,* 39; 1905 Thomas E. Hill, *Hill's Manual . . .,* 420; 1929 Erich Maria Remarque, *All Quiet on the Western Front,* 277; 1949 Marian Castle, *The Golden Fury,* 16.

16. 1961 Henry Miller, *Tropic of Cancer,* 239-40; 1932 D. H. Lawrence, *Lady Chatterley's Lover,* 260; 1939 John Steinbeck, *The Grapes of Wrath,* 157-58.

17. 1957 Ayn Rand, *Atlas Shrugged,* 245, 50, 280.

18. 1893 Sarah Grand, *The Heavenly Twins,* VII, 45.

19. 1890 Arthur Conan Doyle, *A Study in Scarlet,* 25.

20. 1948 Dale Carnegie, *How to Stop Worrying and Start Living,* 101.

21. 1867 Horatio Alger, *Ragged Dick,* 199; 1900 Irving Bacheller, *Eben Holden,* 335-36; 1902 Owen Wister, *The Virginian,* 32-33.

22. 1915 W. Somerset Maugham, *Of Human Bondage,* 90 (first quotation in this paragraph); see also: 1908 Grace Livingston Hill, *Marcia Schuyler,* 156. The second quotation is from 1942 Franz Werfel, *The Song of Bernadette,* 57.

23. 1909 Gene Stratton Porter, *The Girl of the Limberlost,* 21; see also: 1937 A. J. Cronin, *The Citadel,* 116.

24. 1947 Frank Yerby, *The Vixens,* 8; see also: 1916 Edgar Guest, *A Heap o' Livin',* 59; 1944 Niven Busch, *Duel in the Sun,* n.p.; 1946 Taylor Caldwell, *This Side of Innocence,* 406.

25. 1942 Lloyd Douglas, *The Robe,* 296; 1897 Charles Sheldon, *In His Steps,* 262; 1899 Winston Churchill, *Richard*

Carvel, 320; see also: 1874 R. D. Blackmore, *Lorna Doone*, 177; 1888 Mrs. Humphrey Ward, *Robert Elsmere*, 67; 1904 Jack London, *The Sea Wolf*, 69; 1931 Pearl Buck, *The Good Earth*, 100.

26. 1874 E. P. Roe, *Opening a Chestnut Burr*, 14; 1949 Fulton Oursler, *The Greatest Story Ever Told*, 23; 1870 Bret Harte, *The Luck of Roaring Camp*, 77; 1942 Ellery Queen, *Calamity Town*, 73.

27. 1874 E. P. Roe, *Opening a Chestnut Burr*, 14; 1908 Grace Livingston Hill, *Marcia Schuyler*, 155.

28. 1880 Lew Wallace, *Ben-Hur*, 431; 1916 Edgar Guest, *A Heap o' Livin'*, 59.

29. 1945 Betty MacDonald, *The Egg and I*; 1957 Jean Kerr, *Please Don't Eat the Daisies*.

30. 1949 Marian Castle, *The Golden Fury*, 19.

31. 1876 Thomas L. Haines and Levi Yaggy, *The Royal Path of Life*, 129.

32. 1935 M. G. Kains, *Five Acres and Independence*, title page; 1936 Margaret Mitchell, *Gone With the Wind*, 36; 1943 Betty Smith, *A Tree Grows in Brooklyn*, 76.

33. 1958 Boris Pasternak, *Dr. Zhivago*, 40, 406.

34. 1874 E. P. Roe, *Opening a Chestnut Burr*, 23; see also: 1898 Edward N. Westcott, *David Harum*, 215; 1949 Fulton Oursler, *The Greatest Story Ever Told*, 58.

Chapter 3

1. The following books are particularly useful on the subject of women in American literature: Susan Koppelman Cornillon, ed., *Images of Women in Fiction* (Bowling Green, OH: Bowling Green University Popular Press, 1973); Dorothy Yost Deegan, *The Stereotype of the Single Woman in American Novels* (New York: Columbia University Press, 1951); Ann Douglas, *The Feminization of American Culture* (New York: Avon, 1978); Earnest Ernest, *The American Eve in Fact and Fiction, 1775-1914* (Urbana: University of Illinois Press, 1974); Leslie Fiedler, *Love and Death in the American Novel* (London: Paladin, 1970); Judith Fryer, *The Faces of Eve: The Nineteenth Century Novel* (New York: Oxford University Press, 1976); Elizabeth Hardwick, *Seduction and Betrayal: Women and*

Literature (New York: Random House, 1970); Kathryn
Weibel, *Mirror Mirror: Images of Women Reflected in
Popular Culture* (New York: Anchor Press, 1977).

2. 1902 Owen Wister, *The Virginian*, 110; 1909 Harold Bell
Wright, *The Calling of Dan Matthews*, 84, 145; 1912 Zane
Grey, *Riders of the Purple Sage*, 267; 1929 Donald
Henderson Clarke, *Louis Beretti*, 145; 1929 Ernest
Hemingway, *A Farewell to Arms*, 152; 1936 Margaret
Mitchell, *Gone With the Wind*, 16; 1943 Betty Smith, *A
Tree Grows in Brooklyn*, 59, 78, 91; 1949 John O'Hara,
A Rage to Live, 227; 1954 Frances Parkinson Keyes, *The
Royal Box*, 216.

3. 1936 Margaret Mitchell, *Gone With the Wind*, 150, 556,
557; 1943 Betty Smith, *A Tree Grows in Brooklyn*, 210;
1944 W. Somerset Maugham, *The Razor's Edge*, 226.

4. 1894 Anthony Hope, *The Prisoner of Zenda*, 47; see also:
1867 Ouida, *Under Two Flags*, 61; 1896 Henryk
Sienkiewicz, *Quo Vadis*, 4.

5. Intelligence: 1892 A. Conan Doyle, *The Adventures of
Sherlock Holmes*, 13; 1929 Lloyd Douglas, *The Magnificent
Obsession*, 30; 1899 Winston Churchill, *Richard Carvel*,
269; 1958 Rona Jaffe, *The Best of Everything*, 163.

   Courage: 1866 Charles Reade, *Griffith Gaunt*, 302-309;
1902 Owen Wister, *The Virginian*, 331; 1939 William
Faulkner, *The Wild Palms*, 133, 141, 207; 1910 Florence
Barclay, *The Rosary*, 102.

   Business sense: Margaret Mitchell, *Gone With the Wind*;
1944 Elizabeth Goudge, *Green Dolphin Street*.

   Driving: 1916 Edgar Guest, *A Heap o' Livin'*, 122-23;
1944 Bob Hope, *I Never Left Home*, 43; 1958 Robert
Traver, *Anatomy of a Murder*, 39; 1961 Ian Fleming,
Thunderball, 111.

   Honesty: 1894 George Du Maurier, *Trilby*, 76; see also:
1915 W. Somerset Maugham, *Of Human Bondage*, 273.

6. 1944 Ben Ames Williams, *Leave Her to Heaven*, 135; see
also: 1911 Gene Stratton Porter, *The Harvester*, 300.

7. For examples: 1870 Bret Harte, *The Luck of Roaring Camp*,
136; 1876 Thomas L. Haines and Levi Yaggy, *The Royal
Path of Life*, 15, 574; 1892 James M. Barrie, *A Window in
Thrums*, 85; 1914 Edgar Rice Burroughs, *Tarzan of the
Apes*, 171; 1944 Niven Busch, *Duel in the Sun*, 215; 1946
Rosamund Marshall, *Duchess Hotspur*, 238; 1954 Morton
Thompson, *Not as a Stranger*, 689; 1956 William Brinkley,
Don't Go Near the Water, 130; 1959 Morris L. West, *The

Devil's Advocate, 282; 1959 Ian Fleming, *Goldfinger,* 269.

8. Irresponsibility: 1894 Anthony Hope, *The Prisoner of Zenda,* 231; 1899 Paul Leicester Ford, *Janice Meredith,* 386; 1933 Hervey Allen, *Anthony Adverse,* 978; 1956 Grace Metalious, *Peyton Place,* 7.

   Nervousness: 1888 Marie Corelli, *A Romance of Two Worlds,* 89; 1885 Mark Twain, *Huckleberry Finn,*.631; 1904 Gene Stratton Porter, *Freckles,* 204; 1905 Thomas E. Hill, *Hill's Manual of Social and Business Forms,* 167; 1933 Hervey Allen, *Anthony Adverse,* 978; 1940 Agatha Christie, *And Then There Were None,* 16; 1947 Frank Yerby, *The Vixens,* 22.

9. Stubbornness: 1872 E. P. Roe, *Barriers Burned Away,* 360.

   Foolish arguers: 1891 James M. Barrie, *The Little Minister,* 221; see also: 1946 Rosamund Marshall, *Duchess Hotspur,* 201; 1947 Kenneth Roberts, *Lydia Bailey,* 13.

   Gossipers: 1952 Anne Frank, *The Diary of a Young Girl,* 6; see also: 1930 Max Brand, *Destry Rides Again,* 79.

10. 1889 Guy de Maupassant, *Stories,* 16; see also: 1874 R. D. Blackmore, *Lorna Doone,* 220, 446, 643; 1890 Arthur Conan Doyle, *The Sign of the Four,* 198; 1892 Arthur Conan Doyle, *The Adventures of Sherlock Holmes,* 22; 1948 Norman Mailer, *The Naked and the Dead,* 181; 1951 James Jones, *From Here to Eternity,* 31; 1964 Eric Berne, *Games People Play,* 84, 101-104.

11. 1867 Ouida, *Under Two Flags,* 231, 315; see also: 1880 Emile Zola, *Nana;* 1887 H. Rider Haggard, *She,* 153; 1892 James M. Barrie, *A Window in Thrums,* 85-90; 1913 Sax Rohmer, *The Insidious Dr. Fu Manchu,* 103; 1921 E. M. Hull, *The Sheik,* 10; 1876 Thomas L. Haines and Levi Yaggy, *The Royal Path of Life,* 83; 1947 Frank Yerby, *The Vixens,* 254.

12. 1871 Edward Eggleston, *The Hoosier Schoolmaster,* 156-57; see also: 1872 E. P. Roe, *Barriers Burned Away,* 375; 1911 Harold Bell Wright, *The Winning of Barbara Worth,* 64; 1942 Vivian Connell, *The Chinese Room,* 17; see also: 1943 Betty Smith, *A Tree Grows in Brooklyn,* 137.

13. 1866 Augusta J. Evans, *St. Elmo,* 465; 1874 E. P. Roe, *Opening a Chestnut Burr,* 431-32; 1876 Thomas Haines and Levi Yaggy, *The Royal Path of Life,* 79, 416, 422, 577-78; 1880 Lew Wallace, *Ben-Hur,* 303-304; 1892 A. C. Doyle, *The Adventures of Sherlock Holmes,* 107; 1911 Gene Stratton Porter, *The Harvester,* 429-30.

14. 1957 Max Shulman, *Rally Round the Flag*, 35; see also: 1948 Harold Robbins, *Never Love a Stranger*, 267.

15. 1909 Gene Stratton Porter, *The Girl of the Limberlost*, 379; 1910 Florence Barclay, *The Rosary*, 153; 1911 Gene Stratton Porter, *The Harvester,*427, 524, 526; 1944 Lillian Smith, *Strange Fruit*, 67; 1957 Ayn Rand, *Atlas Shrugged*, 205; 1959 Grace Metalious, *Return to Peyton Place*, 55.

16. Reasons for becoming prostitutes: 1867 Ouida, *Under Two Flags*, 54; 1934 John O'Hara, *Butterfield-8*; 1942 Nelson Algren, *Never Came Morning*, 70; 1957 Richard Mason, *The World of Suzie Wong*, 42.

    Hearts of gold: 1870 Bret Harte, *The Luck of Roaring Camp*, 75; 1907 Robert Service, *The Spell of the Yukon and Other Verses*, 68; 1934 Irving Stone, *Lust for Life*, 900; 1936 Margaret Mitchell, *Gone With the Wind*, 818; 1943 Betty Smith, *A Tree Grows in Brooklyn*, 210.

17. Differences between the 1880 and 1972 English trans- lations of *Nana* indicate the new position of sex in the culture. For example, in 1880 Nana at one point throws back her head (40); in 1972 she throws back her head to show her breasts to good advantage (33).

18. 1880 Lew Wallace, *Ben-Hur*, Iras; 1915 W. Somerset Maugham, *Of Human Bondage*, Mildred; 1908 Grace Livingston Hill, *Marcia Schuyler,*Kate; 1934 Sax Rohmer, *The Trail of Dr. Fu Manchu*, 77; 1934 John O'Hara, *Butterfield-8*, 18; 1941 Ben Ames Williams, *Strange Woman*, Jenny; 1944 Ben Ames Williams, *Leave Her to Heaven*, 47; 1950 Bruno Fischer, *The House of Flesh*, murderer; 1964 Irving Wallace, *The Man*, Sally Watson.

19. Note the anagrams for the names of the most famous of al all the cinema vamps: Theda Bara.

20. For examples see: 1933 Hervey Allen, *Anthony Adverse*, 249; 1939 William Faulkner, *The Wild Palms*, 54; 1947 Frank Yerby, *The Vixens*, 61, 164, 226, 302; 1948 Harold Robbins, *Never Love a Stranger*, 39; 1949 John O'Hara, *A Rage to Live*, 221, 252, 379; 1954 Evan Hunter, *The Blackboard Jungle*, 57; 1956 Grace Metalious, *Peyton Place*, 330; 1962 Kyle Onstott, *Drum* 148-51.

21. These romances were evidently aimed at older middle class women. When standing in front of a rich display of romances in a large Woolworth's in New York City, trying to decide which of the Cartland books to use in this study, I had an illustration of the fervor with

which these books are received: an older woman, a
stranger to me, approached and addressed me in tones of
almost religious ardor to recommend the book I was
holding as one that "You will *never* forget."

22. Three years after the publication of *The Sheik* the
edition of *Three Weeks* of 1924 contained ads for three
books, all with the same theme: the conquest of an
Anglo-Saxon woman by a desert lover. It should be noted
that *The Sheik* was reprinted in 1977 in Barbara Cartland's "Library of Love."

23. Jobs held by women outside the home in these best
sellers:
    singers - 12 (in contrast to the single male singer)
    writers - 14 (12 of these were journalists)
    teachers - 11
    nurses - 9
    actresses - 9 (all after 1940)
    artists - 4
    doctors - 4 (all in recent novels)
    detectives - 3
    politicians - 2 (late novels)
    administrators - 2
    preacher - 1
    women in business - 6 (several as managers of brothels)
    exotics: 1 lion-tamer, 1 Indian chief, 1 gang of cat
      burglars, 1 horse-back riding Western thief (all of
      these casually mentioned except for the cat burglar
      gang in 1959 *Goldfinger*)
    many store clerks, maids, cooks
    6 factory workers and 8 office workers (all in late
      books)

24. A delightful parody of this book appeared in 1868:
Charles Henry Webb, *St. Twel'mo or, the Cuneiform
Encyclopedist of Chattanooga*. The heroine, after
discovering the dictionary develops a "fatal fondness
for polysyllables" and "a contempt for common English"
(11). She "erupts with erudition" (12).

25. If I may be forgiven another anecdote: when, in the
course of this study I mentioned that I was about to
read *Little Women,* four friends, all professionally
successful women offered to lend me their copies. This
was the book they had cherished from youth because of
its portrait of Jo.

26. 1958 Harry Golden, *Only in America*, 211-12; see also:
1894 Anthony Hope, *The Prisoner of Zenda,* 7; 1958
Alexander King, *Mine Enemy Grows Older,* 176-79, 203.

Chapter 4

1. 1921 Rafael Sabatini, *Scaramouche,* 34; see also: 1934
   John O'Hara, *Butterfield-8,* 42. Quotations from Harold
   Bell Wright, (1907) *The Shepherd of the Hills* are from
   pages 90, 130; see also the characterization of Jesus'
   father Joseph in *The Greatest Story Ever Told* (1949) by
   Fulton Oursler, 1-22.

2. 1891 Rudyard Kipling, *The Light That Failed,* 220; 1907
   Robert Service, *The Spell of the Yukon and Other Verses,*
   53-54.

3. See also: 1928 Max Brand, *Singing Guns,* 2, 63; 1928 Vina
   Delmar, *Bad Girl,* 12; 1944 Kathleen Winsor, *Forever
   Amber,* 14; 1948 Harold Robbins, *Never Love a Stranger,*
   39, 105, 146, 150; 1961 Ian Fleming, *Thunderball,* 108,
   248; 1961 Barbara Cartland, *The Runaway Heart,* 24.

4. See also: 1929 Donald Henderson Clarke, *Louis Beretti,*
   1937 James M. Cain, *Serenade,* 1938 Damon Runyon, *The
   Best of Damon Runyon;* 1942 Nelson Algren, *Never Came
   Morning,* 1947 Willard Motley, *Knock on Any Door.*

5. *A Supplement to the Oxford English Dictionary,* ed. by
   R. W. Burchfield, Vol. II, 1976.

6. 1911 Gene Stratton Porter, *The Harvester,* 520; see also:
   1909 Gene Stratton Porter, *A Girl of the Limberlost,*
   379.

7. For examples: 1866 Charles Reade, *Griffith Gaunt,* 193-96
   96; 1887 Archibald Gunter, *Mr. Barnes of New York,* 112;
   1963 Georgette Heyer, *The Nonesuch,* 4.

8. Pp. 57-59.

9. For examples: 1867 Ouida, *Under Two Flags,* 231, 315;
   1887 H. Rider Haggard, *She,* 153, 150, 172-73; 1941 Ben
   Ames Williams, *Strange Woman,* 230; 1944 Niven Busch,
   Duel in the Sun, 49; 1946 Rosamund Marshall, *Duchess
   Hotspur,* 86; 1947 Frank Yerby, *The Vixens,* 254.

10. 1928 Vina Delmar, *Bad Girl,* 81, 83; see also: 1939
    William Faulkner, *The Wild Palms,* 87; 1948 Harold
    Robbins, *Never Love a Stranger,* 272-82.

11. Particularly useful on the cowboy in American culture
    are the following: John Cawelti, *Adventure, Mystery and
    Romance: Formula Stories as Art and Popular Culture*
    (Chicago: University of Chicago Press, 1976); David

Brion Davis, "Ten-Gallon Hero" (*American Quarterly,*
Vol. VI, #2, Summer 1954, 111-25); Henry Bamford Parks,
"Metamorphosis of Leatherstocking," in *Literature in
America,* ed. by Philip Rahv (New York: Meridian Books,
1957); Henry Nash Smith, *Virgin Land: The American Past
as Symbol and Myth* (Cambridge: Harvard University Press,
1950).

12. Particularly useful on the detective and crime story
    are the following: John Cawelti, *Adventure, Mystery and
    Romance: Formula Stories as Art and Popular Culture*
    (Chicago: University of Chicago Press, 1976); Martin
    Green, *Transatlantic Patterns: Cultural Comparisons of
    England with America* (New York: Basic Books, 1977);
    Ralph Harper, *The World of the Thriller* (Cleveland:
    The Press of Case Western Reserve University, 1969);
    Ross MacDonald, "The Private Detective," *New York Times
    Book Review* (October 23, 1977); Russel Nye, *The
    Unembarrassed Muse: The Popular Arts in America* (New
    York: The Dial Press, 1970); William Ruehlmann, *Saint
    With a Gun* (New York: New York University Press, 1974);
    Julian Symons, *The Detective in Britain* (London:
    Longmans, Green and Co., 1962); Julian Symons, *Mortal
    Consequences: A History from the Detective Story to the
    Crime Novel* (New York: Harper and Row, 1972); Edmund
    Wilson, "Why Do People Read Detective Stories?" and
    "Who Cares Who Killed Roger Ackroyd?" in *A Literary
    Chronicle, 1920-1950* (New York: Doubleday & Co., Inc.,
    1952).

13. See also: 1934 James Cain, *The Postman Always Rings
    Twice;* 1934 Dashiell Hammett, *The Thin Man;* 1940 Raymond
    Chandler, *Farewell, My Lovely;* 1947 Mickey Spillane,
    I, the Jury; 1951 Richard Prather, *Find This Woman;* 1952
    John MacDonald, *The Damned.*

14. William Ruehlmann, *Saint With a Gun* (New York: New York
    University Press, 1974), 5.

15. Particularly useful on the self-made man and American
    culture are the following: John G. Cawelti, *Apostles of
    the Self-Made Man: Changing Concepts of Success in
    America* (Chicago: University of Chicago Press, 1968);
    Lawrence Chenoweth, *The American Dream of Success,* ed.
    by John Bartlett (North Scituate, MA: Duxbury Press,
    1974); Bruce E. Coad, "The Alger Hero," in *Heroes of
    Popular Culture,* ed. by Ray Browne, Marshall Fishwick,
    and Michael Marsden (Bowling Green, OH: Bowling Green
    University Popular Press, 1972); Richard Huber, *The
    American Dream of Success* (New York: McGraw-Hill Book
    Co., 1971); Donald Meyer, *The Positive Thinkers* (Garden
    City, NY: Doubleday and Co., 1965); John Seelye, "Who

Was Horatio? The Alger Myth and American Scholarship"
(*American Quarterly*, Vol. XVII, Winter 1965, 749-56);
Irvin Wyllie, *The Self-Made Man in America: The Myth of
Rags to Riches* (New Brunswick, NJ: Rutgers University
Press, 1954).

16. Dwight MacDonald, *Against the American Grain: Essays in
the Effects of Mass Culture* (New York: Vintage Books,
1962), 36.

17. For examples: 1908 Mary Roberts Rinehart, *The Circular
Staircase*, 182, 294; 1911 Gene Stratton Porter, *The
Harvester*, 471-72.

18. 1944 W. Somerset Maugham, *The Razor's Edge*, 313; see
also: 1905 Thomas E. Hill, *Hill's Manual of Social and
Business Forms*, 111; 1957 Vance Packard, *The Hidden
Persuaders*, 123; 1958 Harry Golden, *Only in America*,
138; 1961 Harold Robbins, *The Carpetbaggers*, throughout;
1946 Taylor Caldwell, *This Side of Innocence*, 391.

19. 1876 Thomas Haines and Levi Yaggy, *The Royal Path of
Life*, 246; see also: 44, 112, 170-77, 201-206, 213-18,
239, 193; 1904 Gene Stratton Porter, *Freckles*, 56; 1909
Gene Stratton Porter, *A Girl of the Limberlost*, 48;
1916 Edgar Guest, *A Heap o' Livin'*, 14, 52-53; 1926 Paul
DeKruif, *The Microbe Hunters*, 59-60.

20. For example, 1936 Margaret Mitchell, *Gone With the Wind*,
193; 1946 John P. Marquand, *B.F.'s Daughter*, 25; 1946
Frank Yerby, *The Foxes of Harrow*, 31; 1946 Robert
Wilder, *Written on the Wind*, 39-40; 1948 Frances
Parkinson Keyes, *Dinner at Antoine's*, 94, 178; 1949
William Barnard, *Jailbait*, 39.

21. It is interesting to observe that all of these books
offering advice on how to improve one's personality, use
business men as their major examples of successful
personalities. For example: 1960 Maxwell Maltz in
Psycho-Cybernetics discusses successful business men on
the following pages: 49, 50-51, 70, 73, 81, 84-86, 88,
89, 92, 100, 101, 102-103, 105, 111-13, 132, 155, 177,
205, 226, 227, 228.

Chapter 5

Besides the studies of race by psychologists and anthropolo-
gists, Thomas F. Gossett's *Race: The History of an Idea in
America* (New York: Schocken Books, 1965) is particularly

useful. One should also examine *A Dictionary of Inter-national Slurs* by A. Roback (Cambridge, MA: Science-Art Publishers, 1964).

1. 1883 F. Marion Crawford, *A Roman Singer,* 60, 108; 1907 Harold Bell Wright, *The Shepherd of the Hills,* 129; 1936 Daphne Du Maurier, *Jamaica Inn,* 545; 1941 A. J. Cronin, *The Keys of the Kingdom,* 91.

2. 1912 Zane Grey, *Riders of the Purple Sage,*306; 1932 Earl Derr Biggers, *Keeper of the Keys,* 123; 1935 Enid Bagnold, *"National Velvet",* 9; 1936 Margaret Mitchell, *Gone With the Wind,* 62; 1947 Edison Marshall, *Yankee Pasha,* 65; 1954 Lillian Roth, *I'll Cry Tomorrow,* 13; 1957 Art Linkletter, *Kids Say the Darndest Things,* 54.

3. 1914 Edgar Rice Burroughs, *Tarzan of the Apes,* 277; see also: 1907 Harold Bell Wright, *The Shepherd of the Hills,* 81, 83, 129, 132, 165, 241; 1933 Hervey Allen, *Anthony Adverse,* 159; 1944 Elizabeth Goudge, *Green Dolphin Street,* 19; 1947 Frank Yerby, *The Vixens,* 59.

4. 1958 D. C. Jarvis, *Folk Medicine,* 22-23.

5. Paul Bohannon, *Africa and the Africans* (New York: American Museum of Natural History, 1964), 61.

6. 1953 Leon Uris, *Battle Cry,* 365, 381.

7. 1885 Mark Twain, *Huckleberry Finn,*637; 1895 Opie Read, *The Jucklins,* 105; 1905 Rex Beach, *The Spoilers,* 92; 1911 Gene Stratton Porter, *The Harvester,* 403; 1920 E. Phillips Oppenheim, *The Great Impersonation,* 68; 1927 Sinclair Lewis, *Elmer Gantry,* 240; 1928 Max Brand, *Singing Guns,* 149; 1931 Ellery Queen, *The Dutch Shoe Mystery,* 203; 1941 Erle Stanley Gardner, *The Case of the Haunted Husband,* 46, 275; 1948 Frances Parkinson Keyes, *Dinner at Antoine's,* 143; 1956 William Brinkley, *Don't Go Near the Water,* 231; 1959 Grace Metalious, *Return to Peyton Place,* 26.

8. 1947 Irving Shulman, *The Amboy Dukes,* 28; see also: 1943 Betty Smith, *A Tree Grows in Brooklyn,* 16; 1932 James T. Farrell, *Studs Lonigan,* 99.

9. 1890 Arthur Conan Doyle, *A Study in Scarlet,* 58; see also: 1887 Archibald C. Gunter, *Mr. Barnes of New York,* 153; 1937 A. J. Cronin, *The Citadel,* 25.

10. 1884 Helen Hunt Jackson, *Ramona,* 37; 1891 Rudyard Kipling, *The Light that Failed,* 153; 1911 Harold Bell Wright, *The Winning of Barbara Worth,* 448; 1933 Hervey

Allen, *Anthony Adverse,* 695; 1944 Elizabeth Goudge,
Green Dolphin Street, 139; 1951 James Jones, *From Here
to Eternity,* 93; 1957 Kyle Onstott, *Mandingo,* 167.

11. For example: Mark Twain, *Tom Sawyer* and *Huckleberry
Finn,* throughout; 1933 Hervey Allen, *Anthony Adverse,*
316, 897, 1073; 1940 Raymond Chandler, *Farewell, My
Lovely,* 68; 1940 Agatha Christie, *And Then There Were
None,* 74; 1940 Jan Struther, *Mrs. Miniver,* 48, 245; 1948
Frances Parkinson Keyes, *Dinner at Antoine's,* 164; 1951
James Jones, *From Here to Eternity,* throughout; 1956
Grace Metalious, *Peyton Place,* throughout; 1964 John
Le Carré, *The Spy Who Came in from the Cold,* 23; 1926
Paul de Kruif, *The Microbe Hunters,* 32; 1926 Ernest
Hemingway, *The Sun Also Rises,* 65, 72, 73, 74.

12. 1895 Opie Read, *The Jucklins;* 1946 Robert Wilder,
Written on the Wind, 1948 Frances Parkinson Keyes,
Dinner at Antoine's.

13. Russel B. Nye, *The Unembarrassed Muse: The Popular
Arts in America* (New York: Dial Press, 1970), p. 273.
Statistics are from the *New York Times,* 8/29/75, p. 29,
and the *New York Post,* 2/23/76, p. 53.

14. First quotation is from 1899 Paul Leicester Ford,
Janice Meredith, 457; second quotation is from 1900
Winston Churchill, *The Crisis,* 75; see also: 1933 Hervey
Allen, *Anthony Adverse,* 695; 1936 Margaret Mitchell,
Gone With the Wind, 646, 656; 1956 Kathryn Hulme, *The
Nun's Story,* 233; 1957 Kyle Onstott, *Mandingo,*
throughout.

15. 1962 James Baldwin, *Another Country,* 144; see also: 1947
Kenneth Roberts, *Lydia Bailey,* 73, 91; 1948 Harold
Robbins, *Never Love a Stranger,* 179; 1954 Evan Hunter,
The Blackboard Jungle, 57.

16. 1962 James Baldwin, *Another Country,* 134; see also:
1933 Hervey Allen, *Anthony Adverse,* 417; 1939 John
Steinbeck, *Grapes of Wrath,* 14; 1962 Kyle Onstott, *Drum,*
114, 194.

17. J. C. Furnas, *Goodbye to Uncle Tom* (New York: William
Sloane Associates, 1956), 51.

18. For example: 1895 Opie Read, *The Jucklins,* 58.

19. 1890 Arthur Conan Doyle, *A Study in Scarlet,* 58, 60;
see also: 1906 Zane Grey, *The Spirit of the Border,* 42;
1944 Niven Busch, *Duel in the Sun,* 107; 1945 Betty
MacDonald, *The Egg and I,* 22.

20. 1940 Raymond Chandler, *Farewell, My Lovely*, 109; 1941 Ben Ames Williams, *Strange Woman*, 120; 1945 Betty MacDonald, *The Egg and I*, 23, 220; 1958 Anya Seton, *The Winthrop Woman*, 200.

21. 1910 Florence Barclay, *The Rosary*, 32; 1951 William Bradford Huie, *The Revolt of Mamie Stover*, 74, 84; 1959 James Michener, *Hawaii*, 737-38.

22. 1954 Pierre Boulle, *The Bridge Over the River Kwai*, 10 25; 1959 Ian Fleming, *Goldfinger*, 157.

23. 1951 William Bradford Huie, *The Revolt of Mamie Stover*, 74; 1951 James Jones, *From Here to Eternity*, 668.

24. 1934 Sax Rohmer, *The Trail of Fu Manchu*, 69.

25. 1915 W. Somerset Maugham, *Of Human Bondage*, 150; 1943 Betty Smith, *A Tree Grows in Brooklyn*, 122; 1961 Henry Miller, *Tropic of Cancer*, 199.

26. For example: 1929 Donald H. Clarke, *Louis Beretti*, 16-17; 1942 Vivian Connell, *The Chinese Room*, 112.

27. 1930 Earl Derr Biggers, *Charlie Chan Carries On*, 16; and *Keeper of the Keys* (1932), 61.

28. 1874 E. P. Roe, *Opening a Chestnut Burr*, 59; 1880 Lew Wallace, *Ben-Hur*, 89; 1921 H. G. Wells, *The Outline of History*, 496; 1949 Fulton Oursler, *The Greatest Story Ever Told*, 209.

29. 1868 Louisa May Alcott, *Little Women*, 330; 1934 Dashiell Hammett, *The Thin Man*, 77; 1961 Harold Robbins, *The Carpetbaggers*, 445.

30. 1962 Fletcher Knebel and Charles W. Bailey, *Seven Days in May*, 192; see also: 1883 F. Marion Crawford, *A Roman Singer*, 177, 188; 1931 Fannie Hurst, *Back Street*, 119.

31. 1942 Lloyd C. Douglas, *The Robe*, 75; see also: 1929 Lloyd Douglas, *The Magnificent Obsession*, 184; 1957 Jim Bishop, *The Day Christ Died*, 334.

32. For example: 1867 Ouida, *Under Two Flags*, 8, 11, etc.; 1871 Charles Reade, *A Terrible Temptation*, 8, 291, etc.

33. For example: 1874 R. D. Blackmore, *Lorna Doone*, 194; 1874 Jules Verne, *Around the World in Eighty Days*, 80; 1883 Mark Twain, *Life on the Mississippi*, 157; 1932 Charles Nordhoff and James Hall, *Mutiny on the Bounty*, 16.

34. 1883 Mark Twain, *Life on the Mississippi*, 187; 1936 Margaret Mitchell, *Gone With the Wind*, 74; 1949 John O'Hara, *A Rage to Live*, 407; 1957 Kyle Onstott, *Mandingo*, 349.

35. Oscar Handlin, *Adventures in Freedom--300 Years of Jewish Life in America* (New York: McGraw-Hill Book Co., Inc., 1954), 180-81.

36. 1942 Nelson Algren, *Never Came Morning*, 183-84; 1947 Irving Shulman, *The Amboy Dukes*, 28; 1957 Kyle Onstott, *Mandingo*, 169.

37. 1941 James Hilton, *Random Harvest*,234; 1947 Kenneth Roberts, *Lydia Bailey*, 340; 1951 Herman Wouk, *The Caine Mutiny*, 446; 1954 Morton Thompson, *Not as a Stranger*, 176-85; 1956 Eugene Burdick, *The Ninth Wave*, 32; 1960 Harper Lee, *To Kill a Mockingbird*, 157, 259.

Chapter 6

1. Samuel Putnam, *Sequel to the Analytical Reader* (Portland, ME, 1828), 290.

2. Hans Kohn, *The Idea of Nationalism: A Study of Its Origins and Background* (New York: The Macmillan Co., 1948), 15; also useful are: Merle Curti, *The Roots of American Loyalty* (New York: Columbia University Press, 1946); Carlton J. H. Hayes, *Essays in Nationalism* (New York: The Macmillan Co., 1926); *The Historical Evolution of Modern Nationalism* also by Hayes (New York: Richard R. Smith, 1931); Hans Kohn, *American Nationalism* (New York: The Macmillan Co., 1957); Boyd C. Shafer, *Nationalism, Myth and Reality* (New York: Harcourt, Brace and World, Inc., 1955); Louis L. Snyder, ed., *The Dynamics of Nationalism* (Princeton, NJ: D. Van Nostrand, 1964).

3. 1894 George Du Maurier, *Trilby*, 12; 1898 Ralph O'Connor, *Black Rock*, 120; 1900 Irving Bacheller, *Eben Holden*,291; 1904 Gene Stratton Porter, *Freckles*, 4; 1940 Jan Struther, *Mrs. Miniver*, 135; 1941 A. J. Cronin, *The Keys of the Kingdom*, 91.

4. Ruth Miller Elson, *Guardians of Tradition: American Schoolbooks of the Nineteenth Century* (Lincoln: University of Nebraska Press, 1964), 104.

5. 1929 Lloyd Douglas, *The Magnificant Obsession*, 290, 294; 1937 A. J. Cronin, *The Citadel*, 25.

6. Mott, 91-92.

7. Hart, 124.

8. 1886 Frances Hodgson Burnett, *Little Lord Fauntleroy;* 1894 George Du Maurier, *Trilby;* 1907 Eleanor Glyn, *Three Weeks;* 1920 E. Phillips Oppenheim, *The Great Impersonation.*

9. 1929 Ernest Hemingway, *A Farewell to Arms,* 21; 1932 D. H. Lawrence, *Lady Chatterley's Lover,* 289, 1932; Charles Nordhoff and James Hall, *Mutiny on the Bounty,* 3; 1933 Hervey Allen, *Anthony Adverse,* 915; 1934 Barbara Cartland, *A Duel of Hearts,* 27-28; 1950 Tereska Torres, *Women's Barracks,* 109; 1959 Morris West, *The Devil's Advocate,* 16, 32.

10. 1874 R. D. Blackmore, *Lorna Doone,* 327; see also: 1915 W. Somerset Maugham, *Of Human Bondage,* 130.

11. 1894 George Du Maurier, *Trilby,* 214; 1904 Jack London, *The Sea Wolf,* 95-96; 1913 Sax Rohmer, *The Insidious Dr. Fu Manchu,* 72.

12. 1904 Gene Stratton Porter, *Freckles,* 150. It is interesting to note that a shortened form of *Freckles* has been published under the aegis of Barbara Cartland in 1979; it is paper-bound and is sold in mass distribution outlets.

13. For example: 1936 Margaret Mitchell, *Gone With the Wind,* 753; 1958 Harry Golden, *Only in America,* 101; 1941 Ben Ames Williams, *Strange Woman,* 156, 173.

14. 1911 Harold Bell Wright, *The Winning of Barbara Worth,* 14-15; 1943 Betty Smith, *A Tree Grows in Brooklyn,* throughout; 1949 John O'Hara, *A Rage to Live,* 198.

15. 1941 Ben Ames Williams, *Strange Woman,* 166; see also: 1962 Theodore White, *The Making of the President,* 224 ff.

16. 1882 Ludovic Halévy, *L'Abbé Constantin,* 41; see also: 1894 George Du Maurier, *Trilby,* 138; 1899 Winston Churchill, *Richard Carvel,* 243; 1907 Eleanor Glyn, *Three Weeks,* 14; 1946 Frank Yerby, *The Foxes of Harrow,* 40.

17. 1887 Archibald C. Gunter, *Mr. Barnes of New York,* 53; see also: 1927 Sinclair Lewis, *Elmer Gantry,* 255, 410; 1929 Donald Henderson Clarke, *Louis Beretti,* 77; 1929

Lloyd Douglas, *The Magnificent Obsession,* 23; 1953
Annemarie Selinko, *Desirée,* 74.

18. 1944 Elizabeth Goudge, *Green Dolphin Street,* 475; 1951
Herman Wouk, *The Caine Mutiny,* 496; 1961 Henry Miller,
Tropic of Cancer, 162 ff.; 1962 Kyle Onstott, *Drum,* 121.

19. 1934 Irving Stone, *Lust for Life,* 310-11; 1944
W. Somerset Maugham, *The Razor's Edge,* 44.

20. 1958 William J. Lederer and Eugene L. Burdick, *The Ugly
American,* 211; 1965 Robin Moore, *The Green Berets,* 86,
146, 147.

21. 1893 Sarah Grand, *The Heavenly Twins,* 186, 549.

22. 1920 E. Phillips Oppenheim, *The Great Impersonation,* 8,
111, 155; 1929 Ernest Hemingway, *A Farewell to Arms,* 187.

23. 1949 John O'Hara, *A Rage to Live,* 271; see also: 1948
Dale Carnegie, *How to Stop Worrying and Start Living,*
25; 1948 Irwin Shaw, *The Young Lions,* throughout.

24. 1929 Donald Clarke, *Louis Beretti,* 19; see also for
this phrase: 1956 Kathryn Hulme, *The Nun's Story,* 160;
1932 Earl Derr Biggers, *The Keeper of the Keys,* 177.

25. 1942 Ellery Queen, *Calamity Town,* 247-49; 1943 Betty
Smith, *A Tree Grows in Brooklyn,* 102; 1944 Bob Hope,
I Never Left Home, 149; 1948 Harold Robbins, *Never Love
a Stranger,* 13; 1952 Mickey Spillane, *Kiss Me Deadly,*
throughout, 1958 Alexander King, *Mine Enemy Grows Older,*
44; 1959 Ian Fleming, *Goldfinger,* 232.

26. 1937 James Cain, *Serenade,* 115; see also: 1894 George
Du Maurier, *Trilby,* 137-38; 1951 Herman Wouk, *The Caine
Mutiny,* 15.

27. 1929 Donald Clarke, *Louis Beretti,* 1951 James Jones,
From Here to Eternity, 1962 James Baldwin, *Another
Country.*

28. For example: 1884 Helen Hunt Jackson, *Ramona,* 4; 1903
Jack London, *Call of the Wild,* 13-14; 1870 Bret Harte,
The Luck of Roaring Camp, 206-207, 188; 1927 Thornton
Wilder, *The Bridge of San Luis Rey,* 177-78; 1937 James
Cain, *Serenade,* 9, 36; 1946 Rosamund Marshall, *Duchess
Hotspur,* 191, 198; 1949 Hal Ellson, *Duke,* 125; 1953 Leon
Uris, *Battle Cry,* 100, 303; 1954 Evan Hunter, *The
Blackboard Jungle,* 27; 1959 Dariel Telfer, *The Care-
takers,* 285; 1956 Eugene Burdick, *The Ninth Wave,* 2;
1959 Ian Fleming, *Goldfinger,* 9.

29. "greasers": 1870 Bret Harte, *The Luck of Roaring Camp,* 206, 237; 1911 Harold Bell Wright, *The Winning of Barbara Worth,* 215, 315, 245 and throughout; 1957 Ayn Rand, *Atlas Shrugged,* 73.

    "spicks": used by unsympathetic characters in 1947 Irving Shulman, *The Amboy Dukes,* 45; 1952 John MacDonald, *The Damned,* 47; also in 1937 James Cain, *Serenade,* 7.

    "gooks": John MacDonald, *The Damned,* 69 by unsympathetic character.

30. 1953 Leon Uris, *Battle Cry,* 305-306; see also: James Baldwin, *Another Country,* 104, on Puerto Ricans in similar situation.

31. 1946 Frank Yerby, *The Foxes of Harrow,* 338; see also: 1947 Edison Marshall, *Yankee Pasha,* 438; 1946 Taylor Caldwell, *This Side of Innocence,* 441.

32. 1905 Thomas E. Hill, *Hill's Manual of Social and Business Forms,* 92; 1959 Morris West, *The Devil's Advocate,* 255-56; see also: 1926 Will Durant, *The Story of Philosophy,* 530-31.

33. 1869 Mark Twain, *Innocents Abroad,* 1-184; 1874 Jules Verne, *Around the World in Eighty Days,* 167, 186; 1901 G. B. McCutcheon, *Graustark,* 27, 295; 1910 Florence Barclay, *The Rosary,* 133; 1926 Paul de Kruif, *The Microbe Hunters,* 102, 103; 1961 Henry Miller, *Tropic of Cancer,* 150.

34. 1887 Marie Corelli, *Thelma,* 107, 303-304; see also: 1888 Marie Corelli, *A Romance of Two Worlds,* 306; 1915 W. Somerset Maugham, *Of Human Bondage,* 223, 235-36; 1947 Kenneth Roberts, *Lydia Bailey,* 182-83, 264; 1948 Irwin Shaw, *The Young Lions,* 289; 1954 Francis Parkinson Keyes, *The Royal Box,* 16; 1959 Morris West, *The Devil's Advocate,* 256.

35. 1887 Marie Corelli, *Thelma,* 341; 1892 Arthur Conan Doyle, Doyle, *The Adventures of Sherlock Holmes,* 250, 257; 1894 George Du Maurier, *Trilby,* 173; 1910 Florence Barclay, *The Rosary,* 19; 1914 Edgar Rice Burroughs, *Tarzan of the Apes,* 239.

36. 1945 Vera Caspery, *Bedelia,* 25, 29; 1946 Thomas Heggen, *Mr. Roberts,* 17; 1946 Taylor Caldwell, *This Side of Innocence,* 33.

37. 1900 Winston Churchill, *The Crisis,* 1936 Margaret Mitchell, *Gone With the Wind,* 1947 Frank Yerby, *The Vixens.*

38. 1949 Marian Castle, *The Golden Fury,* 19; see also 1906 Zane Grey, *The Spirit of the Border,* 4; 1905 Rex Beach, *The Spoilers,* 2, 10.

Chapter 7

1. 1900 Irving Bacheller, *Eben Holden,* 212; see also: 1868 Louisa May Alcott, *Little Women,* 122; 1905 Thomas E. Hill, *Hill's Manual of Social and Business Forms,* 93; 1911 Gene Stratton Porter, *The Harvester,* 104.

2. 1876 Thomas L. Haines and Levi Yaggy, *The Royal Path of Life,* 61; 1905 Thomas E. Hill, *Hill's Manual . . . ,* 461.

3. God as older brother: 1941 Ben Ames Williams, *Strange Woman,* 260; see also: 1883 Hannah Whitall Smith, *The Christian's Secret of a Happy Life,* 37, 49; 1952 Thomas Costain, *The Silver Chalice,* 71, 100.

   "Be content": 1883 Hannah Smith, *The Christian's Secret of a Happy Life,* 3; 1883 James Whitcomb Riley, *The Old Swimmin' Hole and 'leven More Poems,* 20-22; 1909 Gene Stratton Porter, *A Girl of the Limberlost,* 71.

4. One is reminded of *The Foundations of the Nineteenth Century* by the English expatriate to Germany Houston Stewart Chamberlain, published in Germany in 1899 and in English translation in the United States in 1911. This son-in-law of Richard Wagner made Jesus, Dante, Marco Polo and any contributors to the Italian Renaissance into Teutons with vague tales of the migration of their ancestors from Northern Europe. It was impossible for him to admit that non-Teutons were capable of creative work in scholarship, the arts or science.

5. See also: 1927 Sinclair Lewis, *Elmer Gantry,* 7; 1928 Thornton Wilder, *The Bridge of San Luis Rey,* 177-78; 1944 W. Somerset Maugham, *The Razor's Edge,* 11 ff.; 1945 Thomas Costain, *The Black Rose,* 180.

6. Reverend Dyceworthy in Marie Corelli, *Thelma,* 1887; Dr. Prescott in Donald H. Clarke, (1931) *The Impatient Virgin;* Vicar (676) in Daphne Du Maurier, *Jamaica Inn* (1936); Little Sister Hsia in Pearl Buck, *Pavilion of Women* (1946).

7. 1852 Harriet Beecher Stowe, *Uncle Tom's Cabin,* 225; 1882 Ludovic Halévy, *L'Abbé Constantin,* 5-6; 1887 Marie Corelli, *Thelma,* 35-37, 65, 67; 1894 George Du Maurier,

Trilby, 153; 1932 D. H. Lawrence, *Lady Chatterley's Lover,* 13.

8. See 1941 Father Chisholm in A. J. Cronin, *The Keys of the Kingdom,* 1944 Elizabeth Goudge, *Green Dolphin Street,* 40; 1946 Pearl Buck, *Pavilion of Women,* 153; 1947 James Michener, *Tales of the South Pacific,* 22.

9. 1941 A. J. Cronin, *The Keys of the Kingdom,* 284; see also: 1883 Mark Twain, *Life on the Mississippi,* 12; 1951 William Bradford Huie, *The Revolt of Mamie Stover,* 71; 1959 James Michener, *Hawaii,* 1009.

10. 1888 Mrs. Humphrey Ward, *Robert Elsmere,* 1896 Henryk Sienkiewicz, *Quo Vadis,* 228, 295; 1898 Ralph Connor, *Black Rock,* 12-13, 179, 230, 244; 1921 Rafael Sabatini, *Scaramouche,* 12; 1932 D. H. Lawrence, *Lady Chatterley's Lover,* 212; 1934 Irving Stone, *Lust for Life,* 85; 1946 Taylor Caldwell, *This Side of Innocence,* 407.

11. 1893 Sarah Grand, *The Heavenly Twins,* 155; 1942 Lloyd Douglas, *The Robe,* 16, 213; 1949 Alberto Moravia, *A Woman of Rome,* 1946 Taylor Caldwell, *This Side of Innocence,* 331.

12. Several books on the same theme had already appeared in the 1890s before *In His Steps,* but they never achieved such popularity. See: 1894 Edward Everett Hale, *If Jesus Came to Boston* and 1894 William T. Stead, *If Christ Came to Chicago.*

13. Because the Jews are treated in these books for the most part as a race rather than a religious or ethnic group, they are discussed in the chapter on race, pp. 126-137.

14. 1890 Arthur Conan Doyle, *A Study in Scarlet,* p. 57 in 1927 edition of *The Complete Sherlock Holmes* with preface by Christopher Morley. This edition contains five chapters on the Mormons not printed in the Modern Library edition.

15. Page 62 of the above edition.

16. For example see: 1898 Ralph Connor, *Black Rock,* 5, 42, 159; 1903 John Fox Jr., *The Little Shepherd of Kingdom Come,* 196.

17. See pp. 132-133.

18. William T. Liu and Nathaniel J. Pallone, *Catholics/USA* (New York: John Wiley and Sons, 1970), 5-11; see also: Sidney E. Ahlstrom, *A Religious History of the American*

People (New Haven, CT: Yale University Press, 1972); Philip Gleason, *Contemporary Catholicism in the United States* (Notre Dame, IN: University of Notre Dame Press, 1969); Will Herberg, *Protestant-Catholic-Jew: An Essay in American Religious Sociology* (Garden City, NY: Doubleday and Co., Inc., 1955); Thomas T. McAvoy, ed., *Roman Catholicism and the American Way of Life* (Notre Dame, IN: Notre Dame University Press, 1960).

19. 1876 Mark Twain, *Tom Sawyer,* 381; 1885 Mark Twain, *Huckleberry Finn,* 534; 1887 Marie Corelli, *Thelma,* 35-37; 1894 Ian MacLaren, *Beside the Bonnie Brier Bush,* 36, 59-84; 1929 Lloyd Douglas, *The Magnificent Obsession,* 122; 1944 Lillian Smith, *Strange Fruit,* 81-100; 1949 Marian Castle, *The Golden Fury,* 16; 1960 Harper Lee, *To Kill a Mockingbird,* 5.

Chapter 8

1. See also: 1931 Donald Henderson Clarke, *The Impatient Virgin,* 54-56 and 1941 A. J. Cronin, *The Keys of the Kingdom,* throughout.

2. 1945 Betty MacDonald, *The Egg and I,* 195; see also: 1866 Augusta J. Evans, *St. Elmo,* 28-29; 1871 Edward Eggleston, *The Hoosier School-Master,* 87; 1888 Mrs. Humphrey Ward, *Robert Elsmere,* 30; 1893 Sarah Grand, *The Heavenly Twins,* 168; 1921 Rafael Sabatini, *Scaramouche,* 41; 1927 Sinclair Lewis, *Elmer Gantry,* 389; 1932 James T. Farrell, *Studs Lonigan,* 60; 1934 Dashiell Hammett, *The Thin Man,* 75.

3. 1936 Dale Carnegie, *How to Win Friends and Influence People,* 72, 79, 87, 91, 101; 1937 Napoleon Hill, *Think and Grow Rich,* 16, 24, 31, 76; see also: 1908 John Fox Jr., *The Trail of the Lonesome Pine,* 40; 1946 Taylor Caldwell, *This Side of Innocence,* 450; 1948 Frances Parkinson Keyes, *Dinner at Antoine's,* 221; 1952 Norman Vincent Peale, *The Power of Positive Thinking,* 6.

4. 1943 Betty Smith, *A Tree Grows in Brooklyn,* 136; 1947 Willard Motley, *Knock on Any Door,* 22; 1947 Irving Shulman, *The Amboy Dukes,* 73; 1949 William Barnard, *Jailbait,* 21, 23; 1954 Evan Hunter, *The Blackboard Jungle,* 58-59; 1960 Harper Lee, *To Kill a Mockingbird,* 217.

5. 1947 Irving Shulman, *The Amboy Dukes,* 73; 1954 Evan Hunter, *The Blackboard Jungle, 59.*

6. 1947 Willard Motley, *Knock on Any Door,* 22; 1949 William Barnard, *Jailbait,* 21.

7. 1893 Sarah Grand, *The Heavenly Twins,* 221; 1934 Irving Stone, *Lust for Life,* 333-39.

8. 1931 Fannie Hurst, *Backstreet,* 134; see also: 1945 Vera Caspary, *Bedelia,* 130; 1948 Mary Brinker Post, *Annie Jordan,* 106.

9. 1893 Sarah Grand, *The Heavenly Twins,* 413; 1894 George Du Maurier, *Trilby,* 26.

10. 1934 Irving Stone, *Lust for Life,* 437-38; see also: 1883 F. Marion Crawford, *A Roman Singer,* 238; 1907 Harold Bell Wright, *The Shepherd of the Hills,* 57; 1946 Taylor Caldwell, *This Side of Innocence,* 5; 1959 Morris L. West, *The Devil's Advocate,* 68, 105.

11. 1945 Vera Caspary, *Bedelia,* 23; 1947 Samuel Shellabarger, *The Prince of Foxes,* 8.

12. 1947 Samuel Shellabarger, *The Prince of Foxes,* 81; see also: 1951 James Jones, *From Here to Eternity,* 95.

13. 1908 Grace Livingston Hill, *Marcia Schuyler,* 156; see also: 1937 A. J. Cronin, *The Citadel,* 33.

Chapter 9

1. 1868 Louisa May Alcott, *Little Women,* 101, 121, 231; see also: 1868 Wilkie Collins, *The Moonstone,* 54; 1887 Archibald C. Gunter, *Mr. Barnes of New York,* 125; 1900 Irving Bacheller, *Eben Holden,* 429.

2. 1916 Edgar Guest, *A Heap o' Livin',* 73; see also: 1905 Thomas E. Hill, *Hill's Manual . . .* 143; 1904 Gene Stratton Porter, *Freckles,* 39.

3. 1891 James M. Barrie, *The Little Minister,* 133; see also: 1894 Ian MacLaren, *Beside the Bonnie Brier Bush,* 7.

4. 1943 Betty Smith, *A Tree Grows in Brooklyn,* 12; see also: 1928 Vina Delmar, *Bad Girl,* 97; 1964 Joanne Greenberg, *I Never Promised You a Rose Garden,* 36.

5. 1939 John Steinbeck, *The Grapes of Wrath,* 359, 471; 1944 Lillian Smith, *Strange Fruit,* 117; 1959 James Michener, *Hawaii,* 82.

6. 1959 Ian Fleming, *Goldfinger*, 252; 1960 Barry Goldwater, *The Conscience of a Conservative*, 44-45; 1961 Harold Robbins, *The Carpetbaggers*, 448, 532; 1964 Irving Shulman, *Harlow*, 308.

7. For examples see:
Sex: 1914 Edgar Rice Burroughs, *Tarzan of the Apes*, 372; 1921 Rafael Sabatini, *Scaramouche*, 382; 1931 Fannie Hurst, *Back Street*, 61; 1961 Barbara Cartland, *The Runaway Heart*, 14.

Government and law: 1921 Rafael Sabatini, *Scaramouche*, 47; 1931 Pearl Buck, *The Good Earth*, 284; 1942 Lloyd Douglas, *The Robe*, 66; 1943 Rosamund Marshall, *Kitty*, 74; 1954 Frances P. Keyes, *The Royal Box*, 104.

8. 1948 Norman Mailer, *The Naked and the Dead*, 449; see also: 1926 Agatha Christie, *The Murder of Roger Ackroyd*, 78; 1936 Margaret Mitchell, *Gone With the Wind*, 193; 1946 John P. Marquand, *B. F.'s Daughter*, 4; 1949 Alberto Moravia, *A Woman of Rome*, 141-46.

9. 1887 Marie Corelli, *Thelma*, 278; see also: 1892 James M. Barrie, *A Window in Thrums*, 94; 1894 George Du Maurier, *Trilby*, 24; 1915 W. Somerset Maugham, *Of Human Bondage*, 68.

10. 1887 Marie Corelli, *Thelma*, 276; see also: Harrington in 1956 Grace Metalious, *Peyton Place*, 1959 Ian Fleming, *Goldfinger*, 50; 1961 Harold Robbins, *The Carpetbaggers*, 358.

11. 1894 Anthony Hope, *The Prisoner of Zenda*, 2; see also: 1868 Louisa May Alcott, *Little Women*, 129; 1887 Marie Corelli, *Thelma*, 24; 1905 Thomas E. Hill, *Hill's Manual . . .*, 111; 1908 Mary Roberts Rinehart, *The Circular Staircase*, 275; 1929 Lloyd Douglas, *The Magnificent Obsession*, 28; 1931 Pearl Buck, *The Good Earth*, 259; 1949 John O'Hara, *A Rage to Live*, 20; 1951 J. D. Salinger, *The Catcher in the Rye*, 4; 1953 A. A. Fair, *Some Women Won't Wait*, 37; 1957 Richard Mason, *The World of Suzie Wong*, 137.

12. 1909 Gene Stratton Porter, *A Girl of the Limberlost*, 61; see also: 1866 Augusta J. Evans, *St. Elmo*, 39; 1872 E. P. Roe, *Barriers Burned Away*, 55; 1943 Betty Smith, *A Tree Grows in Brooklyn*, 190-91.

13. 1887 Russell Conwell, *Acres of Diamonds*, see also: 1876 Thomas D. Haines and Levi Yaggy, *The Royal Path of Life*, 112.

14. 1874 Jules Verne, *Around the World in Eighty Days*, 233; 1957 Richard Mason, *The World of Suzie Wong*, 38.

15. 1941 James Hilton, *Random Harvest*, 303; see also: 1946 Taylor Caldwell, *This Side of Innocence*, 355; 1946 Frank Yerby, *The Foxes of Harrow*, 8.

16. 1876 John Habberton, *Helen's Babies*, 17; 1911 Gene Stratton Porter, *The Harvester*, 320; 1945 Vera Caspary, *Bedelia*, 22; 1948 Mary Brinker Post, *Annie Jordan*, 84. Vance Packard in his analysis of the relationship between the American economy and the American population believes the word "servant" is disappearing in 1959 when his best selling book was published, but it never was popular in the United States. He also points out that the cleaning woman expects her employer to prepare her lunch (24). But this may not be a blurring of class lines, but a way to ensure that her time is used exclusively for cleaning.

17. 1866 Augusta J. Evans, *St. Elmo*, 383-84; see also: 1868 Louisa M. Alcott, *Little Women*, 253; 1872 E. P. Roe, *Barriers Burned Away*, 354; 1887 Marie Corelli, *Thelma*, 303, 341; 1892 Arthur Conan Doyle, *The Adventures of Sherlock Holmes*, 250; 1894 George Du Maurier, *Trilby*, 173, 193; 1899 Winston Churchill, *Richard Carvel*, 205, 208; 1901 George Barr McCutcheon, *Graustark*, 233; 1910 Florence Barclay, *The Rosary*, 19; 1914 Edgar Rice Burroughs, *Tarzan of the Apes*, 239.

18. 1903 John Fox Jr., *The Little Shepherd of Kingdom Come*, 40; see also: 1957 Kyle Onstott, *Mandingo*, 160.

19. 1868 Louisa May Alcott, *Little Women*, 222; 1871 Edward Eggleston, *The Hoosier Schoolmaster*, 65; 1871 Charles Reade, *A Terrible Temptation*, 354; 1874 R. D. Blackmore, *Lorna Doone*, 58-59; 1903 John Fox Jr., *The Little Shephers of Kingdom Come*, 40, 213; 1907 Frank Haddock, *The Power of the Will*, 264; 1907 Harold Bell Wright, *The Shepherd of the Hills*, 81, 129; 1911 Kathleen Norris, *Mother*, 82; 1921 E. M. Hull, *The Sheik*, 243; 1933 Hervey Allen, *Anthony Adverse*, 159; 1943 Rosamund Marshall, *Kitty*, 141; 1944 Elizabeth Goudge, *Green Dolphin Street*, 19; 1948 Mary Brinker Post, *Annie Jordan*, 5; 1949 Leslie Turner White, *Lord Johnnie*, 127.

20. 1959 Vance Packard, *The Status Seekers*, 10. In the twenty years since the publication of Packard's book, increasing immigration to England from her former colonies may be altering the British class system with a large dose of ethnicity.

Chapter 10

1. Richard Hofstadter and Michael Wallace, eds., *American Violence: A Documentary History* (New York: Vintage Books, 1970), p. 3; see also: Richard Maxwell Brown, ed., *American Violence* (Englewood Cliffs, NJ: Prentice-Hall, Inc., 1970); Henry Steele Commager, "The Roots of Lawlessness," *The Saturday Review*, 2/13/71; Hugh Davis Graham and Ted Robert Gurr, *Violence in America: Historical and Comparative Perspectives: Report to the National Commission on the Causes and Prevention of Violence*, June, 1969 (New York: New American Library, Inc., 1969); W. M. Frohock, *The Novel of Violence in America, 1920-1950* (Dallas, TX: Southern Methodist University Press, 1950); W. E. Hollon, *Frontier Violence: Another Look* (New York: Oxford University Press, 1974); Richard Slotkin, *Regeneration Through Violence: The Mythology of the American Frontier, 1600-1860* (Middletown, CT: Wesleyan University Press, 1973).

2. 1947 Edison Marshall, *Yankee Pasha*, 310-11; see also 1945 Thomas Costain, *The Black Rose*, 71, 132; 1959 Ian Fleming, *Goldfinger*, 157.

3. 1867 Ouida, *Under Two Flags*, 160; 1874 Jules Verne, *Around the World in Eighty Days*, 161-65; 1944 W. Somerset Maugham, *The Razor's Edge*, 68, 313; 1959 Morris West, *The Devil's Advocate*, 238.

4. 1951 James Jones, *From Here to Eternity*, 209-10; see also: 1929 Lloyd C. Douglas, *The Magnificent Obsession*, 146; 1946 John P. Marquand, *B. F.'s Daughter*, 154; 1958 Harry Golden, *Only in America*, 205.

5. Police brutality: 1929 Donald H. Clarke, *Louis Beretti*, 31 ff.; 1942 Nelson Algren, *Never Came Morning*, 111-19; 1947 Willard Motley, *Knock on Any Door*, 72, 297-98; 1948 Harold Robbins, *Never Love a Stranger*, throughout.

   Police corruption: 1934 John O'Hara, *Butterfield-8*, 174; 1940 Raymond Chandler, *Farewell, My Lovely*, throughout; 1942 Nelson Algren, *Never Came Morning*, 98-100 and throughout; 1947 Willard Motley, *Knock on Any Door*, 157, 175-76; 1952 Mickey Spillane, *Kiss Me Deadly*, throughout; 1953 Polly Adair, *A House Is Not a Home*, 43, 144; 1958 Harry Golden, *Only in America*, 205, 1961 Harold Robbins, *The Carpetbaggers*, 408.

6. 1931 Donald H. Clarke, *The Impatient Virgin*, 78; 1934 Dashiell Hammett, *The Thin Man*, 67; 1939 John Steinbeck, *The Grapes of Wrath*, 407; 1946 Pat Frank, *Mr. Adam*, 100;

1948 Irwin Shaw, *The Young Lions*, 326; 1951 James Jones, *From Here to Eternity*, 5, 46; 1956 Eugene Burdick, *The Ninth Wave*, 248-50; 1958 Harry Golden, *Only in America*, 245; 1948 Alexander King, *Mine Enemy Grows Older*, 155, 261; 1958 William J. Lederer and Eugene Burdick, *The Ugly American*, 55 ff.; 1959 Allen Drury, *Advise and Consent*, throughout; 1961 John Griffin, *Black Like Me*, throughout; 1964 Irving Shulman, *Harlow*, 295; 1964 Irving Wallace, *The Man*, 277.

7. 1954 Morton Thompson, *Not as a Stranger*, 689; 1959 Morris West, *The Devil's Advocate*, 271.

8. I use the masculine pronoun here because the books concerned with vigilante justice were all written by men and described only male vigilantes.

9. R. W. B. Lewis, *The American Adam: Innocence, Tragedy and Tradition in the Nineteenth Century* (Chicago: University of Chicago Press, 1955), 7.

BIBLIOGRAPHY OF BEST SELLERS, U.S., 1865-1965

The basis for inclusion in this list is the formula
developed by Frank Luther Mott in *Golden Multitudes:* each
book must have a sale equal to one percent of the U.S.
population for the decade in which it was published.

Two categories have been added:
An asterisk (*) indicates a book by an author who sold
copiously, but produced no single book that met the above
criterion. (For example, Grace Livingston Hill published
89 popular novels but no single one in the above category.)
A dagger (†) indicates a book included because its concentration on a single subject had enormous influence in that
area although it did not meet the above criterion (for
example, *Uncle Tom's Cabin*).

Books are arranged chronologically with the year of publication in the United States on the left.

(*)1852 Stowe, Harriet Beecher. *Uncle Tom's Cabin, or Life Among the Lowly.* New York: The Modern Library, 1938.

1866 Evans, Augusta J. (Wilson). *St. Elmo.* New York: G. W. Dillingham Co., 1866.

1866 Reade, Charles. *Griffith Gaunt or, Jealousy.* Boston: Dana Estes and Co., 1866.

1867 Alger, Horatio, Jr. *Ragged Dick: or, Street Life in New York.* In *Struggling Upward and Other Works* by Horatio Alger, Jr. New York: Crown Publishers, 1945.

1867 Ouida [Louise de la Ramée]. *Under Two Flags.* New York: Stein and Day, 1967.

1868 Alcott, Louisa May. *Little Women or Mary, Jo, Beth and Amy.* New York: A. L. Burt Co., 1868.

1868 Collins, Wilkie. *The Moonstone.* New York: A. L. Burt Co., 1868.

1868 Phelps, Elizabeth Stuart (Ward). *The Gates Ajar.* Boston: Fields, Osgood and Co., 1869.

1869 Twain, Mark [Samuel Langhorns Clemens]. *The Innocents Abroad.* New York: Harper and Bros., 1869. 2 vols.

1870 Harte, Bret. *The Luck of Roaring Camp and Other Sketches.* Boston: Houghton Mifflin Co., n.d.

1870 Verne, Jules. *Twenty Thousand Leagues Under the Sea.* Cleveland: World Publishing Co., 1946.

1871   Eggleston, Edward. *The Hoosier Schoolmaster: A Story of Backwoods Life in Indiana*. New York: Books, Inc., 1943.

1871   Reade, Charles. *A Terrible Temptation*. Boston: Dana Estes and Co., n.d.

1872   Roe, E. P. *Barriers Burned Away*. New York: Dodd, Mead and Co., 1872.

1874   Blackmore, R. D. *Lorna Doone: A Romance of Exmoor*. New York: Dodd, Mead and Co., 1924.

1874   Roe, E. P. *Opening a Chestnut Burr*. New York: Dodd, Mead and Co., 1874.

1874   Verne, Jules. *Around the World in Eighty Days*. New York: Dodd, Mead and Co., 1956.

1876   Habberton, John. *Helen's Babies*. New York: Hurst and Co., 1876.

1876   Haines, T. L., and Yaggy, L. W. *The Royal Path of Life: or, Aims and Aids to Success and Happiness*. Chicago: Western Publishing Co., 1879.

1876   Twain, Mark [Samuel Clemens]. *Tom Sawyer*. In *The Family Mark Twain*. New York: Harpers, 1935.

1878   Green, Anna Katherine (Rohlfs). *The Leavenworth Case: A Lawyer's Story*. New York: G. P. Putnam's Sons, 1878.

1879   George, Henry. *Progress and Poverty*. New York: The Modern Library, 1929.

1880   Harris, Joel Chandler. *Uncle Remus: His Songs and Sayings*. New York: Grosset and Dunlap, 1921.

1880   Wallace, Lew. *Ben-Hur: A Tale of the Christ*. New York: Harper and Bros., 1880.

1880   Zola, Emile. *Nana*. Translated by John Stirling [Mrs. Mary Neal Sherwood]. Philadelphia: T. B. Peterson and Bros., 1880. 1972 edition translated by George Holden and published by Penguin was also used.

1881   Flaubert, Gustave. *Madame Bovary: A Story of Provincial Life*. Translated by Alan Russell. London: Penguin Books, 1950.

1882   Halévy, Ludovic. *The Abbé Constantin*. New York: Thomas Y. Crowell and Co., n.d.

(*) 1883   Crawford, F. Marion. *A Roman Singer*. New York: P. F. Collier and Son, 1883.

(†) 1883   Phelps, Elizabeth Stuart (Ward). *Beyond the Gates*. Boston: Houghton Mifflin, 1883.

1883   Riley, James Whitcomb. *"The Old Swimmin'-Hole," and 'leven More Poems*. Indianapolis: The Bobbs-Merrill Co., 1883.

1883   Smith, Hannah Whitall. *The Christian's Secret of a Happy Life*. Boston: G. K. Hall and Co., 1973.

1883   Twain, Mark [Samuel Clemens]. *Life on the Mississippi*. In *The Family Mark Twain*. New York: Harper and Bros., 1935.

(†) 1884   [Hay, John]. *The Bread-Winners: A Social Study.*
           New York: Harper and Bros., 1884.
(†) 1884   Jackson, Helen Hunt. *Ramona: A Story.* Boston:
           Little, Brown, 1932.
   1885   Twain, Mark [Samuel Clemens]. *The Adventures of
          Huckleberry Finn.* In *The Family Mark Twain.* New
          York: Harper and Bros., 1935.
   1886   Burnett, Frances Hodgson. *Little Lord Fauntleroy.*
          New York: Charles Scribner's Sons, 1936.
   1886   Haggard, H. Rider. *King Solomon's Mines.* In *Three
          Adventure Novels of H. Rider Haggard.* New York:
          Dover Publications, Inc., 1951.
   1886   Stevenson, Robert Louis. *The Strange Case of Dr.
          Jekyll and Mr. Hyde.* New York: Grosset and Dunlap,
          n.d.
   1887   Conwell, Russell. *Acres of Diamonds.* New York:
          Harper and Bros., 1915.
   1887   Corelli, Marie. *Thelma: A Society Novel.* New
          York: William L. Allison and Co., 1895.
   1887   Gunter, Archibald Clavering. *Mr. Barnes of New
          York.* New York: Hurst and Co., 1887.
   1887   Haggard, H. Rider. *She.* In *Three Adventure Novels
          of H. Rider Haggard.* New York: Dover Publications,
          Inc., 1951.
   1888   Bellamy, Edward. *Looking Backward, 2000-1887.* New
          York: Lancer Books, 1968.
   1888   Caine, Hall. *The Deemster.* London: Chatto and
          Winders, 1893.
   1888   Corelli, Marie. *A Romance of Two Worlds.* New
          York: Grosset and Dunlap, n.d.
   1888   Ward, Mrs. Humphrey. *Robert Elsmere.* London:
          Smith Elder and Co., 1905.
   1889   de Maupassant, Guy. *The Best Stories of Guy de
          Maupassant.* Translated by Michael Monahan. New
          York: The Modern Library, 1925.

   1890   Doyle, Arthur Conan. *The Sign of the Four.* In
          Sherlock Holmes and Dr. Watson. Ed. by Christopher
          Morley. New York: Harcourt Brace and Co., 1944.
   1890   Doyle, Arthur Conan. *A Study in Scarlet.* In
          Sherlock Holmes and Dr. Watson. Ed. by Christopher
          Morley. New York: Harcourt Brace and Co., 1944.
          For Part II "The Country of the Saints", five
          chapters on the Mormons omitted from the above see:
          The Complete Sherlock Holmes. New York: Doubleday
          and Co., Inc., 1927, vol. I.
   1890   Kipling, Rudyard. *Barrack-Room Ballads and Verse.*
          New York: M. K. Mansfield and Co., 1898.
   1891   Barrie, James M. *The Little Minister.* New York:
          Thomas Y. Crowell Co., 1891.
   1891   Kipling, Rudyard. *The Light That Failed.* New York
          York: Book League of America, 1932.

1892   Barrie, James M. *A Window in Thrums*. New York:
        Thomas Y. Crowell and Co., n.d.

1892   Doyle, Arthur Conan. *The Adventures and Memoirs of
        Sherlock Holmes*. New York: The Modern Library,
        n.d.

1893   Grand, Sarah [Frances Elizabeth Clarke McFall].
        The Heavenly Twins. New York: Cassell Publishing
        Co., 1893.

1894   Du Maurier, George. *Trilby*. New York: The Popular
        Library, 1963.

1894   Harvey, William Hope. *Coin's Financial School*.
        Ed. by Richard Hofstadter. Cambridge; MA: The
        Belknap Press of Harvard University Press, 1963.

1894   Hope, Anthony [Anthony Hope Hawkins]. *The
        Prisoner of Zenda*. New York: Henry Holt and Co.,
        1894.

1894   MacLaren, Ian [Rev. John Watson]. *Beside the
        Bonnie Brier Bush*. New York: Dodd, Mead and Co.,
        1894.

1895   Crane, Stephen. *The Red Badge of Courage*. New
        York: W. W. Norton Inc., 1962.

1895   [Tileston, Mary W.]. *Daily Strength for Daily
        Needs*. Boston: Roberts Bros., 1895.

1895   Van Dyke, Henry. *The Other Wise Man*. Privately
        printed for Abbott Kimball, 1951.

1895   Read, Opie. *The Jucklins*. Wright American Fiction
        Vol. III, 1876-1900. #4465 Research Publications
        Inc. Microfilm Reel R-8.

1896   Sienkiewicz, Henryk. *Quo Vadis*. Trans. by Monica
        Gardner. New York: E. P. Dutton, 1952.

1897   Sheldon, Charles M. *In His Steps: "What Would
        Jesus Do?"*. New York: Grosset and Dunlap, n.d.

1897   Trine, Ralph Waldo. *In Tune with the Infinite: or,
        Fullness of Peace, Power and Plenty*. New York:
        Dodd, Mead and Co., 1921.

1898   Connor, Ralph [Charles W. Gordon]. *Black Rock: A
        Tale of the Selkirks*. New York: The Mershon Co.,
        1901.

1898   Hubbard, Elbert. *A Message to Garcia*. New York:
        New York City and Hudson River Railroad, c. 1900.

1898   Westcott, Edward Noyes. *David Harum: A Story of
        American Life*. New York: D. Appleton and Co.,
        1899.

1899   Churchill, Winston. *Richard Carvel*. New York:
        The Macmillan Co., 1900.

1899   Ford, Paul Leicester. *Janice Meredith: A Story of
        the American Revolution*. New York: Dodd, Mead and
        Co., 1899.

1900   Bacheller, Irving. *Eben Holden: A Tale of the
        North Country*. Boston: Lothrop Publishing Co.,
        1900.

1900   Churchill, Winston. *The Crisis*. New York: The Macmillan Co., 1927.

(*) 1901   Libbey, Laura Jean. *Sweetheart, Will You Be True?* New York: Street and Smith, 1901.

1901   McCutcheon, George Baer. *Graustark: The Srory of a Love Behind a Throne*. New York: Grosset and Dunlap, 1901.

1901   Rice, Alice Caldwell Hegan. *Mrs. Wiggs of the Cabbage Patch*. New York: The Century Co., 1901.

1902   Wister, Owen. *The Virginian: A Horseman of the Plains*. New York: The Macmillan Co., 1902.

1903   Fox, John Jr. *The Little Shepherd of Kingdom Come*. New York: Charles Scribner's Sons, 1903.

1903   Knight, William Allen. *The Song of Our Syrian Guest*. Boston: The Pilgrim Press, 1904.

1903   London, Jack. *The Call of the Wild*. New York: The Review of Reviews Co., 1915.

1904   London, Jack. *The Sea Wolf*. New York: The Macmillan Co., 1945.

1904   Porter, Gene Stratton. *Freckles*. New York: Grosset and Dunlap, 1904.

(*) 1905   Beach, Rex. *The Spoilers*. New York: A. L. Burt Co., 1905.

1905   Hill, Thomas E. *Hill's Manual of Social and Business Forms*. Chicago: W. B. Conky Co., 1905.

1906   Grey, Zane. *The Spirit of the Border*. New York: Grosset and Dunlap, 1906.

1907   Glyn, Elinor. *Three Weeks*. New York: The Macauley Co., 1924.

1907   Haddock, Frank Channing. *Power of the Will: A Practical Companion Book for Unfoldment of the Powers of the Mind*. Meriden, CT: The Pelton Publishing Co., 1916.

1907   Service, Robert William. *The Spell of the Yukon and Other Verses*. New York: Barse and Hopkins, 1907.

1907   Wright, Harold Bell. *The Shepherd of the Hills*. New York: A. L. Burt Co., 1907.

1908   Fox, John Jr. *The Trail of the Lonesome Pine*. New York: Charles Scribner's Sons, 1909.

(*) 1908   Hill, Grace Livingston. *Marcia Schuyler*. Philadelphia: J. B. Lippincott Co., 1908.

1908   Rinehart, Mary Roberts. *The Circular Staircase*. New York: The Review of Reviews Co., 1908.

1909   Porter, Gene Stratton. *A Girl of the Limberlost*. New York: Grosset and Dunlap, 1909.

1909   Wright, Harold Bell. *The Calling of Dan Matthews*. New York: A. L. Burt Co., 1909.

1910   Barclay, Florence. *The Rosary*. New York: G. P. Putnam's Sons, 1910.

1911   Norris, Kathleen. *Mother: A Story*. Garden City,
        NY: Doubleday, Page and Co., 1922.
1911   Porter, Gene Stratton. *The Harvester*. Garden
        City, NY: Doubleday, Page and Co., 1913.
1911   Wright, Harold Bell. *The Winning of Barbara Worth*.
        New York: A. L. Burt Co., 1911.
1912   Grey, Zane. *Riders of the Purple Sage*. New York:
        Grosset and Dunlap, 1940.
(*)1913 Rohmer, Sax [Arthur S. Ward]. *The Insidious Dr.
        Fu Manchu*. New York: Pyramid Books, 1976.
1914   Burroughs, Edgar Rice. *Tarzan of the Apes*. New
        York: A. L. Burt Co., 1914.
1915   Maugham, W. Somerset. *Of Human Bondage*. New York:
        Random House, 1956.
1916   Guest, Edgar. *A Heap o' Livin'*. Chicago: The
        Riley and Lee Co., 1916.

1920   Oppenheim, E. Phillips. *The Great Impersonation*.
        In *Five Spy Novels*. Ed. by Howard Haycroft.
        Garden City, NY: Doubleday and Co., 1962.
1921   Hull, E. M. *The Sheik*. Boston: Small, Maynard
        and Co., 1921.
1921   Sabatini, Rafael. *Scaramouche*. New York: Grosset
        and Dunlap, 1921.
1921   Wells, Herbert G. *The Outline of History: Being a
        Plain History of Life and Mankind*. New York: The
        Macmillan Co., 1923.
1923   Gibran, Khalil. *The Prophet*. New York: Alfred A.
        Knopf, 1936.
(†)1924 Barton, Bruce. *The Man Nobody Knows: A Discovery
        of the Real Jesus*. Indianapolis: The Bobbs-Merrill
        Co., 1925.
1924   Wodehouse, P. G. *The Inimitable Jeeves*. London:
        Herbert Jenkins, n.d.
1926   Christie, Agatha. *The Murder of Roger Ackroyd*.
        New York: Pocket Books, Inc., 1964.
1926   De Kruif, Paul. *The Microbe Hunters*. New York:
        Harcourt Brace and Co., 1928.
1926   Durant, Will. *The Story of Philosophy: The Lives
        and Opinions of the Great Philosophers*. New York:
        Simon and Schuster, 1928.
1926   Smith, Thorne. *Topper*. New York: Grosset and
        Dunlap, 1926.
1927   Lewis, Sinclair. *Elmer Gantry*. New York: Harcourt
        Brace and Co., 1927.
1928   Brand, Max [Frederick Faust]. *Singing Guns*.
        Roslyn, NY: Black's Readers Service Co., 1928.
1928   Delmar, Viña. *Bad Girl*. New York: Harcourt Brace
        and Co., 1928.
1928   Hemingway, Ernest. *The Sun Also Rises*. New York:
        The Modern Library, 1930.

1928   Peterkin, Julia. *Scarlet Sister Mary*. Indiana-
       polis: The Bobbs-Merrill Co., 1928.
1928   Wilder, Thornton. *The Bridge of San Luis Rey*.
       New York: Albert and Charles Boni, 1928.
1929   Clarke, Donald Henderson. *Louis Beretti*. New
       York: Grosset and Dunlap, 1929.
1929   Douglas, Lloyd C. *The Magnificent Obsession*.
       Boston: Houghton Mifflin Co., 1929.
1929   Hemingway, Ernest. *A Farewell to Arms*. New York:
       Charles Scribner's Sons, 1969.
1929   Remarque, Erich Maria. *All Quiet on the Western
       Front*. Boston: Little, Brown and Co., 1958.
1929   Sales, Charles (Chic). *The Specialist*. St. Louis:
       Specialist Publishing Co., 1929.

(*) 1930   Biggers, Earl Derr. *Charlie Chan Carries On*.
       London: Tom Stacey, 1972.
1930   Brand, Max [Frederick Faust]. *Destry Rides Again*.
       New York: Pocket Books, 1974.
1931   Buck, Pearl. *The Good Earth*. In *House of Earth*.
       New York: Reynal and Hitchcock, 1935.
1931   Clarke, Donald Henderson. *The Impatient Virgin*.
       New York: The Vanguard Press, 1931.
1931   Faulkner, William. *Sanctuary*. New York: Signet
       Books, 1968.
(*) 1931   Hurst, Fannie. *Back Street*. New York: Grosset
       and Dunlap, 1931.
1931   Queen, Ellery [Frederick Dannay and Manfred B. Lee].
       The Dutch Shoe Mystery. New York: Frederick A.
       Stokes and Co., 1931.
(*) 1932   Biggers, Earl Derr. *The Keeper of the Keys*.
       Indianapolis: The Bobbs-Merrill Co., 1932.
1932   Caldwell, Erskine. *Tobacco Road*. New York: The
       Modern Library, 1940.
1932   Farrell, James T. *Studs Lonigan*. New York: The
       Modern Library, 1932.
1932   Huxley, Aldous. *Brave New World*. New York: Bantam
       Books, 1955.
1932   Lawrence, D. H. *Lady Chatterley's Lover*. Paris:
       The Obelisk Press, 1936.
1932   Lindsay, Norman. *The Cautious Amorist*. New York:
       Farrar and Rinehart, Inc., 1932.
1932   Nordhoff, Charles, and Hall, James Norman. *Mutiny
       on the Bounty*. Boston: Little, Brown and Co.,
       1934.
1933   Allen, Hervey. *Anthony Adverse*. New York: Farrar
       and Rinehart, Inc., 1933.
1933   Caldwell, Erskine. *God's Little Acre*. New York:
       The New American Library, 1958.
1933   Gardner, Erle Stanley. *The Case of the Sulky Girl*.
       New York: William Morrow and Co., 1933.

1933   Hilton, James. *Lost Horizon*. New York: William Morrow and Co., 1957.

1934   Cain, James M. *The Postman Always Rings Twice*. New York: Alfred Knopf, 1934.

1934   Hammett, Dashiell. *The Thin Man*. New York: Vintage, 1972.

(*) 1934   Rohmer, Sax [Arthur S. Ward]. *The Trail of Fu Manchu*. New York: Pyramid Books, 1976.

1934   Stone, Irving. *Lust for Life: A Novel of Vincent Van Gogh*. New York: The Heritage Press, 1936.

1934   Cartland, Barbara. *A Duel of Hearts*. New York: Pyramid Books, 1970.

1935   Bagnold, Enid. *"National Velvet"*. Garden City, NY: Nelson Doubleday, Inc., 1935.

1935   Kains, Maurice Grenville. *Five Acres: A Practical Guide to the Selection and Management of the Small Farm*. New York: Greenberg, 1935.

1935   O'Hara, John. *Butterfield-8*. New York: Bantam Books, 1961.

1936   Carnegie, Dale. *How to Win Friends and Influence People*. New York: Pocket Books, 1974.

1936   Du Maurier, Daphne. *Jamaica Inn*. Garden City, NY: Doubleday and Co., Inc., 1961.

1936   Mitchell, Margaret. *Gone With the Wind*. New York: The Macmillan Co., 1936.

1937   Cain, James M. *Serenade*. New York: Alfred A. Knopf, 1939.

1937   Cronin, Archibald Joseph. *The Citadel*. Boston: Little, Brown and Co., 1937.

1937   Hill, Napoleon. *Think and Grow Rich*. Greenwich, CT: Fawcett Publications, 1963.

1938   Du Maurier, Daphne. *Rebecca*. In *Three Romantic Novels of Cornwall*. Garden City, NY: Doubleday and Co., 1961.

1938   Runyon, Damon. *The Best of Runyon*. Ed. by E. C. Bentley. New York: Frederick A. Stokes Co., 1938.

1939   Faulkner, William. *The Wild Palms*. New York: Vintage, 1966.

1939   Steinbeck, John. *The Grapes of Wrath*. New York: The Modern Library, 1939.

1940   Chandler, Raymond. *Farewell, My Lovely*. New York: The Modern Library, 1940.

1940   Christie, Agatha. *And Then There Were None*. New York: Pocket Books, 1974.

1940   Lindlahr, Victor. *You Are What You Eat*. New York: National Nutrition Society, Inc., 1942.

1940   Struther, Jan [Joyce Maxtone Graham]. *Mrs. Miniver*. New York: Harcourt, Brace and Co., 1940.

1941   Cronin, A. J. *The Keys of the Kingdom*. Boston: Little, Brown and Co., 1941.

1941   Gardner, Erle Stanley. *The Case of the Haunted Husband*. New York: William Morrow and Co., 1941.

1941   Hilton, James. *Random Harvest*. Boston: Little, Brown and Co., 1941.

1941   Williams, Ben Ames. *The Strange Woman*. Cambridge, MA: Houghton Mifflin Co., 1941.

1942   Algren, Nelson. *Never Came Morning*. New York: Harper and Bros., 1942.

1942   Connell, Vivian. *The Chinese Room*. New York: Dial Press, 1942.

1942   Douglas, Lloyd. *The Robe*. Boston: Houghton Mifflin Co., 1942.

1942   Hargrove, Marion. *See Here, Private Hargrove*. New York: Henry Holt and Co., 1942.

1942   Queen, Ellery [Frederick Dannay and Manfred B. Lee]. *Calamity Town*. Boston: Little, Brown and Co., 1942.

1942   Werfel, Franz. *The Song of Bernadette*. Trans. by Ludwig Lewisohn. New York: Viking Press, 1942.

1943   Marshall, Rosamund Van Der Zee. *Kitty*. New York: Duell, Sloan and Pearce, 1943.

1943   Rand, Ayn. *The Fountainhead*. New York: The Bobbs-Merrill Co., Inc., 1943.

1943   Smith, Betty. *A Tree Grows in Brooklyn,* New York: Harper and Bros., 1943.

1943   Willkie, Wendell. *One World*. New York: Simon and Schuster, 1943.

1944   Busch, Niven. *Duel in the Sun*. New York: The Hampton Publishing Co., 1944.

1944   Goudge, Elizabeth. *Green Dolphin Street*. New York: Coward McCann Inc., 1944.

1944   Hope, Bob. *I Never Left Home*. New York: Simon and Schuster, 1944.

1944   Lowell, Juliet. *Dear Sir*. New York: Eagle Books, 1944.

1944   Maugham, W. Somerset. *The Razor's Edge*. New York: Pocket Books, Inc., 1955.

1944   Smith, Lillian. *Strange Fruit*. New York: Reynal and Hitchcock, 1944.

1944   Williams, Ben Ames. *Leave Her to Heaven*. Boston: Houghton Mifflin Co., 1944.

1944   Winsor, Kathleen. *Forever Amber*. New York: The Macmillan Co., 1946.

1945   Caspary, Vera. *Bedelia*. Boston: Houghton Mifflin Co., 1945.

1945   Costain, Thomas B. *The Black Rose*. Garden City, NY: Doubleday Doran and Co., Inc., 1945.

1945   MacDonald, Betty. *The Egg and I*. Philadelphia: J. B. Lippincott Co., 1945.

1945   Steinbeck, John. *Cannery Row*. New York: The Viking Press, 1945.

1946   Buck, Pearl. *Pavilion of Women*. New York: The
        John Day Co., 1946.
1946   Caldwell, Taylor. *This Side of Innocence*. New
        York: Charles Scribner's Sons, 1946.
1946   Frank, Pat. *Mr. Adam*. Philadelphia: J. B.
        Lippincott Co., 1946.
1946   Heggen, Thomas. *Mr. Roberts*. Boston: Houghton
        Mifflin Co., 1946.
1946   Hersey, John. *Hiroshima*. New York: Bantam, 1966.
1946   Marquand, John Phillips. *B. F.'s Daughter*.
        Boston: Little, Brown and Co., 1946.
1946   Marshall, Rosamund.Van Der Zee. *Duchess Hotspur*.
        New York: Prentice-Hall, Inc., 1946.
1946   Spock, Benjamin. *The Common Sense Book of Baby
        and Child Care*. New York: Duell, Sloan and
        Pearce, 1946.
1946   Wilder, Robert. *Written on the Wind*. New York:
        G. P. Putnam's, 1946.
1946   Yerby, Frank. *The Foxes of Harrow*. New York: Dial
        Press, 1946.
1947   Chesser, Eustace. *Love Without Fear: How to
        Achieve Sex Happiness in Marriage*. New York: New
        American Library, 1947.
1947   Marshall, Edison. *Yankee Pasha: The Adventures of
        Jason Starbuck*. New York: Farrar, Straus and Co.,
        1947.
1947   Michener, James A. *Tales of the South Pacific*.
        New York: The Macmillan Co., 1954.
1947   Motley, Willard. *Knock on Any Door*. New York: The
        New American Library, 1947.
1947   Roberts, Kenneth. *Lydia Bailey*. Garden City, NY:
        Doubleday and Co., Inc., 1947.
1947   Shellabarger, Samuel. *Prince of Foxes*. Boston:
        Little, Brown and Co., 1947.
1947   Shulman, Irving. *The Amboy Dukes*. Garden City,
        NY: Doubleday and Co., Inc., 1947.
1947   Spillane, Mickey [Frank Morrison]. *I, the Jury*.
        New York: E. P. Dutton and Co., Inc., 1947.
1947   Yerby, Frank. *The Vixens*. New York: The Dial
        Press, 1947.
1948   Carnegie, Dale. *How to Stop Worrying and Start
        Living*. New York: Simon and Schuster, 1948.
1948   Keyes, Frances Parkinson. *Dinner at Antoine's*.
        New York: Julian Messner, Inc., 1948.
1948   Mailer, Norman. *The Naked and the Dead*. New York:
        Rinehart and Co., Inc., 1948.
1948   Post, Mary Brinker. *Annie Jordan: A Novel of
        Seattle*. Garden City, NY: Doubleday and Co., Inc.,
        1948.
1948   Robbins, Harold. *Never Love a Stranger*. New York:
        Pocket Books, 1975.

1948 Shaw, Irwin. *The Young Lions*. New York: The
Modern Library, 1958.

1948 Webber, Everett, and Webber, Olga. *Rampart Street*.
New York: E. P. Dutton and Co., Inc., 1948.

1949 Bernard, William. *Jailbait: The Story of Juvenile
Delinquency*. New York: Greenberg Publisher, 1949.

1949 Castle, Marian. *The Golden Fury*. New York:
William Morrow and Co., 1949.

1949 Ellson, Hal. *Duke*. New York: Charles Scribner's
Sons, 1949.

1949 Moravia, Alberto. *The Woman of Rome*. Trans. from
the Italian by Lydia Holland. New York: Farrar,
Straus and Co., 1949.

1949 O'Hara, John. *A Rage to Live*. New York: Random
House, 1949.

1949 Orwell, George [Eric Blair]. *Nineteen Eighty-Four*.
New York: Harcourt, Brace and Co., 1949.

1949 Oursler, Fulton. *The Greatest Story Ever Told: A
Tale of the Greatest Life Ever Lived*. Garden City,
NY: Doubleday and Co., Inc., 1949.

1949 Schaefer, Jack. *Shane*. In *The Short Novels of
Jack Schaefer*. Boston: Houghton Mifflin Co., 1961.

1949 White, Leslie Turner. *Lord Johnnie*. New York:
Crown Publishers, 1949.

1950 Fischer, Bruno. *House of Flesh*. New York: Fawcett
Publications, Inc., 1955.

1950 Heyerdahl, Thor. *Kon-Tiki: Across the Pacific by
Raft*. Trans. by F. H. Lyon. Chicago: Rand McNally
and Co., 1962.

1950 Robinson, Henry Morton. *The Cardinal*. New York:
Pocket Books, 1963.

1950 Torres, Tereska. *Women's Barracks*. Trans. by
George Cummings. Greenwich, CT: Fawcett Publications, Inc., 1961.

1951 Carson, Rachel. *The Sea Around Us*. New York:
Oxford University Press, 1951.

1951 Huie, William Bradford. *The Revolt of Mamie
Stover*. New York: Duell, Sloan and Pearce, 1951.

1951 Jones, James. *From Here to Eternity*. New York:
Charles Scribner's Sons, 1951.

1951 Prather, Richard [David Knight]. *Find This Woman*.
Greenwich, Ct: Fawcett Publications, Inc., 1951.

1951 Salinger, J. D. *The Catcher in the Rye*. New York:
Bantam Books, 1966.

1951 Wouk, Herman. *The Caine Mutiny: A Novel of World
War II*. Garden City, NY: International Collectors
Library, American Headquarters, 1951.

1952 Costain, Thomas B. *The Silver Chalice*. Garden
City, NY: Doubleday and Co., Inc., 1952.

1952 Ferber, Edna. *Giant*. Garden City, NY: Doubleday
and Co., Inc., 1952.

1952   Frank, Anne. *Anne Frank: The Diary of a Young Girl.*
        Trans. from the Dutch by B. M. Mooyaart. New York:
        Pocket Books, Inc., 1965.
1952   MacDonald, John. *The Damned.* Greenwich, CT:
        Fawcett Publications, Inc., 1952.
1952   Packer, Vin [Marijane Meaker]. *Spring Fire.*
        Greenwich, CT: Fawcett Publications, Inc., 1952.
1952   Peale, Norman Vincent. *The Power of Positive
        Thinking.* New York: Prentice-Hall, 1952.
1952   Spillane, Mickey [Frank Morrison]. *Kiss Me Deadly.*
        New York: The New American Library, 1964.
1953   Adler, Polly. *A House Is Not a Home.* New York:
        Rinehart and Co., Inc., 1953.
1953   Fair, A. A. [Erle Stanley Gardner]. *Some Women
        Won't Wait.* New York: William Morrow and Co.,
        1953.
1953   Graham, Billy [William Franklin Graham]. *Peace
        with God.* Garden City, NY: Doubleday and Co.,
        Inc., 1956.
1953   Selinko, Annemarie. *Désirée.* New York: William
        Morrow and Co., 1953.
1953   Uris, Leon. *Battle Cry.* New York: Bantam Books,
        1954.
1954   Boulle, Pierre. *The Bridge Over the River Kwai.*
        Trans. by Christian Fielding. New York: The
        Vanguard Press, Inc., 1954.
1954   Geddes, Donald Porter, ed. *An Analysis of the
        Kinsey Report: Reports on Sexual Behavior in the
        Human Male and Female.* New York: E. P. Dutton and
        Co., Inc., 1954.
1954   Hunter, Evan. *The Blackboard Jungle.* New York:
        Simon and Schuster, 1954.
1954   Hyman, Mac. *No Time for Sergeants.* New York:
        Random House, 1954.
1954   Keyes, Frances Parkinson. *The Royal Box.* New
        York: Julian Messner, Inc., 1954.
1954   Roth, Lillian. *I'll Cry Tomorrow.* New York:
        Frederick Fell, Inc., 1954.
1954   Thompson, Morton. *Not as a Stranger.* New York:
        Charles Scribner's Sons, 1954.
1955   Dennis, Patrick [Edward Everett Tanner]. *Auntie
        Mame: An Irreverent Escapade.* New York: Vanguard
        Press, Inc., 1955.
1955   Ilg, Frances L., and Ames, Louise Bates. *Child
        Behavior.* New York: Harper and Bros., 1955.
1955   Prather, Richard S. [David Knight]. *Strip for
        Murder.* Greenwich, CT: Farcett Publications, Inc.,
        1955.
1955   Sagan, Francoise. *Bonjour Tristesse.* Trans. from
        the French by Irene Ash. New York: E. P. Dutton
        and Co., 1955.

1955 Wouk, Herman. *Marjorie Morningstar*. Garden City, NY: Doubleday and Co., Inc., 1955.

1956 Brinkley, William. *Don't Go Near the Water*. New York: Random House, 1956.

1956 Burdick, Eugene. *The Ninth Wave*. Boston: Houghton Mifflin Co., 1956.

1956 Hulme, Kathryn. *The Nun's Story*. Boston: Little, Brown and Co., 1956.

1956 Kennedy, John F. *Profiles in Courage*. New York: Harper and Bros., 1956.

1956 Metalious, Grace. *Peyton Place*. New York: Dell Publishing Co., 1956.

1957 Bishop, Jim [James A.]. *The Day Christ Died*. New York: Harper and Bros., 1977.

1957 Kerr, Jean. *Please Don't Eat the Daisies*. Garden City, NY: Doubleday and Co., Inc., 1957.

1957 Linkletter, Art. *Kids Say the Darndest Things!* New York: Pocket Books, Inc., 1959.

1957 Mason, Richard. *The World of Suzie Wong*. Cleveland: The World Publishing Co., 1957.

1957 Onstott, Kyle. *Mandingo*. Greenwich, CT: Fawcett Publications, n.d.

1957 Packard, Vance. *The Hidden Persuaders*. New York: David McKay Co., Inc., 1957.

1957 Rand, Ayn. *Atlas Shrugged*. New York: Random House, 1957.

1957 Shulman, Max. *Rally Round the Flag, Boys*. Garden City, NY: Doubleday and Co., 1957.

1957 Shute, Nevil [Nevil Shute Norway]. *On the Beach*. New York: William Morrow and Co., 1960.

1958 Dennis, Patrick [Edward Everett Tanner]. *Around the World with Auntie Mame*. New York: Harcourt Brace and Co., 1958.

1958 Golden, Harry. *Only in America*. Cleveland: The World Publishing Co., 1958.

1958 Hoover, J. Edgar. *Masters of Deceit: The Story of Communism in America and How to Fight It*. New York: Henry Holt and Co., 1958.

1958 Jaffe, Rona. *The Best of Everything*. New York: Simon and Schuster, 1958.

1958 Jarvis, D. C. *Folk Medicine: A Vermont Doctor's Guide to Good Health*. New York: Henry Holt and Co., 1958.

1958 King, Alexander. *Mine Enemy Grows Older*. New York: Simon and Schuster, 1958.

1958 Lederer, William., and Burdick, Eugene. *The Ugly American*. New York: W. W. Norton and Co., Inc., 1958.

1958 Mergendahl, Charles. *The Bramble Bush*. New York: G. P. Putnam's Sons, 1958.

1958 Nabokov, Vladimir. *Lolita*. New York: G. P. Putnam's Sons, 1958.

1958   Pasternak, Boris. *Doctor Zhivago*. New York: The New American Library, 1960.

1958   Seton, Anya. *The Winthrop Woman*. Boston: Houghton Mifflin Co., 1958.

1958   Traver, Robert [John Donaldson Voelker]. *Anatomy of a Murder*. New York: St. Martin's Press, 1958.

1958   Uris, Leon. *Exodus*. New York: Bantam Books, 1959.

1959   Drury, Allen. *Advise and Consent*. Garden City, NY: Doubleday and Co., Inc., 1959.

1959   Fleming, Ian. *Goldfinger*. London: Jonathan Cape, 1959.

1959   Metalious, Grace. *Return to Peyton Place*. New York: Julian Messner, Inc., 1959.

1959   Michener, James A. *Hawaii*. New York: Bantam Books, 1970.

1959   Packard, Vance. *The Status Seekers: An Explanation of Class Behavior in America and the Hidden Barriers that Affect You, Your Community, Your Future*. New York: David McKay and Co., Inc., 1959.

1959   Telfer, Dariel. *The Caretakers*. New York: Simon and Schuster, 1959.

1959   West, Morris L. *The Devil's Advocate*. New York: William Morrow and Co., 1959.

1960   Goldwater, Barry. *The Conscience of a Conservative*. Shepherdsville, KY: Victor Publishing Co., 1960.

1960   Lee, Harper. *To Kill a Mockingbird*. Philadelphia: J. B. Lippincott and Co., 1960.

1960   Maltz, Maxwell. *Psycho-Cybernetics*. New York: Pocket Books, 1969.

1960   Shirer, William. *The Rise and Fall of the Third Reich*. New York: Simon and Schuster, 1960.

1960   Wallace, Irving. *The Chapman Report*. New York: Simon and Schuster, 1960.

1961   Cartland, Barbara. *The Runaway Heart*. New York: Pyramid Books, 1974.

1961   Fleming, Ian. *Thunderball*. New York: The Viking Press, 1961.

1961   Griffin, John Howard. *Black Like Me*. Boston: Houghton Mifflin Co., 1961.

1961   Heller, Joseph. *Catch-22*. New York: Dell Publishing Co., Inc., 1977.

1961   Miller, Henry. *Tropic of Cancer*. New York: Grove Press, Inc., 1961.

1961   Robbins, Harold. *The Carpetbaggers*. New York: Pocket Books, 1966.

1961   Stone, Irving. *The Agony and the Ecstasy*. New York: The New American Library, 1963.

1962   Baldwin, James. *Another Country*. New York: The Dial Press, 1962.

1962   Knebel, Fletcher, and Bailey, Charles W. II.
        Seven Days in May. New York: Harper and Row, 1962.
1962   Onstott, Kyle. *Drum*. Greenwich, CT: Fawcett
        Publications, Inc., 1962.
1962   White, Theodore H. *The Making of the President*.
        New York: Atheneum Publishers, 1962.
1963   Heyer, Georgette. *The Nonesuch*. New York: E. P.
        Dutton and Co., Inc., 1963.
1963   McCarthy, Mary. *The Group*. New York: The New
        American Library, 1963.
1964   American Heritage Magazine and United Press
        International. *Four Days: The Historical Record
        of the Death of President Kennedy*. New York:
        American Heritage Publishing Co., Inc., 1964.
1964   Berne, Eric. *Games People Play: The Psychology of
        Human Relationships*. New York: Grove Press, Inc.,
        1967.
1964   Greenberg, Joanne [Hannah Green]. *I Never
        Promised You a Rose Garden*. New York: The New
        American Library, 1964.
1964   Heyer, Georgette. *False Colours*. New York: E. P.
        Dutton and Co., Inc., 1964.
1964   Kaufman, Bel. *Up the Down Staircase*. Englewood
        Cliffs, NJ: Prentice-Hall, Inc., 1964.
1964   le Carré, John. *The Spy Who Came in From the Cold*.
        New York: Coward-McCann, Inc., 1964.
1964   Shulman, Irving. *Harlow: An Intimate Biography*.
        New York: Bernard Geis Associates, 1964.
1964   Wallace, Irving. *The Man*. New York: Simon and
        Schuster, 1964.
1965   Holt, Victoria [Eleanor Hubbert]. *The Legend of
        the Seventh Virgin*. Garden City, NY: Doubleday and
        Co., Inc., 1965.
1965   Moore, Robin. *The Green Berets*. New York: Avon
        Books, 1965.

GENERAL BIBLIOGRAPHY

Banker, Robert. "What Makes a Book Sell?" *Publishers Weekly,* December 4, 1954.

Baritz, Loren. *City on a Hill: A History of Ideas and Myths in America.* New York: John Wiley and Sons, Inc., 1964.

Bassett, Thomas F. *Race: The History of an Idea in America.* New York: Schocken Books, 1965.

Berger, Morroe. *Real and Imagined Worlds: The Novel and Social Science.* Cambridge: Harvard University Press, 1977.

Bocca, Geoffrey. *Best Seller.* New York: Wyndham, 1981.

Bohannon, Paul. *Africa and the Africans.* New York: American Museum of Natural History, 1964.

Brown, Sterling. *The Negro in American Fiction.* Port Washington, NY: Kennikat Press, Inc., 1937.

Browne, Ray B., Fishwick, Marshall, and Marsden, Michael T. *Heroes of Popular Culture.* Bowling Green, OH: Bowling Green University Popular Press, 1972.

Cawelti, John G. *Adventure, Mystery and Romance: Formula Stories as Art and Popular Culture.* Chicago: University of Chicago Press, 1976.

—————. *Apostles of the Self-Made Man: Changing Concepts of Success in America.* Chicago: University of Chicago Press, 1968.

Chenoweth, Lawrence. *The American Dream of Success: The Search for Self in the Twentieth Century.* Edited by John Bartlett. North Scituate, MA: Duxbury Press, 1974.

Cockburn, Claud. *Bestseller: The Books that Everyone Read, 1900-1939.* Harmondsworth, Middlesex, England: Penguin Books, 1972.

Condon, Richard. "On the Role of the Novel." *Harper's Magazine,* September, 1977.

Cornillon, Susan Koppelman, ed. *Images of Women in Fiction.* Bowling Green, OH: Bowling Green University Popular Press, 1973.

Cowley, Malcolm. "Classics and Best Sellers." *The New Republic,* December 22, 1947.

Curti, Merle E. "Dime Novels and the American Tradition." *Yale Review,* June, 1937.

—————. *The Growth of American Thought.* New York: Harper and Bros., 1943.

—————. *Human Nature in American Thought.* Madison: University of Wisconsin Press, 1980.

—————. *The Roots of American Loyalty.* New York: Columbia University Press, 1946.

Davies, Horton. *A Mirror of the Ministry of Modern Novels.*
New York: Oxford University Press, 1959.

Davis, David B. "Ten Gallon Hero." *American Quarterly,*
VI, #2 (Summer, 1954).

Deegan, Dorothy Yost. *The Stereotype of the Single Woman
in American Novels.* New York: Columbia University
Press, 1951.

Denney, Reuel. *The Astonished Muse: Popular Culture in
America.* New York: Grosset and Dunlap, 1964.

Dickinson, A. T., Jr. *American Historical Fiction.* New
York: The Scarecrow Press, 1958.

Douglas, Ann. *The Feminization of American Culture.* New
York: Avon Books, 1978.

Downs, Robert. *Books that Changed America.* New York: The
Macmillan Co., 1970.

Eliot, T. S. "Religion and Literature." *Essays Ancient and
Modern.* New York: Harcourt Brace and Co., 1936.

Elson, Ruth Miller. *Guardians of Tradition: American
Schoolbooks of the Nineteenth Century.* Lincoln:
University of Nebraska Press, 1964.

Ernest, Earnest. *The American Eve in Fact and Fiction,
1775-1914.* Urbana: University of Illinois Press,
1974.

Fiedler, Leslie. *Love and Death in the American Novel.*
London: Paladin, 1970.

Fryer, Judith. *The Faces of Eve: The Nineteenth Century
Novel.* New York: Oxford University Press, 1976.

Furnas, J. C. *Goodbye to Uncle Tom.* New York: William
Sloane Associates, 1956.

Gans, Herbert J. *Popular Culture and High Culture.* New
York: Basic Books, 1975.

Gedin, Per. *Literature in the Marketplace.* Trans. by
George Bisset. London: Faber, 1977.

Green, Martin. *Transatlantic Patterns: Cultural Comparisons
of England with America.* New York: Basic Books,
1977.

Greene, Theodore P. *America's Heroes: The Changing Models
of Success in American Magazines.* New York: Oxford
University Press, 1970.

Hackett, Alice Payne. *70 Years of Best Sellers, 1895-1965.*
New York: R. R. Bowker Co., 1967.

Hackett, Alice Payne, and Burke, James Henry. *80 Years of
Best Sellers.* New York: R. R. Bowker and Co.,
1977.

Handlin, Oscar. *Adventures in Freedom: 300 Years of Jewish
Life in America.* New York: McGraw-Hill Book Co.,
Inc., 1954.

Hardwick, Elizabeth. *Seduction and Betrayal: Women and
Literature.* New York: Random House, 1970.

Harper, Ralph. *The World of the Thriller.* Cleveland: The
Press of Case Western Reserve University, 1969.

Hart, Irving Harlow. "The One Hundred 'Best Sellers' of the Last Quarter Century." *Publishers Weekly,* January 29, 1921.

——————. "Best Sellers in Fiction During the First Quarter of the Twentieth Century." *Publishers Weekly,* February 14, 1925.

——————. "The Most Popular Authors of Fiction Between 1900 and 1925." *Publishers Weekly,* February 21, 1925.

Hart, James D. *The Popular Book: A History of America's Literary Taste.* New York: Oxford University Press, 1950.

Henderson, Harry B. *Versions of the Past: The Historical Imagination in American Fiction.* New York: Oxford University Press, 1974.

Hofstadter, Beatrice. "Popular Culture and the Romantic Heroine." *The American Scholar,* Winter, 1960-61.

Hofstadter, Richard. *Anti-Intellectualism in American Life.* New York: Alfred A. Knopf, 1963.

Huber, Richard M. *The American Dream of Success.* New York: McGraw-Hill Book Co., 1971.

Huth, Hans. *Nature and the American.* Lincoln: University of Nebraska Press, 1972.

Jacobs, Norman, ed. *Culture for the Millions? Mass Media in Modern Society.* Boston: The Beacon Press, 1961.

King, Marian. *Books and People: Five Decades of New York's Oldest Library.* New York: The Macmillan Co., 1956.

Kohn, Hans. *The Idea of Nationalism: A Study of Its Origins and Background.* New York: The Macmillan Co., 1948.

Krutch, Joseph Wood. "Is Our Common Man Too Common?" *Saturday Review,* January 10, 1953.

Lawrence, D. H. *Studies in Classic American Literature.* Garden City, NY: Doubleday and Co., Inc., 1953.

Leavis, Q. D. *Fiction and the Reading Public.* New York: Russell and Russell, 1965.

Lee, Charles. *The Hidden Public: The Story of the Book-of-the-Month Club.* Garden City, NY: Doubleday and Co., Inc., 1958.

Lehmann-Haupt, Hellmut. *The Book in America.* In collaboration with Lawrence C. Wroth and Rollo G. Silver. New York: R. R. Bowker Co., 1951.

Leonard, John. "Are All Novels Created Equal?" *New York Times Book Review,* September 11, 1977.

Lewis, R. W. B. *The American Adam.* Chicago: University of Chicago Press, 1955.

Lindeman, Edward C. "The Common Man as Reader." *Saturday Review,* May 9, 1953.

Lowenthal, David, and Bowden, Martyn, eds. *Geographies of the Mind.* New York: Oxford University Press, 1976.

Lowenthal, Leo. *Literature, Popular Culture and Society.* Englewood Cliffs, NJ: Prentice-Hall, Inc., 1961.

Lynn, Kenneth. *The Dream of Success: A Study of the Modern Imagination.* Boston: Little, Brown and Co., 1955.

MacDonald, Dwight. *Against the Grain: Essays in the Effects of Mass Culture*. New York: Vintage Books, 1962.

MacDonald, Ross. "The Private Detective." *New York Times Book Review*, October 23, 1977.

Madison, Charles. *Book Publishing in America*. New York: McGraw-Hill Book Co., 1966.

Malraux, André. "Art, Popular Art and the Illusion of the Folk." *Partisan Review*, September-October, 1951.

Marx, Leo. *The Machine in the Garden*. New York: Oxford University Press, 1964.

Meyer, Donald. *The Positive Thinkers*. Garden City, NY: Doubleday and Co., Inc., 1965.

Mott, Frank Luther. *Golden Multitudes: The Story of Best Sellers in the United States*. New York: The Macmillan Co., 1947.

Murray, Henry A., ed. *Myth and Mythmaking*. Boston: The Beacon Press, 1968.

Mussell, Kay J. "Beautiful and Damned: The Sexual Woman in Gothic Fiction." *Journal of Popular Culture*. Summer, 1975.

Nash, Roderick. *Wilderness and the American Mind*. New Haven: Yale University Press, 1973.

Nicgorski, Walter, and Weber, Ronald, eds. *An Almost Chosen People: The Moral Aspirations of Americans*. South Bend, IN: University of Notre Dame Press, 1976.

Noble, David W. *The Eternal Adam and the New World Garden*. New York: Braziller, 1968.

Nye, Russel B. *This Almost Chosen People*. East Lansing: Michigan State University Press, 1966.

————. *The Unembarrassed Muse: The Popular Arts in America*. New York: The Dial Press, 1970.

Page, Walter Hines. "Why 'Bad' Novels Succeed and 'Good' Ones Fail." *A Publisher's Confession*. Garden City, NY: Doubleday, Page and Co., 1923.

Papashvily, Helen Waite. *All the Happy Endings*. New York: Harper and Bros., 1956.

Parks, Henry Bamford. "The Metamorphosis of Leather-stocking." *Literature in America*. Ed. by Philip Rahv. New York: Meridian Books, 1957.

Petersen, Clarence. *The Bantam Story: Thirty Years of Paperback Publishing*. New York: Bantam Books, 1973.

Potter, David. *People of Plenty: Economic Abundance and the American Character*. Chicago: University of Chicago Press, 1954.

Rahv, Philip A., ed. *Literature in America*. New York: Meridian Books, 1957.

Roback, A. *A Dictionary of International Slurs*. Cambridge, MA: Science-Art Publishers, 1964.

Roberts, Robert R. "Popular Culture and Public Taste." *The Gilded Age*. Ed. by H. Wayne Morgan. Syracuse, NY: Syracuse University Press, 1970.

Robertson, James Oliver. *American Myth, American Reality*.
    New York: Hill and Wang, 1980.
Rosenberg, Bernard, and White, David Manning, eds. *Mass
    Culture: The Popular Arts in America*. New York:
    The Free Press, 1957.
Roseblatt, Roger. "Love Won't Buy You Money." *The New
    Republic*, March 26, 1977.
Ruehlmann, William. *Saint with a Gun*. New York: New York
    University Press, 1977.
Schick, Frank L. *The Paperbound Book in America*. -New York:
    R. R. Bowker Co., 1958.
Seelye, John. "Who Was Horatio? The Alger Myth and American
    Scholarship." *American Quarterly*, Winter, 1965.
Slotkin, Richard. *Regeneration Through Violence: The
    Mythology of the American Frontier, 1600-1860*.
    Middletown, CT: Wesleyan University Press, 1973.
Smith, Henry Nash. *Democracy and the Novel: Popular
    Resistance to Classic American Writers*. New York:
    Oxford University Press, 1978.
————. "The Scribbling Women and the Cosmic Success
    Story." *Critical Inquiry*, September, 1974.
————. *Virgin Land: The American West as Symbol and
    Myth*. Cambridge: Harvard University Press, 1950.
Starke, Catherine Juanita. *Black Portraiture in American
    Fiction: Stock Characters, Archetypes and
    Individuals*. New York: Basic Books, Inc., 1971.
Steinberg, S. H. *Five Hundred Years of Printing*.
    Harmonsworth, Middlesex, England: Penguin Books,
    1977.
Stevens, George. *Lincoln's Doctor's Dog and Other Famous
    Best Sellers*. Philadelphia: J. B. Lippincott Co.,
    1939.
Sutherland, John. *Bestsellers*. London: Routledge and Kegan
    Paul, 1981.
Symons, Julian. *The Detective in Britain*. London:
    Longmans, Green and Co., 1962.
————. *Mortal Consequences: A History--from the
    Detective Story to the Crime Novel*. New York:
    Schocken Books, 1975.
Thomson, David. *America in the Dark: Hollywood and the Gift
    of Unreality*. New York: William Morrow and Co.,
    1977.
Trilling, Lionel. "Manners, Morals and the Novel." *The
    Liberal Imagination*. Garden City, NY: Doubleday
    and Co., Inc., 1953.
Turner, Alice K. "The Tempestuous, Tumultuous, Turbulent,
    Torrid, and Terribly Profitable World of Paperback
    Passion." *New York Magazine*, February 13, 1978.
Weibel, Kathryn. *Mirror Mirror: Images of Women Reflected
    in Popular Culture*. New York: Anchor Press, 1977.
Wilson, Edmund. *Eight Essays*. Garden City, NY: Doubleday
    Anchor Books, 1954.

—————. *A Literary Chronicle: 1920-1950.* Garden City, NY: Doubleday Anchor Books, 1956.

Wolfe, Don M. *The Image of Man in America.* New York: Thomas Y. Crowell Co., 1970.

Wood, Michael. *America in the Movies.* New York: Basic Books, Inc., 1975.

INDEX